Contents

Chicken & vegetable curry 19

Pork with sweet & sour onion sauce 19

Spicy pepper & tomato soup with cucumber yogurt 20

Mustardy beetroot & lentil salad 21

Warm lemony courgette salad 22

Broccoli & sage pasta 22

Chicken & avocado salad with blueberry balsamic dressing 23

Coleslaw with tahini yogurt dressing 24

Spiced chickpea soup 24

Egg & Puy lentil salad with tamari & watercress 25

Melon & crunchy bran pots 26

Apple & sultana muffins 27

Homemade burgers with sweet potato wedges 28

Salmon with new potato & corn salad & basil dressing 29

Steak, roasted pepper & pearl barley salad 30

Herbed pork fillet with roast vegetables 31

Spiced parsnip & cauliflower soup 31

Red cabbage with apples 32

Indian bean, broccoli & carrot salad 33

Wild salmon veggie bowl 34

Grilled salmon tacos with chipotle lime yogurt 34

Smoked paprika prawn skewers 35

The ultimate makeover: Moussaka 36

Cherry tomato, kale, ricotta & pesto pasta 38

Cod with bacon, lettuce & peas 39

Creamy veggie korma 39

Soy salmon & broccoli traybake	41
BBQ chicken pizza	41
Prawn & lime noodles	42
Simple roast radishes	43
Moroccan tomato & chickpea soup with couscous	44
Salmon noodle soup	45
Quinoa stew with squash, prunes & pomegranate	45
Greek salad omelette	46
Pan-fried scallops with lime & coriander	47
Baked potato with cheesy mince	48
Pea & mint soup with crispy prosciutto strips	48
Red lentil & sweet potato pâté	49
Lemon cod with basil bean mash	50
Spicy cauliflower pilau	50
Indian chickpea & vegetable soup	51
Mixed bean goulash	52
Raid-the-cupboard tuna sweetcorn cakes	52
Oven-baked fish & chips	53
Kale & salmon kedgeree	54
Lemony prawn & chorizo rice pot	55
Lemon spaghetti with tuna & broccoli	55
Pineapple, beef & ginger stir-fry	56
Curry coconut fish parcels	57
Miso chicken & rice soup	57
Roasted carrot, spelt, fennel & blood orange salad	58
Sweet potato salad	59
Superhealthy Singapore noodles	60
Blueberry & lemon pancakes	61

Moroccan lamb with apricots, almonds & mint ... 62

Charred spring onions ... 63

Chipotle black bean soup with lime-pickled onions ... 63

Courgette & quinoa-stuffed peppers ... 64

Tangy trout ... 65

Vegetable & bean chilli ... 65

Pea hummus ... 66

Beef & bean chilli bowl with chipotle yogurt ... 67

Courgette tortilla with toppings ... 68

Spinach & sweet potato tortilla ... 68

Stuffed butternut squash with quinoa ... 69

Quinoa, pea & avocado salad ... 70

Chicken, edamame & ginger pilaf ... 71

Tomatillo salsa ... 72

Barley couscous & prawn tabbouleh ... 72

Turkey tortilla pie ... 73

Feta-stuffed mushrooms with mustard slaw ... 74

Roast chicken thighs with brown rice & salsa verde ... 75

Herby lamb fillet with caponata ... 75

Potato salad with anchovy & quail's eggs ... 77

Chicken with mustard lentils ... 77

Lighter lemon drizzle cake ... 78

Lemon pollock with sweet potato chips & broccoli mash ... 80

Chinese poached chicken & rice ... 81

Masala chicken pie ... 82

Thai red duck with sticky pineapple rice ... 83

Zesty salmon with roasted beets & spinach ... 84

Masala omelette muffins ... 85

Easy ratatouille	86
Lemon & garlic roast chicken with charred broccoli & sweet potato mash	87
Tropical overnight oats	88
Summer vegetable curry	89
Prawn & tomato stew with gremolata topping	89
Tomato & courgette stew	90
Turkey & coriander burgers with guacamole	91
Courgette & couscous salad with tahini dressing	92
Quinoa, squash & broccoli salad	92
Wild garlic & nettle soup	93
Pastry-less pork pie	94
Courgette & tomato soup	95
Instant berry banana slush	96
Sesame chicken salad	96
Fruit & nut breakfast bowl	97
Strawberry & banana almond smoothie	98
Sticky baked meatloaf with avocado & black bean salsa	98
Raspberry coconut porridge	100
Speedy soy spinach	100
Mumsy's vegetable soup	101
Asparagus & lentil salad with cranberries & crumbled feta	102
Spicy mushroom & broccoli noodles	103
Roasted summer vegetable casserole	103
Beetroot & lentil tabbouleh	104
Sweet mustard potato salad	105
Burnt leeks on toast with romesco	105
Corn cups with prawns, mango & chillies	106
Poor man's vongole rosso	107

Butternut squash & sage soup	108
Sushi burrito	108
Seared tuna & anchovy runner beans	109
Green breakfast smoothie	110
Courgette, pea & pesto soup	111
Baba ganoush & crudités	111
Smoky paprika seafood rice	112
Three-grain porridge	113
Sardines & tomatoes on toast	114
Sunshine Cobb salad	115
Low-sugar granola	115
Chicken & basil meatballs	116
Buckwheat & spring lamb stew	117
Barley & bulgur chopped herb salad	118
Cajun prawn pizza	119
Silvana's Mediterranean & basil pasta	120
Apple crunch	121
Egg & avocado open sandwich	122
Simple spicy fish stew	122
Harissa chicken & squash traybake	123
Roast chicken with lemon & rosemary roots	123
Home-style pork curry with cauliflower rice	124
Porcini loaf with summer greens	125
Feta frittatas with carrot & celery salad	127
Spicy Moroccan eggs	128
Pitta pocket	129
Chicken fattoush	129
Spinach soup	130

One-pot chicken with quinoa 131

Vitality chicken salad with avocado dressing 131

Dried fruit energy nuggets 132

Spicy seed mix 133

Prawn & pink grapefruit noodle salad 133

Stuffed Moroccan pitta 134

Spicy bean tostadas with pickled onions & radish salad 135

Artichoke, red onion & rosemary risotto 136

Lighter massaman chicken curry 137

Sesame, edamame & chicken noodle salad 138

Peach crumble 139

Smoked salmon & avocado sushi 140

Hot & sour broth with prawns 141

Herby celery & bulgur salad 141

Crispy fried chicken 142

Chickpea mash 144

Lentil, walnut & apple salad with blue cheese 144

Mango chicken with spiced pilau 145

Stir-fry green curry beef with asparagus & sugar snaps 146

Chicken, butter bean & pepper stew 147

Cheesy turkey nuggets with smoking chips 148

Beetroot hummus 149

Spiced cod with quinoa salad & mint chutney 149

Spicy tuna quinoa salad 150

Mediterranean chicken with roasted vegetables 151

Spring salmon with minty veg 152

Tomato & tamarind fish curry 152

Indian rice salad with chicken 153

Japanese-style brown rice	154
Curried chickpeas	155
Stir-fried beef with hoisin sauce	156
For-the-freezer ratatouille	157
Ceviche	159
Summer vegetable minestrone	160
Spring greens with lemon dressing	161
Harissa aubergine kebabs with minty carrot salad	161
Peanut hummus with fruit & veg sticks	162
Bean & pesto mash	163
Super-green mackerel salad	163
Yellow lentil & coconut curry with cauliflower	164
Charred broccoli, lemon & walnut pasta	165
Creamy yogurt porridge with pear, walnut & cinnamon topping	166
Beetroot & squash salad with horseradish cream	167
Bean, feta & herb dip	167
Easy chicken korma	168
Prawn, rice & mango jar salad	169
Orzo with spinach & cherry tomatoes	169
Kale & apple soup with walnuts	170
Mustardy greens	171
Full English frittata with smoky beans	171
Maple-roasted marrow on cavolo nero salad	172
Griddled lettuce & peas	173
Thai chicken cakes with sweet chilli sauce	174
Herbed lamb cutlets with roasted vegetables	175
Apple crisps	175
Hoisin pork with garlic & ginger greens	176

Roasted balsamic cauliflower	177
Squash & coconut curry	177
Beetroot & mint dip	178
Super berry smoothie	178
Basque-style salmon stew	179
Layered hummus & griddled vegetable salad	180
Storecupboard pasta salad	180
Energy bites	181
Fruity pork steaks	182
Avocado pizza crisps	182
Chicken tikka with spiced rice	184
Baked falafel & cauliflower tabbouleh with avocado, pea & feta smash	185
Veggie olive wraps with mustard vinaigrette	186
Poached eggs with smashed avocado & tomatoes	187
Sticky noodles with homemade hoisin	187
Chicken with Spanish-style butter beans	188
Hearty winter veg soup	189
BBQ chicken drummers with green goddess salad	190
Chicken parmigiana	191
Green pesto minestrone	192
Chipotle chicken wraps	192
Summer egg salad with basil & peas	193
Ratatouille & parmesan bake	194
Raspberry chia jam	195
Tandoori trout	196
Griddled vegetables with melting aubergines	197
Stir-fried chicken with broccoli & brown rice	198
Herb & garlic baked cod with romesco sauce & spinach	198

Carrot & coriander soup	199
Garlicky mushroom penne	200
Staffordshire oatcakes with mushrooms	201
Steak lettuce cups	203
Parmesan pork with tomato & olive spaghetti	204
Rustic vegetable soup	205
Crispy grilled feta with saucy butter beans	206
Crispy paprika chicken with tomatoes & lentils	206
Thai prawn & ginger noodles	207
Chipotle gazpacho	208
Cucumber, pea & lettuce soup	209
Chilli-charred Brussels sprouts	210
Salmon pasta salad with lemon & capers	210
Thai mackerel & sweet potato traybake	211
Slow cooker lasagne	212
Crispy chicken & smashed avocado baps	213
Healthier treacle sponge	214
Spicy meatballs with chilli black beans	215
Smoky veggie nachos	216
Pea & leek open lasagne	217
Penne with broccoli, lemon & anchovies	218
Miso burgers with mint & pomegranate slaw	219
Mozzarella, pepper & aubergine calzone	220
Wild salmon & avocado triangles	221
Baked falafel & cauliflower tabbouleh with pickled carrot, cucumber & chilli salad	222
Lamb & squash biryani with cucumber raita	223
Roasted asparagus & pea salad	224
Roasted red pepper & tomato soup with ricotta	225

Sesame chicken noodles	226
Healthier risotto primavera	226
Spicy peanut pies	228
Meal prep: pasta	229
Fennel spaghetti	230
Three bean spring minestrone	231
Chicken & veg bowl	232
Black-eyed bean mole with salsa	233
Walnut & almond muesli with grated apple	234
Avocado hummus & crudités	234
Spinach dhal with harissa yogurt	235
Thai green pork lettuce cups	235
Tarka dhal	236
Lentil ragu with courgetti	237
Pesto-crusted cod with Puy lentils	238
Squash & spinach fusilli with pecans	238
Coronation chicken salad	239
Spring tabbouleh	240
Salmon & purple sprouting broccoli grain bowl	241
Sweet potato jackets with pomegranate & celeriac slaw	241
Mexican chicken stew with quinoa & beans	242
Lemony chicken stew with giant couscous	243
Porridge with quick berry compote, figs & pistachios	244
Microwave shakshuka	245
Cabbage koshimbir	245
Baked carrot & nigella seed bhajis with raita	246
Fish pie with pea & dill mash	247
Vegetable tagine with chickpeas & raisins	248

Asian pulled chicken salad	248
Chicken piccata with garlicky greens & new potatoes	249
Chicken & aubergine shawarma pittas	250
Little beef & mushroom pies	251
Herby Persian frittata	252
Spiced black bean & chicken soup with kale	253
Chicken waldorf	254
Avocado & strawberry ices	255
Toddler recipe: Mild split pea & spinach dhal	255
Moroccan harira	256
Spinach & tuna pancakes	257
Celeriac, hazelnut & truffle soup	258
Noodle salad with sesame dressing	259
Sesame prawn & smacked cucumber rice noodles	260
Banana & tahini porridge	261
Bombay lamb wraps	261
Creamy leek & bean soup	262
Chicken and mushrooms	263
Spicy 'vedgeree'	263
Creamy mustard mushrooms on toast with a glass of juice	265
Spicy meatball tagine with bulgur & chickpeas	265
Curried pork bulgur salad	266
Brown rice tabbouleh with eggs & parsley	267
Lean turkey burger with sweet potato wedges	268
Broccoli pasta salad with eggs & sunflower seeds	269
Vegan bolognese	269
Sweet potato, coconut & lemongrass soup with coriander sambal	271
Beetroot latkes	272

Baked piri-piri tilapia with crushed potatoes ... 272
Lighter aubergine Parmigiana ... 273
Peruvian toasted sweetcorn, avocado & quinoa salad ... 274
Egg & rocket pizzas ... 275
Apple & penne slaw with walnuts ... 276
Butternut & bacon fusilli ... 277
Prawn fried rice ... 278
Avocado & bean triangles ... 278
White velvet soup with smoky almonds ... 279
Summer pistou ... 280
Chicken with rice & peas ... 281
Chargrilled chicken & kale Caesar salad ... 282
Loaded baked potatoes with slaw ... 283
Potato pancakes with chard & eggs ... 284
Garden salmon salad ... 285
Lighter vegetable lasagne ... 285
Zingy teriyaki beef skewers ... 288
Toasted soda bread with blue cheese & pear ... 289
Harissa trout, beetroot & grapefruit salad with whipped feta ... 290
Spicy harissa chicken with lentils ... 291
Carrot cake overnight oats ... 292
Balsamic beef with beetroot & rocket ... 292
Wasabi chicken rice salad ... 293
Chicken taco salad ... 294
Parsnip gnocchi ... 294
Pork & apple stew with parsley & thyme dumplings ... 295
Roasted squash, pancetta & chestnut risotto ... 297
Bean & pepper chilli ... 298

Cod & smashed celeriac	298
Thai broccoli rice	299
Sausage & butternut squash shells	300
Caramelised onion & goat's cheese pizza	301
Herby quinoa, feta & pomegranate salad	303
Beef goulash soup	303
Falafel burgers	304
Buckwheat with charred baby aubergines	305
Chickpea Bombay mix	306
Green shakshuka	306
Curried parsnip soup shots	307
Chilli tempeh stir-fry	308
Broccoli pasta salad with salmon & sunflower seeds	309
Creamy sprout, hazelnut & leek pasta	310
Roast potatoes with paprika	311
Poached eggs with broccoli, tomatoes & wholemeal flatbread	311
Curried squash, lentil & coconut soup	312
Bang bang chicken cups	313
Meatballs with fennel & balsamic beans & courgette noodles	314
Berry yogurt pots	315
Summer porridge	315
Harissa salmon with zesty couscous	316
Bone broth	317
Blueberry & nut oat bake	318
Chicken korma	319
Prawn jalfrezi	320
Broccoli and kale green soup	320
Smashed cannellini bean tartine	321

Stir-fry with broccoli & brown rice 322

Chicken meatballs 323

Roasted chickpea wraps 324

Creamy squash linguine 325

Easy creamy coleslaw 325

Healthier beef wellington 326

Sweet potato pancakes with orange & grapefruit 328

Vitality chicken salad with avocado dressing 329

Dried fruit energy nuggets 330

Spicy seed mix 330

Prawn & pink grapefruit noodle salad 331

Stuffed Moroccan pitta 331

Spicy bean tostadas with pickled onions & radish salad 332

Artichoke, red onion & rosemary risotto 333

Lighter massaman chicken curry 334

Sesame, edamame & chicken noodle salad 335

Peach crumble 336

Smoked salmon & avocado sushi 337

Hot & sour broth with prawns 338

Herby celery & bulgur salad 339

Crispy fried chicken 339

Chickpea mash 341

Lentil, walnut & apple salad with blue cheese 342

Mango chicken with spiced pilau 343

Stir-fry green curry beef with asparagus & sugar snaps 344

Chicken, butter bean & pepper stew 344

Cheesy turkey nuggets with smoking chips 345

Beetroot hummus 346

Spiced cod with quinoa salad & mint chutney	347
Spicy tuna quinoa salad	348
Mediterranean chicken with roasted vegetables	348
Spring salmon with minty veg	349
Tomato & tamarind fish curry	350
Indian rice salad with chicken	350
Japanese-style brown rice	352
Curried chickpeas	352
Stir-fried beef with hoisin sauce	353
For-the-freezer ratatouille	354
Ceviche	356
Summer vegetable minestrone	357
Spring greens with lemon dressing	358
Harissa aubergine kebabs with minty carrot salad	358
Peanut hummus with fruit & veg sticks	359
Bean & pesto mash	360
Super-green mackerel salad	360
Yellow lentil & coconut curry with cauliflower	361
Charred broccoli, lemon & walnut pasta	362
Creamy yogurt porridge with pear, walnut & cinnamon topping	363
Beetroot & squash salad with horseradish cream	363
Bean, feta & herb dip	364
Easy chicken korma	365
Prawn, rice & mango jar salad	365
Orzo with spinach & cherry tomatoes	366
Kale & apple soup with walnuts	367
Mustardy greens	368
Full English frittata with smoky beans	368

Maple-roasted marrow on cavolo nero salad	369
Griddled lettuce & peas	370
Thai chicken cakes with sweet chilli sauce	371
Herbed lamb cutlets with roasted vegetables	371
Apple crisps	372
Hoisin pork with garlic & ginger greens	373
Roasted balsamic cauliflower	373
Squash & coconut curry	374
Beetroot & mint dip	375
Super berry smoothie	375
Basque-style salmon stew	376
Layered hummus & griddled vegetable salad	376
Storecupboard pasta salad	377
Energy bites	378
Fruity pork steaks	378
Avocado pizza crisps	379
Chicken tikka with spiced rice	380
Chicken & vegetable curry	381
Pork with sweet & sour onion sauce	382
Spicy pepper & tomato soup with cucumber yogurt	383
Mustardy beetroot & lentil salad	384
Warm lemony courgette salad	384
Broccoli & sage pasta	385
Chicken & avocado salad with blueberry balsamic dressing	385
Coleslaw with tahini yogurt dressing	386
Spiced chickpea soup	387
Egg & Puy lentil salad with tamari & watercress	388
Melon & crunchy bran pots	389

Apple & sultana muffins	389
Homemade burgers with sweet potato wedges	390
Salmon with new potato & corn salad & basil dressing	391
Steak, roasted pepper & pearl barley salad	392
Herbed pork fillet with roast vegetables	393
Spiced parsnip & cauliflower soup	394
Chilli chicken & peanut pies	395
Veggie okonomiyaki	396
Curried chicken & baked dhal	397
Broccoli & pea soup with minty ricotta	398
Caponata with cheesy polenta	398
Cauliflower & squash fritters with mint & feta dip	399
Lighter chicken cacciatore	400
Vegan moussaka	401
Lebanese-style meatballs with mujadara	403
Super smoky bacon & tomato spaghetti	404
Slow cooker chilli	405
Root veg lentil bowl with herb pistou	406
Vegan three-bean chilli with potato jackets	407
Oat & chia porridge	408
Moroccan freekeh traybake	409
No-cook chickpea salad	409
Pepper & lemon spaghetti with basil & pine nuts	410
Cod puttanesca with spinach & spaghetti	411
Baked falafel	411
Miso noodles with fried eggs	412
Chocolate chia pudding	413
Rosemary, garlic & chilli popcorn	414

Lime prawn cocktail pitta salad 414

Pasta e fagioli 415

Steak & Vietnamese noodle salad 416

Turkey escalopes & giant couscous 417

Roasted cauli-broc bowl with tahini hummus 418

Creamy chicken, squash & pecan pasta 418

Squash & pesto pasta 419

Simple fish stew 420

Super-quick sesame ramen 421

Jerk-style chicken pilaf 422

Spinach & barley risotto 422

Chia & oat breakfast scones with yogurt and berries 423

Hearty mushroom soup 424

Chicken & vegetable curry

Prep: 15 mins **Cook:** 30 mins Plus marinating

Serves 2

Ingredients

- 100g coconut yogurt
- 2 heaped tbsp tandoori spice mix
- 2 skinless chicken breasts, cut into chunks
- 1 large onion, chopped
- 1 red pepper, cut into chunks
- 250ml passata
- 250g pouch cooked basmati rice
- 100g frozen pea
- small bunch coriander, roughly chopped

Method

STEP 1

Mix together 75g of the yogurt with 1 tbsp of the spice mix and some seasoning. Add the chicken and leave to marinate for at least 15 mins or up to overnight in the fridge. Heat the remaining spices, the onion and a good splash of water, and soften for 5 mins, stirring often.

STEP 2

Tip in the pepper chunks and passata, and simmer while you cook the chicken. Heat the grill to High, remove the chicken from the marinade and shake off any excess. Grill under a high heat until starting to char at the edges.

STEP 3

Tip the rice and peas into a pan with a splash of water and heat through. Stir most of the coriander into the sauce. Serve the rice alongside the chicken and sauce, scattered with the remaining coriander and the remaining yogurt on the side.

Pork with sweet & sour onion sauce

Prep: 10 mins **Cook:** 20 mins

Serves 4

Ingredients

- 250g mixed basmati rice and wild rice
- 600g pork fillet, cut into 4cm-thick slices
- 2 tbsp coarse black pepper (freshly ground)
- 2 tbsp olive oil
- 1 large red onion, halved and sliced
- 150ml cider vinegar
- 75ml maple syrup
- small bunch parsley, chopped

Method

STEP 1

Boil the rice in plenty of water, following pack instructions, until cooked. Drain, return to the pot and cover to keep warm.

STEP 2

Meanwhile, sprinkle the meat on all sides with the black pepper and some salt. Heat 1 tbsp of the oil in a large frying pan. Sear the meat on both sides until nicely browned. Remove from the pan.

STEP 3

Add the remaining oil and the onion to the pan. Cook for 5 mins, then pour in the vinegar and let reduce for 1 min. Stir in the maple syrup, then return the pork to the pan and heat for 5 mins until cooked through. Serve the pork and sauce spooned over the rice and scattered with the parsley.

Spicy pepper & tomato soup with cucumber yogurt

Prep: 15 mins **Cook:** 25 mins - 30 mins

Serves 4

Ingredients

- 2 tbsp olive oil, plus extra to serve
- 2 onions, finely sliced
- 1 carrot, finely chopped
- 3 red peppers, roughly chopped
- 3 garlic cloves, sliced
- 1 red chilli, sliced
- 400g can chopped tomato

- 850ml-1 litre/1½-1¾pts vegetable stock or bouillon
- 4 tbsp Greek-style yogurt
- ½ cucumber, halved, deseeded, coarsely grated and squeezed of excess water
- a few mint leaves, chopped

Method

STEP 1

Heat the oil in a large saucepan. Tip in the onions, carrot and peppers. Cook gently for 15 mins, to soften. Add the garlic and chilli, and cook for a few mins more. Pour over the chopped tomatoes and 800ml of the stock. Bring to the boil and simmer for 10-15 mins until the veg is completely tender.

STEP 2

Meanwhile, mix the yogurt, cucumber and mint in a bowl, and season.

STEP 3

Blitz the soup with a hand blender until smooth, using the extra stock to thin if it has become too thick. Heat through, season and spoon into bowls. Serve with a dollop of the yogurt mixture on top and a drizzle of olive oil.

Mustardy beetroot & lentil salad

Prep: 5 mins **Cook:** 20 mins plus cooling

Serves 5 - 6

Ingredients

- 200g puy lentils (or use 2 x 250g packs pre-cooked lentils)
- 1 tbsp wholegrain mustard (or gluten-free alternative)
- 1 ½ tbsp extra virgin olive oil
- 300g pack cooked beetroot (not in vinegar), sliced

- large handful tarragon, roughly chopped

Method

STEP 1

If not using pre-cooked lentils, cook the lentils following pack instructions, drain and leave to cool. Meanwhile, combine the mustard, oil and some seasoning to make a dressing.

STEP 2

Tip the lentils into a bowl, pour over the dressing and mix well. Stir through the beetroot, tarragon and some seasoning, then serve.

Warm lemony courgette salad

Prep: 10 mins **Cook:** 5 mins

Serves 2

Ingredients

- 2 courgettes
- 1 tbsp olive oil
- zest 1 lemon, plus a squeeze of lemon
- 1 garlic clove, crushed
- ¼ small pack basil, roughly torn

Method

STEP 1

Use a vegetable peeler to slice the courgettes into wide strips, discarding the central, seedy part. Heat the oil in a large frying pan, add the lemon zest and garlic, and fry over a medium heat for 1 min. Add the courgette strips and cook, stirring regularly, for a further 1-2 mins until the courgettes are slightly softened. Add a squeeze of lemon juice and toss the basil through.

Broccoli & sage pasta

Prep: 5 mins **Cook:** 12 mins

Serves 2

Ingredients

- 140g quick-cook spaghetti
- 140g long-stem broccoli, trimmed and cut into 5cm lengths
- 3 tbsp olive oil
- 2 shallots, sliced
- 1 garlic clove, finely chopped
- ¼ tsp crushed chillies
- 12 sage leaves, shredded
- grated parmesan (or vegetarian alternative), to serve (optional)

Method

STEP 1

Boil the spaghetti for 1 min. Add the broccoli and cook for 4 mins more.

STEP 2

Meanwhile, heat the oil in a frying pan and add the shallots and garlic. Gently cook for 5 mins until golden. Add the chillies and sage to the pan and gently cook for 2 mins. Drain the pasta, mix with the shallot mixture in the pan, then scatter with Parmesan, if you like.

Chicken & avocado salad with blueberry balsamic dressing

Prep: 15 mins **Cook:** 5 mins

Serves 2

Ingredients

- 1 garlic clove
- 85g blueberries
- 1 tbsp extra virgin rapeseed oil
- 2 tsp balsamic vinegar
- 125g fresh or frozen baby broad beans
- 1 large cooked beetroot, finely chopped
- 1 avocado, stoned, peeled and sliced
- 85g bag mixed baby leaf salad
- 175g cooked chicken
- **Method**

STEP 1

Finely chop the garlic. Mash half the blueberries with the oil, vinegar and some black pepper in a large salad bowl.

STEP 2

Boil the broad beans for 5 mins until just tender. Drain, leaving them unskinned.

STEP 3

Stir the garlic into the dressing, then pile in the warm beans and remaining blueberries with the beetroot, avocado, salad and chicken. Toss to mix, but don't go overboard or the juice from the beetroot will turn everything pink. Pile onto plates or into shallow bowls to serve.

Coleslaw with tahini yogurt dressing

Prep: 15 mins No cook

Serves 6

Ingredients

- 1 ½ tbsp tahini paste
- 5 tbsp Greek-style natural yogurt
- ½ garlic clove, crushed
- 1 small red cabbage, quartered and finely sliced
- 3 small carrots, cut into fine matchsticks
- 1 small onion, halved and finely sliced

Method

STEP 1

Put the tahini, yogurt, garlic, and some seasoning in a large bowl and mix until smooth. The dressing will thicken so add 2-3 tbsps cold water to loosen it. Add the vegetables to the dressing, and toss together until everything is well coated.

Spiced chickpea soup

Prep: 10 mins **Cook:** 25 mins

Serves 4

Ingredients

- 1 tbsp olive oil
- 1 onion , chopped
- 2 garlic cloves , crushed
- 1 red chilli , deseeded and roughly chopped
- 1 tbsp grated fresh ginger
- 1 tsp cumin
- 1 tsp ras-el-hanout
- ¼ tsp cinnamon
- 200g roasted red pepper , from a jar
- 2 x 400g cans chopped tomato
- 400ml vegetable stock
- 400g can chickpea , drained and rinsed
- 2 preserved lemons , rind chopped (discard the pulp and seeds)
- 1 tbsp clear honey
- 50g wholewheat couscous

Method

STEP 1

Heat the oil in a large lidded pan. Add the onion and garlic, put on the lid and cook for 5 mins, stirring halfway through. Stir the chilli, ginger, cumin, ras el hanout and cinnamon into the pan and cook for 1 min. Add the peppers, tomatoes and stock. Bring to the boil, turn down to a simmer, put on the lid and cook for 10 mins.

STEP 2

Blitz the soup with a stick blender, or in a food processor until smooth. Return to the pan and add more liquid to thin the soup, if you like. Stir in the chickpeas, preserved lemons, honey and some seasoning. If eating straight away, add the couscous and heat through for 5 mins. (If taking to work, add the couscous just before reheating).

Egg & Puy lentil salad with tamari & watercress

Prep: 10 mins **Cook:** 35 mins plus optional overnight soaking

Serves 2

Ingredients

- 75g dried puy lentils
- 175g cauliflower florets , broken into smaller pieces
- 1 tbsp rapeseed oil , plus a drizzle
- 1 large carrot , chopped into small pieces
- 2 celery sticks , chopped into small pieces
- 2 garlic cloves
- 3 omega-3 enriched eggs
- 1 tbsp wheat-free tamari
- 10 cherry tomatoes , halved

- 4 spring onions, finely sliced
- 2 generous handfuls watercress, large stems removed

Method

STEP 1

If you want to activate the lentils (see tip below), do this the night, or up to 8 hrs, before eating. Pour water over them and leave to soak at room temperature. Drain and rinse.

STEP 2

When ready to eat, heat oven to 220C/ 200C fan/gas 7. Toss the cauliflower with a drizzle of the oil, then roast for 20 mins on a parchment-lined baking tray until tender and tinged with gold round the edges.

STEP 3

Meanwhile, put the drained lentils in a pan with the carrot and celery. Pour in water to cover, put on a lid and boil for 20 mins until the lentils are tender. Check before they are ready in case they are boiling dry and, if necessary, top up with a little more water.

STEP 4

While they are cooking, finely grate the garlic and set aside in a large bowl. Boil the eggs for 6 mins, this will give you eggs with a soft yolk. When they are ready, plunge into cold water, then shell.

STEP 5

Mix the tamari and oil into the garlic to make a dressing. Check the lentils and drain, if necessary, then toss in the bowl with the dressing, tomatoes, spring onions and watercress. Pile onto plates and top with the eggs, adding any remaining dressing from the bowl over the top.

Melon & crunchy bran pots

Prep: 10 mins No cook

Serves 1

Ingredients

- ½ x 200g pack melon medley
- 150g pot fat-free yogurt
- 2 tbsp fruit & fibre cereal
- 1 tbsp mixed seed
- 1 tsp clear honey

Method

STEP 1

Top melon medley with yogurt, then sprinkle over cereal mixed with seeds. Drizzle over honey and eat immediately.

Apple & sultana muffins

Prep: 15 mins **Cook:** 25 mins

Makes 12

Ingredients

- 200g self-raising flour
- 1 tsp baking powder
- 1 tsp cinnamon
- 50g wholemeal flour
- 100g golden caster sugar
- 2 eggs
- 125ml semi-skimmed milk
- 4 tbsp sunflower oil
- 2 apples , grated
- 100g sultana

Method

STEP 1

Heat oven to 180C/160C fan/gas 4. In a large bowl mix the self-raising flour, baking powder, cinnamon, wholemeal flour and golden caster sugar.

STEP 2

In another bowl, mix the eggs, semi-skimmed milk and sunflower oil. Pour the wet ingredients into the dry and mix well, then stir in the grated apples and sultanas.

STEP 3

Divide the mix between 12 muffin cases and bake for 25 mins. Cool on a wire rack, then pack in a container for lunch.

Homemade burgers with sweet potato wedges

Prep: 15 mins **Cook:** 40 mins Plus chilling

Serves 6

Ingredients

For the burgers

- 1 tbsp olive oil , plus extra for drizzling
- 1 red onion , finely chopped
- 500g lean minced beef or turkey
- 1 egg
- 12 cream crackers, bashed to fine crumbs
- 2 tsp chilli paste
- 2 tsp garlic paste
- 1 tsp each, tomato ketchup and brown sauce
- 2 tbsp plain flour
- 6 hamburger rolls , toasted, to serve
- toppings of your choice (relish, chutney and salad), to serve

For the wedges

- 4 sweet potatoes , cut into wedges
- 2 tbsp olive oil
- 1 tsp paprika

Method

STEP 1

Heat the oil in a frying pan and fry the onion for about 5 mins or until soft. Leave to cool slightly. When cool, put the onion in a large bowl with the mince, egg, bashed crackers, chilli, garlic, ketchup and brown sauce, and mix well to combine. Divide the mince into 6, roll into balls and flatten each into a nice fat burger.

STEP 2

Put the flour on a plate, dab each burger to the flour on both sides, then transfer to a baking tray. Wrap with cling film and pop in the fridge for a couple of hours.

STEP 3

Heat oven to 200C/180C fan/gas 6. To make the wedges, put the sweet potato on a baking tray and drizzle with olive oil. Sprinkle with paprika, season, then give them a good shake or shuffle around with your hands to make sure they're well coated. Roast for 30-40 mins depending on how crisp you like them. Make sure you give them a good shake a couple of times to ensure they cook evenly.

STEP 4

When the wedges have been cooking for 10 mins, drizzle the burgers with a little olive oil and put them in the oven to cook with the wedges for the remaining 20-30 mins, flipping them halfway. 5 Serve the burgers in the rolls with your choice of toppings, and a good helping of wedges on the side.

Salmon with new potato & corn salad & basil dressing

Prep: 15 mins **Cook:** 15 mins

Serves 4

Ingredients

- 400g baby new potatoes
- 2 sweetcorn cobs
- 4 skinless salmon fillets
- 2 very large tomatoes , like beefsteak

For the dressing

- 2 tbsp red wine vinegar
- 2 tbsp extra-virgin olive oil
- 1 shallot , finely chopped
- 1 tbsp capers , finely chopped
- handful basil leaves

Method

STEP 1

Cook potatoes in boiling water until tender, adding corn for final 5 mins, then drain and allow to cool a little.

STEP 2

For the dressing, mix the vinegar, oil, shallot, capers, basil and some seasoning.

STEP 3

Heat grill to high. Rub a little dressing on the salmon and cook, skinned-side down, for 7-8 mins. Slice tomatoes and place on a serving plate. Slice the potatoes, cut the corn from the cobs and arrange over the tomatoes. Top with the salmon, then drizzle over the remaining dressing.

Steak, roasted pepper & pearl barley salad

Prep: 10 mins **Cook:** 30 mins

Serves 2

Ingredients

- 85g pearl barley , rinsed
- 1 red pepper , deseeded and cut into strips
- 1 yellow pepper , deseeded and cut into strips
- 1 red onion , cut into 8 wedges, leaving root intact
- 1 tbsp olive oil , plus a little extra
- 1 large lean steak , around 300g, trimmed of any excess fat
- ½ x 100g bag watercress , roughly chopped
- juice ½ lemon , plus wedges to serve (optional)

Method

STEP 1

Put the pearl barley in a large pan of water. Bring to the boil and cook vigorously for 25-30 mins or until tender. Drain thoroughly and transfer to a bowl.

STEP 2

Meanwhile, heat oven to 200C/ 180C fan/gas 6. Put the peppers on a baking tray with the onion wedges, toss in 1 tbsp olive oil and roast for about 20 mins until tender.

STEP 3

While the peppers are roasting, rub the steak with a little bit of oil and season. Cook in a non-stick frying pan for 3-4 mins each side, or to your liking. Set aside to rest for a few mins. Mix the cooked peppers and onions into the barley. Stir though the watercress, lemon juice and some seasoning. Thinly slice the steaks, place on top of the salad and serve with lemon wedges, if you like.

Herbed pork fillet with roast vegetables

Total time 1 hr and 45 mins Takes around 1½ - 1¾ hours

Serves 4

Ingredients

- 4 medium parsnips, peeled and quartered lengthways
- 1 butternut squash (about 650g/1lb 7oz), peeled, seeded and cut into chunks
- 2 red onions, each cut into 8 wedges
- 1 tbsp olive oil
- grated zest of 1 lemon
- 2 tsp pork seasoning or dried mixed Italian herbs
- 500g lean pork tenderloin, in one or two pieces
- 1 medium Bramley apple
- 400ml hot chicken stock

Method

STEP 1

Preheat the oven to 200C/ gas 6/fan 180C. Put all the vegetables into a roasting tin. Drizzle with the olive oil, season with salt and pepper, then toss everything together.

STEP 2

On a plate, mix together the lemon zest and pork seasoning or herbs. Roll the pork tenderloin in the mixture, then put it on top of the vegetables. Roast for 40 minutes.

STEP 3

Peel and core the apple and cut it into chunks. Scatter the pieces into the roasting tin, then pour in the hot stock and cook for a further 15-20 minutes. Slice the pork, arrange on a platter with the veg, then spoon the pan juices on top.

Spiced parsnip & cauliflower soup

Prep: 15 mins **Cook:** 50 mins

Serves 6 - 8

Ingredients

- 1 tbsp olive oil
- 1 medium cauliflower, cut into florets
- 3 parsnips, chopped
- 2 onions, chopped
- 1 tbsp fennel seed
- 1 tsp coriander seed
- ½ tsp turmeric
- 3 garlic cloves, sliced
- 1-2 green chillies, deseeded and chopped
- 5cm piece ginger, sliced
- zest and juice 1 lemon
- 1l vegetable stock
- handful coriander, chopped

Method

STEP 1

Heat the oil in a large saucepan and add the vegetables. Cover partially and sweat slowly for 10-15 mins until soft but not brown. In a separate pan, dry-roast the spices with a pinch of salt for a few mins until fragrant. Grind with a pestle and mortar to a fine powder.

STEP 2

Add the garlic, chilli, ginger and spices to the vegetables, and cook for about 5 mins, stirring regularly. Add the lemon zest and juice. Pour in the stock, topping up if necessary to just cover the veg. Simmer for 25-30 mins until all the vegetables are tender.

STEP 3

Purée with a blender until smooth. Dilute the consistency with more water if needed, until you get a thick but easily pourable soup. Season generously, stir in the coriander and add more lemon juice to balance the taste. Eat straight away or chill in the fridge to reheat. This also freezes beautifully. Serve with crusty bread, if you like.

Red cabbage with apples

Prep: 10 mins **Cook:** 45 mins

Serves 8

Ingredients

- 1 red cabbage, finely shredded
- 2 bay leaves
- 5 star anise
- ½ tsp ground cinnamon

- 200ml vegetable stock or water
- 50g golden caster sugar
- 75ml cider vinegar
- 2 apples, cored and cut into wedges

Method

STEP 1

Place all the ingredients except for the apples in a large saucepan and season. Place over a medium heat, bring to the boil, then turn down the heat and simmer for 30 mins. Add the apples, then continue cooking for 15 mins until tender.

Indian bean, broccoli & carrot salad

Prep: 15 mins **Cook:** 15 mins

Serves 4

Ingredients

- 250g green bean, trimmed
- 1 head of broccoli, cut into florets
- 2 tsp vegetable oil
- 2 tsp black mustard seed
- ½ tsp dried chilli flakes
- 100g frozen pea (or use fresh)
- 3 large carrots, grated
- large bunch coriander, roughly chopped
- 3 tbsp sunflower seed

For the raita

- 200ml natural yogurt
- ½ cucumber, peeled and grated
- thumb-sized piece ginger, grated
- ½ tsp ground cumin
- juice and zest 1 lime
- 1 tbsp chopped mint leaves
- pitta bread, to serve (optional)

Method

STEP 1

Cook the green beans in a large pan of boiling salted water for 4-5 mins, adding the broccoli after the first 2 mins. Once all the vegetables are tender, drain well. Meanwhile, mix all the raita ingredients together, then set aside.

STEP 2

Heat the oil in a large frying pan and toast the mustard seeds and chilli flakes for a few mins until fragrant. Add the peas, green beans and broccoli, tossing until heated through. Turn off the heat and stir in the carrots and coriander.

STEP 3

Serve the salad warm (or cold for a working lunch) with a dollop of raita, sprinkled with sunflower seeds and some pitta bread, if you like.

Wild salmon veggie bowl

Prep: 10 mins no cook

Serves 2

Ingredients

- 2 carrots
- 1 large courgette
- 2 cooked beetroot, diced
- 2 tbsp balsamic vinegar
- ⅓ small pack dill, chopped, plus some extra fronts (optional)
- 1 small red onion, finely chopped
- 280g poached or canned wild salmon
- 2 tbsp capers in vinegar, rinsed

Method

STEP 1

Shred the carrots and courgette into long spaghetti strips with a julienne peeler or spiralizer, and pile onto two plates.

STEP 2

Stir the beetroot, balsamic vinegar, chopped dill and red onion together in a small bowl, then spoon on top of the veg. Flake over chunks of the salmon and scatter with the capers and extra dill, if you like.

Grilled salmon tacos with chipotle lime yogurt

Prep: 15 mins **Cook:** 10 mins

Serves 4

Ingredients

- 1 tsp garlic salt
- 2 tbsp smoked paprika
- good pinch of sugar
- 500g salmon fillet

To serve

- 8 small soft flour tortillas, warmed
- ¼ small green cabbage, finely shredded
- small bunch coriander, picked into sprigs
- 200ml fat-free yogurt
- 1 tbsp chipotle paste or hot chilli sauce
- juice 1 lime
- few pickled jalapeno chillies, sliced
- lime wedges, to serve
- hot chilli sauce to serve, (optional)

Method

STEP 1

Rub the garlic salt, paprika, sugar and some seasoning into the flesh of the salmon fillet. Heat grill to high.

STEP 2

Mix the yogurt, chipotle paste or hot sauce and lime juice together in a bowl with some seasoning, and set aside. Place the salmon on a baking tray lined with foil and grill, skin-side down, for 7-8 mins until cooked through. Remove from the grill and carefully peel off and discard the skin.

STEP 3

Flake the salmon into large chunks and serve with the warmed tortillas, chipotle yogurt, shredded cabbage, coriander, jalapeños and lime wedges. Add a shake of hot sauce, if you like it spicy.

Smoked paprika prawn skewers

Prep: 10 mins **Cook:** 10 mins plus marinating

Serves 6 - 8

Ingredients

- 12 large raw prawns
- ½ tbsp smoked Spanish paprika (sweet or hot, whichever you prefer)
- 2 large garlic cloves, finely chopped
- 1 tsp cumin seeds, toasted and ground
- couple of oregano sprigs, leaves finely chopped, or 1/2 tsp dried
- juice and zest of 1 large lemon
- 2 tbsp olive oil

You will also need:

- 12 mini wooden skewers

Method

STEP 1

Soak the skewers in a bowl of water for 10 mins. Meanwhile, peel the prawns, leaving the tails intact, and devein. To do this, run a sharp knife down the back, making a tiny incision just enough to remove the visible black vein. Wash the prawns and pat dry with kitchen paper.

STEP 2

In a medium-sized bowl, mix together the paprika, garlic, cumin, oregano, lemon zest and 1 tbsp olive oil. Add the prawns and leave to marinate for 15 mins at room temperature. Then skewer a prawn onto each stick.

STEP 3

Heat the remaining oil in a roomy frying pan and fry the prawns for 3-4 mins, turning halfway through until just cooked. You may need to do this in batches. Season, squeeze over some lemon juice and serve.

The ultimate makeover: Moussaka

Prep: 30 mins **Cook:** 2 hrs and 5 mins

Serves 6

Ingredients

- 2½ tbsp olive oil
- 1 onion, chopped
- 2 plump garlic cloves, finely chopped
- 2 large carrots (350g total weight), diced
- 450g 5% fat minced beef

- 100ml white wine
- 1 tsp ground cinnamon , plus extra
- ¼ tsp ground allspice
- 400g can plum tomatoes
- 2 tbsp tomato purée
- 1 heaped tbsp chopped oregano leaves
- 2 good handfuls chopped flat-leaf parsley , plus extra to garnish
- 3 aubergines (about 750g/1lb 10oz total weight), ends trimmed
- 1 tbsp lemon juice

For the topping

- 2 eggs
- 1 tbsp cornflour
- 300g 2% Greek yogurt
- 50g parmesan , grated

To serve

- halved cherry tomatoes and thinly sliced red onion and rocket salad

Method

STEP 1

Heat 1 tbsp oil in a large, wide sauté pan. Tip in the onion and garlic, then fry for 6-8 mins until turning golden. Add the carrots and fry for 2 mins more. Stir the meat into the pan, breaking it up as you stir. Cook and stir over a high heat until the meat is no longer pink. Pour in the wine and briefly cook until most of the liquid has evaporated. Stir in the cinnamon and allspice. Tip in the tomatoes, tomato purée and 1 tbsp water (mixed with any juices left in the can), then stir to break up the tomatoes. Season with some pepper, add all the oregano and half the parsley, cover, then simmer on a low heat for 50 mins, stirring occasionally. Season to taste. Mix in the remaining parsley. Can be done a day ahead and refrigerated overnight.

STEP 2

While the meat cooks (unless you are doing this a day ahead) prepare the aubergines. Heat oven to 200C/fan 180C/ gas 6. Brush a little of the remaining oil onto 2 large baking sheets. Mix the rest of the oil with the lemon juice. Slice the aubergines into 1cm thick lengthways slices, then lay them on the oiled baking sheets. Brush with the oil and lemon mix, then season with pepper. Bake for 20-25 mins until soft, then set aside. Lower oven to 180C/fan 160C/gas 4.

STEP 3

Spread 2 big spoonfuls of the meat mixture on the bottom of an ovenproof dish (about 28 x 20 x 6cm deep). Lay the aubergine slices on top, slightly overlapping. Spoon the rest of the meat mixture on top. Beat the eggs in a bowl. Slacken the cornflour with a little of the yogurt, stir in the rest of the yogurt, then mix this into the eggs with half the cheese. Season with pepper. Pour and spread this over the meat to cover it. Sprinkle with the rest of the cheese, a little cinnamon and a grating of pepper. Bake for 50 mins-1 hr until bubbling and golden.

STEP 4

Leave moussaka to settle for 8-10 mins, then scatter over some chopped parsley and cut into squares. Serve with a salad of tomato, red onion and rocket.

Cherry tomato, kale, ricotta & pesto pasta

Prep: 10 mins **Cook:** 15 mins

Serves 4

Ingredients

- 2 tbsp olive oil
- 3 garlic cloves , chopped
- 1 tsp crushed chilli flakes
- 2 x 400g cans cherry tomatoes
- 500g penne
- 200g kale , chopped
- 4 tbsp ricotta
- 4 tbsp fresh pesto
- parmesan or vegetarian alternative, to serve (optional)

Method

STEP 1

Heat the oil in a large saucepan, add the garlic and cook for 2 mins until golden. Add the chilli flakes and tomatoes, season well, and simmer for 15 mins until the sauce is thick and reduced.

STEP 2

While the sauce is cooking, cook the pasta following pack instructions – add the kale for the final 2 mins of cooking. Drain well and stir into the sauce, then divide between 4 bowls. Top each with a dollop of ricotta, a drizzle of pesto and shavings of Parmesan, if you like.

Cod with bacon, lettuce & peas

Prep: 8 mins **Cook:** 12 mins

Serves 2

Ingredients

- 2 tsp sunflower oil
- 2 rashers rindless smoked streaky bacon, cut into small pieces
- 1 long shallot or small onion, very finely sliced
- 1 garlic clove, crushed
- 2 x 140g/5oz thick skinless cod fillets
- 140g frozen pea
- 200ml chicken stock, fresh or made with ½ cube
- 2 Little Gem lettuces, thickly shredded
- 2 tbsp half-fat crème fraîche
- 2 thick slices crusty wholegrain bread, to serve

Method

STEP 1

Heat the sunflower oil in a medium non-stick frying pan. Add the bacon, shallot or onion, and garlic. Cook gently, stirring, for 2 mins, then push to one side of the pan.

STEP 2

Season the cod with ground black pepper. Fry in the pan for 2 mins, then turn over. Add the peas and stock, and bring to a simmer. Cook over a medium heat for a further 2 mins, then add the lettuce and crème fraîche. Cook for a couple mins more, stirring the vegetables occasionally, until the fish is just cooked and the lettuce has wilted. Serve with bread to mop up the broth.

Creamy veggie korma

Prep: 15 mins **Cook:** 30 mins

Serves 4

Ingredients

- 1 tbsp vegetable oil
- 1 onion, finely chopped
- 3 cardamom pods, bashed
- 2 tsp each ground cumin and coriander
- ½ tsp ground turmeric
- 1 green chilli, deseeded (if desired) and finely chopped
- 1 garlic clove, crushed
- thumb-size piece ginger, finely chopped
- 800g mixed vegetable, such as carrots, cauliflower, potato and courgette, chopped
- 300-500ml hot vegetable stock
- 200g frozen peas
- 200ml yogurt
- 2 tbsp ground almonds (optional)

Make it non-veggie

- ½ small raw chicken breast per portion

To serve

- toasted flaked almonds, chopped coriander, basmati rice or naan bread

Method

STEP 1

Heat the oil in a large pan. Cook onion with the dry spices over a low heat for 5-6 mins until the onion is light golden. Add the chilli, garlic and ginger and cook for 1 min, then throw in the mixed vegetables and cook for a further 5 mins.

STEP 2

Divide the mixture appropriately between two pans if serving vegetarians and meat eaters. Chop the chicken into small chunks and stir into one pan. Add the stock, dividing between the pans appropriately, and simmer for 10 mins (if only cooking the veggie version in one pan, use 300ml stock; if dividing between two pans, add 250ml to each). Divide the peas, if necessary, and add, cooking for 3 mins more until the veg are tender and the chicken is cooked through.

STEP 3

Remove from the heat and stir through the yogurt and ground almonds, if using. Serve sprinkled with the toasted almonds and coriander, with basmati rice or naan bread on the side.

Soy salmon & broccoli traybake

Prep: 10 mins **Cook:** 20 mins

Serves 4

Ingredients

- 4 skin-on salmon fillets
- 1 head broccoli , broken into florets
- juice ½ lemon , ½ lemon quartered
- small bunch spring onions , sliced
- 2 tbsp soy sauce

Method

STEP 1

Heat oven to 180C/160C fan/gas 4. Put the salmon in a large roasting tin, leaving space between each fillet.

STEP 2

Wash and drain the broccoli and, while still a little wet, arrange in the tray around the fillets. Pour the lemon juice over everything, then add the lemon quarters.

STEP 3

Top with half the spring onions, drizzle with a little olive oil and put in the oven for 14 mins. Remove from the oven, sprinkle everything with the soy, then return to the oven for 4 mins more until the salmon is cooked through. Sprinkle with the remaining spring onions just before serving.

BBQ chicken pizza

Prep: 25 mins **Cook:** 30 mins

Serves 4

Ingredients

For the base

- 250g wholemeal flour , plus a little for kneading if necessary
- 1 tsp instant yeast
- ¼ tsp salt

- 1 tbsp rapeseed oil , plus extra for greasing

For the topping

- pack of 3 peppers
- 1 large onion
- 1 tbsp rapeseed oil
- 1 tsp fennel seeds
- 2 tbsp barbecue sauce
- 2 tbsp tomato purée
- 1 large skinless chicken breast fillet (about 225g), diced
- 175g baby plum tomatoes , quartered
- 50g Applewood smoked cheese , grated

Method

STEP 1

Heat oven to 220C/200C fan/gas 7. Tip the flour into a mixer with a dough hook, or a bowl. Add the yeast, salt, oil and 200ml warm water then mix well to a very soft dough. Knead in the food mixer for about 5 mins, but if making this by hand, tip onto a work surface and knead for about 10 mins. The dough is sticky, but try not to add too much extra flour. Leave in the bowl and cover with a tea towel while you halve and slice the peppers and onions. There is no need to prove the dough for a specific time, just let it sit while you make the topping.

STEP 2

For the topping: toss the peppers and onions with the oil and fennel seeds then roast for 15 mins. Meanwhile mix the barbecue sauce and tomato purée with 5 tbsp water.

STEP 3

Take the dough from the bowl and press into the base and up the sides of an oiled 25x35cm Swiss roll tin. Don't knead the dough first otherwise it will be too elastic and will keep shrinking back. Spread with two thirds of the barbecue sauce mix then add the remainder to the chicken and toss well to coat it.

STEP 4

Take the roasted pepper mixture from the oven and spread on top of the pizza. Scatter over the tomatoes then evenly spoon on the barbecue chicken. Scatter with the cheese and bake for 15 mins. Serve with a salad or healthy coleslaw.

Prawn & lime noodles

Prep: 20 mins No cook

Serves 2

Ingredients

- 100g dried vermicelli rice noodle
- 2 tbsp each soy sauce , fish sauce and sesame oil
- juice 1 lime , plus wedges to serve
- ½ red chilli , deseeded and finely chopped
- 6 spring onions , finely shredded
- 2 large carrots , coarsely grated
- handful mint leaves, torn
- 150g pack ready-cooked king prawns
- 25g cashews or peanuts

Method

STEP 1

Put the noodles in a bowl, pour over boiled water from a kettle to cover and set aside for 5 mins. Drain and rinse under cold running water, then place in a large bowl.

STEP 2

Mix the soy, fish sauce, sesame oil, lime juice and chilli to make a dressing. Pour over the noodles and stir to coat. Add the spring onions, carrots, mint, prawns and nuts. Mix again and divide between 2 bowls to serve, with lime wedges on the side.

Simple roast radishes

Cook: 20 mins

Easy

Ingredients

- 450g radishes
- 2 tbsp olive oil

Method

STEP 1

Heat oven to 180C/160C fan/gas 4. Remove the leaves from the radishes and if they are nice and fresh, set aside. Halve the radishes and tip into a roasting tin with the olive oil.

STEP 2

Roast for 20 mins until shrivelled and softened, then remove from the oven. Season with salt, toss with some of the leaves to wilt and serve.

Moroccan tomato & chickpea soup with couscous

Prep: 20 mins **Cook:** 45 mins

Serves 4

Ingredients

- 75g couscous
- 3 tbsp olive oil
- 750ml low-sodium hot vegetable stock
- 1 large onion, finely chopped
- 1 carrot, chopped into small cubes
- 4 garlic cloves, crushed
- half a finger of ginger, peeled and finely chopped
- 1-2 tbsp ras-el-hanout
- 1 tbsp harissa paste, plus extra to serve
- 400g tin chopped tomato
- 400g tin chickpea
- juice ½ lemon
- roughly chopped coriander, to serve

Method

STEP 1

Tip the couscous into a bowl, season with salt and pepper and stir through 1 tbsp of the oil. Pour over enough hot stock just to cover and cover the bowl with cling film and set aside.

STEP 2

Heat the rest of the oil in a saucepan and cook the onion and carrot gently for 8 mins until softened. Add the garlic and ginger and cook for 2 mins more then stir in the ras el hanout and harissa and cook for another minute. Pour in the tomatoes and stock and give everything a good stir. Season, add the chickpeas and simmer everything gently for 20 mins until thickened slightly then squeeze over the lemon.

STEP 3

Uncover the couscous and fluff up with a fork. Spoon the soup into bowls, top each with a mound of couscous, scatter with coriander and serve with extra harissa for those who want it.

Salmon noodle soup

Prep: 15 mins **Cook:** 20 mins

Serves 4

Ingredients

- 1l low-salt chicken stock
- 2 tsp Thai red curry paste
- 100g flat rice noodle
- 150g pack shiitake mushroom , sliced
- 125g pack baby corn , sliced
- 2 skinless salmon fillets , sliced
- juice 2 limes
- 1 tbsp reduced-salt soy sauce
- pinch brown sugar
- small bunch coriander , chopped

Method

STEP 1

Pour the stock into a large pan, bring to the boil, then stir in the curry paste. Add the noodles and cook for 8 mins. Tip in the mushrooms and corn and cook for 2 mins more.

STEP 2

Add the salmon to the pan and cook for 3 mins or until cooked through. Remove from the heat and stir in the lime juice, soy sauce and a pinch of sugar. Ladle into 4 bowls and sprinkle over the coriander just before you serve.

Quinoa stew with squash, prunes & pomegranate

Prep: 15 mins **Cook:** 40 mins

Serves 4

Ingredients

- 1 small butternut squash, deseeded and cubed
- 2 tbsp olive oil
- 1 large onion, thinly sliced
- 1 garlic clove, chopped
- 1 tbsp finely chopped ginger
- 1 tsp ras-el-hanout or Middle Eastern spice mix
- 200g quinoa
- 5 prunes, roughly chopped
- juice 1 lemon
- 600ml vegetable stock
- seeds from 1 pomegranate
- small handful mint leaves

Method

STEP 1

Heat oven to 200C/180C fan/gas 6. Put the squash on a baking tray and toss with 1 tbsp of the oil. Season well and roast for 30-35 mins or until soft.

STEP 2

Meanwhile, heat the remaining oil in a big saucepan. Add the onion, garlic and ginger, season and cook for 10 mins. Add the spice and quinoa, and cook for another couple of mins. Add the prunes, lemon juice and stock, bring to the boil, then cover and simmer for 25 mins.

STEP 3

When everything is tender, stir the squash through the stew. Spoon into bowls and scatter with pomegranate seeds and mint to serve.

Greek salad omelette

Cook: 20 mins **Serves 4 - 6**

Ingredients

- 10 eggs
- handful of parsley leaves, chopped (optional)

- 2 tbsp olive oil
- 1 large red onion, cut into wedges
- 3 tomatoes, chopped into large chunks
- large handful black olives, (pitted are easier to eat)
- 100g feta cheese, crumbled

Method

STEP 1

Heat the grill to high. Whisk the eggs in a large bowl with the chopped parsley, pepper and salt, if you want. Heat the oil in a large non-stick frying pan, then fry the onion wedges over a high heat for about 4 mins until they start to brown around the edges. Throw in the tomatoes and olives and cook for 1-2 mins until the tomatoes begin to soften.

STEP 2

Turn the heat down to medium and pour in the eggs. Cook the eggs in the pan, stirring them as they begin to set, until half cooked, but still runny in places – about 2 mins. Scatter over the feta, then place the pan under the grill for 5-6 mins until omelette is puffed up and golden. Cut into wedges and serve straight from the pan.

Pan-fried scallops with lime & coriander

Cook: 2 mins Ready in 10-15 mins

Serves 2 as a starter

Ingredients

- 6-8 scallops
- 1 tbsp olive oil
- 2 large chopped garlic cloves
- 1 tsp chopped fresh red chilli
- juice of half a lime
- roughly chopped coriander
- salt and pepper

Method

STEP 1

Fry the scallops in the olive oil for about 1 min until golden, then flip them over and sprinkle over the garlic cloves and chopped fresh red chilli into the pan. Cook for about 1 min more, then squeeze over the juice of the lime.

STEP 2

Finish off with roughly chopped coriander and salt and pepper. Serve straight away.

Baked potato with cheesy mince

Total time 1 hr Ready in around 1 hour

Serves 4

Ingredients

- 2 tbsp olive oil
- 1 finely chopped onion
- 1 crushed garlic clove
- 1 carrot , finely diced
- 1 celery stick
- 450g minced lamb
- 2 tbsp sun-dried tomato paste
- 1 tbsp Worcestershire sauce
- 300ml beef stock
- 2 tsp cornflour
- 2 tsp water
- baked potato with grated cheddar, to serve

Method

STEP 1

Heat the olive oil in a large pan and fry the onion, garlic, diced carrot and celery stick for 6-8 minutes. Stir in the minced lamb and cook for 3-4 minutes until browned, then add the sun-dried tomato paste and Worcestershire sauce. Stir in the beef stock and cover and simmer for 35-40 minutes until very tender. Season well. Mix the cornflour with cold water to a paste, stir in and cook for 1 minute. Serve over baked potatoes and top with grated cheddar.

Pea & mint soup with crispy prosciutto strips

Prep: 5 mins **Cook:** 15 mins

Serves 2

Ingredients

- 2 leeks , well washed and thinly sliced
- 200g potato (unpeeled), scrubbed and grated
- 500ml chicken or vegetable stock
- 200g frozen pea
- 150g pot 0% bio yogurt
- 2 tbsp chopped mint
- 2 slices prosciutto , all excess fat removed

Method

STEP 1

Put the leeks, potato and stock in a pan and bring to the boil. Cover and simmer for 8 mins.

STEP 2

Tip in the peas, cover and cook for 5 mins more. Take off the heat and blitz with a hand blender (or in a food processor) until smooth, then stir in the yogurt and mint.

STEP 3

Meanwhile, lay the slices of prosciutto in a large non-stick frying pan in a single layer and heat until crisp. Allow to cool a little, then tear into strips, ready to sprinkle over the soup with some ground black pepper. Will keep in the fridge for 2 days.

Red lentil & sweet potato pâté

Cook: 30 mins Prep 10 mins plus chilling

Serves 4

Ingredients

- 1 tbsp olive oil , plus extra for drizzling
- ½ onion , finely chopped
- 1 tsp smoked paprika , plus a little extra
- 1 small sweet potato , peeled and diced
- 140g red lentil
- 3 thyme sprigs, leaves chopped, plus a little extra to decorate (optional)
- 500ml low-sodium vegetable stock (choose a vegan brand, if desired)
- 1 tsp red wine vinegar (choose a vegan brand, if desired)
- pitta bread and vegetable sticks, to serve

Method

STEP 1

Heat the oil in a large pan, add the onion and cook slowly until soft and golden. Tip in the paprika and cook for a further 2 mins, then add the sweet potato, lentils, thyme and stock. Bring to a simmer, then cook for 20 mins or until the potato and lentils are tender.

STEP 2

Add the vinegar and some seasoning, and roughly mash the mixture until you get a texture you like. Chill for 1 hr, then drizzle with olive oil, dust with the extra paprika and sprinkle with thyme sprigs, if you like. Serve with pitta bread and vegetable sticks.

Lemon cod with basil bean mash

Prep: 8 mins **Cook:** 18 mins

Serves 2

Ingredients

- 2 small bunches cherry tomatoes, on the vine
- 1 tbsp olive oil
- chunks skinless cod or other white fish fillet
- zest 1 lemon, plus juice of 0.5
- 240g pack frozen soya beans
- 1 garlic clove
- bunch basil, leaves and stalks separated
- 100ml low-sodium chicken or vegetable stock

Method

STEP 1

Heat oven to 200C/fan 180C/gas 6. Put the tomatoes onto a baking tray, rub with a little oil and some seasoning, then roast for 5 mins until the skins are starting to split. Add the fish to the tray, top with most of the lemon zest and some more seasoning, then drizzle with a little more oil. Roast for 8-10 mins until the fish flakes easily.

STEP 2

Meanwhile, cook the beans in a pan of boiling water for 3 mins until just tender. Drain, then tip into a food processor with the rest of the oil, garlic, basil stalks, lemon juice and stock, then pulse to a thick, slightly rough purée. Season to taste.

STEP 3

Divide the tomatoes and mash between two plates, top with the cod, then scatter with basil leaves and the remaining lemon zest to serve.

Spicy cauliflower pilau

Prep:10 mins **Cook:**5 mins

Serves 2

Ingredients

- 225g cauliflower florets (not the stalk)
- 3 cloves
- ½ cinnamon stick
- ½ tsp turmeric
- 6 curry leaves

Method

STEP 1

Put the cauliflower florets in a food processor and pulse to make grains the size of rice. Tip into a microwaveable bowl and stir in the cloves, cinnamon stick, turmeric and curry leaves.

STEP 2

Mix well, cover with cling film, pierce and microwave on High for 3 mins. Fluff up with a fork and serve.

Indian chickpea & vegetable soup

Prep:10 mins **Cook:**15 mins

Makes 4 lunches

Ingredients

- 1 tbsp vegetable oil
- 1 large onion , chopped
- 1 tsp finely grated fresh root ginger
- 1 garlic clove , chopped
- 1 tbsp garam masala
- 850ml vegetable stock
- 2 large carrots , quartered lengthways and chopped
- 400g can chickpea , drained
- 100g green bean , chopped

Method

STEP 1

Heat the oil in a medium saucepan, then add the onion, ginger and garlic. Fry for 2 mins, then add the garam masala, give it 1 min more, then add the stock and carrots. Simmer for 10 mins, then add the chickpeas. Use a stick blender to whizz the soup a little. Stir in the beans and simmer for 3 mins. Pack into a flask or, if you've got a microwave at work, chill and heat up for lunch. Great with naan bread.

Mixed bean goulash

Prep: 5 mins **Cook:** 20 mins Ready in 25 minutes

Serves 2

Ingredients

- 2 tbsp olive oil
- 1 large onion , finely chopped
- 1 tbsp smoked paprika
- 400g can chopped tomato with garlic
- 400g can mixed bean , drained and rinsed

Method

STEP 1

Heat the oil in a large saucepan, then fry the onion for 5 mins until beginning to soften. Add the paprika and cook for a further min, then stir in the tomatoes and 1/2 a can of water. Simmer gently for 10 mins until thickened and glossy.

STEP 2

Tip in the mixed beans and continue to cook for a further 2 mins to just heat through the beans. Spoon into warm bowls and serve with soured cream and toasted ciabatta slices, drizzled with olive oil.

Raid-the-cupboard tuna sweetcorn cakes

Prep: 15 mins **Cook:** 25 mins Plus chilling

Makes 4

Ingredients

- 450g potato , quartered
- 2 tbsp mayonnaise , plus extra to serve
- 2 x 185g cans tuna , drained
- 198g can sweetcorn , drained
- small bunch chives , snipped, or 1 tsp dried parsley
- 2 eggs , beaten
- 100g dried breadcrumb

- sunflower oil, for frying
- salad and your favourite dressing, to serve

Method

STEP 1

Cook the potatoes in boiling salted water until really tender. Drain and allow to steam-dry in a colander. Tip into a bowl, season and mash. Stir in the mayonnaise, tuna, sweetcorn and chives or parsley. Shape into 4 cakes and chill until cold and firm.

STEP 2

Dip each cake into the egg, letting the excess drip off, then coat in the breadcrumbs. Chill for 15 mins.

STEP 3

Heat a little of the oil in a pan and gently fry the cakes for 2-3 mins on each side until golden. You may need to do this in batches – keep warm in a low oven. Serve with extra mayonnaise and salad leaves.

Oven-baked fish & chips

Prep: 15 mins **Cook:** 40 mins

Serves 4

Ingredients

- 800g/ 1lb 12 oz floury potato, scrubbed and cut into chips
- 2 tbsp olive oil
- 50g fresh breadcrumb
- zest 1 lemon
- 2 tbsp chopped flat-leaf parsley
- 4 x 140g/5oz thick sustainable white fish fillets
- 200g/ 7oz cherry tomato

Method

STEP 1

Heat oven to 220C/200C fan/gas 7. Pat chips dry on kitchen paper, then lay in a single layer on a large baking tray. Drizzle with half the olive oil and season with salt. Cook for 40 mins, turning after 20 mins, so they cook evenly.

STEP 2

Mix the breadcrumbs with the lemon zest and parsley, then season well. Top the cod evenly with the breadcrumb mixture, then drizzle .0with the remaining oil. Put in a roasting tin with the cherry tomatoes, then bake in the oven for the final 10 mins of the chips' cooking time.

Kale & salmon kedgeree

Prep: 10 mins **Cook:** 30 mins

Serves 4

Ingredients

- 300g brown rice
- 2 salmon fillets (about 280g)
- 4 eggs
- 1 tbsp vegetable oil
- 1 onion , finely chopped
- 100g curly kale , stalks removed, roughly chopped
- 1 garlic clove , crushed
- 1 tbsp curry powder
- 1 tsp turmeric
- zest and juice 1 lemon

Method

STEP 1

Cook the rice following pack instructions. Meanwhile, season the salmon and steam over a pan of simmering water for 8 mins or until just cooked. Keep the pan of water on the heat, add the eggs and boil for 6 mins, then run under cold water.

STEP 2

Heat the oil in a large frying pan or wok, add the onion and cook for 5 mins. Throw in the kale and cook, stirring, for 5 mins. Add the garlic, curry powder, turmeric and rice, season and stir until heated through.

STEP 3

Peel and quarter the eggs. Flake the salmon and gently fold through the rice, then divide between plates and top with the eggs. Sprinkle over the lemon zest and squeeze over a little juice before serving.

Lemony prawn & chorizo rice pot

Prep: 15 mins **Cook:** 25 mins

Serves 4

Ingredients

- 1 tbsp olive oil
- 1 onion, sliced
- 2 small red peppers, deseeded and sliced
- 50g chorizo, thinly sliced
- 2 garlic cloves, crushed
- 1 red chilli (deseeded if you don't like it too hot)
- ½ tsp turmeric
- 250g long grain rice
- 200g raw peeled prawn, defrosted if frozen
- 100g frozen pea
- zest and juice 1 lemon, plus extra wedges to serve

Method

STEP 1

Boil the kettle. Heat the oil in a shallow pan with a lid, add the onion, peppers, chorizo, garlic and chilli, then fry over a high heat for 3 mins. Add the turmeric and rice, stirring to ensure the rice is coated. Pour in 500ml boiling water, cover, then cook for 12 mins.

STEP 2

Uncover, then stir – the rice should be almost tender. Stir in the prawns and peas, with a splash more water if the rice is looking dry, then cook for 1 min more until the prawns are just pink and the rice tender. Stir in the lemon zest and juice with seasoning and serve with extra lemon wedges on the side.

Lemon spaghetti with tuna & broccoli

Prep: 5 mins **Cook:** 10 mins

Serves 4

Ingredients

- 350g spaghetti
- 250g broccoli, cut into small florets

- 2 shallots , finely chopped
- 85g pitted green olive , halved
- 2 tbsp caper , drained
- 198g can tuna in oil
- zest and juice 1 lemon
- 1 tbsp olive oil , plus extra for drizzling

Method

STEP 1

Boil the spaghetti in salted water for 6 mins. Add the broccoli and boil for 4 mins more or until both are just tender.

STEP 2

Meanwhile, mix the shallots, olives, capers, tuna and lemon zest and juice in a roomy serving bowl. Drain the pasta and broccoli, add to the bowl and toss really well with the olive oil and lots of black pepper. Serve with a little extra olive oil drizzled over.

Pineapple, beef & ginger stir-fry

Prep: 15 mins **Cook:** 10 mins

Serves 2

Ingredients

- 400g rump steak, thinly sliced
- 3tbsp soy sauce
- 2tbsp soft brown sugar
- 1tbsp chilli sauce
- 1tbsp rice wine vinegar
- 2tsp vegetable oil
- thumb-sized piece ginger, cut into fine matchsticks
- 4 spring onions, cut into 3cm lengths
- 200g pineapple, cut into chunks
- handful coriander leaves, to serve
- rice and greens, to serve (optional)

Method

STEP 1

Mix the steak, soy sauce, sugar, chilli sauce and vinegar together, and set aside for 10 mins.

STEP 2

Heat a wok with 1 tsp of the oil. Lift the steak from the marinade and sear, in batches, then remove. Add a bit more oil and fry the ginger until golden. Add the spring onions and pineapple, and return the steak to the pan. Stir to heat through for 1 min, then add any remaining marinade. Keep stirring until the marinade becomes thick and everything is hot. Serve sprinkled with coriander, and with rice and greens, if you like.

Curry coconut fish parcels

Prep: 10 mins **Cook:** 10 mins - 15 mins

Serves 2

Ingredients

- 2 large tilapia fillets , about 125g/4½oz each
- 2 tsp yellow or red curry paste
- 2 tsp desiccated coconut
- zest and juice 1 lime , plus wedges to serve
- 1 tsp soy sauce
- 140g basmati rice
- 2 tbsp sweet chilli sauce
- 1 red chilli , sliced
- 200g cooked thin-stemmed broccoli , to serve

Method

STEP 1

Heat oven to 200C/180C fan/gas 6. Tear off 4 large pieces of foil, double them up, then place a fish fillet in the middle of each. Spread over the curry paste. Divide the coconut, lime zest and juice, and soy between each fillet. Bring up the sides of the foil, then scrunch the edges and sides together to make 2 sealed parcels.

STEP 2

Put the parcels on a baking tray and bake for 10-15 mins. Tip the rice into a pan with plenty of water, and boil for 12-15 mins or until cooked. Drain well. Serve the fish on the rice, drizzle over the chilli sauce and scatter with sliced chilli. Serve with broccoli and lime wedges.

Miso chicken & rice soup

Prep: 10 mins **Cook:** 10 mins

Serves 2

Ingredients

- 500ml chicken stock
- 2 skinless chicken breasts
- 50g long grain rice
- 8 Chanteney carrots, halved lengthways
- 2 tbsp miso paste
- 1 tbsp soy sauce
- 1 tbsp mirin
- 2 spring onions, sliced

Method

STEP 1

Bring the stock to a gentle boil in a medium saucepan. Add the chicken breasts and simmer for 8 mins until cooked through. Remove from the pan and shred the meat.

STEP 2

Add the rice and carrots to the hot stock. Bring back up to the boil, cover with a lid, then reduce the heat and cook for 10 mins until the rice is cooked and the carrots are tender.

STEP 3

Return the chicken to the pan and add the miso, soy and mirin. Scatter over the spring onions just before serving.

Roasted carrot, spelt, fennel & blood orange salad

Prep: 35 mins **Cook:** 25 mins

Serves 6

Ingredients

- 400g spelt
- 1 vegetable stock cube
- 4 tbsp extra virgin olive oil
- 400g baby carrots, scrubbed
- 3 blood oranges, 2 zested and 1 juiced
- 1 tbsp olive oil
- 2 tsp clear honey
- 2 fennel bulbs, thinly sliced
- 4 tbsp red wine vinegar
- 1 small red onion, finely chopped
- large bunch parsley, chopped
- 70g pack pitted, dry black olives or 85g couchillo (the very small black ones) or Kalamata olives
- small pack parsley, chopped (optional)

Method

STEP 1

Heat oven to 200C/180C fan/gas 6 and cook the spelt with the stock cube following pack instructions – don't overcook it, as it should still have a little nutty bite. When the spelt is done, drain it very well and toss on a platter with 1 tbsp of the extra virgin olive oil to stop it from sticking together too much.

STEP 2

Meanwhile, toss the carrots with the olive oil, blood orange zest and some seasoning in a roasting tin, then roast for 15 mins. Carefully stir through half the honey with the fennel. Continue roasting for another 10 mins, then cool for 5 mins. Cut away the pith and peel from the 2 zested oranges, then roughly chop or slice.

STEP 3

Whisk together the remaining extra virgin olive oil, 1 tsp honey, red wine vinegar and the blood orange juice with some seasoning. Scrape the roasted carrots and fennel plus any cooking juices on top of the spelt, along with the orange chunks, red onion, herbs and olives. Drizzle over the dressing and toss everything together well. The salad will happily hold at room temperature for a few hours, but the spelt will soak up the dressing – so if you're making it ahead, add half the dressing when assembling and stir through the rest just before you serve it. As you serve, stir through the parsley, if you like.

Sweet potato salad

Prep: 15 mins **Cook:** 35 mins

Serves 6

Ingredients

- 1.2kg sweet potato , peeled and cut into biggish chunks
- 1 tbsp olive oil

For the dressing

- 2 shallots (or half a small red onion), finely chopped
- 4 spring onions , finely sliced
- small bunch chives , snipped into quarters or use mini ones
- 5 tbsp sherry vinegar
- 2 tbsp extra-virgin olive oil

- 2 tbsp honey

Method

STEP 1

Heat oven to 200C/180C fan/gas 6. Toss the sweet potato chunks with the olive oil and some seasoning, and spread on a baking parchment-lined baking sheet. Roast for 30 - 35 mins until tender and golden. Cool at room temperature.

STEP 2

When just about cool whisk together all the dressing ingredients with a little more seasoning and gently toss through the potato chunks – use your hands to avoid breaking them up.

Superhealthy Singapore noodles

Prep: 20 mins **Cook:** 10 mins

Serves 4

Ingredients

- 3 nests medium egg noodles
- 2 tbsp sunflower oil
- 100g tenderstem broccoli , stems sliced at an angle
- 1 red pepper , deseeded, quartered then cut into strips
- 85g baby corn , quartered lenthways
- 2 garlic cloves , shredded
- 1 red chilli , deseeded and chopped
- thumb-sized piece fresh ginger , peeled and finely chopped
- 2 skinless chicken breasts , sliced
- 100g shelled raw king prawns
- 1 heaped tbsp Madras curry paste
- 2 tsp soy sauce
- 100g beansprouts
- 15g pack coriander , chopped
- 4 spring onions , shredded
- lime wedges, for squeezing

Method

STEP 1

Pour boiling water over the noodles and leave to soften. Meanwhile, heat half the oil in a large non-stick wok and stir-fry all the vegetables, except the beansprouts and onions, with the garlic, chilli and ginger until softened. If the broccoli won't soften, add a splash of water to the wok and cover to create some steam.

STEP 2

Tip the veg on to a plate, add the rest of the oil to the wok then briefly stir-fry the chicken and prawns until just cooked. Set aside with the vegetables and add the curry paste to the pan. Stir-fry for a few secs then add 150ml water and the soy sauce. Allow to bubble then add the drained, softened noodles and beansprouts, and toss together to coat.

STEP 3

Return the vegetables, chicken and prawns to the wok with the coriander and spring onions. Toss well over the heat and serve with lime wedges.

Blueberry & lemon pancakes

Prep: 10 mins **Cook:** 20 mins

Makes 14-16

Ingredients

- 200g plain flour
- 1 tsp cream of tartar
- ½ tsp bicarbonate of soda
- 1 tsp golden syrup
- 75g blueberry
- zest 1 lemon
- 200ml milk
- 1 large egg
- butter , for cooking

Method

STEP 1

First, put the flour, cream of tartar and bicarbonate of soda in the bowl. Mix them well with the fork. Drop the golden syrup into the dry ingredients along with the blueberries and lemon zest.

STEP 2

Pour the milk into a measuring jug. Now break in the egg and mix well with a fork. Pour most of the milk mixture into the bowl and mix well with a rubber spatula. Keep adding more milk until you get a smooth, thick, pouring batter.

STEP 3

Heat the frying pan and brush with a little butter. Then spoon in the batter, 1 tbsp at a time, in heaps. Bubbles will appear on top as the pancakes cook – turn them at this stage, using the metal spatula to help you. Cook until brown on the second side, then keep warm on a plate, covered with foil. Repeat until all the mixture is used up.

Moroccan lamb with apricots, almonds & mint

Prep: 2 hrs **Serves 4**

Ingredients

- 2 tbsp olive oil
- 550g lean lamb, cubed
- 1 onion, chopped
- 2 garlic cloves, crushed
- 700ml lamb or chicken stock
- grated zest and juice 1 orange
- 1 cinnamon stick
- 1 tsp clear honey
- 175g ready-to-eat dried apricots
- 3 tbsp chopped fresh mint
- 25g ground almonds
- 25g toasted flaked almonds
- steamed broccoli and couscous, to serve

Method

STEP 1

Heat the oil in a large flameproof casserole. Add the lamb and cook over a medium-high heat for 3-4 minutes until evenly browned, stirring often. Remove the lamb to a plate, using a slotted spoon.

STEP 2

Stir the onion and garlic into the casserole and cook gently for 5 minutes until softened. Return the lamb to the pot. Add the stock, zest and juice, cinnamon, honey and salt and pepper. Bring to the boil then reduce the heat, cover and cook gently for 1 hour.

STEP 3

Add the apricots and two-thirds of the mint and cook for 30 minutes until the lamb is tender. Stir in the ground almonds to thicken the sauce. Serve with the remaining mint and toasted almonds scattered over the top.

Charred spring onions

Prep: 5 mins **Cook:** 10 mins - 12 mins

Serves 6

Ingredients

- 2 bunches of spring onions (about 20)

Method

STEP 1

If your barbecue hasn't already been heated, light and heat until the ashes turn grey, or heat a griddle pan. Wash the spring onions and pat dry. Trim off the ends, then place the onions directly on the barbecue or in a hot griddle pan.

STEP 2

When the spring onions have softened and blackened, take off the heat and move to a hot spot on the barbecue top to keep warm before serving.

Chipotle black bean soup with lime-pickled onions

Prep: 10 mins **Cook:** 25 mins Plus pickling

Serves 2

Ingredients

- juice 2 limes
- 2 small red onions, thinly sliced
- ½ tbsp olive oil
- 2 garlic cloves, finely chopped
- ½ tbsp ground cumin
- ½ tbsp smoked paprika
- ½ tbsp chipotle paste, or Tabasco, to taste
- 400g can black bean, drained and rinsed
- 400ml vegetable stock
- half-fat soured cream, to serve
- coriander leaves, to serve
- crisp tortilla chips, to serve

Method

STEP 1

To make the lime-pickled onions, combine ½ the lime juice and ½ the onions in a small bowl, and season. Leave to pickle for 30 mins.

STEP 2

Meanwhile, heat the olive oil in a saucepan over a medium-high heat. Add the garlic and remaining onions, and season. Cook for 8 mins or until the onions are translucent. Add the spices and chipotle purée, cook for 1 min, then add the beans, stock and remaining lime juice. Simmer for 15 mins, then purée in a blender.

STEP 3

Pour the soup into a clean pan to reheat. Serve with a little of the drained pickled onions, topped with a small drizzle of soured cream and some coriander, and the tortillas on the side.

Courgette & quinoa-stuffed peppers

Prep: 10 mins **Cook:** 20 mins

Serves 4

Ingredients

- 4 red peppers
- 1 courgette , quartered lengthways and thinly sliced
- 2 x 250g packs ready-to-eat quinoa
- 85g feta cheese , finely crumbled
- handful parsley , roughly chopped

Method

STEP 1

Heat oven to 200C/180C fan/gas 6. Cut each pepper in half through the stem, and remove the seeds. Put the peppers, cut-side up, on a baking sheet, drizzle with 1 tbsp olive oil and season well. Roast for 15 mins.

STEP 2

Meanwhile, heat 1 tsp olive oil in a small frying pan, add the courgette and cook until soft. Remove from the heat, then stir through the quinoa, feta and parsley. Season with pepper.

STEP 3

Divide the quinoa mixture between the pepper halves, then return to the oven for 5 mins to heat through. Serve with a green salad, if you like.

Tangy trout

Prep: 10 mins **Cook:** 5 mins

Serves 4

Ingredients

- 4 trout fillets
- 50g breadcrumbs
- 1 tbsp butter, softened
- 1 small bunch parsley, chopped
- zest and juice of 1 lemon, plus lemon wedges to serve
- 25g pine nuts, toasted and half roughly chopped
- 1 tbsp olive oil

Method

STEP 1

Heat the grill to high. Lay the fillets, skin side down, on an oiled baking tray. Mix together the breadcrumbs, butter, parsley, lemon zest and juice, and half the pine nuts. Scatter the mixture in a thin layer over the fillets, drizzle with the oil and place under the grill for 5 mins. Sprinkle over the remaining pine nuts, then serve with the lemon wedges and a potato salad.

Vegetable & bean chilli

Prep: 10 mins **Cook:** 30 mins - 35 mins

Serves 4

Ingredients

- 1 tbsp olive oil
- 1 clove garlic, finely chopped

- thumb-sized piece ginger, finely chopped
- 1 large onion, chopped
- 2 courgettes, diced
- 1 red pepper, deseeded and chopped
- 1 yellow pepper, deseeded and chopped
- 1 tbsp chilli powder
- 100g red lentils, washed and drained
- 1 tbsp tomato purée
- x cans chopped tomatoes
- 195g can sweetcorn, drained
- 420g can butter beans, drained
- 400g can kidney beans in water, drained

Method

STEP 1

Heat the oil in a large pan. Cook the garlic, ginger, onion, courgettes and peppers for about 5 mins until starting to soften. Add the chilli powder and cook for 1 min more.

STEP 2

Stir in the lentils, tomato purée, tomatoes and 250ml water. Bring to the boil and cook for 15-20 mins.

STEP 3

Add the sweetcorn and beans, and cook for a further 10 mins.

Pea hummus

Prep: 10 mins No cook

Serves 4

Ingredients

- 200g cooked peas
- 1 garlic clove, crushed
- 1 tbsp tahini
- squeeze of lemon
- 1 tbsp cooked cannellini beans, from a can
- 2 tbsp olive oil
- strips of pitta bread, to serve
- raw vegetable sticks, to serve

Method

STEP 1

Blitz all the ingredients together using a hand blender or food processor. Add 1-2 tbsp water, then blitz again. Transfer a portion to a pot and add to a lunchbox with pitta bread strips and veg sticks. Keep the rest chilled for up to 3 days.

Beef & bean chilli bowl with chipotle yogurt

Prep: 5 mins **Cook:** 45 mins

Serves 4

Ingredients

- 1 tbsp olive oil
- 1 large onion , chopped
- 250g pack extra-lean minced beef
- 1 tbsp chipotle paste , plus a little extra to serve
- 1 tbsp Cajun seasoning mix
- 2 x 400g cans mixed bean salad, drained
- 400g can chopped tomato
- 1 low-sodium beef stock cube
- 2 squares 70% cocoa dark chocolate
- small pack coriander , chopped
- cooked brown rice and low-fat Greek yogurt, to serve

Method

STEP 1

Heat the oil in a frying pan and cook the onion on a medium heat until softened. Add the beef with some black pepper and a little salt, breaking up any lumps with a wooden spoon, and cook until browned. Add the chipotle and Cajun seasoning. Give it a good stir and cook for 1 min more.

STEP 2

Tip in the beans and tomatoes, then crumble over the stock cube. Add a can of water and simmer for about 20-30 mins, until thickened. Add the chocolate, and stir until melted, then add most of the coriander.

STEP 3

Serve the chilli in bowls on top of the rice sprinkled with the rest of the coriander, with a dollop of low-fat yogurt, and an extra drizzle of chipotle paste on top.

Courgette tortilla with toppings

Prep: 5 mins **Cook:** 6 mins

Serves 2

Ingredients

- 1 tbsp olive oil
- 1 large courgette , coarsely grated
- 1 tsp harissa
- 4 large eggs
- 3 tbsp reduced-fat hummus
- 1 large red pepper from a jar, torn into strips
- 3 pitted queen olives , quartered
- handful coriander

Method

STEP 1

Heat the oil in a 20cm non-stick frying pan, add the courgette and cook for a few mins, stirring occasionally, until softened. Meanwhile, beat the harissa with the eggs and pour into the pan. Cook gently, stirring, to allow the uncooked egg to flow onto the base of the pan. When it is two-thirds cooked, leave it untouched for 2 mins to set. Slide onto a plate, then return to the pan, uncooked-side down, to finish cooking.

STEP 2

To serve, tip onto a board and spread with the hummus. Scatter with the pepper, olives and coriander. Cut into quarters and eat warm or cold.

Spinach & sweet potato tortilla

Prep: 10 mins **Cook:** 1 hr

Serves 6 - 8

Ingredients

- 300g bag baby spinach leaves
- 8 tbsp light olive oil
- 2 large onions , thinly sliced
- 4 medium sweet potatoes (800g/ 1lb 12oz), peeled, cut into thin slices
- 2 garlic cloves , finely chopped
- 8 large eggs

Method

STEP 1

Put the spinach in a large colander and pour over a kettleful of boiling water. Drain well and, when cooled a little, squeeze dry, trying not to mush up the spinach too much.

STEP 2

Heat 3 tbsp oil in a 25cm non-stick pan with a lid, then sweat the onions for 15 mins until really soft but not coloured. Add another 3 tbsp oil and add the potatoes and garlic. Mix in with the onions, season well, cover and cook over a gentle heat for another 15 mins or so until the potatoes are very tender. Stir occasionally to stop them catching.

STEP 3

Whisk the eggs in a large bowl, tip in the cooked potato and onion, and mix together. Separate the spinach clumps, add to the mix and fold through, trying not to break up the potato too much.

STEP 4

Add 2 tbsp more oil to the pan and pour in the sweet potato and egg mix. Cover and cook over a low-medium heat for 20 mins until the base and sides are golden brown and the centre has mostly set. Run a palette knife around the sides to stop it from sticking. 5 To turn the tortilla over, put a plate face down onto the pan, then flip it over. Slide the tortilla back into the pan and cook for a further 5-10 mins until just set and golden all over. (Don't worry if it breaks up a little on the edges as you're turning it – it will look perfect when it's cooked through and set.) Continue cooking on the other side until just set and golden all over. Again use a palette knife to release the tortilla from the sides. Allow to rest for 5 mins, then tip onto a board before cutting into wedges.

Stuffed butternut squash with quinoa

Prep: 10 mins **Cook:** 1 hr

Serves 2 with filling leftover

Ingredients

- 1 medium butternut squash
- olive oil, for roasting
- pinch dried oregano

- 150g ready-to-eat quinoa (we used Merchant Gourmet Red and White Quinoa)
- 100g feta cheese
- 50g toasted pine nut
- 1 small carrot, grated (around 50g)
- small bunch chives, snipped
- juice half lemon
- 1 red pepper, chopped
- 50g pitted black olive
- 2 spring onions, chopped

Method

STEP 1

Heat the oven to 200C/fan 180C/gas 6. Halve the butternut squash, scoop out the seeds and score the flesh with a sharp knife.

STEP 2

Arrange the two halves on a baking tray, drizzle with a little olive oil, season with freshly ground black pepper and sea salt, sprinkle with dried oregano and cook for 40 minutes. Take out the oven, add the chopped peppers to the tray alongside the squash and cook for a further 10 minutes.

STEP 3

Meanwhile mix the rest of the ingredients. Take the tray out of the oven and carefully transfer the peppers to the stuffing mix. Stir together and spoon the filling onto the butternut squash. Return to the oven for 10 mins. Serve.

Quinoa, pea & avocado salad

Prep: 20 mins No cook

Serves 4

Ingredients

- 100g frozen peas
- juice 1 lemon
- 2 tbsp olive oil
- ½ small pack mint, leaves only, chopped
- ½ small pack chives, snipped
- 250g pack ready-to-eat red & white quinoa mix (we used Merchant Gourmet)

- 1 avocado, stoned, peeled and chopped into chunks
- 75g bag pea shoots

Method

STEP 1

Put the peas in a large heatproof bowl, pour over just-boiled water, then set aside.

STEP 2

Pour the lemon juice into a small bowl and whisk in some seasoning. Keep whisking as you slowly add the olive oil, followed by the mint and chives.

STEP 3

Drain the peas and tip into a large serving dish. Stir in the quinoa, breaking up any clumps. Pour over the dressing, then fold in the avocado and pea shoots. Serve immediately.

Chicken, edamame & ginger pilaf

Prep: 10 mins **Cook:** 17 mins

Serves 4

Ingredients

- 2 tbsp vegetable oil
- 1 onion, thinly sliced
- thumb-sized piece ginger, grated
- 1 red chilli, deseeded and finely sliced
- 3 skinless chicken breasts, cut into bite-sized pieces
- 250g basmati rice
- 600ml vegetable stock
- 100g frozen edamame / soya beans
- coriander leaves and fat-free Greek yoghurt (optional), to serve

Method

STEP 1

Heat the oil in a medium saucepan, then add the onion, ginger and chilli, along with some seasoning. Cook for 5 mins, then add the chicken and rice. Cook for 2 mins more, then add the stock and bring to the boil. Turn the heat to low, cover and cook for 8-10 mins until the rice is just cooked. During the final 3 mins of cooking, add the edamame beans. Sprinkle some coriander leaves on top and serve with a dollop of Greek yogurt, if you like.

Tomatillo salsa

Prep: 5 mins **Cook:** 5 mins plus cooling

Serves 4

Ingredients

- 400g tomatillos
- small pack coriander
- 1 white onion, chopped
- 2 green chillies, roughly chopped
- 1 garlic clove, roughly chopped
- 1 lime, juiced
- 1 avocado, cut into small cubes

Method

STEP 1

Put the tomatillos in a pan of boiling water, cook for 3 mins or until the skins split, remove with a slotted spoon and cool for 5-10 mins. Blitz in a food processor with the coriander, onion, chilli, garlic and lime. Tip into a bowl, stir in the avocado and season to taste.

Barley couscous & prawn tabbouleh

Prep: 10 mins **Cook:** 25 mins

Serves 2

Ingredients

- 125g barley couscous
- zest 1 lemon, juice of 0.5
- 1 tbsp extra virgin rapeseed oil
- ½ small pack dill, finely chopped
- good handful mint leaves, chopped
- ½ cucumber, chopped
- 2 nectarines, chopped
- 125g peeled prawns, or a handful of cashews or pecans for a vegetarian version.

Method

STEP 1

Tip the couscous into a bowl and pour over just enough boiling water to cover, following pack instructions. Leave for no more than 5 mins, drain thoroughly, then fluff up with a fork and tip into a bowl. Stir in the lemon zest and juice with the oil, dill and mint, then add the cucumber and nectarines.

STEP 2

Toss through the prawns or nuts and serve on plates or pack into lunch containers.

Turkey tortilla pie

Prep: 5 mins **Cook:** 25 mins

Serves 4

Ingredients

- 2 onions, finely chopped
- 1 tbsp olive oil, plus a little extra if needed
- 2 tsp ground cumin
- 500g pack turkey mince
- 1 ½ tbsp chipotle paste
- 400g can chopped tomato
- 400g can kidney bean, drained and rinsed
- 198g can sweetcorn, drained
- 2 corn tortillas, snipped into triangles
- small handful grated cheddar
- 2 spring onions, finely sliced

Method

STEP 1

In a deep flameproof casserole dish, cook the onions in the oil for 8 mins until soft. Add the cumin and cook for 1 min more. Stir in the mince and add a bit more oil, if needed. Turn up the heat and cook for 4-6 mins, stirring occasionally, until the mince is browned.

STEP 2

Stir in the chipotle paste, tomatoes and half a can of water, and simmer for 5 mins. Mix in the beans and sweetcorn, and cook for a few mins more until thick, piping hot and the mince is cooked.

STEP 3

Heat the grill. Take the pan off the heat and put the tortilla triangles randomly on top. Scatter over the cheese and grill for a few mins until the topping is crisp, taking care that it doesn't burn. Sprinkle with the spring onions and serve.

Feta-stuffed mushrooms with mustard slaw

Prep: 20 mins **Cook:** 35 mins

Serves 2

Ingredients

- 4 large Portobello mushrooms , each about 10cm across
- 1-2 tsp rapeseed oil
- 100g bulghar wheat
- 2 garlic cloves , finely grated
- 50g feta , crumbled
- 2 tsp finely chopped rosemary leaves
- 6 walnut halves , roughly broken
- 2 tbsp chopped parsley (optional)

For the slaw

- 2 carrots , coarsely grated
- 1 red onion , finely sliced
- 200g red cabbage , finely shredded
- 40g raisins
- 1 tbsp rapeseed oil
- 1 tbsp apple cider vinegar
- 1 tsp English mustard powder
- 4 tbsp four-seed mix (sesame, sunflower, golden linseed and pumpkin)

Method

STEP 1

Heat oven to 200C/180C fan/ gas 6 and snap the stalks from the mushrooms. Put the stalks in a large, shallow ovenproof dish along with the caps, turned upside down. Brush the caps with the oil and bake in the oven for 15 mins.

STEP 2

Meanwhile, boil the bulghar for 8 mins, then drain and toss with the garlic, feta, rosemary, walnuts and parsley (if using).

STEP 3

Take the mushrooms from the oven and turn the caps round the other way. Roughly chop the stalks, add to the bulghar mixture and pile it on top of the mushroom caps. Return to the oven for 10 mins while you make the slaw.

STEP 4

Put all the slaw ingredients in a bowl and toss well. Serve half with the mushrooms and chill the rest to serve for lunch with the Masala omelette muffins (see goes well with) another day.

Roast chicken thighs with brown rice & salsa verde

Prep: 10 mins **Cook:** 35 mins

Serves 2

Ingredients

- 3 skinless boneless chicken thighs , cut in half
- 2 tbsp rapeseed oil
- 2 garlic cloves , bashed
- ½ small pack coriander
- ½ small pack parsley
- 1 anchovy fillet
- ½ tbsp capers
- ½ lemon , zested and juiced
- 200g pouch cooked wholegrain rice
- 200g baby leaf spinach

Method

STEP 1

Heat oven to 200C/180C fan/gas 6. Season the chicken, rub with ½ tbsp oil, then put in a large roasting tin with the garlic and roast for 25-30 mins.

STEP 2

Meanwhile, blitz the herbs, anchovy, capers, lemon juice and remaining oil with some seasoning in a food processor until finely chopped. Set aside.

STEP 3

Once the chicken is cooked, remove the tin from the oven and squeeze the garlic out of their skins. Tip in the rice and use a wooden spoon to break it up, then add the spinach and lemon zest and toss. Return to the oven for 5 mins. Divide between bowls and dollop on the salsa verde.

Herby lamb fillet with caponata

Prep: 10 mins **Cook:** 25 mins

Serves 2

Ingredients

- 3 garlic cloves

For the caponata

- 2 tsp rapeseed oil
- 1 red onion, cut into wedges
- 1 aubergine, sliced and quartered
- 500g carton passata
- 1 green pepper, quartered, deseeded and sliced
- 6 pitted Kalamata olives, halved and rinsed
- 2 tsp capers, rinsed
- 1 tsp chopped rosemary
- 1 tsp balsamic vinegar

For the lamb & potatoes

- 4 baby new potatoes, halved
- 1 tsp chopped rosemary
- 1 tsp rapeseed oil
- 250g lean lamb loin fillet, all visible fat removed
- 240g bag baby spinach
- finely chopped parsley (optional)

Method

STEP 1

Slice 2 of the garlic cloves for the caponata, finely grate the other for the lamb and set aside. Heat the oil for the caponata in a wide pan, add the onion and fry for 5 mins to soften. Tip in the aubergine and cook, stirring, for 5 mins more. Add the passata and pepper with the olives, capers, rosemary and balsamic vinegar, then cover and cook for 15 mins, stirring frequently.

STEP 2

Meanwhile, heat oven to 190C/170C fan/ gas 5. Boil the potatoes for 10 mins, then drain. Mix the grated garlic with the rosemary and some black pepper, then rub all over the lamb. Toss the potatoes in the oil with some more black pepper, place in a small roasting tin with the lamb and roast for 15-20 mins. Meanwhile, wilt the spinach in the microwave or in a pan, and squeeze to drain any excess liquid.

STEP 3

Stir the garlic into the caponata and serve with the lamb, either whole or sliced, rolled in parsley if you like, with the potatoes and spinach.

Potato salad with anchovy & quail's eggs

Prep: 10 mins **Cook:** 20 mins

Serves 1

Ingredients

- 4 quail's eggs
- 100g green beans
- 100g new potatoes, halved or quartered if very large
- 1 anchovy, finely chopped
- 1 tbsp chopped parsley
- 1 tbsp chopped chives
- juice 0.5 lemon

Method

STEP 1

Bring a medium pan of water to a simmer. Lower the quail's eggs into the water and cook for 2 mins. Lift out the eggs with a slotted spoon and put into a bowl of cold water. Add the beans to the pan, simmer for 4 mins until tender, then remove from the pan with a slotted spoon and plunge into the bowl of cold water.

STEP 2

Put the potatoes in the pan and boil for 10-15 mins until tender. Drain the potatoes in a colander and leave them to cool. While the potatoes are cooling, peel the eggs and cut them in half. Toss the potatoes and beans with the chopped anchovy, herbs and lemon juice. Top with the quail's eggs to serve.

Chicken with mustard lentils

Prep: 15 mins **Cook:** 1 hr and 15 mins

Serves 4

Ingredients

- 1 tbsp vegetable oil
- pack of 4 chicken thighs and 4 chicken drumsticks
- 1 red onion , thinly sliced
- 2 garlic cloves , crushed
- 250g puy lentils
- 750ml hot chicken stock
- 2 tbsp crème fraîche
- zest and juice 1 lemon
- 1 tbsp Dijon mustard
- small bunch parsley , chopped
- green vegetables , to serve (optional)

Method

STEP 1

Heat the oil in a large flameproof casserole. Season the chicken pieces, then brown in the hot oil for 3 mins each side, until golden on all sides. Remove and set aside. Pour away all but 1 tbsp oil.

STEP 2

Add the onion to the pan and cook for 5 mins, then add the garlic and cook for 1 min more. Add the lentils and stock and stir well. Put the chicken on top, put the lid on and leave to simmer over a medium heat for 30 mins. Remove the lid and increase the heat. Bubble for another 20 mins until the lentils are tender, most of the stock has been absorbed, and the chicken is cooked through.

STEP 3

Stir in the crème fraîche, lemon zest and juice, mustard, parsley and seasoning. Serve with green veg, if you like.

Lighter lemon drizzle cake

Prep: 25 mins **Cook:** 40 mins

Cuts into 12 slices

Ingredients

- 75ml rapeseed oil , plus extra for the tin
- 175g self-raising flour
- 1 ½ tsp baking powder
- 50g ground almond
- 50g polenta
- finely grated zest 2 lemons
- 140g golden caster sugar
- 2 large eggs
- 225g natural yogurt

For the lemon syrup

- 85g caster sugar
- juice 2 lemon (about 5 tbsp)

Method

STEP 1

Heat oven to 180C/160C fan/gas 4. Lightly oil a 20cm round x 5cm deep cake tin and line the base with baking parchment. For the cake, put the flour, baking powder, ground almonds and polenta in a large mixing bowl. Stir in the lemon zest and sugar, then make a dip in the centre. Beat the eggs in a bowl, then stir in the yogurt. Tip this mixture along with the oil into the dip (see step-by-step number 1), then briefly and gently stir with a large metal spoon so everything is just combined, without overmixing.

STEP 2

Spoon the mixture into the tin and level the top (step 2). Bake for 40 mins or until a skewer inserted into the centre of the cake comes out clean. Cover loosely with foil for the final 5-10 mins if it starts to brown too quickly.

STEP 3

While the cake cooks, make the lemon syrup. Tip the caster sugar into a small saucepan with the lemon juice and 75ml water. Heat over a medium heat, stirring occasionally, until the sugar has dissolved. Raise the heat, boil for 4 mins until slightly reduced and syrupy, then remove from the heat.

STEP 4

Remove the cake from the oven and let it cool briefly in the tin. While it is still warm, turn it out of the tin, peel off the lining paper and sit the cake on a wire rack set over a baking tray or similar. Use a skewer to make lots of small holes all over the top of the cake (step 3). Slowly spoon over half the lemon syrup (step 4) and let it soak in. Spoon over the rest in the same way, brushing the edges and sides of the cake too with the last of the syrup.

Lemon pollock with sweet potato chips & broccoli mash

Prep: 15 mins **Cook:** 35 mins

Serves 2

Ingredients

- 2 garlic cloves
- For the chips
- 2 sweet potatoes (175g/6oz), scrubbed and cut into chips

- 2 tsp rapeseed oil , plus extra for the fish
- ½ tsp smoked paprika

For the fish & dressing

- 2 pollock fillets (about 100g/4oz each)
- ½ unwaxed lemon
- 2 tbsp extra virgin olive oil

- 1 ½ tsp capers , rinsed and chopped
- 1 tbsp chopped dill

For the broccoli mash

- 1 leek , chopped
- 4 broccoli spears (about 200g/7oz)

- 85g frozen peas
- handful mint

Method

STEP 1

Heat oven to 200C/180C fan/gas 6. Finely chop the garlic, put half in a bowl for the dressing and set the rest aside for the chips. Toss the sweet potatoes with the oil and spread out on a large baking sheet. Bake for 25 mins, turning halfway through.

STEP 2

Put the fish on a sheet of baking parchment on a baking sheet, brush with a little oil, then grate over the lemon zest and season with black pepper. Set aside.

STEP 3

Boil the leek for 5 mins, then add the broccoli and cook for 5 mins more. Tip in the peas for a further 2 mins. Drain, return to the pan and blitz with a stick blender to make a thick purée. Add the mint, then blitz again.

STEP 4

Meanwhile, toss the garlic and paprika with the chips and return to the oven with the fish for 10 mins. Add the olive oil to the garlic, with the capers and dill and 1 tbsp water. Serve everything together with the caper dressing spooned over the fish.

Chinese poached chicken & rice

Prep: 20 mins **Cook:** 40 mins

Serves 4

Ingredients

- large piece of ginger , 1 tbsp finely grated, the rest sliced
- 3 garlic cloves
- 1 tsp black peppercorns
- 1 tbsp soy sauce , plus 2-3 tsp (optional)
- 8 chicken legs
- 3 tbsp sesame oil
- 2 bunches spring onions , chopped
- 4 pak choi , halved
- cooked long-grain rice , to serve

Method

STEP 1

Put the sliced ginger, the garlic, peppercorns and half the soy in a large pan with the chicken legs. Add enough water to cover, and season with a little salt. Bring to the boil, then reduce to a low simmer, put on the lid and poach for 30 mins.

STEP 2

Meanwhile, heat a pan and add the sesame oil and spring onions. Soften for 1 min, then remove from the heat and stir in the grated ginger and remaining soy sauce to make a relish.

STEP 3

When the chicken is ready, remove from the pan, set aside 4 of the legs and chill for tomorrow. Add the pak choi to the poaching liquid and cook for 3-4 mins. Strain the poaching liquid to remove the ginger, garlic and peppercorns, reserving the liquid. Pull the skin from the remaining 4 chicken legs and discard. Tear the meat into thick pieces. Serve in bowls with rice, the pak choi, a ladle of the hot chicken broth, the spring onion relish and extra soy sauce, if you like.

Masala chicken pie

Prep: 15 mins - 20 mins **Cook:** 1 hr and 30 mins

Serves 6

Ingredients

- 2 tbsp vegetable oil
- 4 skinless chicken breasts
- 2 onions , chopped
- finger-length piece ginger , grated
- 3 garlic cloves , crushed
- 2 tbsp medium curry powder
- 2 tsp ground coriander
- 2 tsp ground cumin
- 2 tsp black or brown mustard seed
- 2 tsp white or red wine vinegar
- 2 tsp sugar (white or brown)
- 2 x 400g cans chopped tomatoes
- 150ml light coconut milk (buy a 400ml can- you'll need more for the topping)
- 1 large red pepper , deseeded and cut into large chunks
- 1 large green pepper , deseeded and cut into large chunks
- ½ a small bunch coriander , leaves roughly chopped, stalks reserved (see below)

For the topping

- 1 ½kg floury potato , cut into very large chunks
- 150ml light coconut milk
- 1 tsp turmeric
- juice 1 lemon
- 1 bunch spring onions , finely chopped
- stalks from ½ a small bunch coriander , finely chopped
- 1 tsp kalonji seeds (also known as nigella or onion seeds)
- naan bread , to serve (optional)

Method

STEP 1

Heat a deep frying pan or flameproof casserole dish and add 2 tsp of the oil. Brown the chicken breasts quickly but well on both sides, then remove to a plate. Turn down the heat and add the remaining oil, the onions, ginger and garlic. Fry gently until soft. Add the spices and cook for a few mins, stirring.

STEP 2

Stir in the vinegar, sugar, tomatoes and coconut milk. Bring to a simmer and bubble for 10 mins. Roughly chop the chicken breasts and stir into the pan with any chicken juices and the peppers. Simmer for another 20 mins until the chicken is cooked through and the sauce reduced a little. Take off the heat, stir in the coriander leaves and season to taste – it will need a good seasoning.

STEP 3

To make the topping, put the potatoes in a big pan of water, bring to the boil, then boil until cooked – 10-15 mins depending on how big your chunks are. Drain really well, then tip back into the pan and steam-dry for a few mins.

STEP 4

Add the coconut milk and turmeric to the pan, and mash really well. Season with the lemon juice and some salt, then stir through the spring onions and coriander stalks.

STEP 5

Spoon the chicken masala into a baking dish. Dollop on spoonfuls of mash to cover, then sprinkle over the kalonji seeds. Can be covered and chilled for up to 2 days (or frozen for up to a month).

STEP 6

Heat oven to 200C/180C fan/gas 6 and bake for 25-30 mins (or 45 mins from chilled) until hot through and crisping on top. Serve with naan bread, if you like.

Thai red duck with sticky pineapple rice

Prep: 20 mins **Cook:** 15 mins plus marinating and steaming

Serves 2

Ingredients

- 2 duck breasts, skin removed and discarded
- 1 tbsp Thai red curry paste

- zest and juice 1 lime , plus extra wedges to serve
- 140g jasmine rice
- 125ml light coconut milk , from a can
- 140g frozen peas
- 50g beansprouts
- ½ red onion , diced
- 100g fresh pineapple , cubed
- 1 red chilli , deseeded and finely chopped
- ¼ small pack coriander , stalks finely chopped, leaves roughly chopped

Method

STEP 1

Sit a duck breast between 2 sheets of cling film on a chopping board. Use a rolling pin to bash the duck until it is 0.5cm thick. Repeat with the other breast, then put them both in a dish. Mix the curry paste with the lime zest and juice, and rub all over the duck. Leave to marinate at room temperature for 20 mins.

STEP 2

Meanwhile, tip the rice into a small saucepan with some salt. Pour over the coconut milk with 150ml water. Bring to a simmer, then cover the pan, turn the heat down low and cook for 5 more mins. Stir in the peas, then cover, turn the heat off and leave for another 10 mins. Check the rice - all the liquid should be absorbed and the rice cooked through. Boil the kettle, put the beansprouts and red onion in a colander and pour over a kettleful of boiling water. Stir the beansprouts and onion into the rice with the pineapple, chilli and coriander stalks, and some more salt if it needs it, and put the lid back on to keep warm.

STEP 3

Heat a griddle pan and cook the duck for 1-2 mins each side or until cooked to your liking. Slice the duck, stir most of the coriander leaves through the rice with a fork to fluff up, and serve alongside the duck, scattered with the remaining coriander.

Zesty salmon with roasted beets & spinach

Prep: 10 mins **Cook:** 1 hr

Serves 2

Ingredients

- 4 small fresh beetroots , about 200g
- 1 ½ tbsp rapeseed oil

- 1 tsp coriander seeds, lightly crushed
- 2 skinless salmon or trout fillets
- 2 ½ small oranges, zest of 1 and juice of half
- 3 tbsp pumpkin seeds
- 1 garlic clove
- 1 red onion, finely chopped
- 4 handfuls baby spinach leaves
- 1 avocado, thickly sliced

Method

STEP 1

Heat oven to 180C, 160C fan, gas 4. Trim the stems of the beetroot and reserve any tender leaves that are suitable for eating in the salad. Cut the beetroots into quarters then toss with 1/2 tbsp oil, the coriander seeds, and some seasoning then pile into the centre of a large sheet of foil and wrap up like a parcel. Bake for 45 mins or until the beetroots are tender then top with the salmon, scatter over half the orange zest and return to the oven for 15 mins. If you want to toast the pumpkin seeds, put them in the oven for 10 mins.

STEP 2

Meanwhile cut the peel and pith from 2 oranges then cut out the segments with a sharp knife working over a bowl to catch the juices. Finely grate the garlic and leave for 10 mins to allow the enzymes to activate. Stir the garlic into the orange juice and remaining oil with seasoning to make a dressing.

STEP 3

Remove the parcel from the oven and carefully lift off the fish. Tip the beetroot into a bowl with the red onion, remaining orange zest, pumpkin seeds and spinach leaves and toss well. Gently toss through the orange segments and avocado with any beet leaves then pile onto plates and top with the warm salmon. Drizzle over the dressing and serve while still warm.

Masala omelette muffins

Prep: 10 mins **Cook:** 20 mins - 25 mins

makes 4

Ingredients

- rapeseed oil, for greasing
- 2 medium courgettes, coarsely grated
- 6 large eggs
- 2 large or 4 small garlic cloves, finely grated

- 1 red chilli , deseeded and finely chopped
- 1 tsp chilli powder
- 1 tsp ground cumin
- 1 tsp ground coriander
- handful fresh coriander , chopped
- 125g frozen peas
- 40g feta

Method

STEP 1

Heat oven to 220C/200C fan/ gas 7 and lightly oil four 200ml ramekins. Grate the courgettes and squeeze really well, removing as much liquid as possible. Put all the ingredients except the feta in a large jug and mix really well.

STEP 2

Pour into the ramekins, scatter with the feta and bake on a baking sheet for 20-25 mins until risen and set. You can serve the muffins hot or cold with salad, slaw or cooked vegetables.

Easy ratatouille

Prep: 25 mins **Cook:** 40 mins

Serves 4

Ingredients

- 2 aubergines
- 3 medium courgettes
- 2 red peppers
- 2 tbsp olive oil
- 1 large onion , finely diced
- 3 garlic cloves , crushed
- 2 x 400g cans chopped tomatoes
- 1 tsp dried oregano , basil or Italian mixed herbs
- small bunch basil , chopped, plus a few leaves to serve
- 1 tbsp red wine vinegar
- 1-2 tbsp sugar

Method

STEP 1

Dice the aubergine, courgette and pepper into 3cm chunks. Heat the olive oil in a large casserole or deep frying pan over a medium heat. Fry the onion for 10 mins until soft and translucent. Add the chopped veg, turn the heat to high and fry for another 10 mins until softened.

STEP 2

Stir the garlic into the pan, and toss everything together, frying for 1 min more. Tip in the chopped tomatoes, plus half a can of water (200ml), the dried herbs and the chopped basil. Simmer for 20 minutes on a medium heat, stirring occasionally, until the veg is tender and the tomatoes are thick and coating the veg. Season and add the vinegar and sugar to balance the sweet and acidity of the tomatoes. Scatter with the basil leaves, and serve with rustic bread, or pasta.

Lemon & garlic roast chicken with charred broccoli & sweet potato mash

Prep: 10 mins **Cook:** 1 hr - 1 hr and 15 mins

Serves 2

Ingredients

- 1 small free-range chicken (about 1kg)
- 2 garlic cloves
- 1 tsp rapeseed oil
- small bunch thyme
- 1 lemon , halved
- 1 small head broccoli (about 200g), cut into small florets
- 200g sweet potato , peeled and cubed (cook 100g extra if you are using for Chicken wrap with sticky sweet potato, see 'goes well with')
- 1 tbsp low-fat cream cheese

Method

STEP 1

Heat oven to 200C/180C fan/gas 6 and put the chicken in a large non-stick roasting tin. Halve 1 garlic clove and rub it over the chicken. Drizzle with oil, rub in with your fingers, then stuff the cavity with the thyme, 1 lemon half and the garlic you just used.

STEP 2

Cut the other lemon half into quarters and scatter around the chicken with the other garlic clove, halved.

STEP 3

Cover the tin with foil and bake for 40 mins, then remove the foil and spoon over the hot juices. Arrange the broccoli around the chicken, turning well in the juices, and return the tin to the oven for another 20-30 mins. To check that it is cooked through, pierce between the leg and thigh – if the juices run clear, the chicken is ready. Re-cover with foil and set aside while you prepare the sweet potatoes.

STEP 4

Put the sweet potatoes in a pan of boiling water, return to the boil, then simmer for 7-10 mins until tender. Drain well, then mash. Set aside 100g of sweet potato mash if using for Chicken wrap with sticky sweet potato, see 'goes well with', then add the cream cheese to the rest and stir well.

STEP 5

Remove the broccoli from the roasting tin and divide between 2 plates. Put the chicken on a serving plate, discard the lemon and garlic from the tin and remove as much of the fat from the juices as possible. Pour the remaining juices into a serving jug.

STEP 6

Carve the chicken and serve about 100g (1-2 slices) per person (keep the rest of the chicken for Chicken wrap with sticky sweet potato if making, see 'goes well with'). Serve with the broccoli and mashed sweet potatoes, and a drizzle of the lemony-garlic juices on top.

Tropical overnight oats

Prep: 10 mins No cook

Serves 1

Ingredients

- 50g rolled porridge oats
- 20g coconut yogurt
- 2 sliced kiwis
- 1 passion fruit
- ½ tsp toasted mixed seeds

Method

STEP 1

Soak the oats in 150ml water with a pinch of salt, then cover and chill in the fridge overnight.

STEP 2

The next day spoon half the oats into a bowl. Layer with the coconut yogurt, sliced kiwis, the pulp of the passion fruit and the rest of the oats, then top with the toasted mixed seeds.

Summer vegetable curry

Prep: 10 mins **Cook:** 35 mins

Serves 4

Ingredients

- 1-2 tbsp red Thai curry paste (depending on taste)
- 500ml low-sodium vegetable stock
- 2 onions, chopped
- 1 aubergine, diced
- 75g red lentil
- 200ml can reduced-fat coconut milk
- 2 red or yellow peppers, deseeded and cut into wedges
- 140g frozen pea
- 100g bag baby spinach, roughly chopped
- brown basmati rice and mango chutney, to serve

Method

STEP 1

Heat the curry paste in a large non-stick saucepan with a splash of the stock. Add the onions and fry for 5 mins until starting to soften. Stir in the aubergine and cook for a further 5 mins – add a little more stock if starting to stick.

STEP 2

Add the lentils, coconut milk and the rest of the stock, and simmer for 15 mins or until the lentils are tender. Add the peppers and cook for 5-10 mins more. Stir through the peas and spinach and cook until spinach has just wilted. Serve the curry with rice and mango chutney.

Prawn & tomato stew with gremolata topping

Prep: 10 mins **Cook:** 35 mins

Serves 4

Ingredients

- 500g new potato
- 2 tbsp olive oil
- 1 large onion , sliced
- 4 celery sticks, cut into pieces
- 2 garlic cloves , chopped
- 2 anchovy fillets, chopped
- pinch chilli flakes
- 400g can chopped tomato
- 250ml white wine
- 200ml vegetable stock
- 400g raw king prawn , peeled
- zest and juice 1 lemon
- 1 tsp salted baby caper , rinsed
- large handful parsley , chopped
- toasted bread , to serve

Method

STEP 1

Put the potatoes in a saucepan of cold salted water and bring to the boil. Reduce the heat to medium and simmer for 15-20 mins or until cooked but still firm. Drain and, when cool enough to handle, thickly slice.

STEP 2

Meanwhile, heat the oil in a large saucepan over a low-medium heat. Add the onion, celery, garlic, anchovy and chilli, season and cook for 8 mins or until softened. Increase the heat to medium-high, add the tomatoes, wine and stock, and cook for 15 mins. Add the prawns, lemon juice, capers and potatoes. Cook for 5 mins more, or until the prawns turn pink and are just cooked. Mix together the parsley and lemon zest, then scatter over the stew, then serve with toasted bread, for dunking.

Tomato & courgette stew

Prep: 10 mins **Cook:** 1 hr

Serves 4

Ingredients

- 1 tbsp olive oil
- 1 onion , chopped
- 2 garlic cloves , crushed
- 3 courgettes , quartered lengthways and cut into chunks
- 2 x 400g cans chopped tomatoes
- small bunch basil , torn
- 25g parmesan (or vegetarian alternative), finely grated

Method

STEP 1

Heat the oil in a large frying pan over a medium heat. Add the onion and cook for about 10 mins until softened and starting to go golden brown. Add the garlic and cook for 5 mins more.

STEP 2

Add the courgettes and cook for about 5 mins until starting to soften. Tip in the tomatoes and give everything a good stir. Simmer for 35-40 mins or until tomatoes are reduced and courgettes soft, then stir in the basil and Parmesan.

Turkey & coriander burgers with guacamole

Prep: 15 mins **Cook:** 15 mins

Serves 4

Ingredients

- 400g turkey mince
- 1 tsp Worcestershire sauce
- 85g fresh breadcrumb
- 1 tbsp chopped coriander
- 1 red onion , finely chopped
- 1 large ripe avocado , or 2 small
- 1 chilli , deseeded and finely chopped
- juice 1 lime
- 4 ciabatta rolls, cut in half
- 1 tsp sunflower oil
- 8 hot peppadew peppers, roughly chopped

Method

STEP 1

Mix the mince, Worcestershire sauce, breadcrumbs, half each of the coriander and onion, and some seasoning until combined. Form into 4 burgers, then chill until ready to cook.

STEP 2

To make the guacamole, mash the avocado with the remaining coriander and onion, the chilli and lime juice, and season.

STEP 3

Heat a griddle pan or barbecue until hot. Griddle the rolls, cut-side down, for 1 min, then keep warm. Brush the burgers with the oil to keep them from sticking. Cook for 7-8 mins on each side until charred and cooked through. Fill the rolls with the burgers, guacamole and peppadews.

Courgette & couscous salad with tahini dressing

Prep: 10 mins no cook

Serves 4

Ingredients

- 200g couscous
- zest and juice 1 lemon
- 2 tbsp olive oil
- 2 tbsp tahini paste
- 1 garlic clove, crushed
- griddled courgettes
- 4 tomatoes, roughly chopped
- 200g pack feta cheese, crumbled
- small pack mint, leaves picked
- small pack parsley, leaves picked
- 1 red chilli, deseeded and sliced

Method

STEP 1

Put the couscous in a heatproof bowl and pour over boiling water to just cover. Cover with cling film and leave to stand for 5 mins.

STEP 2

Mix the lemon zest and juice, oil, tahini and garlic, and season to taste. Fluff the prepared couscous and season. Spoon onto a large serving platter and scatter over the courgettes, tomatoes, feta, herbs and chilli. Drizzle over the dressing.

Quinoa, squash & broccoli salad

Prep: 10 mins **Cook:** 10 mins

Serves 2

Ingredients

- 2 tsp rapeseed oil
- 1 red onion, halved and sliced
- 2 garlic cloves, sliced
- 175g frozen butternut squash chunks
- 140g broccoli, stalks sliced, top cut into small florets
- 1 tbsp fresh thyme leaf
- 250g pack ready-to-eat red & white quinoa
- 2 tbsp chopped parsley
- 25g dried cranberries
- handful pumpkin seeds (optional)
- 1 tbsp balsamic vinegar
- 50g feta cheese, crumbled

Method

STEP 1

Heat the oil in a wok with a lid, add the onion and garlic, and fry for 5 mins until softened, then lift from the wok with a slotted spoon. Add the squash, stir round the wok until it starts to colour, then add the broccoli. Sprinkle in 3 tbsp water and the thyme, cover the pan and steam for about 5 mins until the veg is tender.

STEP 2

Meanwhile, tip quinoa into a bowl and fluff it up. Add the parsley, cranberries, seeds (if using), cooked onion and garlic, and balsamic vinegar, and mix well. Toss through the vegetables with the feta. Will keep in the fridge for 2 days.

Wild garlic & nettle soup

Prep: 15 mins **Cook:** 35 mins

Serves 4 - 6

Ingredients

- 1 tbsp rapeseed oil, plus extra for drizzling
- 25g butter
- 1 onion, finely diced
- 1 leek, finely diced
- 2 celery sticks, thinly sliced
- 1 carrot, finely diced
- 1 small potato, peeled and diced
- 1.2l good-quality vegetable stock
- 300g young nettle leaves
- 200g wild garlic leaves (keep any flowers if you have them)
- 3 tbsp milk

Method

STEP 1

Heat the oil and butter in a large saucepan. Add the onion, leek, celery, carrot, potato and a good pinch of salt, and stir until everything is well coated. Cover and sweat gently for 15-20 mins, stirring every so often to make sure that the vegetables don't catch on the bottom of the pan.

STEP 2

Pour in the stock and simmer for 10 mins. Add the nettles in several batches, stirring, then add the wild garlic leaves and simmer for 2 mins.

STEP 3

Remove from the heat and blend using a stick blender or tip into a blender. Return to the heat and stir through the milk, then taste for seasoning. Ladle into bowls and drizzle over a little extra oil, then top with a few wild garlic flowers, if you have them.

Pastry-less pork pie

Prep: 55 mins **Cook:** 1 hr and 15 mins plus cooling

Serves 6 - 8

Ingredients

- 4-5 large courgettes
- 1 tbsp olive or rapeseed oil , plus a drizzle
- 50g dried breadcrumbs , plus 2 tbsp
- 1 red onion , finely chopped
- 2 garlic cloves , crushed
- 290g jar red peppers , drained and chopped
- small bunch parsley , chopped
- zest 1 lemon
- 1 large egg
- 500g minced pork
- 2 tsp chilli flakes
- 2 tsp fennel seeds

Method

STEP 1

Cut the courgettes lengthways into thin slices (use a mandolin if you have one), stopping when you reach the seedy middle (set this aside). Heat a griddle pan. Toss the courgettes in a little oil to coat, then cook in batches until soft and marked with griddle lines. Drizzle a little oil into an 18cm springform tin and brush all over the base and sides. Line the base with a circle of baking parchment. Use the courgettes to line the tin, overlapping them across the base, up the sides and over the edge – you need enough overhang to cover the top and the filling, so you may need to double up on slices up the sides. Scatter 2 tbsp breadcrumbs over the base.

STEP 2

Heat the oil in a large frying pan. Add the onion and cook for 5 mins until softened a little. Meanwhile, finely chop the centre pieces of courgette and add to the pan with the garlic. Cook for about 5 mins until the courgette has softened, then set aside to cool.

STEP 3

Heat oven to 180C/160C fan/gas 4. Mix the cooled veg, the peppers, parsley, lemon zest, breadcrumbs, egg, pork, chilli, fennel seeds and plenty of seasoning in a bowl. Pack the mixture into the courgette-lined tin, pressing it firmly into the edges and flattening the top – try not to move the courgette slices too much. Fold over the overhanging courgettes to cover the top of the pie and press down firmly.

STEP 4

Place the tin on a baking tray – some juice may leak out of the tin so you will need the tray to catch this. Bake for 1 hr 15 mins – if you have a meat thermometer, the temperature should read at least 70C. Cool in the tin for 10 mins.

STEP 5

Remove the pie from the tin, pouring away any juices, and flip over so that the neater side is facing up. Remove the baking parchment and leave to cool completely, then store in the fridge. Transport in a cooler bag and serve in wedges.

Courgette & tomato soup

Prep: 10 mins **Cook:** 35 mins

Serves 8

Ingredients

- 1 tbsp butter
- 2 onions , chopped
- 1kg courgette , sliced
- 1kg tomato , chopped

- 2 tbsp plain flour
- ½ tsp turmeric
- 2l low-sodium chicken or vegetable stock from cubes
- crusty bread, to serve (optional)

Method

STEP 1

Melt the butter in a large pan, add the onions and courgettes, and cook for 5 mins on a medium heat, stirring occasionally.

STEP 2

Add the tomatoes and flour. Cook for a couple of mins, stirring around to stop the flour from becoming lumpy. Add the turmeric and stock, cover and simmer for 30 mins.

STEP 3

Purée with a stick blender, then sieve if you want a really smooth texture. Serve hot with crusty bread, if you like, or chill, then freeze for up to 2 months.

Instant berry banana slush

Prep: 5 mins no cook

Serves 2

Ingredients

- 2 ripe bananas
- 200g frozen berry mix (blackberries, raspberries and currants)

Method

STEP 1

Slice the bananas into a bowl and add the frozen berry mix. Blitz with a stick blender to make a slushy ice and serve straight away in two glasses with spoons.

Sesame chicken salad

Prep: 10 mins **Cook:** 10 mins

Serves 2

Ingredients

- 2 skinless chicken breasts
- 85g frozen soya bean
- 1 large carrot , finely cut into thin matchsticks
- 4 spring onions , finely sliced
- 140g cherry tomato , halved
- small bunch coriander , chopped
- small handful Thai or ordinary basil leaves , chopped if large
- 85g herb or baby salad leaves
- 1 tsp toasted sesame seeds

For the dressing

- grated zest and juice 1 small lime
- 1 tsp fish sauce
- 1 tsp sesame oil
- 2 tsp sweet chilli sauce

Method

STEP 1

Put the chicken in a pan and pour over cold water to cover. Tip the soya beans into a steamer. Bring the pan to a gentle simmer, then cook the chicken for 8 mins with the beans above.

STEP 2

Meanwhile, mix the dressing ingredients in a large bowl. When the chicken is cooked, slice and toss in the dressing along with the beans, carrot, onions, tomatoes, coriander and basil. Mix really well, pile onto the salad leaves and sprinkle with the sesame seeds.

Fruit & nut breakfast bowl

Prep: 5 mins **Cook:** 5 mins - 10 mins

Serves 2

Ingredients

- 6 tbsp porridge oats
- 2 oranges
- just under ½ x 200ml tub 0% fat Greek-style yogurt
- 60g pot raisins , nuts, goji berries and seeds

Method

STEP 1

Put the oats in a non-stick pan with 400ml water and cook over the heat, stirring occasionally for about 4 mins until thickened.

STEP 2

Meanwhile, cut the peel and pith from the oranges then slice them in half, cutting down either side, as closely as you can, to where the stalk would be as this will remove quite a tough section of the membrane. Now just chop the oranges.

STEP 3

Pour the porridge into bowls, spoon on the yogurt then pile on the oranges and the fruit, nut and seed mixture.

Strawberry & banana almond smoothie

Prep: 5 mins No cook

Serves 1

Ingredients

- 1 small banana
- 7 strawberries, hulled
- 3 tbsp 0% bio-yogurt
- 3 tbsp skimmed milk
- 2 tbsp ground almond

Method

STEP 1

Slice the banana into the bowl of a food processor, or a jug if using a hand blender. Add the strawberries, yogurt, milk and ground almonds, and blitz until completely smooth. Pour into a glass and enjoy.

Sticky baked meatloaf with avocado & black bean salsa

Prep: 25 mins **Cook:** 1 hr

Serves 4

Ingredients

For the meatloaf

- 1 tbsp rapeseed oil , plus a little for greasing
- 2 large onions , halved and thinly sliced
- 4 large garlic cloves , grated
- 1 tsp allspice or mixed spice
- 1 ½ tsp fennel seeds
- 2 tbsp smoked paprika
- 2 tbsp tomato purée
- 50g quinoa
- 160g grated carrot
- 1 tsp dried oregano
- ½ tsp ground cumin
- 400g pack turkey leg and breast mince
- 1 large egg
- 1 tsp black treacle

For the salsa

- 400g black beans , drained
- 1 small red onion , finely chopped
- 1 avocado , finely chopped
- 2 tomatoes , finely chopped
- ½ small pack fresh coriander , chopped
- 1 red chilli deseeded and finely chopped (optional)
- juice 1 lime

Method

STEP 1

Heat oven to 180C/160C fan/gas 4. Grease and line a deep 500g loaf tin with baking parchment. Heat the oil in a large, non-stick frying pan. Add the onions and fry for 10 mins, stirring occasionally until golden. Stir in the garlic and spices, toast over the heat for 3 mins, then add the purée. Scrape half into a small bowl for the topping.

STEP 2

Stir the quinoa and 4 tbsp water into the frying pan and cook for 2 mins. Tip into a bowl, leave to cool for 5 mins, then add the carrot, oregano, cumin, turkey mince and egg. Season with black pepper and mix well. Pack into the greased tin and bake, uncovered, for 35 mins until firm.

STEP 3

Meanwhile, mix all the salsa ingredients in a serving bowl, and add 3 tbsp water to the remaining onion mixture with the black treacle.

STEP 4

When the meatloaf is cooked, carefully turn it out of the tin onto a shallow ovenproof dish and spread the onion mixture over the top. Return to the oven, bake for 10 mins more, then slice and serve with the salsa.

Raspberry coconut porridge

Prep: 10 mins **Cook:** 10 mins plus overnight soaking

Serves 4

Ingredients

- 100g rolled porridge oats (not instant)
- 25g creamed coconut, chopped
- 200g frozen raspberries
- 125g pot coconut yogurt (we used COYO)
- a few mint leaves, to serve (optional)

Method

STEP 1

Tip the oats and creamed coconut into a large bowl, pour on 800ml cold water, cover and leave to soak overnight.

STEP 2

The next day, tip the contents of the bowl into a saucepan and cook over a medium heat, stirring frequently, for 5 -10 mins until the oats are cooked. Add the raspberries to the pan with the yogurt and allow to thaw and melt into the oats off the heat. Reserve half for the next day and spoon the remainder into bowls. Top each portion with mint leaves, if you like.

Speedy soy spinach

Prep: 5 mins **Cook:** 5 mins

Serves 4 as a side dish

Ingredients

- 1 tbsp vegetable oil
- 1 garlic clove
- 200g bag spinach
- 2 tbsp soy sauce
- 1 tbsp toasted sesame seeds

Method

STEP 1

Heat the oil in a pan and cook the garlic for a few secs. Tip in the spinach and cook for 2 mins, stirring often until just beginning to wilt. Drizzle over the soy sauce, toss through and scatter with sesame seeds. Great served with chicken or grills.

Mumsy's vegetable soup

Prep: 10 mins **Cook:** 30 mins

Serves 4

Ingredients

- 200g sourdough bread, cut into croutons
- 1 tbsp caraway seeds
- 3 tbsp olive oil
- 1 garlic clove, chopped
- 1 carrot, chopped
- 1 potato, chopped
- 600ml vegetable stock (we use bouillon)
- 100g cherry tomatoes, halved
- 400g can chopped tomatoes
- pinch of golden caster sugar
- 1 bouquet garni (2 bay leaves, 1 rosemary sprig and 2 thyme sprigs tied together with string)
- 1 celery stick, chopped
- 200g cauliflower, cut into florets
- 150g white cabbage, shredded
- 1 tsp Worcestershire sauce
- 2 tsp mushroom ketchup

Method

STEP 1

Heat oven to 180C/160C fan/gas 4. Put the bread on a baking tray with the caraway seeds, half the oil and some sea salt, and bake for 10-15 mins or until golden and crisp. Set aside.

STEP 2

Meanwhile, heat the remaining oil in a large saucepan over a medium heat. Add the garlic, carrot and potato and cook for 5 mins, stirring frequently, until a little softened.

STEP 3

Add the stock, tomatoes, sugar, bouquet garni, celery and seasoning and bring to a rolling boil. Reduce the heat, simmer for 10 mins, then add the cauliflower and cabbage. Cook for 15 mins until the veg is tender.

STEP 4

Stir in the Worcestershire sauce and mushroom ketchup. Remove the bouquet garni and serve the soup in bowls with the caraway croutons.

Asparagus & lentil salad with cranberries & crumbled feta

Prep: 10 mins **Cook:** 20 mins

Serves 2

Ingredients

- 1 garlic clove
- 125g puy lentils
- 100g pack fine asparagus tips
- 3 spring onions , finely sliced
- 25g dried cranberries
- 1 tbsp extra virgin rapeseed oil , plus a little extra (optional)
- 2 tsp organic apple cider vinegar
- 140g cherry tomatoes , halved
- 50g feta (read back of pack for vegetarian option)

Method

STEP 1

Finely grate the garlic and put in a bowl. Boil the lentils for 25 mins, and put the asparagus in a steamer over them for the last 5 mins until just tender.

STEP 2

Meanwhile, put the onions, cranberries, oil and vinegar in the bowl with the garlic and stir well. When the lentils are ready, drain and toss them into the dressing with the tomatoes. Tip into plastic containers (for a packed lunch), or onto plates, then top with the asparagus and crumble over the feta. Drizzle with a little extra oil, if you like.

Spicy mushroom & broccoli noodles

Prep: 10 mins **Cook:** 10 mins

Serves 2

Ingredients

- 1 low-salt vegetable stock cube
- 2 nests medium egg noodles
- 1 small head broccoli, broken into florets
- 1 tbsp sesame oil, plus extra to serve
- 250g pack shiitake or chestnut mushroom, thickly sliced
- 1 fat garlic clove, finely chopped
- ½ tsp chilli flakes, or crumble one dried chilli into pieces
- 4 spring onions, thinly sliced
- 2 tbsp hoisin sauce
- handful roasted cashew nuts

Method

STEP 1

Put the stock cube into a pan of water, then bring to the boil. Add the noodles, bring the stock back to the boil and cook for 2 mins. Add the broccoli and boil for 2 mins more. Reserve a cup of the stock, then drain the noodles and veg.

STEP 2

Heat a frying pan or wok, add the sesame oil and stir-fry the mushrooms for 2 mins until turning golden. Add the garlic, chilli flakes and most of the spring onions, cook 1 min more, then tip in the noodles and broccoli. Splash in 3 tbsp of the stock and the hoisin sauce, then toss together for 1 min using a pair of tongs or 2 wooden spoons. Serve the noodles scattered with the cashew nuts and remaining spring onions. Add a dash more sesame oil to taste, if you like.

Roasted summer vegetable casserole

Prep: 15 mins **Cook:** 1 hr

Serves 2 - 3

Ingredients

- 3 tbsp olive oil

- 1 garlic bulb, halved through the middle
- 2 large courgettes, thickly sliced
- 1 large red onion, sliced
- 1 aubergine, halved and sliced on the diagonal
- 2 large tomatoes, quartered
- 200g new potatoes, scrubbed and halved
- 1 red pepper, deseeded and cut into chunky pieces
- 400g can chopped tomatoes
- 0.5 small pack parsley, chopped

Method

STEP 1

Heat oven to 200C/180C fan/gas 6 and put the oil in a roasting tin. Tip in the garlic and all the fresh veg, then toss with your hands to coat in the oil. Season well and roast for 45 mins.

STEP 2

Remove the garlic from the roasting tin and squeeze out the softened cloves all over the veg, stirring to evenly distribute. In a medium pan, simmer the chopped tomatoes until bubbling, season well and stir through the roasted veg in the tin. Scatter over the parsley and serve.

Beetroot & lentil tabbouleh

Prep: 15 mins No cook

Serves 4

Ingredients

- 1 small pack flat-leaf parsley, plus extra leaves to serve (optional)
- 1 small pack mint
- 1 small pack chives
- 200g radishes
- 2 beetroot, peeled and quartered
- 1 red apple, cored, quartered and sliced
- 1 tsp ground cumin
- 4 tbsp olive oil
- 250g pack cooked quinoa
- 400g can chickpeas, drained and rinsed
- 400g can green lentils, drained
- 2 lemons, juiced

Method

STEP 1

Put the herbs, radishes and beetroot in a food processor and blitz until chopped into small pieces. Stir in the rest of the ingredients, adding the lemon juice a bit at a time to taste – you may not need all of it. Season, then place on a large platter topped with a few parsley leaves, if you like, and serve straight away.

Sweet mustard potato salad

Prep: 10 mins **Cook:** 10 mins

Serves 10

Ingredients

- 1.2kg waxy potatoes , such as Charlotte, cut into small chunks
- 400g good-quality mayonnaise
- 2 tbsp American mustard
- 2 tbsp cider vinegar
- 2 tbsp honey
- hard-boiled eggs , finely chopped
- 8 spring onions , sliced

Method

STEP 1

Put the potatoes in a pan of salted water, bring to the boil, then cover and simmer for 8-10 mins or until cooked through – a cutlery knife should easily pierce them. Drain and leave to cool in a colander.

STEP 2

Combine the mayo, mustard, vinegar, honey and eggs, then season well. Stir through the potatoes and half the spring onions, transfer to a serving dish and scatter over the remaining onions. Chill until you're ready to serve. Can be made 1 day ahead.

Burnt leeks on toast with romesco

Prep: 20 mins **Cook:** 25 mins

Serves 6

Ingredients

- 50g whole blanched almonds
- 100g cooked red peppers from a jar, drained

- 1 large ciabatta loaf, sliced
- ½ tbsp olive oil , plus 2 tsp
- 1 tsp sherry vinegar
- 1 red chilli , deseeded
- ¼ tsp smoked paprika
- 1 garlic clove , crushed
- 3 leeks , each cut into 4 pieces

Method

STEP 1

Toast the almonds in a dry pan until golden. Put the almonds, peppers, 1 small ciabatta slice (about 10g – an end piece is ideal), 1/ 2 tbsp olive oil, the vinegar, chilli, paprika , garlic and some seasoning in a food processor (or use a stick blender). Blend until smooth, then transfer to a bowl and chill in the fridge until needed. Can be done a day in advance.

STEP 2

Put the leeks in a saucepan and cover with water. Bring to the boil and cook for 5 mins. Drain on kitchen paper until needed.

STEP 3

When you're ready to serve, heat grill to high. Put the cooked leeks on a baking tray, season and drizzle with 2 tsp olive oil. Grill the leeks until starting to blacken, about 8-10 mins, turning once during cooking.

STEP 4

Toast the remaining ciabatta slices and spread with a little of the romesco. Gently pull the leeks into ribbons and pile them on top. Season well and serve immediately.

Corn cups with prawns, mango & chillies

Prep: 15 mins **Cook:** 10 mins

Makes 24

Ingredients

- 8-10 corn tortillas
- 3 tbsp vegetable oil
- 100g small shelled prawns
- juice 1 lime
- ½ mango , peeled, deseeded and finely diced
- 2 tbsp finely diced red onion
- 1 red chilli , finely diced

- handful coriander, finely chopped and some whole leaves reserved

Method

STEP 1

Heat oven to 200C/180C fan/gas 6. Using a 6cm pastry cutter, cut out circles from the tortillas. Heat the tortilla circles from the tortillas. Heat the tortilla circles for 5 secs in a microwave, then press into a mini muffin tin. Brush with the oil and bake for 8-10 mins until golden and crisp. Remove and leave to cool completely.

STEP 2

Chop the prawns into small pieces and marinate in the lime juice for 5 mins. Put the prawns and lime juice in a bowl with the mango, red onion, chilli and coriander. Season, mix together and use to fill the corn cups just before serving. Top with coriander leaves.

Poor man's vongole rosso

Prep: 10 mins **Cook:** 25 mins

Serves 4

Ingredients

- 2 tbsp olive oil
- 3 garlic cloves, thinly sliced
- 400g can cherry tomatoes
- glass of white wine
- small pinch of golden caster sugar
- 750g cockles, rinsed
- 400g linguine
- 1 tbsp good-quality extra virgin olive oil

Method

STEP 1

Heat the olive oil in a large saucepan with a lid. Add the garlic and sizzle for 1 min, then tip in the tomatoes. Use the white wine to swirl round and rinse out the tomato can, then tip it into the pan, sprinkle over the sugar and turn up the heat. Simmer until everything becomes thick, making sure you stir occasionally so it doesn't burn on the bottom of the pan – this will take 15-20 mins.

STEP 2

Once the tomatoes have had about 10 mins, cook the pasta in a big pan of salted water until just cooked – this will take about 10 mins – then drain. When the tomatoes and wine have reduced to a thick sauce, throw the cockles into the pan, stir once, cover with a lid and turn the heat up to max. Cook for 3-4 mins until all the cockles have opened, then stir again. Turn off the heat and stir through the pasta with the extra virgin olive oil until everything is coated. Try a strand of pasta and season with salt to taste. Bring the pan to the table with a separate bowl for the shells, and serve straight from the pan.

Butternut squash & sage soup

Prep: 20 mins **Cook:** 40 mins

Serves 8

Ingredients

- 1 tbsp olive oil
- 1 tbsp butter
- 3 onions , chopped
- 2 tbsp chopped sage
- 1.4kg peeled, deseeded butternut squash - buy whole squash and prepare, or buy bags of ready-prepared
- 1 tbsp clear honey
- 1 ½l vegetable stock
- bunch chives , snipped, and cracked black pepper, to serve

Method

STEP 1

Melt the oil and butter in a large saucepan or flameproof casserole. Add the onions and sage, and gently cook until really soft – about 15 mins. Tip in the squash and cook for 5 mins, stirring. Add the honey and stock, bring to a simmer and cook until the squash is tender.

STEP 2

Let the soup cool a bit so you don't burn yourself, then whizz until really smooth with a hand blender, or in batches in a blender. Season to taste, adding a drop more stock or water if the soup is too thick. Reheat before serving, sprinkled with chives and cracked black pepper.

Sushi burrito

Prep: 45 mins **Cook:** 10 mins

Serves 4

Ingredients

- 150g sushi rice
- 2 tsp rice wine vinegar
- ½ cucumber , cut into matchsticks
- 1 carrot , cut into matchsticks
- 1 tbsp soy sauce
- 4 nori sheets
- 2 tsp wasabi paste
- 50g pickled ginger , finely chopped
- 1 lime , juiced
- 2 very ripe avocados , halved, stoned, peeled and sliced
- 200g sushi grade tuna steak , sliced
- small pack coriander , leaves picked

Method

STEP 1

Put the rice in a bowl, cover with cold water and massage to remove the starch. Drain and repeat until the water runs clear. Put the rice in a small saucepan, cover with 2.5cm of water and put on a tight-fitting lid. Simmer on a medium heat for 10 mins, then take off the heat (leaving the lid on) and steam for a further 15 mins. Stir in the vinegar, then cool completely.

STEP 2

Toss the cucumber and carrot matchsticks in the soy and leave to marinate.

STEP 3

Lay out a sushi mat and put a nori sheet, shiny-side down, on top of it. Spread a quarter of the rice over the nori, leaving a 1cm border at the top. Mix the wasabi, ginger and lime juice.

STEP 4

Layer with the avocado, cucumber and carrot, and tuna. Top with the wasabi mix and coriander. Dampen the top border with a little water, fold in both sides of the nori sheet, then use the sushi mat to help roll. Wrap in foil, slice in half and serve.

Seared tuna & anchovy runner beans

Prep: 5 mins **Cook:** 10 mins

Serves 2

Ingredients

- 3 tbsp snipped chives
- 12 basil leaves
- 2 tbsp chopped mint , plus a few small leaves, for serving
- zest and juice 1 small lemon
- 2 tbsp extra virgin olive oil
- 1 tbsp Dijon mustard
- 1 tbsp small capers
- 6 anchovies (smoked or unsmoked), chopped
- 300g runner beans , sliced diagonally
- 2 tuna steaks
- small handful flat-leaf parsley
- 2 tbsp toasted flaked almonds

Method

STEP 1

Put the chives, basil and mint in a small food processor with the lemon zest and juice, oil and mustard. Blitz to a purée. Take out 2 tbsp to use as a coating for the fish, then stir the capers and anchovies into the rest.

STEP 2

Cook the runner beans in boiling salted water or steam for 5 mins until tender but still with a little bite.

STEP 3

Brush the tuna with the reserved herby mixture and griddle for 2-3 mins each side until cooked but still a little pink in the centre. Toss half the caper dressing through the warm beans with the parsley and pile onto plates. Top with the tuna, spoon over the remaining dressing and scatter with the almonds and mint leaves.

Green breakfast smoothie

Prep: 10 mins No cook

Serves 2

Ingredients

- 1 handful spinach (about 50g/2oz), roughly chopped
- 100g broccoli florets, roughly chopped
- 2 celery sticks
- 4 tbsp desiccated coconut
- 1 banana
- 300ml rice milk (good dairy alternative - we used one from Rude Health)

- ¼ tsp spirulina or 1 scoop of greens powder or vegan protein powder (optional)

Method

STEP 1

Whizz 300ml water and the ingredients in a blender until smooth.

Courgette, pea & pesto soup

Prep: 10 mins **Cook:** 15 mins

Serves 4

Ingredients

- 1 tbsp olive oil
- 1 garlic clove, sliced
- 500g courgettes, quartered lengthways and chopped
- 200g frozen peas
- 400g can cannellini beans, drained and rinsed
- 1l hot vegetable stock
- 2 tbsp basil pesto, or vegetarian alternative

Method

STEP 1

Heat the oil in a large saucepan. Cook the garlic for a few seconds, then add the courgettes and cook for 3 mins until they start to soften. Stir in the peas and cannellini beans, pour on the hot stock and cook for a further 3 mins.

STEP 2

Stir the pesto through the soup with some seasoning, then ladle into bowls and serve with crusty brown bread, if you like. Or pop in a flask to take to work.

Baba ganoush & crudités

Prep: 15 mins **Cook:** 30 mins plus draining

Serves 6

Ingredients

For the baba ganoush

- 4 large aubergines (about 1.2kg), pricked all over with a fork
- zest and juice of 1 lemon
- 2 fat garlic cloves, chopped
- 3 tbsp tahini
- 4 tbsp extra virgin olive oil, plus a little extra for drizzling

For the crudités (optional)

- 4 large carrots, ends trimmed and spiralized into thick noodles
- 1 large cucumber, ends trimmed, spiralized into thick ribbons and patted dry to remove excess water
- 1 large courgette (about 145g), ends trimmed and spiralized into thick noodles
- 150g pack mixed radishes, cut into random shapes

Method

STEP 1

Cover the hob in tin foil for ease of cleaning then put each aubergine on a single gas hob and cook, turning occasionally with tongs until the aubergines are completely charred and collapsed, this will take 10–15 mins. Alternatively, heat the grill to its highest setting, lay the aubergines on a baking tray and cook, turning occasionally, for 30 mins to achieve the same effect. While the aubergine is cooking, prep the vegetables if using.

STEP 2

Allow the aubergines to cool slightly then scoop out the soft flesh into a colander. Leave to drain for 30 mins to remove any excess water then blitz the aubergine along with the other baba ganoush ingredients and some seasoning in a food processor to however smooth or chunky you like.

STEP 3

Spoon the dip into a bowl and serve in the centre of the vegetable crudités.

Smoky paprika seafood rice

Prep: 15 mins **Cook:** 35 mins

Serves 4

Ingredients

- 1.3l fish or chicken stock
- large pinch of saffron (optional, see tip)
- 4 tbsp olive oil
- 4 garlic cloves , 1 left whole, 3 finely chopped
- 12 large prawns , shells on
- 4 baby squid (about 250g), cleaned and sliced
- 1 onion , very finely chopped
- 2 celery sticks , very finely chopped
- 1 tsp fennel seeds , lightly crushed
- 2 tbsp tomato purée
- 1 tsp smoked paprika (hot or sweet)
- 300g paella rice
- 250ml fino sherry or dry white wine
- 300g fresh mussels , cleaned (discard any that are open)
- large handful parsley , roughly chopped
- 1 lemon , cut into wedges, to serve

Method

STEP 1

Heat the stock in a large saucepan. Add the saffron to infuse, if you like. Take off the heat and set aside. In a large deep-sided frying pan or paella pan, heat 1 tbsp of the oil. Smash the whole garlic clove and add to the oil. Throw in the prawns and cook for 2 mins until just turning pink but not cooked through. Push to one side of the pan and add the squid to the garlicky oil for 1 min or so, again just to colour. Remove the seafood to a plate.

STEP 2

Add the remaining oil to the pan, and cook the onion and celery slowly for 15 mins until very soft and beginning to caramelise. Add the finely chopped garlic, the fennel seeds, tomato purée and paprika, and cook for 5 mins more. Meanwhile, bring the stock to a simmer. Add the rice to the pan with the onion mixture, give everything a good stir, then add the sherry and 1 litre of the hot stock. Bring to the boil and simmer gently for 15 mins, shaking the pan from time to time.

STEP 3

When the rice is almost cooked but still has a little bite, dot over the prawns, squid and the mussels. Add the cooking juices and the rest of the stock. Cover and cook for 5 mins until the seafood is cooked through, the mussels have opened and the rice is just tender. (You may have to add a splash more water if the rice looks dry.) Discard any mussels that haven't opened. Sprinkle over some chopped parsley and serve with lemon wedges to squeeze over.

Three-grain porridge

Prep: 5 mins **Cook:** 5 mins

Serves 18

Ingredients

- 300g oatmeal
- 300g spelt flakes
- 300g barley flakes
- agave nectar and sliced strawberries, to serve (optional)

Method

STEP 1

Working in batches, toast the oatmeal, spelt flakes and barley in a large, dry frying pan for 5 mins until golden, then leave to cool and store in an airtight container.

STEP 2

When you want to eat it, simply combine 50g of the porridge mixture in a saucepan with 300ml milk or water. Cook for 5 mins, stirring occasionally, then top with a drizzle of honey and strawberries, if you like (optional). Will keep for 6 months.

Sardines & tomatoes on toast

Prep: 10 mins no cook

Serves 1

Ingredients

- 2 slices sourdough bread, toasted
- 1 large garlic clove , halved
- 135g can sardines in olive oil
- 130g cherry tomatoes , halved
- handful watercress
- 1 tbsp parsley , roughly chopped
- 1/2 lemon , to serve (optional)

Method

STEP 1

Rub each piece of toast with the garlic. In a small bowl, mix the sardines and their oil with the tomatoes and the watercress, then season. Sit half the mixture on each slice of toast, piled high. Scatter over the parsley and squeeze over the lemon, if you like.

Sunshine Cobb salad

Prep: 20 mins **Cook:** 10 mins

Serves 2

Ingredients

- 1 large egg
- 400g can black beans, drained and rinsed
- 1 red, orange or yellow pepper, deseeded and diced
- thumb-sized piece cucumber, diced
- 8 cherry tomatoes, halved
- 198g can sweetcorn, drained
- 150g pack cooked prawns
- handful of watercress

For the chilli-lime dressing

- 1 red chilli, deseeded and finely chopped
- zest and juice 1 lime
- 1 tbsp white wine vinegar
- 2 tsp clear honey
- 1 tbsp extra virgin olive oil or rapeseed oil

Method

STEP 1

Bring a small pan of water to the boil. Add the egg and cook for 8 mins. Drain, then run under cold water to cool.

STEP 2

To assemble the salad, arrange the remaining ingredients in 2 containers. When the egg is cool, peel and quarter it and divide between the containers too.

STEP 3

Mix together the dressing ingredients in a small bowl and transfer to 2 mini jars or containers to take with the salads to work. Dress and toss together just before eating.

Low-sugar granola

Prep: 10 mins **Cook:** 30 mins - 35 mins

Makes 500g

Ingredients

- 200g rolled oats
- 150g bag mixed nuts
- 150g mixed seeds
- 1 orange , zested
- 2 tsp mixed spice
- 2 tsp cinnamon
- 2 tbsp cold pressed rapeseed oil
- 1½ tbsp maple syrup

Method

STEP 1

Heat oven to 160C/140C fan/gas 4. Mix all the ingredients in a bowl with a pinch of salt, then spread out on a baking tray.

STEP 2

Roast for 30-35 mins until golden, pulling the tray out of the oven twice while cooking to give everything a good stir – this will help the granola toast evenly. Leave to cool. Will keep in an airtight container for one month.

Chicken & basil meatballs

Prep: 20 mins **Cook:** 20 mins

24 (12 of each flavour)

Ingredients

- 1 shallot
- 250g chicken breast
- 25g seeded bread
- ⅓ pack fresh basil leaves
- 1 clove garlic
- rapeseed oil , for frying

For the Thai chicken chicory bites

- 12 chicory leaves , red or green
- sriracha or Thai sweet chilli sauce, to serve
- 1 spring onion , cut lengthways and shredded into fine strips
- 25g salted peanuts , finely chopped

For the roasted pepper sticks

- 2 roasted red peppers , cut into 24 chunks
- 24 fresh basil leaves

You will need

- 24 cocktail sticks

Method

STEP 1

Put the shallot into a food processor and pulse briefly to chop. Add all the remaining meatball ingredients, except for the oil, and blitz to make a soft purée. Shape into 24 mini meatballs with wet hands.

STEP 2

Heat a drizzle of the oil in a large non-stick frying pan. Add half the meatballs and fry for 5 mins, moving them around the pan to evenly colour them. Remove from the pan and cook the remaining meatballs. Keep chilled until ready to serve. Will keep in the fridge for up to one day.

STEP 3

To serve, warm the meatballs, if you like, at 180C/160C fan/gas 4 for 10 mins, then arrange half in the chicory leaves, top with some chilli sauce and sprinkle with the onion and peanuts.

STEP 4

For the pepper version, thread the meatballs onto 12 cocktail sticks with the 2 chunks of pepper and 2 fresh basil leaves either side.

Buckwheat & spring lamb stew

Prep: 25 mins **Cook:** 3 hrs and 15 mins

Serves 4

Ingredients

- 2 tbsp cold pressed rapeseed oil
- 400g stewing lamb , excess fat trimmed
- 1 onion , finely chopped
- 3 leeks , cut into 1 cm rounds
- 250g baby chantenay carrots
- 3 garlic cloves , finely chopped
- 2 tbsp plain flour
- 3 lemon thyme sprigs

- 1 bay leaf
- 150ml white wine
- 600ml low-salt veg stock
- 80g buckwheat
- 1 large unwaxed lemon, zested
- 1 small bunch parsley, leaves finely chopped

Method

STEP 1

Heat 1 tbsp oil in a casserole dish over a high heat. Fry the lamb in two batches for 5 mins each until evenly browned. Remove from the pan and set aside.

STEP 2

Heat the remaining oil in the same pan and fry the onion and leeks over a medium heat for 7 mins. Tip in the carrots and two-thirds of the garlic, then fry for 1 min. Stir the meat into the pan along with the plain flour and fry for another 2 mins. Add the thyme and bay leaf, then the wine and bring to a bubble before pouring in the stock. Mix everything together well. Put a lid on the pan and cook over a low heat for 2½-3 hrs or until the meat is tender. Add the buckwheat for the last 20 mins of cooking time.

STEP 3

Mix the remaining garlic with the lemon zest and parsley. Serve the stew in bowls, scattered with the parsley and lemon mixture.

Barley & bulgur chopped herb salad

Prep: 20 mins **Cook:** 25 mins plus 1 hr chilling

Serves 6

Ingredients

- 150g pearl barley
- 150g bulgur wheat
- 3 tbsp olive oil
- 3 white onions, halved and sliced
- 4 garlic cloves, crushed
- ¼ tsp ground cloves
- small bunch of parsley
- small bunch of dill
- small bunch of mint
- ½ cucumber, finely chopped
- 4 tomatoes, finely chopped
- 2 lemons, juiced

Method

STEP 1

Bring a pan of water to the boil and add the barley. Cover and cook for 25 mins, or until tender. Meanwhile, pour boiling water over the bulgur wheat to just cover, and set aside.

STEP 2

Heat 2 tbsp oil in a large frying pan and add the onions. Cook for 20-25 mins, stirring regularly, until golden and caramelised. Stir in the garlic and cloves for 30 secs.

STEP 3

Drain the barley and bulgur well and tip into a bowl. Add the remaining oil, the onions, and plenty of seasoning. Mix well and chill until you're ready to serve (up to 24 hrs ahead is fine, or at least 1 hr). Remove from the fridge 30 mins before you want to serve.

STEP 4

Toss through the remaining ingredients and serve on a large platter or in a bowl.

Cajun prawn pizza

Prep: 10 mins **Cook:** 20 mins

Serves 2

Ingredients

For the base

- 200g wholemeal flour, plus a little for kneading if necessary
- 1 tsp instant yeast
- pinch of salt
- 2 tsp rapeseed oil, plus extra greasing

For the topping

- 1 tbsp rapeseed oil, plus extra for greasing
- 2 large sticks celery, finely chopped
- 1 yellow pepper or green pepper, de-seeded and diced
- 225g can chopped tomatoes
- 1 tsp smoked paprika
- 165g pack raw, peeled king prawns
- 2-3 tbsp chopped coriander
- ½ - 1 tsp Cajun spice mix
- 2 handfuls rocket, optional

Method

STEP 1

Heat oven to 220C/200C fan/gas 7. Tip the flour into a mixer with a dough hook, or a bowl. Add the yeast, salt, oil and 150ml warm water then mix well to a soft dough. Knead in the food mixer for about 5 mins, but if making this by hand, tip onto a work surface and knead for about 10 mins. The dough is sticky, but try not to add too much extra flour. Leave in the bowl and cover with a tea towel while you make the topping. There is no need to prove the dough for a specific time, just let it sit while you get on with the next step.

STEP 2

For the topping: heat the oil in a non-stick pan or wok. Add the celery and pepper and fry for 8 mins, stirring frequently, until softened. Tip in the tomatoes and paprika then cook for 2 mins more. Set aside to cool a little then stir in the prawns.

STEP 3

With an oiled knife, cut the dough in half and shape each piece into a 25cm round with lightly oiled hands on oiled baking sheets. Don't knead the dough first otherwise it will be too elastic and will shrink back. Spread each with half of the tomato and prawn mix then scatter with the coriander and sprinkle with the Cajun spice. Bake for 10 mins until golden. Serve with a green salad.

Silvana's Mediterranean & basil pasta

Prep: 5 mins **Cook:** 30 mins

Serves 4

Ingredients

- 2 red peppers, seeded and cut into chunks
- 2 red onions, cut into wedges
- 2 mild red chillies, seeded and diced

- 3 garlic cloves, coarsley chopped
- 1 tsp golden caster sugar
- 2 tbsp olive oil, plus extra to serve
- 1kg small ripe tomatoes, quartered
- 350g dried pasta
- a handful of fresh basil leaves and 2 tbsp grated parmesan (or vegetarian alternative), to serve

Method

STEP 1

To roast the veg, preheat the oven to 200C/gas 6/fan 180C. Scatter the peppers, red onions, chillies and garlic in a large roasting tin. Sprinkle with sugar, drizzle over the oil and season well with salt and pepper. Roast for 15 minutes, toss in the tomatoes and roast for another 15 minutes until everything is starting to soften and look golden.

STEP 2

While the vegetables are roasting, cook the pasta in a large pan of salted boiling water according to packet instructions, until tender but still with a bit of bite. Drain well.

STEP 3

Remove the vegetables from the oven, tip in the pasta and toss lightly together. Tear the basil leaves on top and sprinkle with Parmesan to serve. If you have any leftovers it makes a great cold pasta salad – just moisten with extra olive oil if needed.

Apple crunch

Prep: 1 min **Serves 1**

Ingredients

- 1 small eating apple
- 1 tbsp organic unsalted crunchy peanut butter

Method

STEP 1

Cut the apple in half and spread with the peanut butter.

Egg & avocado open sandwich

Prep: 10 mins **Cook:** 10 mins

Serves 1

Ingredients

- 2 medium eggs
- 1 ripe avocado
- juice 1 lime
- 2 slices rye bread
- 2 tsp hot chilli sauce - we used sriracha
- handful cress , to serve

Method

STEP 1

Bring a medium pan of water to the boil. Add the eggs and cook for 8-9 mins until hard-boiled. Meanwhile, halve the avocado and scoop the flesh into a bowl. Add the lime juice, season well and mash with a fork.

STEP 2

When the eggs are cooked, run under cold water for 2 mins before removing the shells. Spread the avocado on the rye bread. Slice the eggs into thin rounds and place on top of the avocado. Drizzle some chilli sauce over the eggs, scatter the cress on top and add a good grinding of black pepper.

Simple spicy fish stew

Prep: 5 mins **Cook:** 15 mins

Serves 4

Ingredients

- 1 tbsp olive oil
- 2 garlic cloves , crushed
- 1 tsp ground cumin
- ½ tsp paprika
- 200g can chopped tomato
- 1 red pepper , deseeded, cut into chunks
- 450g white fish fillets, cut into chunks
- handful coriander , roughly chopped
- 1 lemon , cut into wedges

Method

STEP 1

Heat oil in a saucepan. Tip in the garlic, cumin and paprika and cook for 1 min. Add 100ml water and the tomatoes. Bring to the boil, then turn down the heat. Add the pepper, simmer for 5 mins. Add the fish, simmer for 5 mins. Serve with coriander and a wedge of lemon.

Harissa chicken & squash traybake

Prep: 15 mins **Cook:** 35 mins

Serves 4

Ingredients

- 3 tbsp harissa
- ½ x 500g pot low-fat natural yogurt
- 4 skinless chicken breasts, slashed
- 1 small butternut squash, peeled, deseeded and cut into long wedges
- 2 red onions, cut into wedges

Method

STEP 1

Heat oven to 200C/180C fan/ gas 6. Mix 2 tbsp of the harissa with 3 tbsp of the yogurt. Rub all over the chicken breasts and set aside to marinate while you start the veg.

STEP 2

Toss the squash and the onions with remaining harissa, mixed with 2 tbsp oil (sunflower, vegetable or olive is fine), and some seasoning in a large roasting tin. Roast for 10 mins.

STEP 3

Remove veg from the oven, add the chicken to the tin, then roast for a further 20-25 mins until the chicken and veg are cooked through. Serve with the remaining yogurt on the side, and a big bowl of couscous or rice.

Roast chicken with lemon & rosemary roots

Prep: 20 mins **Cook:** 1 hr and 30 mins

Serves 4

Ingredients

- 4 large carrots (about 400g), cut into big chunks
- 1 celeriac (about 575g peeled weight), cut into roastie-sized chunks
- 1 large swede (550g unpeeled), quartered and cut into thick slices
- 2 red onions, cut into wedges
- 1 garlic bulb
- 2 tbsp rapeseed oil
- 2 tsp sprigs rosemary leaves and woody stalks separated
- 1 lemon
- 1 medium chicken (about 1.4kg)
- 2 x 200g bags curly kale

Method

STEP 1

Heat oven to 200C/180C fan/gas 6. Tip the carrots, celeriac, swede, onions and garlic into a large roasting tin with the oil, rosemary leaves and a grinding of black pepper. Toss well and roast for 5-10 mins while you get the chicken ready.

STEP 2

Grate the zest and squeeze the juice from the lemon, set aside and put the lemon shells and the woody stalks from the rosemary inside the chicken. Stir the veg, scatter over the lemon zest and drizzle over the juice, then sit the chicken on top of the veg and roast for 1-1 1/4 hrs until the chicken is tender but still moist. Take the chicken from the oven and leave to rest for 10 mins. Keep the veg in the oven and steam one of the bags of kale (if you're eating this over two days for the Healthy Diet Plan, otherwise steam both).

STEP 3

Squeeze the garlic from the skins, carve the chicken and serve with the vegetables.

Home-style pork curry with cauliflower rice

Prep: 15 mins **Cook:** 1 hr

Serves 4

Ingredients

For the curry

- 425g lean pork fillet (tenderloin), cubed
- 2 tbsp Madras curry powder

- 2 tbsp red wine vinegar
- 1 tbsp rapeseed oil
- 1 large onion , finely chopped
- 2 tbsp finely shredded ginger
- 1 tsp fennel , toasted in a pan then crushed

For the cauliflower rice

- 1 medium cauliflower
- good handful coriander , chopped

- 1 tsp cumin , toasted in a pan then crushed
- 400g can chopped tomatoes
- 2 tbsp red lentils
- 350g pack baby aubergine , quartered
- 1 reduced-salt vegetable stock cube
- cumin seeds , toasted (optional)

Method

STEP 1

Tip the pork into a bowl and stir in the curry powder and vinegar. Set aside. Heat the oil in a heavy-based pan and fry the onion and ginger for 10 mins, stirring frequently, until golden. Tip in the pork mixture and fry for a few mins more. Remove the pork and set aside. Stir in the toasted spices, then tip in the tomatoes, lentils and aubergine, and crumble in the stock cube. Cover and leave to simmer for 40 mins, stirring frequently, until the aubergine is almost cooked. If it starts to look dry, add a splash of water. Return the pork to the pan and cook for a further 10-20 mins until the pork is cooked and tender.

STEP 2

Just before serving, cut the hard core and stalks from the cauliflower and pulse the rest in a food processor to make grains the size of rice. Tip into a heatproof bowl, cover with cling film, then pierce and microwave for 7 mins on High – there is no need to add any water. Stir in the coriander and serve with the curry. For spicier rice, add some toasted cumin seeds.

Porcini loaf with summer greens

Prep: 20 mins **Cook:** 50 mins

Serves 4

Ingredients

For the vegetables

- 450g salad potatoes , halved

- 2 tsp cold-pressed rapeseed oil, plus extra for the tin
- 1 lemon, zested and juiced (you'll need 2 tbsp lemon juice)
- 1 tsp vegetable bouillon powder
- 2 leeks, cut into rings

For the loaf

- 410g can jackfruit, drained
- 1 tbsp chopped tarragon leaves
- 1 garlic clove, finely grated
- ½ tsp smoked paprika
- 350g asparagus (250g pack and 100g pack), ends trimmed, cut crosswise into quarters
- 320g frozen peas
- 260g bag young leaf spinach
- 2 tbsp bio Greek yogurt
- 1 tbsp chopped tarragon leaves
- 3 eggs
- 40g dried porcini mushrooms
- 200g pack chestnut purée
- 40g roasted unsalted cashews

Method

STEP 1

Heat the oven to 190C/170C fan/gas 5. Oil and line a 500g loaf tin with two strips of baking parchment so it's fully lined, with an overhang at the top that could be folded over. Toss the potatoes with the oil and put in a small roasting tin.

STEP 2

To make the loaf, weigh out 125g jackfruit, choosing the pieces that have the most 'open' texture, then thinly slice. Tip into a bowl and stir in the tarragon, garlic and paprika.

STEP 3

Tip the rest of the jackfruit into a bowl with the eggs and dried mushrooms and blitz with a stick blender until very smooth. Add the chestnut purée, then blitz again until well mixed. Stir 150g of the mushroom mix with the sliced jackfruit. Spoon half of the remaining dried mushroom mix into the tin, then add the mushroom and sliced jackfruit mix, and cover with the rest of the dried mushroom mix. Press down and scatter over the cashews. Fold over the baking parchment and bake alongside the potatoes for 45 mins, or until firm.

STEP 4

Toss the lemon zest with the potatoes. Cover the loaf and leave it to rest while you cook the veg.

STEP 5

Tip 150ml water into a pan with the bouillon and leeks. Cover and cook over a medium heat for 2 mins. Add the asparagus and peas, then cover and cook for 2 mins more. Finally, add the spinach and stir to wilt. Add the lemon juice and the yogurt to the veg mix and stir well. If you're following our Healthy Diet Plan, serve half the veg with four slices of the loaf, reserving the remaining four slices and the rest of the veg for another night. Will keep for up to three days, covered, in the fridge. To serve on the second night, reheat the leftovers in the microwave until piping hot.

Feta frittatas with carrot & celery salad

Prep: 15 mins **Cook:** 25 mins

Serves 2

Ingredients

For the frittatas

- 2 tsp rapeseed oil , plus a drizzle for the salad (optional)
- 1 large leek , well washed and thinly sliced
- 25g baby spinach
- 3 large eggs
- ⅓ pack dill , stalks removed, fronds chopped
- 2 tbsp natural bio-yogurt
- 50g feta , crumbled
- 1 garlic clove , finely grated

For the salad

- 2 tsp balsamic vinegar
- 2 tsp tahini
- 2 celery sticks , sliced
- 2 carrots , peeled into ribbons
- 1 very small red onion , thinly sliced
- 2 romaine lettuces leaves, torn into pieces
- 6 pitted black Kalamata olive , rinsed and halved

Method

STEP 1

Heat oven to 220C/200C fan/gas 7 with a muffin tin inside. Heat the oil in a frying pan and fry the leek for about 4 mins, stirring regularly, over a medium-high heat to soften it. Stir in the spinach and cook for 1 min until wilted down, then set aside to cool slightly.

STEP 2

Beat the eggs, dill, yogurt and feta together in a jug with black pepper and the garlic. Add the leeks and spinach, and stir well. Take the muffin tin out of the oven and drop in four muffin cases, add the egg mixture and bake for 15-18 mins until set and golden.

STEP 3

Meanwhile, mix the balsamic vinegar with the tahini and 1-2 tbsp water in a bowl to make a dressing, then toss with the vegetables and olives. Pile onto plates, carefully remove the paper cases from the frittatas and serve.

Spicy Moroccan eggs

Prep: 10 mins **Cook:** 15 mins - 20 mins

Serves 4

Ingredients

- 2 tsp rapeseed oil
- 1 large onion, halved and thinly sliced
- 3 garlic cloves, sliced
- 1 tbsp rose harissa
- 1 tsp ground coriander
- 150ml vegetable stock
- 400g can chickpea
- 2 x 400g cans cherry tomatoes
- 2 courgettes, finely diced
- 200g bag baby spinach
- 4 tbsp chopped coriander
- 4 large eggs

Method

STEP 1

Heat the oil in a large, deep frying pan, and fry the onion and garlic for about 8 mins, stirring every now and then, until starting to turn golden. Add the harissa and ground coriander, stir well, then pour in the stock and chickpeas with their liquid. Cover and simmer for 5 mins, then mash about one-third of the chickpeas to thicken the stock a little.

STEP 2

Tip the tomatoes and courgettes into the pan, and cook gently for 10 mins until the courgettes are tender. Fold in the spinach so that it wilts into the pan.

STEP 3

Stir in the chopped coriander, then make 4 hollows in the mixture and break in the eggs. Cover and cook for 2 mins, then take off the heat and allow to settle for 2 mins before serving.

Pitta pocket

Prep: 2 mins **Serves 1**

Ingredients

- ½ wholemeal pitta bread
- 25g cooked skinless chicken breast
- ¼ cucumber, cut into chunks
- 4 cherry tomatoes, halved

Method

STEP 1

Fill the pitta half with the chicken breast, cucumber and cherry tomatoes.

Chicken fattoush

Prep: 15 mins No cook

Serves 4

Ingredients

- juice 2 lemons
- 2 tbsp olive oil
- 1 Cos lettuce, chopped
- 2 tomatoes, chopped into chunks
- small pack flat-leaf parsley, chopped
- ½ cucumber, chopped into chunks
- 200g pack cooked chicken pieces (or leftover cooked chicken)
- 2 spring onions, sliced
- 2 pitta breads
- 1-2 tsp ground sumac

Method

STEP 1

Pour the lemon juice into a large bowl and whisk while you slowly add the oil. When all the oil has been added and the mixture starts to thicken, season.

STEP 2

Add the lettuce, tomatoes, parsley, cucumber, chicken pieces and spring onions, and stir well to coat the salad in the dressing.

STEP 3

Put the pitta breads in the toaster until crisp and golden, then chop into chunks. Scatter the toasted pitta pieces over the salad and sprinkle over the sumac. Serve straight away.

Spinach soup

Prep: 10 mins **Cook:** 25 mins

Serves 4

Ingredients

- 25g butter
- 1 bunch spring onions, chopped
- 1 leek (about 120g), sliced
- 2 small sticks celery (about 85g), sliced
- 1 small potato (about 200g), peeled and diced
- ½ tsp ground black pepper
- 1l stock (made with two chicken or vegetable stock cubes)
- 2 x 200-235g bags spinach
- 150g half-fat crème fraîche

Method

STEP 1

Heat the butter in a large saucepan. Add the spring onions, leek, celery and potato. Stir and put on the lid. Sweat for 10 minutes, stirring a couple of times.

STEP 2

Pour in the stock and cook for 10 – 15 minutes until the potato is soft.

STEP 3

Add the spinach and cook for a couple of minutes until wilted. Use a hand blender to blitz to a smooth soup.

STEP 4

Stir in the crème fraîche. Reheat and serve.

One-pot chicken with quinoa

Prep: 5 mins **Cook:** 30 mins

Serves 2

Ingredients

- 1 tbsp cold-pressed rapeseed oil
- 2 skinless chicken breasts (about 300g/11oz)
- 1 medium onion , sliced into 12 wedges
- 1 red pepper , deseeded and sliced
- 2 garlic cloves , finely chopped
- 100g green beans , trimmed and cut in half
- 1/4-1/2 tsp chilli flakes , according to taste
- 2 tsp ground cumin
- 2 tsp ground coriander
- 100g uncooked quinoa
- 85g frozen sweetcorn
- 75g kale , thickly shredded

Method

STEP 1

Heat the oil in a large, deep frying pan or sauté pan. Season the chicken and fry over a medium-high heat for 2-3 mins each side or until golden. Transfer to a plate. Add the onion and pepper to the pan and cook for 3 mins, stirring, until softened and lightly browned.

STEP 2

Tip in the garlic and beans, and stir-fry for 2 mins. Add the chilli and spices, then stir in the quinoa and sweetcorn. Pour in 700ml just-boiled water with 1/2 tsp flaked sea salt and bring to the boil.

STEP 3

Return the chicken to the pan, reduce the heat to a simmer and cook for 12 mins, stirring regularly and turning the chicken occasionally. Add the kale and cook for a further 3 mins or until the quinoa and chicken are cooked through.

Vitality chicken salad with avocado dressing

Prep: 5 mins **Cook:** 3 mins

Serves 1

Ingredients

- handful frozen soya beans
- 1 skinless cooked chicken breast, shredded
- ¼ cucumber, peeled, deseeded and chopped
- ½ avocado, flesh scooped out
- few drops Tabasco sauce
- juice ½ lemon, plus a lemon wedge
- 2 tsp extra-virgin olive oil
- 5-6 Little Gem lettuce leaves
- 1 tsp mixed seed

Method

STEP 1

Blanch the soya beans for 3 mins. Rinse in cold water and drain thoroughly. Put the chicken, beans and cucumber in a bowl.

STEP 2

Blitz the avocado, Tabasco, lemon juice and oil in a food processor or with a hand blender. Season, pour into the bowl and mix well to coat.

STEP 3

Spoon the mixture into the lettuce leaves (or serve it alongside them) and sprinkle with the seeds. Chill until lunch, then serve with a lemon wedge.

Dried fruit energy nuggets

Prep: 10 mins No cook

Makes 6

Ingredients

- 50g soft dried apricot
- 100g soft dried date
- 50g dried cherry
- 2 tsp coconut oil
- 1 tbsp toasted sesame seed

Method

STEP 1

Whizz apricots with dates and cherries in a food processor until very finely chopped. Tip into a bowl and use your hands to work in coconut oil. Shape the mix into walnut-sized balls, then roll in sesame seeds. Store in an airtight container until you need a quick energy fix.

Spicy seed mix

Prep: 5 mins **Cook:** 20 mins

Makes 250g

Ingredients

- 250g mixed seed (sunflower, pumpkin, linseed)
- 1 tsp rapeseed oil
- 1 tsp ras-el-hanout
- ¼ tsp low-sodium salt
- 1 tsp reduced salt soy sauce
- 1 tsp agave syrup
- pinch cayenne

Method

STEP 1

Preheat the oven to 160C/ 140 fan/ Gas mark 3.

STEP 2

Mix all the ingredients together in a bowl and spread onto a baking sheet. Cook for 15 - 20 mins until dry and golden. Stir once during cooking. Allow to cool and store in a sealed container for up to 3 weeks.

Prawn & pink grapefruit noodle salad

Prep: 25 mins No cook

Serves 6

Ingredients

- 200g thin rice noodle (vermicelli)
- 12 cherry tomatoes, halved
- 1 tbsp fish sauce
- juice 1 lime
- 2 tsp palm sugar or soft brown sugar
- 1 large red chilli, ½ diced, ½ sliced
- 2 pink grapefruits, segmented

- ½ cucumber , peeled, deseeded and thinly sliced
- 2 carrots , cut into matchsticks
- 3 spring onions , thinly sliced
- 400g cooked large prawn
- large handful mint , leaves picked
- large handful coriander , leaves picked

Method

STEP 1

Put the noodles in a bowl, breaking them up a little, and cover with boiling water from the kettle. Leave to soak for 10 mins until tender. Drain, rinse under cold running water, then leave the noodles to drain thoroughly.

STEP 2

In the same bowl, lightly squash the cherry tomatoes – we used the end of a rolling pin. Stir in the fish sauce, lime juice, sugar and diced chilli. Taste for the right balance of sweet, sour and spicy – adjust if necessary (see tip, below).

STEP 3

Toss through the noodles, then add all the remaining ingredients, except the sliced chilli. Season and give everything a good stir, then divide the noodle salad between 6 serving dishes and sprinkle over the chilli before serving.

Stuffed Moroccan pitta

Prep: 5 mins No cook

Serves 2

Ingredients

- 2 wheat-free pitta bread pockets
- 4 falafels , halved (from Falafels with hummus recipe, in 'goes well with', below right)
- 4 tbsp hummus (from Falafels with hummus recipe, see 'goes well with')
- ½ red pepper , deseeded and sliced
- handful rocket leaves

Method

STEP 1

Spread the hummus on the inside of each pitta, then layer with the falafels, pepper and rocket.

Spicy bean tostadas with pickled onions & radish salad

Prep: 15 mins **Cook:** 12 mins

Serves 4

Ingredients

- 2 red onions , 1 thinly sliced, 1 finely chopped
- 2 limes , juice of 1 and 1 cut into wedges
- 1 ½ tbsp sunflower oil
- 2 garlic cloves , finely chopped
- 2 tsp ground cumin
- 1 tbsp tomato purée
- 1 tbsp chipotle paste
- 400g can kidney bean , drained and rinsed
- 4 corn tortillas
- 140g radish , thinly sliced
- large handful coriander , roughly chopped

Method

STEP 1

Heat oven to 220C/200C fan/gas 7. Put the sliced onion, lime juice and seasoning in a bowl, and set aside.

STEP 2

Heat 1 tbsp of the oil in a pan and fry the chopped onion and garlic until tender. Stir in the cumin and fry for 1 min more. Add the tomato purée, chipotle paste and beans, stir, then tip in half a can of water. Simmer for 5 mins, season, then roughly mash to a purée. (You can cook for a few mins more if it is a bit runny, or add a few splashes of water to thin.)

STEP 3

Meanwhile, brush the tortillas with the remaining oil and place on a baking sheet. Bake for 8 mins until crisp. Spread the tortillas with the bean mixture. Mix the radishes and coriander with the pickled onions, then spoon on top. Serve with lime wedges.

Artichoke, red onion & rosemary risotto

Prep: 15 mins **Cook:** 35 mins

Serves 4

Ingredients

- 1 tbsp olive oil
- 2 red onions , sliced into thin wedges
- 2 red peppers , cut into chunks
- 2 tbsp rosemary needles
- 140g arborio risotto rice
- 150ml white wine
- 850ml low-salt vegetable stock
- 400g tin artichoke heart in water, drained and halved
- 2 tbsp grated parmesan or vegetarian alternative
- 2 tbsp toasted pine nuts

Method

STEP 1

Heat the oil in a large frying pan or wok. Cook the onions gently for 6-7 mins until softened and browning. Add the peppers and rosemary and cook for a further 5 mins. Add rice and stir well.

STEP 2

Pour in the wine and of the stock. Bring to the boil then reduce the heat and simmer gently, stirring occasionally until almost all the liquid is absorbed.

STEP 3

Stir in another of the stock and simmer again, until it's all absorbed. Add the final with the artichokes and simmer again until rice is tender.

STEP 4

Season and stir in the Parmesan and ½ the pine nuts. Scatter over the remainder and serve.

Lighter massaman chicken curry

Prep:35 mins **Cook:**35 mins

Serves 4

Ingredients

For the curry paste

- 1 tbsp coriander seed
- 2 tsp cumin seed
- seeds from 5 cardamom pods
- 3 cloves
- ½ tsp crushed dried chilli
- 2 tsp rapeseed oil
- 100g shallot , finely chopped
- 3 garlic cloves , finely chopped
- 2.5cm piece ginger , finely grated
- 1 plump lemongrass stalk, tough ends and outside layer removed, finely chopped
- 4 tbsp light coconut milk (from the can, below)
- ¼ tsp ground black pepper

For the curry

- 25g unsalted, unroasted peanut
- 2 tsp rapeseed oil
- 140g small shallot (6-7), halved
- 1 cinnamon stick , broken in half
- 400ml can light coconut milk
- 500g skinless, boneless chicken breast , cut into bite-sized pieces
- 200g sweet potato , cut into 2.5cm chunks
- 175g green bean , stem ends trimmed
- 1 tbsp fish sauce
- 2 tsp tamarind paste
- 75ml chicken stock
- coriander or Thai basil leaves (or both), to garnish
- a small handful of peanuts , to garnish

Method

STEP 1

To make the curry paste, heat a small heavy-based frying pan and drop in all the seeds and the cloves. Dry-fry over a medium heat, shaking the pan often, for 1-2 mins to release their flavours – until they start popping in the pan. Mix in the chillies, then grind finely using a pestle and mortar or a spice grinder. Set aside.

STEP 2

Heat the oil in the same pan. Tip in the shallots and garlic, and fry over a medium heat for 5-6 mins, stirring occasionally, until a deep, rich golden brown. Stir in the ground spices and stir-fry for 1 min. Spoon into a mini processor with the ginger, lemongrass and coconut milk. Blitz until it is as smooth as you can get it, then stir in the black pepper. Can be kept in the fridge for several days.

STEP 3

To make the curry, dry-fry the peanuts in a small frying pan for about 2 mins to give them extra colour and flavour. Set aside. Heat the oil in a large sauté pan, tip in the shallots and fry over a medium heat, turning occasionally, for 8-10 mins until they are well browned all over and softened. Remove and set aside. Put the cinnamon stick and curry paste in the sauté pan and cook for 1 min. Pour in 100ml of the coconut milk. Let it bubble for 2 mins, stirring occasionally, until it's like a thick paste. Tip in the chicken and stir-fry in the paste over a high-ish heat for 6-8 mins or until cooked.

STEP 4

Meanwhile, steam the sweet potato chunks for 8-10 mins and the beans for about 5 mins. Remove the pan of chicken from the heat and stir in the remaining coconut milk, the fish sauce, tamarind paste and stock. Lay the sweet potatoes and shallots in the curry and warm through gently over a very low heat – overheating or overcooking may cause the coconut milk to curdle and thicken. If you need to thin the sauce slightly, stir in 1-2 spoons of water. Remove the cinnamon.

STEP 5

Lay a bunch of the beans to one side of each serving bowl or plate. Spoon the curry over one end of the beans and serve scattered with the coriander, Thai basil and peanuts.

Sesame, edamame & chicken noodle salad

Prep: 15 mins **Cook:** 5 mins

Serves 3 (or 2 adults and 2 children)

Ingredients

- 2 chicken legs, cooked
- 1½ tbsp sesame seeds
- 4 wholewheat noodle nests
- 160g frozen edamame beans
- 160g long-stemmed broccoli, cut into small florets

- 1 tbsp tahini
- 2 tbsp sesame oil
- 2 tsp honey
- 1½ tbsp low-sodium soy sauce
- 1 tbsp rice wine vinegar

Method

STEP 1

Boil the kettle. Remove the chicken skin, then shred the meat and discard the bones. Set aside. In a large pan, toast the sesame seeds for 1 min until golden, then tip into a large bowl (big enough to hold the noodles).

STEP 2

Fill the pan with water from the kettle and bring back to the boil. Add the noodles and cook following pack instructions. Tip in the beans and broccoli for the last 2 mins.

STEP 3

Meanwhile, mix the tahini, sesame oil, honey, soy sauce and vinegar into the sesame seeds. Drain the noodles, reserving a cup of the cooking water, and run under cold water to cool. Drain again and toss through the sauce along with the chicken. Add a splash of the cooking water to make the sauce thin enough to coat the noodles (it will thicken as it cools). Transfer to containers and chill until ready to eat, if not eating straight away.

Peach crumble

Prep: 10 mins **Cook:** 35 mins

Serves 6

Ingredients

- 3 x 410g cans peach slices in juice
- zest 1 lemon , plus juice ½
- 1 tbsp agave syrup
- 140g plain flour
- 50g porridge oat
- 25g cold butter , grated

Method

STEP 1

Heat oven to 200C/180C fan/gas 6. Drain the peaches, but reserve the juice. Tip the peaches into a deep baking dish, roughly 20 x 30cm. Scatter over the lemon zest and juice and 1 tbsp of the agave, then toss everything together.

STEP 2

In a bowl, combine the flour, oats, butter, remaining agave and 4 tbsp of the reserved peach juice. Mix together, first with a spoon, then with your fingers, until you have a rough crumbly mixture. Scatter over the peaches, then bake for 35 mins until golden and crunchy on top.

Smoked salmon & avocado sushi

Prep: 20 mins **Cook:** 10 mins

Makes 32

Ingredients

- 300g sushi rice
- 2 tbsp rice or white wine vinegar
- 1 tsp caster sugar
- 1 large avocado
- juice ½ lemon
- 4 sheets nori seaweed
- 4 large slices smoked salmon
- 1 bunch chives
- sweet soy sauce (kecap manis), to serve

Method

STEP 1

Put the rice in a small pan with 600ml water. Bring to the boil and cook for 10 mins until the water is absorbed and the rice is tender. Stir through the vinegar and sugar, cover and cool.

STEP 2

Skin, stone and slice the avocado. Put in a bowl and squeeze over the lemon juice, turning the avocado to ensure the pieces are covered.

STEP 3

Divide the rice between the nori sheets and spread it out evenly, leaving a 1cm border at the top and bottom. Lay the salmon over the rice, followed by the chives and finally position the avocado across the centre.

STEP 4

Fold the bottom edge of the seaweed over the filling, then roll it up firmly. Dampen the top border with a little water to help it seal the roll. Repeat to make 4 rolls. At this stage, the rolls can be wrapped individually in cling film and chilled until ready to serve.

STEP 5

Using a serrated knife, cut each roll into 8 rounds. Serve with sweet soy sauce for dipping.

Hot & sour broth with prawns

Prep: 10 mins **Cook:** 5 mins

Serves 4

Ingredients

- 3 tbsp rice vinegar or white wine vinegar
- 500ml chicken stock
- 1 tbsp soy sauce
- 1-2 tbsp golden caster sugar
- thumb-size piece ginger, peeled and thinly sliced
- 2 small hot red chillies, thinly sliced
- 3 spring onions, thinly sliced
- 300g small raw peeled prawns, from a sustainable source

Method

STEP 1

Put the vinegar, stock, soy sauce, sugar (start with 1 tbsp and add the second at the end if you want the soup sweeter), ginger, chillies and spring onions in a saucepan and bring to a simmer. Cook for 1 min, then add the prawns to heat through. Serve in small bowls or cups.

Herby celery & bulgur salad

Prep: 30 mins No cook

Serves 6

Ingredients

- 200g bulgur wheat
- 1 bunch celery
- 1 dessert apple
- juice 1 lemon
- 4 tbsp olive oil
- handful toasted hazelnuts, roughly chopped
- 1 red chilli, deseeded and chopped
- large handful pomegranate seeds
- small bunch parsley, chopped
- small bunch mint, chopped
- small bunch tarragon, chopped

Method

STEP 1

Put the bulgur wheat in a large bowl and just cover with boiling water. Cover the bowl with cling film and leave for 30 mins to absorb all the water.

STEP 2

Meanwhile, separate the sticks of celery and set the leaves aside. Very finely slice the celery and roughly chop the leaves. Cut the apple into fine matchsticks and toss in a little lemon juice. In a bowl, mix the remaining lemon juice with the oil and some seasoning to make a dressing.

STEP 3

Gently fluff up the bulgur with a fork. Mix the sliced celery and apple through the bulgur, followed by the nuts, chilli, pomegranate seeds and herbs. Drizzle over the dressing and toss everything together gently. Scatter with the celery leaves and serve.

Crispy fried chicken

Prep: 15 mins **Cook:** 20 mins plus 1 hr or overnight marinating

Serves 4

Ingredients

- 150ml buttermilk
- 2 plump garlic cloves, crushed

- 4 x skinless, boneless chicken breasts (total weight 550g), preferably organic
- 50g Japanese panko breadcrumbs
- 2 tbsp self-raising flour
- ½ rounded tsp paprika
- ¼ rounded tsp English mustard powder
- ¼ rounded tsp dried thyme
- ¼ tsp hot chilli powder
- ½ tsp ground black pepper
- 3 tbsp rapeseed oil

Method

STEP 1

Pour the buttermilk into a wide shallow dish and stir in the garlic. Slice the chicken into chunky slices, about 9.5cm long x 3-4cm wide. Lay the chicken in the dish and turn it over in the buttermilk so it is well coated. Leave in the fridge for 1-2 hrs, or preferably overnight.

STEP 2

Meanwhile, heat a large, non-stick frying pan and tip in the panko crumbs and flour. Toast them in the pan for 2-3 mins, stirring regularly so they brown evenly and don't burn. Tip the crumb mix into a bowl and stir in the paprika, mustard, thyme, chilli powder, pepper and a pinch of fine sea salt. Set aside.

STEP 3

When ready to cook, heat oven to 230C/210C fan/gas 8. Line a baking tin with foil and sit a wire rack (preferably non-stick) on top. Transfer half the crumb mix to a medium-large plastic bag. Lift half the chicken from the buttermilk, leaving the marinade clinging to it. Transfer it to the bag of seasoned crumbs. Seal the end of the bag and give it a good shake so the chicken gets well covered (you could do all the crumbs and chicken together if you prefer, but it's easier to coat evenly in 2 batches).

STEP 4

Remove the chicken from the bag. Heat 1 tbsp of the oil in a large, non-stick frying pan, then add the chicken pieces and fry for 1½ mins without moving them. Turn the chicken over, pour in another ½ tbsp of the oil to cover the base of the pan and fry for 1 min more, so both sides are becoming golden. Using tongs, transfer to the wire rack. Repeat with the remaining seasoned crumbs, oil and chicken.

STEP 5

Bake all the chicken on the rack for 15 mins until cooked and crisp, then serve with the Crunchy coleslaw (see 'Goes well with', below right).

Chickpea mash

Prep: 5 mins **Cook:** 1 hr and 10 mins plus overnight soaking

Serves 6

Ingredients

- 500g pack of dried chickpeas
- 1 tsp fennel seeds
- 1 banana shallot , quartered lengthways
- 1 red chilli , deseeded and halved lengthways
- 2 rosemary sprigs
- 2 bay leaves
- 250ml white wine
- 1.3l vegetable stock (we used Marigold bouillon)
- extra virgin olive oil , to serve

Method

STEP 1

In a large bowl, cover the chickpeas with cold water and soak overnight. The next day, drain and rinse well.

STEP 2

Tip the chickpeas into a large pan with all the other ingredients except the olive oil. Bring to the boil, then leave to simmer for 1 hr-1 hr 10 mins until the chickpeas are tender but not mushy.

STEP 3

Remove the bay leaves and rosemary sprigs. Working in batches, blitz the chickpeas in a food processor along with their cooking liquid and the shallot until smooth.

STEP 4

Reheat the mash if necessary and serve sharing-style with a generous drizzle of olive oil and some cracked black pepper on top.

Lentil, walnut & apple salad with blue cheese

Prep: 30 mins **Cook:** 25 mins

Serves 4

Ingredients

- 250g Puy lentil
- 1l chicken stock or water
- 1 celery heart, finely chopped
- 1 Granny Smith, peeled, cored and finely sliced
- 2 shallots, finely sliced

For the vinaigrette

- 2 tbsp extra-virgin olive oil or walnut oil
- 2 tbsp red wine vinegar
- 1 tsp Dijon mustard
- 1 garlic clove, crushed

- 25g walnut, toasted and chopped
- 2 tbsp flat-leaf parsley, finely chopped
- a few handfuls mixed leaf salad
- 1 tbsp strong blue cheese, crumbled (we used Roquefort)

Method

STEP 1

Put the lentils and stock or water in a large saucepan and bring to the boil. Reduce the heat and simmer for 20-25 mins, or until al dente. Drain and pour into a bowl. Add the celery, apple, shallots, walnuts, parsley and salad leaves, then mix together well.

STEP 2

To make the vinaigrette, put all the ingredients in a small glass jar with a lid. Season and shake well. Keep the lid on until ready to serve. Pour the dressing over the salad, toss well, then scatter over the blue cheese.

Mango chicken with spiced pilau

Prep: 10 mins **Cook:** 30 mins

Serves 4

Ingredients

- 4 skinless, boneless chicken breasts
- 4 tbsp chunky mango chutney

- 1 tbsp medium curry powder
- 4 tsp cumin seeds
- 4 tsp sunflower oil
- 2 small onions , thinly sliced
- 4 bay leaves
- 1 cinnamon stick
- 200g basmati rice
- 4 tbsp chopped coriander
- lime wedges, to serve (optional)

Method

STEP 1

Heat oven to 200C/180C fan/gas 6 and line a baking tray with foil. Cut a horizontal pocket in each chicken breast, taking care not to cut all the way through to the other side. Stuff with the mango chutney, then seal the pocket closed around the chutney with a cocktail stick.

STEP 2

Mix the curry powder and 2 tsp cumin seeds with 3 tsp oil, then brush all over the chicken. Place on the baking tray and roast for 25-30 mins until cooked through.

STEP 3

Meanwhile, heat remaining oil and fry the onions for 6-8 mins until golden. Add remaining cumin, bay and cinnamon then cook, stirring, for 1 min. Stir in the rice. Pour over 450ml boiling water, add a pinch of salt, bring to the boil, stir and cover. Reduce heat; simmer for 15 mins.

STEP 4

Remove bay and cinnamon, stir in coriander and serve with the chicken.

Stir-fry green curry beef with asparagus & sugar snaps

Prep: 10 mins **Cook:** 10 mins

Serves 2

Ingredients

- 250g very lean sirloin steak , sliced
- 1 tsp Thai fish sauce
- zest and juice 1/2 lime
- ½ tsp green peppercorns in brine, rinsed and chopped
- 3 garlic cloves , chopped

- 1 tbsp rapeseed oil
- 1 large banana shallot , chopped
- 10 asparagus spears , sliced at an angle
- 4 handfuls sugar snap peas
- 4 broccoli florets (about 275g/10oz), cut into smaller pieces
- 175ml reduced-fat coconut milk
- 2-3 tsp green Thai curry paste (if you like it spicy, use a yellow paste)
- good handful basil leaves (about 25)

Method

STEP 1

Stir the beef with the fish sauce, lime zest, peppercorns and garlic, then set aside. Heat half the oil in a large non-stick wok and pile in the shallot, asparagus, sugar snaps and broccoli. Stir-fry over a high heat for 5 mins. (There are a lot of vegetables, so you can speed up the process by adding a dash of water to the wok every now and then to steam them at the same time.)

STEP 2

Stir the coconut milk, curry paste and lime juice together, pour into the pan and stir well. Simmer for 2 mins, adding a few tbsp water until the vegetables are tender but still have a lot of bite. Tip into bowls and keep warm.

STEP 3

Add the remaining oil to the pan, tip in the beef and stir-fry for 1-2 mins until just cooked. Stir through the basil leaves and serve on top of the vegetables.

Chicken, butter bean & pepper stew

Prep: 10 mins **Cook:** 55 mins

Serves 4

Ingredients

- 1 tbsp olive oil
- 1 large onion , chopped
- 2 celery sticks, chopped
- 1 yellow pepper , deseeded and diced
- 1 red pepper , deseeded and diced
- 1 garlic clove , crushed
- 2 tbsp paprika
- 400g can chopped tomato
- 150ml chicken stock

- 2 x 400g cans butter beans, drained and rinsed
- 8 skinless chicken thighs

Method

STEP 1

Heat oven to 180C/160C fan/gas 4. Heat the oil in a large flameproof casserole dish. Add the onion, celery and peppers, and fry for 5 mins. Add the garlic and paprika, and cook for a further 3 mins.

STEP 2

Stir in the tomatoes, stock and butter beans, and season well. Bring to the boil, then nestle the chicken thighs into the sauce. Cover with a tight-fitting lid and put in the oven for 45 mins.

Cheesy turkey nuggets with smoking chips

Prep: 15 mins **Cook:** 30 mins

Serves 4

Ingredients

- 1 egg
- 3 tbsp finely grated parmesan
- 3 garlic cloves, 1 crushed, 2 finely chopped
- 500g pack turkey breast pieces, large chunks halved to make 16 pieces in all
- 750g large potato, cut into thick chips
- 2 tbsp sunflower oil
- 65g fresh breadcrumb (all crusts if possible)
- ½-1 tsp smoked paprika
- salad, to serve

Method

STEP 1

Heat oven to 220C/200C fan/gas 7. Beat the egg in a bowl with the Parmesan, crushed garlic and some seasoning, then stir in the turkey pieces.

STEP 2

Toss potatoes in the oil, then spread out on a baking tray and bake for 15 mins.

STEP 3

Meanwhile, toss the turkey into the breadcrumbs and spread out on another baking tray. Take the chips from the oven and tip in a bowl with the chopped garlic, paprika and sea salt. Mix well, then spread back out on the tray and return to the oven with the turkey. Bake for 10-12 mins, then serve with a salad.

Beetroot hummus

Prep: 15 mins **Cook:** 45 mins Plus cooling

Serves 8-10

Ingredients

- 500g raw beetroot , leaves trimmed to 1 inch, but root left whole
- 2 x 400g cans chickpeas , drained
- juice 2 lemons
- 1 tbsp ground cumin
- yogurt, toasted cumin seeds, mint and crusty bread, to serve

Method

STEP 1

Cook the beetroot in a large pan of boiling water with the lid on for 30-40 mins until tender. When they're done, a skewer or knife should go all the way in easily. Drain, then set aside to cool.

STEP 2

Pop on a pair of rubber gloves. Pull off and discard the roots, leaves/stalk and peel of the cooled beetroot. Roughly chop the flesh. Whizz the beetroot, chickpeas, lemon juice, cumin, 2 tsp salt and some pepper. Serve swirled with a little yogurt, some toasted cumin seeds, a little torn mint and some crusty bread.

Spiced cod with quinoa salad & mint chutney

Prep: 5 mins **Cook:** 25 mins

Serves 2

Ingredients

- 40g quinoa (or 85g pre-cooked quinoa)
- 3 tbsp chopped mint

- 3 tbsp chopped coriander
- 150g pot 0% natural yogurt
- 1 garlic clove
- ¼ tsp turmeric
- pinch of cumin seeds
- 2 x 150g chunky fillets skinless white fish , such as sustainable cod
- ¼ cucumber , finely diced
- 1 small red onion , finely chopped
- 4 tomatoes , chopped
- good squeeze of lemon juice

Method

STEP 1

Tip the quinoa (if not pre-cooked) into a pan, cover with water and boil, covered, for 25 mins, checking the water level to make sure it doesn't boil dry. Drain well.

STEP 2

Meanwhile, put 2 tbsp each of the mint and coriander in a bowl. Add the yogurt and garlic, and blitz with a hand blender until smooth. Stir 2 tbsp of the herby yogurt with the turmeric and cumin, then add the fish and turn in the mixture to completely coat.

STEP 3

Turn the grill to High. Arrange the fish in a shallow heatproof dish and grill for 8-10 mins, depending on thickness, until it flakes. Toss the quinoa with the cucumber, onion, tomatoes, lemon juice and remaining herbs. Spoon onto a plate, add the fish and spoon round the mint chutney, or add it at the table.

Spicy tuna quinoa salad

Prep: 10 mins **Cook:** 10 mins

Serves 4

Ingredients

- 1 onion , sliced
- 350g pepper , sliced
- 1 tbsp olive oil
- 1 red chilli , finely chopped
- 225g pouch ready-to-eat quinoa
- 350g cherry tomato , halved

- handful black olives, chopped
- 225g jar albacore tuna in olive oil, flaked

Method

STEP 1

Fry the onion and peppers in the oil until soft. Add the chilli and cool slightly.

STEP 2

Mix the quinoa, onion mixture, cherry tomatoes, olives and tuna together. Divide between 4 plates, pour over a little of the oil from the tuna jar, season and serve.

Mediterranean chicken with roasted vegetables

Prep: 50 mins - 55 mins **Serves 2**

Ingredients

- 250g baby new potatoes, thinly sliced
- 1 large courgette, diagonally sliced
- 1 red onion, cut into wedges
- 1 yellow pepper, seeded and cut into chunks
- 6 firm plum tomatoes, halved
- 12 black olives, pitted
- 2 skinless boneless chicken breast fillets, about 150g/5oz each
- 3 tbsp olive oil
- 1 rounded tbsp green pesto

Method

STEP 1

Preheat the oven to 200C/ Gas 6/fan oven 180C. Spread the potatoes, courgette, onion, pepper and tomatoes in a shallow roasting tin and scatter over the olives. Season with salt and coarsely ground black pepper.

STEP 2

Slash the flesh of each chicken breast 3-4 times using a sharp knife, then lay the chicken on top of the vegetables.

STEP 3

Mix the olive oil and pesto together until well blended and spoon evenly over the chicken. Cover the tin with foil and cook for 30 minutes.

STEP 4

Remove the foil from the tin. Return to the oven and cook for a further 10 minutes until the vegetables are juicy and look tempting to eat and the chicken is cooked through (the juices should run clear when pierced with a skewer).

Spring salmon with minty veg

Prep: 10 mins **Cook:** 10 mins

Serves 4

Ingredients

- 750g small new potato , thickly sliced
- 750g frozen pea and beans (we used Waitrose pea and bean mix, £2.29/1kg)
- 3 tbsp olive oil
- zest and juice of 1 lemon
- small pack mint , leaves only
- 4 salmon fillets about 140g/5oz each

Method

STEP 1

Boil the potatoes in a large pan for 4 mins. Tip in the peas and beans, bring back up to a boil, then carry on cooking for another 3 mins until the potatoes and beans are tender. Whizz the olive oil, lemon zest and juice and mint in a blender to make a dressing(or finely chop the mint and whisk into the oil and lemon).

STEP 2

Put the salmon in a microwave-proof dish, season, then pour the dressing over. Cover with cling film, pierce, then microwave on High for 4-5 mins until cooked through. Drain the veg, then mix with the hot dressing and cooking juices from the fish. Serve the fish on top of the vegetables.

Tomato & tamarind fish curry

Prep: 10 mins **Cook:** 25 mins

Serves 4

Ingredients

- 6 garlic cloves
- 1 red chilli , roughly chopped (deseeded if you don't like it too hot)
- thumb-sized piece ginger , peeled and roughly chopped
- 1 tsp turmeric
- 1 tbsp ground coriander
- 1 tbsp rapeseed oil
- 2 tsp cumin seed
- 1 tsp fennel seed
- 2 x 400g cans chopped tomatoes
- 200g green bean , trimmed and halved
- 1 tbsp tamarind paste
- 4 firm white fish fillets (we used hake)
- handful coriander leaves, roughly chopped
- cooked basmati rice , to serve

Method

STEP 1

Blitz together the garlic, chilli, ginger, turmeric and ground coriander with 3 tbsp water. Heat the oil in a large pan and toast the cumin and fennel seeds, letting them sizzle until aromatic. Add the ginger paste and fry for 3 mins.

STEP 2

Empty the tomatoes into the spice pan, plus a can of water. Add the beans, bring to the boil, then turn down the heat and simmer for 5 mins. Stir in the tamarind paste. Add the fish fillets, generously season with ground black pepper, cover and simmer for 10 mins. Take off the lid, carefully turn the fillets, then bubble the sauce until the fish is cooked through and the sauce is thick. Sprinkle over the coriander leaves and serve with rice.

Indian rice salad with chicken

Prep:20 mins **Cook:**20 mins

Serves 6 - 8

Ingredients

- 500g bag long grain rice
- 1 tsp turmeric
- small bunch coriander , leaves roughly chopped, stalks reserved

- 100g bag toasted cashew , ½ very roughly chopped
- 1 cucumber , deseeded and cut into chunks
- 1 large red onion , finely chopped
- about 110g pack pomegranate seeds

For the dressing

- 4 tbsp mango chutney
- 1 tbsp sunflower oil
- 1 tbsp brown sugar
- 400g can black bean , drained and rinsed
- 2 x roughly 130g packs cooked chicken tikka pieces, chopped
- natural yogurt and mini poppadum crisps, to serve (optional)
- 1 tbsp medium curry powder , plus 1 tsp for the rice
- juice 1½-2 lemon , depending on size

Method

STEP 1

Cook the rice following pack instructions but add the turmeric and 1 tsp curry powder to the cooking water. Drain well and spread on a tray lined with kitchen paper to cool.

STEP 2

Meanwhile, finely chop the coriander stalks and whisk with all the other dressing ingredients, plus seasoning.

STEP 3

Tip the rice into a big mixing bowl. Using a fork, break up any large lumps, then mix in the cashews, cucumber, onion, coriander leaves, pomegranate seeds, beans and chicken. Pour over the dressing and lightly stir in, then cover and keep in the fridge. Eat over the next 2 days (as long as it's within the chicken use-by date). Keep a big spoon in the bowl so kids can easily help themselves. Top with a dollop of yogurt and add a handful of poppadum crisps, if you like.

Japanese-style brown rice

Prep: 5 mins **Cook:** 25 mins

Serves 4

Ingredients

- 250g brown rice
- 175g frozen soya bean
- 1 tbsp low-salt soy sauce
- 1 tbsp extra virgin olive oil
- 2 tsp finely grated ginger
- 1 garlic clove , crushed
- 4 spring onions , thinly sliced on the diagonal

Method

STEP 1

Cook the brown rice following pack instructions, adding the soya beans for the final 2 mins of cooking. Meanwhile, mix together the soy sauce, olive oil, ginger and garlic.

STEP 2

Drain the cooked rice and beans, transfer to a serving bowl and stir in the soy sauce mixture. Scatter with the spring onions and serve.

Curried chickpeas

Prep: 15 mins **Cook:** 15 mins

Serves 4

Ingredients

- 2 tbsp vegetable oil
- 1 tsp cumin seeds
- 1-2 red chillies , deseeded and chopped
- 1 clove
- 1 small cinnamon stick
- 1 bay leaf
- 1 onion , finely chopped
- ½ tsp ground turmeric
- 2 garlic cloves , finely chopped
- 400g can chickpeas , rinsed and drained
- 1 tsp paprika
- 1 tsp ground coriander
- 2 small tomatoes , chopped
- 1 tbsp chopped coriander

Method

STEP 1

Heat the oil in a heavy-bottomed pan. Fry the cumin, chillies, clove, cinnamon and bay leaf together until the cumin starts to crackle. Tip in the onion, turmeric and a pinch of salt. Cook for 2 mins until starting to soften, then add the garlic.

STEP 2

Continue cooking 4-5 mins until the onion is soft, then add chickpeas, paprika, black pepper and ground coriander. Give everything a good stir so the chickpeas are well coated in the spices.

STEP 3

Add the tomatoes and 2 tbsp water. Cook on a medium heat until tomatoes are soft and the sauce is thick and pulpy. Take off the heat and sprinkle on the coriander.

Stir-fried beef with hoisin sauce

Prep: 20 mins - 25 mins Plus 20 minutes marinating

Serves 2

Ingredients

- 1 tbsp soy sauce
- 1 tbsp dry sherry
- 2 tsp sesame oil
- 1 fat garlic clove , crushed
- 1 tsp finely chopped fresh root ginger (or fresh ginger paste in a jar)
- 200g lean sirloin steak , thinly sliced across the grain
- 1 tbsp sesame seeds
- 1 tbsp sunflower oil
- 1 large carrot , cut into matchsticks
- 100g mangetout , halved lengthways
- 140g mushrooms , sliced
- 3 tbsp hoisin sauce
- Chinese noodles , to serve

Method

STEP 1

Mix together the soy sauce, sherry, sesame oil, garlic and ginger in a shallow dish. Add the steak and leave to marinate for about 20 minutes (or longer, if you have time).

STEP 2

Heat a large heavy-based frying pan or wok, add the sesame seeds and toast over a high heat, stirring, for a few minutes until golden. Tip on to a plate.

STEP 3

When ready to cook, heat the sunflower oil in a large frying pan or wok until hot. Add the steak with the marinade and stir fry for 3-4 minutes over a high heat until lightly browned. Remove, using a slotted spoon, on to a plate, leaving the juices in the pan.

STEP 4

Toss the carrots in the pan and stir fry for a few minutes, then add the mangetout and cook for a further 2 minutes.

STEP 5

Return the steak to the pan, add the mushrooms and toss everything together. Add the hoisin sauce and stir fry for a final minute. Sprinkle with the toasted sesame seeds and serve immediately.

For-the-freezer ratatouille

Prep: 15 mins **Cook:** 1 hr and 55 mins for the basic ratatouille

Serves 10

Ingredients

- 250g red onion , cut into 3cm chunks
- 250g white onion , cut into 3cm chunks
- 600g red and yellow pepper - after deseeding and removing stalks, cut into chunks
- 1kg courgette , cut into 3cm chunks
- 1kg aubergine
- 20g garlic clove , crushed
- 800g cherry tomato
- 3 x 400g cans chopped tomatoes
- 1 tbsp sugar
- 2 tbsp red wine vinegar

To serve as Greek veg bake with feta (serves 1)

- 1 tsp dried thyme or oregano , plus a pinch extra
- 1 tbsp wholemeal breadcrumb
- 25g light feta cheese
- 30g Little Gem lettuce leaves
- 25g sliced spring onion
- 50g sliced cucumber
- squeeze of lemon juice

To serve as veggie chilli jackets (serves 1)

- 1 small baking potato weighing 100g
- 1 tsp cumin seed
- 1 tsp mild chilli powder
- 2 tbsp chopped coriander
- 25g fat-free Greek yogurt
- 10g rocket leaves

- squeeze of lemon juice

To serve as cheesy stuffed peppers (serves 2)

- 2 small peppers of any colour
- 25g lighter mature cheddar
- 200g cooked broccoli
- 20g baby spinach leaves
- 1 tsp balsamic vinegar

Method

STEP 1

Heat oven to 200C/180C fan/gas 6. Scatter the onions in a roasting tin, season and roast for 25 mins, stirring occasionally, until charred and softened. Repeat with the peppers for 20 mins, then the courgette for just 15 mins.

STEP 2

Heat a non-stick frying pan. Slice the aubergines into 2-3cm thick rounds and arrange in the pan (only cut what you can fit in your pan at a time – cooking freshly cut slices in batches should prevent them going brown). Cook over a high heat until charred on both sides, then remove to a microwave-proof plate. Repeat in batches until all are nicely crisped and browned. Cover the plate with cling film, poke in a couple of holes, then microwave the aubergines on High for about 5 mins until soft. You may need to do this in batches. Quarter the slices, or cut into chunks. (Because you're frying without oil, they'll burn before they're cooked through, so finishing in a microwave is ideal. If you don't have one, just add to the sauce for the final 10-15 mins simmering, but they may break up a bit.)

STEP 3

While roasting the veg, put the garlic in the non-stick frying pan or a large pan with a small glass of water. Simmer until the water is nearly gone, then tip in the cherry and chopped tomatoes, sugar, vinegar and plenty of seasoning. Simmer for 20 mins until thickened and saucy. Taste for seasoning, then turn off and combine with the veg. Cool, divide into 10 portions and freeze.

STEP 4

To serve as Greek veg bake with feta (serves 1, prep 10 mins, cook 15 mins): Stir herbs through 1 serving defrosted ratatouille and tip into a small dish. Sprinkle with breadcrumbs, then add feta with a pinch more herbs. Bake at 200C/180C fan/gas 6 for 15 mins if defrosted, or 25-30 mins from frozen. Toss Baby Gem leaves with spring onion, cucumber and lemon juice. Serve with the bake.

Per serving: 236 kcals, protein 13g, carbs 34g, fat 5g, sat fat 3g, fibre 10g, sugar 20g, salt 1.0g

STEP 5

To serve as veggie chilli jackets (serves 1, prep 5 mins, cook about 1hr): Bake potato in the oven. Add a few tbsp water to a pan with cumin seeds and chilli powder. Simmer, and just before the water evaporates, stir in 1 serving of defrosted ratatouille. Heat through, then stir in coriander. Halve the potato, top with veggie chilli and Greek yogurt. Serve with rocket leaves dressed with lemon juice.

Per serving: 270kcals, protein 14g, carbs 50g, fat 3g, sat fat 0g, fibrew 12g, sugar 20g, salt 0.4g

STEP 6

To serve as cheesy stuffed peppers (serves 2, prep 15 mins, cook 20 mins): Halve peppers down the stalks and scrape out any seeds. Divide 1 serving of defrosted ratatouille between the pepper halves. Grate over cheddar, then bake for 15-20 mins at 200C/180C fan/gas 6. Serve with broccoli and spinach tossed with balsamic vinegar.

Per serving: 173 kcals, protein 12g, carbs 21g, fat 4g, sat fat 2g, fibre 10g, sugar 20g, salt 0.4g

Ceviche

Prep: 20 mins Plus 1hr 30 mins in lime juice no cook

Serves 6 as a starter

Ingredients

- 500g firm white fish fillets, such as haddock, halibut or pollack, skinned and thinly sliced
- juice 8 limes (250ml/9fl oz), plus extra wedges to serve
- 1 red onion , sliced into rings
- handful pitted green olives , finely chopped
- 2-3 green chillies , finely chopped
- 2-3 tomatoes , seeded and chopped into 2cm pieces
- bunch coriander , roughly chopped

- 2 tbsp extra-virgin olive oil
- good pinch caster sugar
- tortilla chips, to serve

Method

STEP 1

In a large glass bowl, combine the fish, lime juice and onion. The juice should completely cover the fish; if not, add a little more. Cover with cling film and place in the fridge for 1 hr 30 mins.

STEP 2

Remove the fish and onion from the lime juice (discard the juice) and place in a bowl. Add the olives, chilies, tomatoes, coriander and olive oil, stir gently, then season with a good pinch of salt and sugar. This can be made a couple of hours in advance and stored in the fridge. Serve with tortilla chips to scoop up the ceviche and enjoy with a glass of cold beer.

Summer vegetable minestrone

Prep: 10 mins **Cook:** 30 mins

Serves 4

Ingredients

- 3 tbsp olive oil
- 2 leeks, finely sliced
- 2 celery sticks, finely chopped
- 2 courgettes, quartered lengthways then sliced
- 4 garlic cloves, finely chopped
- 1l vegetable stock
- 250g asparagus, woody ends removed, chopped
- 100g pea, fresh or frozen
- 200g broad bean, double-podded if you have time
- small bunch basil, most chopped
- crusty bread, to serve

Method

STEP 1

Heat the oil in a large saucepan, add the leeks and celery, and cook for 8 mins until soft. Add the courgettes and garlic. Cook gently for 5 mins more.

STEP 2

Pour in the stock and simmer, covered, for 10 mins. Add the asparagus, peas and broad beans, and cook for a further 4 mins, until just cooked through. Stir in the chopped basil and season well. Scatter with basil leaves and serve with crusty bread.

Spring greens with lemon dressing

Prep: 10 mins **Cook:** 5 mins

Serves 8

Ingredients

- 250g broccoli , thicker stalks halved
- 400g spring green , thick stalks removed and shredded

For the dressing

- 2 garlic cloves , crushed
- zest and juice 1 lemon
- 2 tbsp olive oil

Method

STEP 1

To make the dressing, mix the garlic, lemon juice and zest, olive oil and some seasoning together. Bring a large pan of water to the boil, then add the broccoli and greens, and cook for about 5 mins until tender. Drain well, then toss through the dressing and serve.

Harissa aubergine kebabs with minty carrot salad

Prep: 10 mins **Cook:** 15 mins

Serves 2

Ingredients

- 2 tbsp harissa paste
- 2 tbsp red wine vinegar

- 1 aubergine, cut into 4cm cubes
- 2 carrots, finely shredded
- 1 small red onion, sliced
- small handful mint, chopped, plus extra leaves to serve
- 2 Middle Eastern flatbreads
- 2 heaped tbsp hummus
- Greek yoghurt, to serve

Method

STEP 1

Mix the harissa and vinegar in a bowl. Remove half and reserve. Toss the aubergine in the remaining harissa sauce and season. Thread onto metal or soaked wooden skewers. Heat a griddle or grill until hot, then cook the kebabs until golden on all sides and cooked through.

STEP 2

Meanwhile, mix together the carrots, onion and mint with some seasoning.

STEP 3

Top the flatbreads with the hummus, carrot salad and kebabs. Scatter over the extra mint and serve with yogurt and a drizzle of reserved harissa sauce.

Peanut hummus with fruit & veg sticks

Prep: 10 mins No cook

Serves 2

Ingredients

- 380g carton chickpeas
- zest and juice 0.5 lemon (use the other 1/2 to squeeze over the apple to stop it browning, if you like)
- 1 tbsp tahini
- 0.5-1 tsp smoked paprika
- 2 tbsp roasted unsalted peanuts
- 1 tsp rapeseed oil
- 2 crisp red apples, cored and cut into slices
- 2 carrots, cut into sticks
- 4 celery sticks, cut into batons lengthways

Method

STEP 1

Drain the chickpeas, reserving the liquid. Tip three-quarters of the chickpeas into a food processor and add the lemon zest and juice, tahini, paprika, peanuts and oil with 3 tbsp chickpea liquid. Blitz in a food processor until smooth, then stir in the reserved chickpeas. Serve with the fruit and veg sticks.

Bean & pesto mash

Prep: 5 mins **Cook:** 5 mins

Serves 4

Ingredients

- 1 tbsp olive oil , plus a drizzle to serve (optional)
- 2 x 400g cans cannellini beans , rinsed and drained
- 2 tbsp pesto

Method

STEP 1

Heat the oil in a large saucepan. Add the beans and cook for 3-4 mins until hot through. Lightly mash with a potato masher for a chunky texture. Stir through the pesto and season. To serve, drizzle with a little olive oil, if you like.

Super-green mackerel salad

Prep: 10 mins **Cook:** 10 mins

Serves 1

Ingredients

- 85g green bean
- 85g thin-stemmed broccoli
- large handful baby spinach leaves
- 2 hot-smoked mackerel fillets (about 75g), skinned and flaked
- 2 tsp sunflower seed , toasted

For the dressing

- 75ml low-fat natural yogurt
- 1 tsp lemon juice
- 1 tsp wholegrain mustard
- 2 tsp dill , chopped, plus extra to serve

Method

STEP 1

Boil a pan of water. Add the green beans and cook for 2 mins, then add the broccoli and cook for 4 mins more. Drain, run under cold water until cool, then drain well.

STEP 2

To make the dressing, combine all the ingredients in a small jam jar with a twist of black pepper, put the lid on and give it a good shake.

STEP 3

To serve, mix together the cooked veg with the spinach and mackerel and pack into a lunchbox. Just before eating, pour over the dressing, scatter over the sunflower seeds and add a grind of black pepper and extra dill.

Yellow lentil & coconut curry with cauliflower

Prep: 15 mins **Cook:** 50 mins

Serves 4

Ingredients

- 1 tbsp vegetable oil
- 1 onion , thinly sliced
- 2 garlic cloves , crushed
- thumb-sized piece ginger , finely chopped
- 3 tbsp curry paste (we used Bart Veeraswamy Gujurat Masala curry paste)
- 200g yellow lentil , rinsed
- 1 ½l vegetable stock
- 3 tbsp unsweetened desiccated coconut , plus extra to sprinkle if you like
- 1 cauliflower , broken into little florets
- cooked basmati rice and coriander leaves, plus mango chutney and naan bread (optional), to serve

Method

STEP 1

Heat the oil in a large saucepan, then add the onion, garlic and ginger. Cook for 5 mins, add the curry paste, then stir-fry for 1 min before adding the lentils, stock and coconut. Bring the mixture to the boil and simmer for 40 mins or until the lentils are soft.

STEP 2

During the final 10 mins of cooking, stir in the cauliflower to cook. Spoon rice into 4 bowls, top with the curry and sprinkle with coriander leaves, and coconut if you like. Serve with mango chutney and naan bread (optional).

Charred broccoli, lemon & walnut pasta

Prep: 5 mins **Cook:** 15 mins

Serves 2

Ingredients

- 1 head broccoli , cut into small florets and stalk cut into small pieces
- 3 tsp olive oil
- 150g penne or fusilli
- 2 garlic cloves , crushed
- 1 tbsp roughly chopped walnuts
- pinch of chilli flakes
- ½ lemon , zested and juiced

Method

STEP 1

Heat the grill to high. Put the broccoli on a baking tray and drizzle over 1 tsp of the oil. Season, and toss together. Grill for 8-10 mins, tossing around halfway through, until crispy and charred.

STEP 2

Cook the pasta in salted water following pack instructions. Drain, reserving a cup of the cooking water.

STEP 3

In a frying pan, heat the remaining 2 tsp oil over a medium heat, and fry the garlic, walnuts and chilli for 3-4 mins until golden.

STEP 4

Tip in the pasta, broccoli, lemon zest and juice, reserving a little of the zest. Add a splash of the reserved cooking water and toss everything together to coat the pasta. Serve in warmed bowls with the remaining lemon zest scattered over.

Creamy yogurt porridge with pear, walnut & cinnamon topping

Prep: 6 mins **Cook:** 3 mins

Serves 1

Ingredients

For the porridge

- 3 tbsp (25g) porridge oat
- 150g 0% fat probiotic plain yogurt

For the topping

- 1 ripe pear, sliced (keep the skin on)
- 4 broken walnut halves
- couple pinches of cinnamon

Method

STEP 1

For the porridge: Tip 200ml water into a small non-stick pan and stir in porridge oats. Cook over a low heat until bubbling and thickened. (To make in a microwave, use a deep container to prevent spillage as the mixture will rise up as it cooks, and cook for 3 mins on High.) Stir in yogurt – or swirl in half and top with the rest.

STEP 2

For the topping: Add pear and walnut halves to the finished porridge, then sprinkle on cinnamon.

Beetroot & squash salad with horseradish cream

Prep: 30 mins **Cook:** 45 mins

Serves 12

Ingredients

- 1kg raw beetroot
- 6 red onions
- 1 ¼kg large butternut squash, peeled and deseeded
- 2 tbsp red wine vinegar
- 1 tbsp soft brown sugar
- 50ml olive oil

For the horseradish cream

- 175ml soured cream
- 3 tbsp creamed horseradish
- juice 1 lemon
- 85g watercress, large stalks removed

Method

STEP 1

Heat oven to 200C/180C fan/gas 6. Peel the beetroot and cut each into 8 wedges. Cut the onions and butternut squash into roughly the same size. Spread out in a large roasting tin. Mix the vinegar and sugar until dissolved, then whisk in the oil. Pour over the vegetables, toss and roast for 40-45 mins until charred and soft, stirring halfway through cooking.

STEP 2

To make the horseradish cream, mix together the soured cream, horseradish, lemon juice and some seasoning.

STEP 3

To serve, put the roasted veg in a large bowl or on a platter, followed by the watercress, then drizzle over the horseradish cream. Serve warm or cold.

Bean, feta & herb dip

Prep: 10 mins No cook

Serves 4

Ingredients

- 400g can cannellini bean
- 200g feta cheese
- 1 tbsp lemon juice
- 1 garlic clove , crushed
- 3 tbsp chopped dill, mint or chives (or 1 tbsp each)

Method

STEP 1

Drain and rinse beans. Tip into a food processor with feta, lemon juice and garlic, and whizz until smooth. Add dill, mint or chives, and season with pepper.

Easy chicken korma

Prep: 15 mins **Cook:** 20 mins

Serves 4

Ingredients

- small knob fresh ginger , peeled and finely sliced
- 1 garlic clove
- 1 onion , sliced
- 1 tbsp vegetable oil
- 4 skinless chicken breasts, cut into bite-size pieces
- 1 tsp garam masala
- 100ml chicken stock
- 3 tbsp low-fat fromage frais
- 2 tbsp ground almonds
- handful toasted, sliced almonds , to serve
- coriander leaves, plain rice , naan bread or chapatis, to serve

Method

STEP 1

Cook the ginger, garlic and onion in a large pan with the oil until softened. Tip in the chicken and cook until lightly browned, about 5 mins, then add in garam masala and cook for 1 min further.

STEP 2

Pour over the stock and simmer for 10 mins until the chicken is cooked through. Mix together the fromage frais and ground almonds. Take the pan off the heat and stir in the fromage frais mixture. Sprinkle over sliced almonds, garnish with coriander and serve with boiled rice, chapatis or plain naan bread.

Prawn, rice & mango jar salad

Prep: 15 mins No cook

Serves 1

Ingredients

- 125g cooked rice (we used brown basmati)
- handful baby spinach
- 50g cooked prawn
- ¼ ripe mango, cut into small pieces

- ½ red chilli, deseeded and finely chopped
- small handful coriander, roughly chopped

For the dressing

- ½ tbsp low-salt soy sauce
- 1 tsp sesame oil

- 1 tsp rice vinegar
- ½ tsp brown sugar

Method

STEP 1

Make the dressing by whisking together all the ingredients. Tip the dressing into the bottom of a big jar, top with the rice and put in the fridge if making the night before.

STEP 2

Layer the spinach, prawns, mango, chilli and coriander on top of the rice. Leave a little space at the top so that when lunchtime arrives, you can shake up the salad to eat.

Orzo with spinach & cherry tomatoes

Prep: 5 mins **Cook:** 25 mins

Serves 4

Ingredients

- 400g orzo pasta
- 2 tbsp olive oil
- 1 celery heart, chopped
- 1 red onion, chopped
- 3 garlic cloves, chopped
- 2 x 400g cans cherry tomato
- 250g baby spinach
- 10 black olives, halved
- small handful dill, chopped
- small handful mint, chopped

Method

STEP 1

Cook the orzo following pack instructions. Drain, rinse under cold water, drain again and toss with half the olive oil.

STEP 2

Meanwhile, heat the remaining oil in a large sauté pan. Add the celery, onion and some seasoning, and cook for 8 mins until soft. Add the garlic, cook for 1 min, then tip in the cherry tomatoes and simmer for 10 mins. Add the spinach, cover with a lid to wilt the leaves, then add the orzo, olives, dill and mint. Season and serve.

Kale & apple soup with walnuts

Prep: 20 mins **Cook:** 15 mins

Serves 2

Ingredients

- 8 walnut halves, broken into pieces
- 1 onion, finely chopped
- 2 carrots, coarsely grated
- 2 red apples, unpeeled and finely chopped
- 1 tbsp cider vinegar
- 500ml reduced-salt vegetable stock
- 200g kale, roughly chopped
- 20g pack of dried apple crisps (optional)

Method

STEP 1

In a dry, non-stick frying pan, cook the walnut pieces for 2-3 mins until toasted, turning frequently so they don't burn. Take off the heat and allow to cool.

STEP 2

Put the onion, carrots, apples, vinegar and stock in a large saucepan and bring to the boil. Reduce the heat and simmer for 10 mins, stirring occasionally.

STEP 3

Once the onion is translucent and the apples start to soften, add the kale and simmer for an additional 2 mins. Carefully transfer to a blender or liquidiser and blend until very smooth. Pour into bowls and serve topped with the toasted walnuts, and a sprinkling of apple crisps, if you like.

Mustardy greens

Prep: 10 mins **Cook:** 5 mins

Serves 4

Ingredients

- 300g spring green
- 300g frozen pea
- 25g butter
- 1 tbsp wholegrain mustard
- 2 tbsp Dijon mustard

Method

STEP 1

Heat 250ml water in a large pan. Add the greens and peas, cover with a lid and boil for 4 mins. Drain into a colander, put the pan back on the heat, and add the butter and mustards. When the butter has melted, add the veg back to the pan, season well and toss everything together. Serve straight away.

Full English frittata with smoky beans

Prep: 5 mins **Cook:** 30 mins

Serves 4

Ingredients

- 2 low-fat sausages, sliced
- 4 rashers extra lean bacon, all fat removed, chopped
- 150g pack button mushroom, halved, or larger ones quartered
- 8 egg whites, or use 350ml liquid egg whites from a carton
- 3 tbsp milk
- 140g cherry tomato, halved
- 2 x 400g cans reduced salt and sugar baked beans
- 1 ½ tsp smoked paprika
- small bunch chives, snipped

Method

STEP 1

Heat oven to 180C/160C fan/gas 4. Line a roasting tin about the size of A4 paper with enough baking parchment to cover the base and sides. Fry the sausages and bacon in a non-stick pan until golden, stirring them often to stop them sticking. Scoop into the tin.

STEP 2

Place the pan back on the heat and fry the mushrooms for about 5 mins until golden, then add these to the tray, too. Whisk the egg whites with the milk and lots of seasoning. Pour into the tin, then dot the tomatoes on top.

STEP 3

Bake in the oven for 20-25 mins, until set. Meanwhile, tip the beans into a pan with the paprika and heat through. Scatter the frittata with the chives and serve with the beans on the side.

Maple-roasted marrow on cavolo nero salad

Prep: 15 mins **Cook:** 30 mins

Serves 4

Ingredients

- 1 medium marrow
- 1 tbsp olive oil
- 1 garlic clove, crushed
- 1 tbsp maple syrup
- 3 tbsp hazelnuts, halved
- 2 slices toasted sourdough bread, blitzed into crumbs
- 200g cavolo nero, stalks removed, shredded
- 10 radishes, quartered

- 16 shavings of vegetarian-style Parmesan

For the dressing

- 2 tbsp red wine vinegar
- 1 tbsp lemon juice
- 3 tbsp extra virgin olive oil
- 1 shallot, finely diced
- 1 tsp Dijon mustard
- pinch golden caster sugar

Method

STEP 1

Heat oven to 220C/200C fan/gas 7. Slice the marrow open lengthways and scoop out the seeds. Cut the marrow into slices and place on a baking tray. Toss with the olive oil, garlic, maple syrup and some seasoning. Roast for 20 mins, then sprinkle the hazelnuts and breadcrumbs over. Roast for another 8 mins, then remove.

STEP 2

While the marrow is roasting, prepare the rest of the salad. Shred the cavolo nero leaves into bite-sized pieces. Put on a large platter or shallow bowl and top with the radishes.

STEP 3

Combine the dressing ingredients in a small bowl, adding some salt. Mix well.

STEP 4

Just before the marrow has finished cooking, drizzle the dressing over the cavolo nero. Use your hands to massage it into the cavolo nero for a few mins so that it softens it, then top with the marrow, breadcrumbs and hazelnuts. Sprinkle the Parmesan shavings over and serve.

Griddled lettuce & peas

Prep: 5 mins **Cook:** 10 mins

Serves 2

Ingredients

- 3 tsp white wine vinegar
- 1 tbsp olive oil
- 1 garlic clove, crushed
- 1 tbsp chopped parsley

- 1 tbsp chopped mint
- 2 Baby Gem lettuces, halved
- 140g frozen peas

Method

STEP 1

To make a dressing, mix the vinegar, 2 tsp of the oil, the garlic and herbs in a small bowl. Heat a griddle pan. Brush the lettuces in the remaining oil and cook on the griddle for 3 mins each side until charred. Bring a small pan of water to the boil, add the peas and cook for 3 mins. Drain the peas and mix with the lettuce and dressing. Serve straight away.

Thai chicken cakes with sweet chilli sauce

Total time 25 mins Ready in 20-25 minutes

Serves 2 - 3

Ingredients

- 2 large boneless, skinless chicken breasts (about 175g), cubed
- 1 garlic clove, roughly chopped
- small piece fresh root ginger, peeled and roughly chopped
- 1 small onion, roughly chopped
- 4 tbsp fresh coriander, plus a few sprigs to garnish
- 1 green chilli, seeded and roughly chopped
- 2 tbsp olive oil
- sweet chilli sauce, lime wedges, shredded spring onion and red chilli, to serve

Method

STEP 1

Toss the chicken, garlic, ginger, onion, coriander and chilli into a food processor and season well. Blitz until the chicken is finely ground and everything is well mixed. Use your hands to shape six small cakes.

STEP 2

Heat the oil in a frying pan, then fry the cakes over a medium heat for about 6-8 mins, turning once. Serve hot, with sweet chilli sauce, lime wedges, coriander, shredded spring onion and red chilli.

Herbed lamb cutlets with roasted vegetables

Prep: 15 mins **Cook:** 45 mins

Serves 4

Ingredients

- 2 peppers, any colour, deseeded and cut into chunky pieces
- 1 large sweet potato, peeled and cut into chunky pieces
- 2 courgettes, sliced into chunks
- 1 red onion, cut into wedges
- 1 tbsp olive oil
- 8 lean lamb cutlets
- 1 tbsp thyme leaf, chopped
- 2 tbsp mint leaves, chopped

Method

STEP 1

Heat oven to 220C/200C fan/gas 7. Put the peppers, sweet potato, courgettes and onion on a large baking tray and drizzle over the oil. Season with lots of ground black pepper. Roast for 25 mins.

STEP 2

Meanwhile, trim the lamb of as much fat as possible. Mix the herbs with a few twists of ground black pepper and pat all over the lamb.

STEP 3

Take the vegetables out of the oven, turn over and push to one side of the tray. Place the cutlets on the hot tray and return to the oven for 10 mins.

STEP 4

Turn the cutlets and cook for a further 10 mins or until the vegetables and lamb are tender and lightly charred. Mix everything on the tray and serve.

Apple crisps

Prep: 5 mins **Cook:** 40 mins

Makes roughly 16

Ingredients

- 1 apple

Method

STEP 1

Heat oven to 140C/120C fan/gas 1. Thinly slice the apple through the core – use a mandolin, if you have one, to get thin slices. Arrange the slices on a baking tray lined with parchment and bake for 40 mins. Cool until crisp.

Hoisin pork with garlic & ginger greens

Prep: 10 mins **Cook:** 10 mins Plus marinating

Serves 4

Ingredients

- 500g pork loin steak, cut into 2cm-thick slices
- 4 tbsp hoisin sauce
- 1 tbsp light soy sauce, plus a dash
- 350g thin-stemmed broccoli
- 1 tbsp sunflower oil
- 2 garlic cloves, thinly sliced
- 5cm-piece ginger, shredded
- 1 bunch spring onion, halved lengthways
- 350g bok choi, halved lengthways
- rice or noodles, to serve (optional)

Method

STEP 1

Put the pork, hoisin and soy sauce in a bowl and allow to stand for 10 mins. Heat the grill to high, shake off any excess sauce, then lay the pork on a tray. Grill for 5 mins, turning halfway, until cooked through. Remove and leave to rest in a warm place for 5 mins.

STEP 2

Meanwhile, put the broccoli in a microwave-safe bowl with 4 tbsp water, cover with cling film, then microwave on High for 3 mins. Heat the oil in a wok, add the garlic and ginger, and stir-fry for 1 min. Add the spring onions and bok choi, then stir-fry for a further 2 mins. Tip in the broccoli with a dash of soy sauce and stir-fry for 1-2 mins more until the veg is warmed through. Serve the pork with the greens, a drizzle of any resting pork juices and rice or noodles, if you like.

Roasted balsamic cauliflower

Prep: 5 mins **Cook:** 25 mins - 30 mins

Serves 2

Ingredients

- 1 large cauliflower , cut into bite-sized florets
- 2 tbsp olive oil
- 1 garlic clove , finely chopped
- 2 tbsp balsamic glaze
- 1 red chilli (deseeded if you don't like it too hot), finely sliced

Method

STEP 1

Heat oven to 200C/180C fan/gas 6. Put the cauliflower on a large baking sheet. Combine the oil and garlic, and drizzle over the cauliflower and roast in the oven for 10 mins.

STEP 2

Drizzle the balsamic glaze over the cauliflower and roast for a further 15-20 mins until it is cooked through. Serve immediately with the chilli scattered over.

Squash & coconut curry

Prep: 10 mins **Cook:** 20 mins Ready in 30 minutes

Serves 2

Ingredients

- 2 tbsp Madras curry paste
- 1 large butternut squash (600g/1lb 5oz peeled weight), chopped into medium size chunks
- 1 red pepper , halved, deseeded and roughly chopped into chunks
- 400g can reduced-fat coconut milk

- small bunch coriander, roughly chopped

Method

STEP 1

Heat a large frying pan or wok, tip in the curry paste and fry for 1 min. Add the squash and red pepper, then toss well in the paste.

STEP 2

Pour in the coconut milk with 200ml water and bring to a simmer. Cook for 15-20 mins or until the butternut squash is very tender and the sauce has thickened. Season to taste, then serve scattered with chopped coriander and naan bread or rice.

Beetroot & mint dip

Prep: 10 mins No cook

Serves 4

Ingredients

- 250g vacuum-packed beetroot
- ½ tsp ground cumin
- 2 tsp chopped mint, plus a few leaves for sprinkling
- squeeze lemon juice
- 3 tbsp half-fat crème fraîche
- a few pinches nigella seeds

Method

STEP 1

Put beetroot and cumin in the small bowl of a food processor, season and blend until smooth. Tip into a bowl, add the mint and lemon juice, then gently stir through crème fraîche to get a rippled effect. Sprinkle with mint leaves and nigella seeds.

Super berry smoothie

Prep: 10 mins No cook

Serves 4

Ingredients

- 450g bag frozen berry
- 450g pot fat-free strawberry yogurt
- 100ml milk
- 25g porridge oat
- 2 tsp honey (optional)

Method

STEP 1

Whizz the berries, yogurt and milk together with a stick blender until smooth. Stir through the porridge oats, then pour into 4 glasses and serve with a drizzle of honey, if you like.

Basque-style salmon stew

Prep: 10 mins **Cook:** 25 mins

Serves 4

Ingredients

- 1 tbsp olive oil
- 3 mixed peppers , deseeded and sliced
- 1 large onion , thinly sliced
- 400g baby potatoes , unpeeled and halved
- 2 tsp smoked paprika
- 2 garlic cloves , sliced
- 2 tsp dried thyme
- 400g can chopped tomatoes
- 4 salmon fillets
- 1 tbsp chopped parsley , to serve (optional)

Method

STEP 1

Heat the oil in a large pan and add the peppers, onion and potatoes. Cook, stirring regularly for 5-8 mins until golden. Then add the paprika, garlic, thyme and tomatoes. Bring to the boil, stir and cover, then turn down heat and simmer for 12 mins. Add a splash of water if the sauce becomes too thick.

STEP 2

Season the stew and lay the salmon on top, skin side down. Place the lid back on and simmer for another 8 mins until the salmon is cooked through. Scatter with parsley, if you like, and serve.

Layered hummus & griddled vegetable salad

Prep: 15 mins **Cook:** 45 mins

Serves 4

Ingredients

- 3 red peppers , halved
- 3 tbsp olive oil
- 2 courgettes , thinly sliced lengthways
- 1 large aubergine , thinly sliced lengthways
- 8 tbsp hummus
- juice 1 lemon
- small garlic clove , crushed
- 1 tsp sumac
- 2 large handfuls rocket
- ciabatta , to serve

Method

STEP 1

Heat oven to 200C/180C fan/ gas 6. Rub the peppers with a little oil and roast for 30 mins, turning halfway through, until soft and slightly charred. Place in a bowl, cover with cling film and set aside.

STEP 2

Meanwhile, heat a large griddle pan (or two, if you have them, for speed) until hot. Drizzle the courgettes and aubergine with oil, then griddle for a few mins each side until char lines appear. Peel the peppers and discard the seeds. Tear the peppers into thick strips.

STEP 3

Spread the hummus over a serving plate. Mix together the lemon juice and garlic. Toss with the vegetables and half the sumac, then arrange over the hummus. Top with the rocket leaves and sprinkle over the remaining sumac. Serve with ciabatta.

Storecupboard pasta salad

Prep: 5 mins **Serves 2**

Ingredients

- 2 tsp finely chopped red onion
- 1 tsp caper
- 1 tbsp pesto
- 2 tsp olive oil
- 185g can of tuna in spring water, drained
- 100g leftover pasta shapes
- 3 sundried tomatoes, chopped

Method

STEP 1

Mix the onion, capers, pesto and oil. Flake the tuna into a bowl with the pasta and tomatoes, then stir in the pesto mix.

Energy bites

Prep: 10 mins Plus chilling no cook

Makes 8

Ingredients

- 100g pecan
- 75g raisin
- 1 tbsp ground flaxseed (or a mix- we used milled flaxseed, almond, Brazil nut and walnut mix)
- 1 tbsp cocoa powder
- 1 tbsp agave syrup
- 50g desiccated coconut
- 2 tbsp peanut butter

Method

STEP 1

Put pecans in a food processor and blitz to crumbs. Add raisins, peanut butter, flaxseeds, cocoa powder and agave syrup, then pulse to combine.

STEP 2

Shape mixture into golf ball-sized balls and roll in desiccated coconut to coat. Put in the fridge to firm for 20 mins, then eat whenever you need a quick energy boost.

Fruity pork steaks

Prep: 10 mins **Cook:** 22 mins

Serves 4

Ingredients

- 4 boneless pork loin steaks , trimmed of any fat
- 2 tsp Chinese five-spice powder
- 1 tbsp sunflower oil
- 1 large red onion , cut into thin wedges through the root
- 4 red apples , cored and cut into eighths
- 2 tbsp redcurrant jelly
- 1 tbsp red wine vinegar or cider vinegar
- 200ml chicken stock

Method

STEP 1

Dust the pork steaks with the Chinese five-spice powder. Heat half the oil in a frying pan and fry the pork for about 3 mins on each side until browned and cooked through. Transfer to a plate.

STEP 2

Add the remaining oil to the frying pan, reduce the heat slightly, then fry the onion wedges for 2 mins. Add the apples and cook, stirring occasionally, for another 3 mins.

STEP 3

Add the redcurrant jelly to the pan, followed by the vinegar and then the stock. Bring to the boil and simmer rapidly, uncovered, for 8-10 mins until the sauce is slightly syrupy and the apples are tender. Gently reheat the pork in the sauce, turning to glaze each side.

Avocado pizza crisps

Prep: 15 mins **Cook:** 28 mins

Serves 2

Ingredients

For the topping

- 2 tsp rapeseed oil
- 1 red or orange pepper, deseeded, quartered and sliced
- 2 garlic cloves, finely chopped
- 160g cherry tomatoes
- 1 small avocado, halved, destoned and sliced
- 2 good handfuls of rocket
- 1 small red onion, thinly sliced
- 4 Kalamata olives, sliced
- 1 tsp balsamic vinegar

For the base

- 150g wholemeal flour
- 1 ½ tsp baking powder
- 2 tsp rapeseed oil

Method

STEP 1

Heat oven to 200C/180C fan/gas 6 and line two baking sheets with baking parchment. Heat the oil in a non-stick pan and fry the pepper for 5 mins, stirring every now and then until softened. Add the garlic, stir well and remove from the heat. Stir in the cherry tomatoes.

STEP 2

Meanwhile, make the base. Tip the flour into a bowl with the baking powder. Mix 80ml water with the oil, then add to the flour and stir in with the blade of a knife. Set aside for 5 mins.

STEP 3

Cut the dough in half and knead on the work surface until smooth – you shouldn't need to add any extra flour. Roll out to a very thin 20cm circle, then lift onto the baking sheet. Do the same with the other half of the dough. Bake the two bases for 8 mins, then turn them over and top with the pepper and tomato mixture. Return to the oven for 10 mins more.

STEP 4

Toss the avocado, rocket, onion and olives with the balsamic vinegar. Remove the bases from the oven and squash the tomatoes a little to fill any areas that aren't covered with the topping. Pile the avocado mixture on top and eat while still hot.

Chicken tikka with spiced rice

Prep: 10 mins **Cook:** 20 mins Plus marinating

Serves 4

Ingredients

- 4 skinless chicken breasts
- 150g pot low-fat natural yogurt
- 50g tikka paste
- 100g/4oz cucumber , diced
- 1 tbsp roughly chopped mint leaves
- 1 red onion , cut into thin wedges
- 140g easy-cook long grain rice
- 1 tbsp medium curry powder
- 50g frozen pea
- 1 small red pepper , diced

Method

STEP 1

Slash each chicken breast deeply with a knife 3-4 times on one side. Put in a bowl and add 50g of the yogurt and the tikka paste. Mix well, cover and marinate in the fridge for 30 mins. Make the raita by stirring the cucumber and most of the mint into the rest of the yogurt. Season with black pepper, cover and chill.

STEP 2

Heat oven to 240C/220C fan/gas 9. Scatter the onion wedges over a foil-lined baking tray. Remove the chicken from the marinade, shake off any excess and place on top of the onion wedges. Cook for 20 mins.

STEP 3

Meanwhile, tip the rice, curry powder, peas and pepper into a pan of boiling water and simmer for 10 mins or until the rice is just tender. Drain well and divide the rice between 4 plates. Add the chicken, roasted onion and remaining mint. Serve with the cucumber raita.

Baked falafel & cauliflower tabbouleh with avocado, pea & feta smash

Prep: 35 mins **Cook:** 23 mins

Serves 2

Ingredients

- 400g can chickpeas , drained (or 85g dried chickpeas soaked in 500ml cold water overnight, then drained)
- 1 tsp ground cumin
- 1 tsp ground coriander
- ¼ tsp cayenne pepper
- ½ small red onion , quartered
- 1 garlic clove
- 1 tbsp sesame seeds
- ½ tsp baking powder (gluten free if you like)
- small pack parsley , stalks and leaves separated, leaves chopped
- 1 tbsp olive oil
- ½ small cauliflower , cut into florets
- ½ small pack mint , leaves chopped
- 1 lemon , juiced and ½ zested
- 200g frozen peas
- ½ medium, ripe avocado
- 30g feta
- 2 handfuls rocket

Method

STEP 1

Heat oven to 200C/180C fan/gas 6. Line a baking sheet with baking parchment. Tip the chickpeas, ½ tsp ground cumin, ½ tsp ground coriander, cayenne pepper, red onion, garlic, sesame seeds, baking powder, parsley stalks and ½ tbsp water into a food processor. Blitz until everything is combined but not mushy – you want the falafel to have some texture, rather than being like hummus. Season to taste, then roll into 18 even-sized balls. Flatten each ball into a disc shape and put them on the baking sheet (the more surface area the crisper they will become). Brush them with ½ tbsp oil. Bake for 20 mins, turning halfway, until golden and crisp.

STEP 2

Meanwhile, clean the food processor. Briefly pulse the cauliflower until you have a couscous consistency. Mix the cauliflower with the remaining ground spices, olive oil and seasoning. Tip onto a baking tray and roast for 10-12 mins, stirring occasionally, until slightly toasted.

Once cool, mix through the chopped parsley, mint and a squeeze of lemon juice. Season to taste.

STEP 3

Put the frozen peas in a microwavable bowl, cover and cook on high for 2-3 mins. Drain off all the water, then roughly mash. Add the avocado and mash again to combine. Crumble in the feta, mix, then add the lemon zest and another squeeze of lemon juice, and seasoning to taste.

STEP 4

Toss the rocket leaves in a final squeeze of lemon juice, then serve with the falafel and cauliflower tabbouleh, rocket and the pea and avocado smash.

Veggie olive wraps with mustard vinaigrette

Prep: 10 mins no cook

Serves 1

Ingredients

- 1 carrot , shredded or coarsely grated
- 80g wedge red cabbage , finely shredded
- 2 spring onions , thinly sliced
- 1 courgette , shredded or coarsely grated
- handful basil leaves
- 5 green olives , pitted and halved
- ½ tsp English mustard powder
- 2 tsp extra virgin rapeseed oil
- 1 tbsp cider vinegar
- 1 large seeded tortilla

Method

STEP 1

Mix all the ingredients except for the tortilla and toss well.

STEP 2

Put the tortilla on a sheet of foil and pile the filling along one side of the wrap – it will almost look like too much mixture, but once you start to roll it firmly it will compact. Roll the tortilla from the filling side, folding in the sides as you go. Fold the foil in at the ends to keep stuff inside the wrap. Cut in half and eat straight away. If taking to work, leave whole and wrap up like a cracker in baking parchment.

Poached eggs with smashed avocado & tomatoes

Prep: 10 mins **Cook:** 10 mins

Serves 2

Ingredients

- 2 tomatoes, halved
- ½ tsp rapeseed oil
- 2 eggs
- 1 small ripe avocado
- 2 slices seeded wholemeal soda bread (see goes well with)
- 2 handfuls rocket

Method

STEP 1

Heat a non-stick frying pan, very lightly brush the cut surface of the tomatoes with a little oil, then cook them, cut-side down, in the pan until they have softened and slightly caramelised. Meanwhile, heat a pan of water, carefully break in the eggs and leave to poach for 1-2 mins until the whites are firm but the yolks are still runny.

STEP 2

Halve and stone the avocado, then scoop out the flesh and smash onto the bread. Add the eggs, grind over black pepper and add a handful of rocket to each portion. Serve the tomatoes on the side.

Sticky noodles with homemade hoisin

Prep: 10 mins **Cook:** 20 mins - 25 mins

Serves 2

Ingredients

For the hoisin

- 2 tbsp raisins
- 1 garlic clove
- 1 tbsp apple cider vinegar
- 2 tsp tomato purée
- 1 tsp tamari, plus extra to serve (optional)
- 1 tsp Chinese five spice
- 2 tbsp crunchy peanut butter (without palm oil or sugar)

For the stir-fry

- 2 nests wholemeal noodles (75g)
- 1 tsp rapeseed oil
- 1 tbsp chopped ginger
- 1 yellow pepper, deseeded and thinly sliced
- 2 red onions (173g), thinly sliced
- 100g Tenderstem broccoli, halved
- 100g frozen soya beans, thawed
- 1 red chilli, seeded and chopped
- handful basil leaves

Method

STEP 1

Put the raisins in a measuring jug or small, high-sided bowl, pour over 100ml boiling water then stir in the garlic, vinegar, tomato purée, tamari and five spice. Blitz with a hand blender until smooth, then stir in the peanut butter until well mixed.

STEP 2

Pour boiling water over the noodles and soak for 5 mins. Heat the oil in a non-stick wok, add the ginger with the vegetables and chilli and stir-fry for 5 mins or more until the veg have softened, but still have some bite.

STEP 3

Drain the noodles and add to the pan with the hoisin. Toss well adding a little extra water if necessary to moisten, then toss through the basil leaves.

Chicken with Spanish-style butter beans

Prep: 5 mins No cook

Serves 2

Ingredients

- 2 roasted garlic clove
- 1½ tbsp olive oil

- ½ lemon , zested and juiced
- ½ tsp smoked paprika
- 400g can of butter beans , drained and rinsed
- 2 roasted peppers
- 150g cherry tomatoes , halved
- 100g rocket
- 150g leftover roast chicken
- 25g feta

Method

STEP 1

Squeeze the garlic out of the skins and whisk together with the oil, lemon zest, juice, smoked paprika and some seasoning in a large bowl. Add the butter beans, peppers, tomatoes and rocket, and give everything a good mix. Divide between lunchboxes. Top with the chicken on one side and crumble over the feta.

Hearty winter veg soup

Prep: 5 mins **Cook:** 20 mins

Serves 4

Ingredients

- 1 tbsp olive oil
- 2 garlic cloves , crushed
- 1 swede , peeled and cut into chunks
- 4 large carrots , peeled and cut into chunks
- 3 sprigs thyme , leaves removed and roughly chopped
- 850ml vegetable stock
- 500ml semi-skimmed milk
- 2 x 410g cans mixed beans in water, drained

Method

STEP 1

Heat the oil in a large saucepan, then gently soften the garlic without colouring. Tip in the swede, carrots and two-thirds of the thyme, then pour in the stock and milk. Bring to the boil, then simmer for 15 mins.

STEP 2

Ladle a third of the soup into a blender, whizz until smooth, then pour back into the pan along with the beans. Check for seasoning, then return to the heat and warm through. Serve sprinkled with the remaining thyme and some warm, crusty bread rolls.

BBQ chicken drummers with green goddess salad

Prep: 20 mins **Cook:** 30 mins

Serves 2

Ingredients

- 2 tsp tomato purée
- 2 tsp balsamic vinegar
- ¼ tsp smoked paprika
- 1 pitted medjool date
- 1 tsp rapeseed oil
- 1 large garlic clove, chopped

For the dressing

- 1 small avocado, halved and stoned
- 2 tbsp bio yogurt
- 1 tbsp lemon juice
- 4 large skinless chicken drumsticks
- 1 romaine lettuce, shredded
- 2 handfuls watercress
- 2 chunks cucumber, halved and sliced
- 2 jacket potatoes, to serve

- 4 spring onions, chopped
- ½ tsp dried tarragon
- ¼ tsp English mustard powder

Method

STEP 1

Blitz the tomato purée, vinegar, paprika, date, oil, garlic and 2-3 tbsp water until smooth. Slash the drumsticks a few times, then toss in the sauce. Heat the oven to 200C/180C fan/gas 6, then roast for 30 mins.

STEP 2

To make the dressing, scoop the avocado into a bowl with the yogurt, lemon juice, spring onions, tarragon and mustard powder, then blitz with a hand blender until smooth.

STEP 3

Toss the lettuce, watercress and cucumbers together and pile onto plates. Spoon over the dressing and serve with the chicken and potatoes.

Chicken parmigiana

Prep: 15 mins **Cook:** 15 mins

Serves 4

Ingredients

- 2 large, skinless chicken breasts, halved through the middle
- 2 eggs, beaten
- 75g breadcrumb
- 75g parmesan, grated
- 1 tbsp olive oil
- 2 garlic cloves, crushed
- half a 690ml jar passata
- 1 tsp caster sugar
- 1 tsp dried oregano
- half a 125g ball light mozzarella, torn

Method

STEP 1

Halve 2 large skinless chicken breasts through the middle then place the 4 pieces between cling film sheets and bash out with a rolling pin until they are the thickness of a £1 coin.

STEP 2

Dip in 2 beaten eggs, then 75g breadcrumbs, mixed with half of the 75g grated parmesan. Set aside on a plate in the fridge while you make the sauce.

STEP 3

Heat 1 tbsp olive oil and cook 2 crushed garlic cloves for 1 min, then tip in half a 690ml jar passata, 1 tsp caster sugar and 1 tsp dried oregano. Season and simmer for 5-10 mins.

STEP 4

Heat grill to High and cook the chicken for 5 mins each side, then remove.

STEP 5

Pour the tomato sauce into a shallow ovenproof dish and top with the chicken.

STEP 6

Scatter over torn pieces of half a 125g ball light mozzarella, and the remaining grated parmesan and grill for 3-4 mins until the cheese has melted and the sauce is bubbling.

STEP 7

Serve with vegetables or salad and some pasta or potatoes, if you like.

Green pesto minestrone

Prep: 10 mins **Cook:** 25 mins

Serves 4

Ingredients

- 2 tbsp olive oil
- 1 large onion , finely chopped
- 2 celery sticks , finely chopped
- 1.4l vegetable stock
- 2 small lemons , zested and juiced
- 170g orzo
- 120g frozen peas
- 250g frozen spinach
- 50g pesto
- garlic flatbreads , to serve (optional)
- 60g parmesan (or vegetarian alternative), grated

Method

STEP 1

Heat the oil in a large saucepan, add the onion, celery and a pinch of salt, and fry for 8 mins until soft. Add the stock with the zest and juice of the lemons, and season. Stir in the orzo and cook for 5 mins, then add the peas and spinach, and cook for a further 5 mins. Swirl though the pesto and season.

STEP 2

Heat the flatbreads, if using, following pack instructions. Ladle the soup generously into bowls and top with a handful of parmesan. Serve with the flatbread to dip.

Chipotle chicken wraps

Prep: 15 mins **Cook:** 25 mins

Serves 4

Ingredients

- 1 tbsp vegetable oil
- 1 onion , finely sliced
- 1 garlic clove
- 2 chicken breasts , sliced into strips
- 2 tbsp chipotle paste
- 400g can chopped tomatoes
- 400g can black beans , drained
- 4 large corn or flour tortilla wraps
- ½ avocado , stoned, peeled and sliced
- ½ Baby Gem lettuce , shredded
- 1 lime , halved

Method

STEP 1

Heat the oil in a frying pan over a low-medium heat. Toss in the onion and cook for 10 mins until softened. Crush in the garlic and stir for 1 min before adding the chicken. Turn up the heat and brown the chicken all over. Spoon over the chipotle and stir to coat for 1 min. Pour in the tomatoes and bring to the boil. Season well and reduce the heat to a gentle simmer.

STEP 2

Cook for 5-6 mins or until the chicken is cooked through and any excess liquid has evaporated. Stir the beans through until warmed, then remove from the heat. Warm the wraps following pack instructions.

STEP 3

Divide the mix between the wraps, top with the avocado and shredded lettuce, and squeeze over the lime. Roll up and cut in half before serving.

Summer egg salad with basil & peas

Prep: 10 mins **Cook:** 12 mins

Serves 2

Ingredients

- 150g new potatoes , thickly sliced
- 160g French beans , trimmed
- 160g frozen peas
- 3 eggs
- 160g romaine lettuce , roughly torn into pieces

For the dressing

- 1 tbsp extra virgin olive oil
- 2 tsp cider vinegar
- ½ tsp English mustard powder
- 2 tbsp chopped mint
- 3 tbsp chopped basil
- 1 garlic clove , finely grated
- 1 tbsp capers

Method

STEP 1

Cook the potatoes in a pan of simmering water for 5 mins. Add the beans and cook 5 mins more, then tip in the peas and cook for 2 mins until all the vegetables are just tender. Meanwhile, boil the eggs in another pan for 8 mins. Drain and run under cold water, then carefully shell and halve.

STEP 2

Mix all the dressing ingredients together in a large bowl with a good grinding of black pepper, crushing the herbs and capers with the back of a spoon to intensify their flavours.

STEP 3

Mix the warm vegetables into the dressing to coat, then add the lettuce and toss everything together. Pile onto plates, top with the eggs and grind over some black pepper to serve.

Ratatouille & parmesan bake

Prep: 20 mins **Cook:** 25 mins

2 (with leftovers for other meals)

Ingredients

- 1 large aubergine
- 2 tsp rapeseed oil , plus extra for brushing
- 2 red onions , halved and sliced
- 2 peppers (any colours), diced
- 2 large courgettes , diced
- 2 garlic cloves , chopped
- 400g can chopped tomatoes
- 2 tsp gluten-free vegetable bouillon
- 1 thyme sprig , plus a few extra leaves for the top
- handful basil , stalks chopped, leaves torn and kept separate

For the topping

- 1 large egg
- 150g pot bio yogurt

- 15-25g vegetarian parmesan-style cheese, finely grated
- 2 handfuls rocket, dressed with balsamic vinegar, to serve

Method

STEP 1

Heat oven to 220C/200C fan/gas 7. Cut the aubergine lengthways into long thin slices – once you have six slices, chop the remainder. Brush the slices very lightly with oil, place on a baking sheet lined with baking parchment and cook for 15 mins, turning once, until softened and pliable. Turn oven down to 180C/160C fan/gas 4.

STEP 2

Meanwhile, heat the oil in a large non-stick frying pan and fry the onions until softened. Stir in the chopped aubergine, the peppers, courgettes and garlic, and cook, stirring, for a few mins more. Tip in the tomatoes and a half a can of water, then stir in the bouillon, thyme and basil stalks. Cover and simmer for 20 mins or until tender. You can add up to half a can of water if the mixture is getting too dry. Stir through the basil leaves.

STEP 3

If you are following our Healthy Diet Plan, set aside half of the ratatouille when it is ready - you'll need to chill this for our ratatouille pasta salad with rocket later in the week. If you're not following the plan, you can serve the extra ratatouille on the side or set it aside to enjoy for another meal.

STEP 4

Beat the eggs with the yogurt, cheese and 1 tbsp water. Spoon the remaining ratatouille into a shallow ovenproof dish, top with the aubergine slices, then cover with the yogurt mixture and scatter with thyme. Bake for 10-15 mins until the topping is set and starting to colour. Serve with dressed rocket on the side.

Raspberry chia jam

Prep: 5 mins **Cook:** 15 mins Plus cooling

Makes 1 jar (about 400g)

Ingredients

- 500g raspberries
- 1 tsp vanilla bean paste
- 3 tbsp honey
- 3 tbsp chia seeds

Method

STEP 1

Put the raspberries in a pan with the vanilla and honey, then cook over a low heat for 5 mins or until the berries have broken down.

STEP 2

Stir through the chia and cook for 10 mins. Set aside to cool completely (it will thicken significantly as it cools). Spoon into a bowl or sterilised jar. Great on toast, swirled through porridge or in yogurt. Will keep in the fridge for up to one week.

Tandoori trout

Prep: 5 mins **Cook:** 35 mins

Serves 4

Ingredients

- 4 thick trout fillets
- 1 tbsp tandoori curry paste
- 500g new potatoes, larger ones halved
- 2 tbsp vegetable oil
- 1 garlic clove, chopped
- 1 tsp ground cumin
- 1 tsp garam masala (or ground coriander)
- ½ tsp ground turmeric
- 320g frozen peas
- yogurt, coriander leaves and mango chutney, to serve

Method

STEP 1

Coat the trout in the curry paste. Put the potatoes in a large pan of cold salted water, bring to the boil and cook for 15-20 mins until tender but still retaining their shape. Drain and leave to steam-dry.

STEP 2

Heat the grill. Put the trout fillets on a baking tray lined with foil and cook until tender, about 6-8 mins.

STEP 3

Meanwhile, heat the oil in a large frying pan and add the garlic and spices. Cook for a few mins until fragrant, then tip in the potatoes. Fry for 3 mins until crisp at the edges, then throw in the frozen peas. Cook for 2-3 mins more until warmed through. Season well and serve with the trout, coriander sprinkled over, and yogurt and chutney on the side.

Griddled vegetables with melting aubergines

Prep:10 mins **Cook:**25 mins

Serves 2

Ingredients

- 1 large aubergine
- ½a lemon , zested and juiced
- 3cloves of garlic , 1 crushed, 2 chopped
- 2 tbsp chopped parsley , plus extra to serve
- 1 tsp extra virgin olive oil , plus a little for drizzling
- 4 tsp omega seed mix (see tip)
- 2 tsp thyme leaves
- 1 tbsp rapeseed oil
- 1 red pepper , deseeded and cut into quarters
- 1 large onion , thickly sliced
- 2 courgettes , sliced on the angle
- 2 large tomatoes , each cut into 3 thick slices
- 8 Kalamata olives , halved

Method

STEP 1

Grill the aubergine, turning frequently, until soft all over and the skin is blistered, about 8-10 mins. Alternatively, if you have a gas hob, cook it directly over the flame. When it is cool enough to handle, remove the skin, finely chop the flesh and mix with the lemon juice, 1 chopped clove garlic, 1 tbsp parsley, 1 tsp extra virgin olive oil and the seeds. Mix the remaining parsley with the remaining chopped garlic and the lemon zest.

STEP 2

Meanwhile, mix the thyme, crushed garlic and rapeseed oil and toss with the vegetables, keeping the onions as slices rather than breaking up into rings. Heat a large griddle pan and char the vegetables until tender and marked with lines – the tomatoes will need the least time. Pile onto plates with the aubergine purée and olives, drizzle over a little extra olive oil and scatter with the parsley, lemon zest and garlic.

Stir-fried chicken with broccoli & brown rice

Prep: 10 mins **Cook:** 20 mins

Serves 2

Ingredients

- 200g trimmed broccoli florets (about 6), halved
- 1 chicken breast (approx 180g), diced
- 15g ginger, cut into shreds
- 2 garlic cloves, cut into shreds
- 1 red onion, sliced
- 1 roasted red pepper, from a jar, cut into cubes
- 2 tsp olive oil
- 1 tsp mild chilli powder
- 1 tbsp reduced-salt soy sauce
- 1 tbsp honey
- 250g pack cooked brown rice

Method

STEP 1

Put the kettle on to boil and tip the broccoli into a medium pan ready to go on the heat. Pour the water over the broccoli then boil for 4 mins.

STEP 2

Heat the olive oil in a non-stick wok and stir-fry the ginger, garlic and onion for 2 mins, add the mild chilli powder and stir briefly. Add the chicken and stir-fry for 2 mins more. Drain the broccoli and reserve the water. Tip the broccoli into the wok with the soy, honey, red pepper and 4 tbsp broccoli water then cook until heated through. Meanwhile, heat the rice following the pack instructions and serve with the stir-fry.

Herb & garlic baked cod with romesco sauce & spinach

Prep: 10 mins **Cook:** 20 mins

Serves 2

Ingredients

- 2 x 140g skinless cod loin or pollock fillets
- 1 tbsp rapeseed oil, plus 2 tsp
- 1 tsp fresh thyme leaves
- 1 large garlic clove, finely grated
- ½ lemon, zested and juiced
- 1 large red pepper, sliced
- 2 leeks, well washed and thinly sliced
- 2 tbsp flaked almonds
- 1 tbsp tomato purée
- ¼ tsp vegetable bouillon powder
- 1 tsp apple cider vinegar
- 100g baby spinach, wilted in a pan or the microwave

Method

STEP 1

Heat oven to 220C/200C fan/ gas 7 and put the fish fillets in a shallow ovenproof dish so they fit quite snugly in a single layer. Mix 1 tbsp rapeseed oil with the thyme and garlic, spoon over the fish, then grate over the lemon zest. Bake for 10-12 mins until the fish is moist and flakes easily when tested.

STEP 2

Meanwhile, heat the remaining oil in a non-stick pan and fry the pepper and leeks for 5 mins until softened. Add the almonds and cook for 5 mins more. Tip in the tomato purée, 5 tbsp water, the bouillon powder and vinegar, and cook briefly to warm the mixture through.

STEP 3

Add the juice of up to half a lemon and blitz with a stick blender until it makes a thick, pesto-like sauce. Serve with the fish and the wilted spinach.

Carrot & coriander soup

Prep: 15 mins **Cook:** 25 mins

Serves 4

Ingredients

- 1 tbsp vegetable oil
- 1 onion, chopped
- 1 tsp ground coriander
- 1 potato, chopped
- 450g carrots, peeled and chopped
- 1.2l vegetable or chicken stock
- handful coriander (about ½ a supermarket packet)

Method

STEP 1

Heat 1 tbsp vegetable oil in a large pan, add 1 chopped onion, then fry for 5 mins until softened.

STEP 2

Stir in 1 tsp ground coriander and 1 chopped potato, then cook for 1 min.

STEP 3

Add the 450g peeled and chopped carrots and 1.2l vegetable or chicken stock, bring to the boil, then reduce the heat.

STEP 4

Cover and cook for 20 mins until the carrots are tender.

STEP 5

Tip into a food processor with a handful of coriander then blitz until smooth (you may need to do this in two batches). Return to pan, taste, add salt if necessary, then reheat to serve.

Garlicky mushroom penne

Prep: 20 mins **Cook:** 15 mins

Serves 2

Ingredients

- 210g can chickpeas , no need to drain
- 1 tbsp lemon juice
- 1 large garlic clove
- 1 tsp vegetable bouillon
- 2 tsp tahini
- ¼ tsp ground coriander
- 115g wholemeal penne
- 2 tsp rapeseed oil
- 2 red onions , halved and sliced
- 200g closed cup mushrooms , roughly chopped
- ½ lemon , juiced
- generous handful chopped parsley

Method

STEP 1

To make the hummus, tip a 210g can chickpeas with the liquid into a bowl and add 1 tbsp lemon juice, 1 large garlic clove, 1 tsp vegetable bouillon, 2 tsp tahini and ¼ tsp ground coriander.

STEP 2

Blitz to a wet paste with a hand blender, still retaining some texture from the chickpeas.

STEP 3

Cook 115g wholemeal penne pasta according to the pack instructions.

STEP 4

Meanwhile, heat 2 tsp rapeseed oil in a non-stick wok or large frying pan and add 2 halved and sliced red onions and 200g roughly chopped closed cup mushrooms, stirring frequently until softened and starting to caramelise.

STEP 5

Toss together lightly, squeeze over the juice of ½ a lemon and serve, adding a dash of water to loosen the mixture a little if needed. Scatter with a generous handful of chopped parsley.

Staffordshire oatcakes with mushrooms

Prep: 15 mins **Cook:** 20 mins plus at least 2 hrs proving

Serves 4

Ingredients

For the oatcakes

- 85g porridge oats
- 85g plain wholemeal flour
- ½ tsp dried yeast

For the topping

- 4 tsp rapeseed oil , plus a little for frying
- 320g button mushrooms , sliced
- 4 tomatoes , each cut into 8 wedges
- 4 tbsp milled seeds with flax and chia
- 4 tbsp tahini
- a few coriander sprigs, chopped

Method

STEP 1

For the oatcakes, tip the oats and 350ml water into a bowl and blitz with a stick blender until smooth (alternatively you can use a food processor or liquidizer). Stir in the flour and yeast, cover and leave in the fridge overnight, or leave at room temperature for 2-3 hrs until bubbles appear.

STEP 2

Use kitchen paper to rub ½ tsp oil round a non-stick frying pan, then heat. Ladle in a quarter of the batter and swirl the pan to cover the base (the oatcakes should be a few millimeters thick, like a crêpe). Cook for 2 mins, then turn and cook for 2 mins more until golden. Make four oatcakes in the same way. If you're following our Healthy Diet Plan, chill two for another day. Will keep, covered in the fridge, for two days.

STEP 3

To make the topping for two oatcakes, heat 2 tsp oil in a non-stick pan, add 160g mushrooms and fry for 2-3 mins, stirring until softened. Stir in 2 tomatoes, then add 2 tbsp ground seeds and cook for 2 mins more. Reheat the oatcakes in a dry frying pan or the microwave if necessary, then spread each one with 1 tbsp tahini, the mushroom mixture and scatter with a little coriander before serving. On the second day, repeat step 3 with the remaining ingredients.

Steak lettuce cups

Prep: 10 mins **Cook:** 5 mins

Makes 20

Ingredients

- 200g fillet steak , excess fat trimmed
- 4 Baby Gem lettuces
- ½ tbsp cold pressed rapeseed oil

For the chimichurri

- 1 tbsp chopped parsley
- ½ tbsp cold pressed rapeseed oil
- 1 small garlic clove , crushed
- 1 tsp red wine vinegar
- pinch of dried oregano

For the chilli & lime sauce

- ¼ red chilli , finely chopped
- 1 lime , zested and juiced
- ½ tsp fish sauce
- 1 tsp groundnut oil
- pinch of sugar

Method

STEP 1

Take the steak out of the fridge 30 mins ahead of frying it. Mix the chimichurri ingredients with 1 tbsp water, season and set aside. Mix the ingredients for the chilli & lime sauce and set aside. Separate the Baby Gem lettuces so you have 20 leaves ('cups').

STEP 2

Heat a non-stick frying pan over a medium-high heat. Coat the steak in the oil, season, then fry for 2-3 mins on each side. Set aside for 10 mins, then cut into 20 slices. Place a steak strip on each cup. To serve, top half with the chimichurri and half with the chilli & lime sauce.

Parmesan pork with tomato & olive spaghetti

Prep: 10 mins **Cook:** 30 mins

Serves 2

Ingredients

- 300g lean pork fillet , cut into 6 equal slices
- 3 tsp rapeseed oil
- 3 tsp finely chopped fresh sage
- 4 garlic cloves , finely grated
- 15g very finely grated parmesan
- 1 large carrot (215g), chopped
- 3 celery sticks (165g), chopped
- 6 Kalamata olives , thinly sliced
- 2 tbsp tomato purée
- 1 ½ tsp vegetable bouillon powder
- 150g wholemeal spaghetti
- 100g cherry tomatoes , halved
- large handful chopped parsley (about 10g)

Method

STEP 1

Put the pork in a bowl with 1 tsp oil, 1 tsp sage, 1 garlic clove and lots of black pepper. Mix well, put on a tray and scatter with the cheese.

STEP 2

Heat the remaining 2 tsp oil in a pan and fry the carrot, celery and remaining garlic and sage for 5 mins, stirring frequently. Add the olives, tomato purée, bouillon and 200ml water, cover and cook for 5-8 mins or until the veg is tender.

STEP 3

Meanwhile, cook the spaghetti following pack instructions and heat the grill. Grill the pork for 6 mins, then leave to rest. Drain the spaghetti, reserving a little water, and toss into the veg with the tomatoes and parsley. Add the water to loosen, then serve with the pork.

Rustic vegetable soup

Prep: 15 mins Cook: 30 mins

Serves 4

Ingredients

- 1 tbsp rapeseed oil
- 1 large onion, chopped
- 2 carrots, chopped
- 2 celery sticks, chopped
- 50g dried red lentils
- 1½ l boiling vegetable bouillon (we used Marigold)
- 2 tbsp tomato purée
- 1 tbsp chopped fresh thyme
- 1 leek, finely sliced
- 175g bite-sized cauliflower florets
- 1 courgette, chopped
- 3 garlic cloves, finely chopped
- ½ large Savoy cabbage, stalks removed and leaves chopped
- 1 tbsp basil, chopped

Method

STEP 1

Heat the oil in a large pan with a lid. Add the onion, carrots and celery and fry for 10 mins, stirring from time to time until they are starting to colour a little around the edges. Stir in the lentils and cook for 1 min more.

STEP 2

Pour in the hot bouillon, add the tomato purée and thyme and stir well. Add the leek, cauliflower, courgette, and garlic, bring to the boil, then cover and leave to simmer for 15 mins.

STEP 3

Add the cabbage and basil and cook for 5 mins more until the veg is just tender. Season with pepper, ladle into bowls and serve. Will keep in the fridge for a couple of days. Freezes well. Thaw, then reheat in a pan until piping hot.

Crispy grilled feta with saucy butter beans

Prep: 2 mins **Cook:** 18 mins

Serves 4

Ingredients

- 500ml passata
- 2 x 400g cans butter beans, drained and rinsed
- 2 garlic cloves, crushed
- 1 tsp dried oregano, plus a pinch
- 200g spinach
- 2 roasted red peppers, sliced
- 1/2 lemon, zested and juiced
- 100g block of feta, cut into chunks
- 1/2 tsp olive oil
- 4 small pittas

Method

STEP 1

Put a large ovenproof frying pan over a medium-high heat, and tip in the passata, butter beans, garlic, oregano, spinach and peppers. Stir together and cook for 6-8 mins until the sauce is bubbling and the spinach has wilted. Season, then add the lemon juice.

STEP 2

Heat the grill to high. Scatter the feta over the sauce, so it's still exposed, drizzle with the olive oil and sprinkle over the lemon zest plus a pinch of oregano, then grind over some black pepper. Grill for 5-8 mins until the feta is golden and crisp at the edges.

STEP 3

Meanwhile, toast the pittas under the grill or in the toaster, then serve with the beans and feta.

Crispy paprika chicken with tomatoes & lentils

Prep: 10 mins **Cook:** 20 mins

Serves 2

Ingredients

- 2 chicken breasts
- ½ tsp smoked paprika
- ½ lemon, zested and juiced
- 1½ tbsp cold-pressed rapeseed oil
- 1 garlic clove
- 1 tsp fennel seeds
- 1 fennel bulb, sliced
- 400g can cherry tomatoes
- 1 tbsp sherry vinegar
- 200g pouch puy lentils
- 100g watercress
- 2 tbsp natural yogurt
- handful of dill, leaves picked

Method

STEP 1

Put the chicken breasts between two sheets of baking parchment and, using a rolling pin, roll to a 1cm thickness. Rub with the paprika, lemon zest, ½ tbsp oil, salt and pepper. Cover and set aside while you start the lentils.

STEP 2

Heat the remaining oil in a pan and add the garlic, fennel seeds and fennel slices with a pinch of salt. Cook for 5 mins until starting to soften, then tip in the tomatoes, vinegar and lentils. Turn down the heat and leave to bubble away.

STEP 3

Heat another non-stick frying pan over a high heat, add the chicken breasts and cook for 7 mins, turning halfway, until golden brown and cooked through. Add the watercress to the lentils and stir to wilt, then squeeze in the lemon juice. Slice the chicken then serve it alongside the lentils with a dollop of yogurt and dill.

Thai prawn & ginger noodles

Prep: 15 mins **Cook:** 15 mins plus soaking

Serves 2

Ingredients

- 100g folded rice noodles (sen lek)
- zest and juice 1 small orange
- 1½-2 tbsp red curry paste
- 1-2 tsp fish sauce
- 2 tsp light brown soft sugar
- 1 tbsp sunflower oil
- 25g ginger, scraped and shredded
- 2 large garlic cloves, sliced

- 1 red pepper, deseeded and sliced
- 85g sugar snap peas, halved lengthways
- 140g beansprouts
- 175g pack raw king prawns
- handful chopped basil
- handful chopped coriander

Method

STEP 1

Put the noodles in a bowl and pour over boiling water to cover them. Set aside to soak for 10 mins. Stir together the orange juice and zest, curry paste, fish sauce, sugar and 3 tbsp water to make a sauce.

STEP 2

Heat the oil in a large wok and add half the ginger and the garlic. Cook, stirring, for 1 min. Add the pepper and stir-fry for 3 mins more. Toss in the sugar snaps, cook briefly, then pour in the curry sauce. Add the beansprouts and prawns, and continue cooking until the prawns just turn pink. Drain the noodles, then toss these into the pan with the herbs and remaining ginger. Mix until the noodles are well coated in the sauce, then serve.

Chipotle gazpacho

Prep: 25 mins Plus 2 hrs chilling; no cook

Serves 4

Ingredients

- 1kg ripe tomatoes , roughly chopped
- 1 large red pepper , deseeded and roughly chopped
- 1/2 cucumber , sliced
- 4 spring onions , finely sliced
- 1 small garlic clove , grated
- 40g blanched almonds , roughly chopped
- 3 limes , juiced
- 2 tbsp olive oil
- 2 tsp chipotle paste
- 1 large, ripe avocado , cubed
- 1 small red chilli , deseeded and finely chopped
- 1/2 small bunch coriander , finely chopped

Method

STEP 1

Put the tomatoes, pepper, cucumber, two of the spring onions, the garlic, half the almonds, half the lime juice, and all the olive oil and chipotle paste into a blender. Whizz until almost smooth. Pour into a jug and chill for at least 2 hrs.

STEP 2

When ready to eat, toss the remaining spring onion, avocado, chilli and coriander with the remaining lime juice. Ladle the soup into four bowls and top with the avocado salsa and reserved almonds.

Cucumber, pea & lettuce soup

Prep: 5 mins **Cook:** 15 mins

Serves 4

Ingredients

- 1 tsp rapeseed oil
- small bunch spring onions , roughly chopped
- 1 cucumber , roughly chopped
- 1 large round lettuce , roughly chopped
- 225g frozen peas
- 4 tsp vegetable bouillon
- 4 tbsp bio yogurt (optional)
- 4 slices rye bread

Method

STEP 1

Boil 1.4 litres water in a kettle. Heat the oil in a large non-stick frying pan and cook the spring onions for 5 mins, stirring frequently, or until softened. Add the cucumber, lettuce and peas, then pour in the boiled water. Stir in the bouillon, cover and simmer for 10 mins or until the vegetables are soft but still bright green.

STEP 2

Blitz the mixture with a hand blender until smooth. Serve hot or cold, topped with yogurt (if you like), with rye bread alongside.

Chilli-charred Brussels sprouts

Prep: 15 mins **Cook:** 25 mins

Serves 6

Ingredients

- 600g Brussels sprouts , trimmed at the base
- 60ml olive oil
- 4 garlic cloves , peeled and bashed
- 1-2 tsp chilli flakes
- 1 lemon , zested and juiced

Method

STEP 1

Bring a pan of salted water to the boil. Add the Brussels sprouts and cook for 4-5 mins until just tender, then drain and leave to cool a little before slicing in half vertically.

STEP 2

Meanwhile, heat 3 tbsp olive oil in a large frying pan over a medium heat, add the garlic and cook until golden but not burnt, around 4 mins. Use a slotted spoon to remove the garlic and discard. Add the chilli flakes and a big pinch of salt to the oil, then put the sprouts cut-side down in the pan, and leave them to cook for around 10 mins. Don't be tempted to move them – this ensures that they get some colour. Add the remaining olive oil and the lemon juice, then cook for a few mins more.

STEP 3

Tip onto a large serving platter, top with lemon zest and season. These will hold in a low oven for 20 mins while you get everything else ready.

Salmon pasta salad with lemon & capers

Prep: 10 mins **Cook:** 20 mins

Serves 2

Ingredients

- 85g wholewheat penne
- 1 tbsp rapeseed oil

- 1 large red pepper, roughly chopped
- 2 frozen, skinless wild salmon fillets (about 120g each)
- 1 lemon, zested and juiced
- 2 garlic cloves, finely grated
- 1 shallot, very finely chopped
- 2 tbsp capers
- 6 pitted Kalamata olives, sliced
- 1 tsp extra virgin olive oil
- 2 handfuls rocket

Method

STEP 1

Cook the pasta following pack instructions. Meanwhile, heat the rapeseed oil in a frying pan, add the pepper, cover and leave for about 5 mins until it softens and starts to char a little. Stir, then push the pepper to one side and add the salmon. Cover and fry for 8-10 mins until just cooked.

STEP 2

Meanwhile, mix the lemon zest and juice in a large bowl with the garlic, shallot, capers and olives.

STEP 3

Add the cooked pepper and salmon to the bowl. Drain the pasta and add it too, with black pepper and the olive oil. Toss everything together, flaking the salmon as you do so. If eating now, toss through the rocket; if packing a lunch, leave to cool, then put in a container with the rocket on top and mix through just before eating.

Thai mackerel & sweet potato traybake

Prep: 30 mins **Cook:** 45 mins

Serves 4

Ingredients

- 2 red chillies, deseeded and roughly chopped, plus extra sliced chillies to serve
- 4 shallots, roughly chopped
- 2 garlic cloves
- 1 thumb-sized piece ginger, peeled and chopped
- 1 lemongrass stalk
- 1 tbsp hot smoked paprika
- 2 limes, zested and juiced, plus wedges to serve

- 200g sweet potato, peeled and cut into 1cm cubes
- 1 tbsp rapeseed oil
- 2 red peppers, deseeded and sliced
- 3 dried kaffir lime leaves
- 4 raw mackerel fillets
- 4 spring onions, trimmed and sliced
- small bunch coriander, chopped
- 320g broccoli, steamed, to serve

Method

STEP 1

Put the chillies, shallots, garlic cloves, ginger, lemongrass, paprika, lime zest and juice and 1 tbsp water into a small food processor and blitz to a smooth paste.

STEP 2

Heat oven to 200C/180C fan/gas 6. Put the sweet potato in a large roasting tin and toss with the oil. Add the curry paste, peppers and kaffir lime leaves and roast for 35-40 mins until the potato is tender. Heat the grill to high.

STEP 3

Slash the mackerel skin a few times with a sharp knife. Arrange the fish over the veg, skin-side up, then grill for 4-5 mins until the skin is blistered and the flesh is cooked through.

STEP 4

Scatter over the spring onions, coriander and extra chillies, then squeeze over the lime wedges. Serve with the steamed broccoli.

Slow cooker lasagne

Prep: 1 hr and 15 mins **Cook:** 3 hrs

Serves 4

Ingredients

- 2 tsp rapeseed oil
- 2 onions, finely chopped
- 4 celery sticks (about 175g), finely diced
- 4 carrots (320g), finely diced
- 2 garlic cloves, chopped
- 400g lean (5% fat) mince beef
- 400g can chopped tomatoes
- 2 tbsp tomato purée
- 2 tsp vegetable bouillon

- 1 tbsp balsamic vinegar
- 1 tbsp fresh thyme leaves
- 6 wholewheat lasagne sheets (105g)

For the sauce

- 400ml whole milk
- 50g wholemeal flour
- 1 bay leaf
- generous grating of nutmeg
- 15g finely grated parmesan

Method

STEP 1

Heat the slow cooker if necessary. Heat the oil in a large non-stick pan and fry the onions, celery, carrots and garlic for 5-10 mins, stirring frequently until softened and starting to colour. Tip in the meat and break it down with a wooden spoon, stirring until it browns. Pour in the tomatoes with a quarter of a can of water, the tomato purée, bouillon, balsamic vinegar, thyme and plenty of black pepper, return to the boil and cook for 5 mins more.

STEP 2

Spoon half the mince in the slow cooker and top with half the lasagne, breaking it where necessary so it covers as much of the meat layer as possible. Top with the rest of the meat, and then another layer of the lasagne. Cover and cook on Low while you make the sauce.

STEP 3

Tip the milk and flour into a pan with the bay leaf and nutmeg and cook on the hob, whisking continuously until thickened. Carry on cooking for a few mins to cook the flour. Remove the bay leaf and stir in the cheese. Pour onto the pasta and spread out with a spatula, then cover and cook for 3 hours until the meat is cooked and the pasta is tender. Allow to settle for 10 mins before serving with salad.

Crispy chicken & smashed avocado baps

Prep: 30 mins **Cook:** 10 mins

Serves 4

Ingredients

- 2 large skinless chicken breasts
- 100g plain flour
- 1 egg, beaten
- splash of milk

- 3 tbsp ground almonds
- 1 tbsp sesame seeds
- 3 tbsp vegetable or rapeseed oil
- 2 small avocados, stoned, peeled and halved
- ½ lime, juiced
- 4 baps or rolls, split
- 1 Little Gem lettuce, leaves separated

Method

STEP 1

Put the chicken on a board and cover with a sheet of baking parchment. Bash with a rolling pin to an even thickness, then cut both breasts in half diagonally.

STEP 2

Put the flour on a plate. Season. Combine the egg and milk in a wide, shallow bowl. Dust the chicken in the flour, shake off the excess, then dunk into the egg mix. Add the almonds and sesame seeds to any remaining flour on the plate and coat the chicken in the mixture.

STEP 3

Heat half the oil in a large frying pan over a medium heat and fry the chicken for 4-5 mins on each side until crisp and golden, adding the rest of the oil when you turn the pieces over. Cut into the thickest part of one of the pieces to check it's cooked through, then leave to cool for 5 mins.

STEP 4

Scoop the avocado flesh into a bowl with the lime juice and a pinch of salt, then mash. Spread over the baps, top with the lettuce, then the chicken. Cut in half.

Healthier treacle sponge

Prep: 25 mins **Cook:** 20 mins

Makes 6

Ingredients

- 2 tbsp rapeseed oil, plus ¼ tsp
- 5 tbsp golden syrup
- 1 small orange (½ tsp finely grated zest and 2 tbsp plus 1 tsp juice)
- 175g self-raising flour

- 1 ½ tsp baking powder
- 100g light muscovado sugar
- 25g ground almond
- 2 large eggs
- 175g natural yogurt
- 1 tsp black treacle
- 25g butter , melted

Method

STEP 1

Heat oven to 180C/160C fan/gas 4. Brush 6 x 200ml pudding tins with the ¼ tsp oil, then sit them on a baking tray. Stir together 4 tbsp of the golden syrup, the orange zest and 2 tbsp orange juice and spoon a little into the bottom of each tin (step 1).

STEP 2

Tip the flour, baking powder, sugar (breaking up any lumps with your fingers) and ground almonds into a large mixing bowl and make a dip in the centre. Beat the eggs in a separate bowl, then stir in the yogurt and treacle. Pour this mixture, along with the melted butter and remaining 2 tbsp oil, into the dry mixture (step 2) and stir together briefly with a large metal spoon, just so everything is well combined. Divide the mixture evenly between the tins (step 3). Bake for 20-25 mins or until the puddings have risen to the top of the tins and feel firm.

STEP 3

Mix together the remaining 1 tbsp golden syrup and 1 tsp orange juice to drizzle over as a sauce. To serve, if the pudding tops have peaked slightly, slice off to level so they sit upright when turned out. Loosen around the sides with a round-bladed knife (step 4), then turn them out onto plates. Scrape out any syrupy bits remaining in the tins and put on top of the puddings, then drizzle a little of the syrup sauce over and around each one.

Spicy meatballs with chilli black beans

Prep:20 mins **Cook:**25 mins

Serves 4

Ingredients

- 1 red onion, halved and sliced
- 2 garlic cloves, sliced
- 1 large yellow pepper, quartered, deseeded and diced
- 1 tsp ground cumin
- 2-3 tsp chipotle chilli paste
- 300ml reduced-salt chicken stock

- 400g can cherry tomatoes
- 400g can black beans or red kidney beans, drained

For the meatballs

- 500g pack turkey breast mince
- 50g porridge oats
- 2 spring onions, finely chopped
- 1 tsp ground cumin
- 1 avocado, stoned, peeled and chopped
- juice ½ lime
- 1 tsp coriander
- small bunch coriander, chopped, stalks and leaves kept separate
- 1 tsp rapeseed oil

Method

STEP 1

First make the meatballs. Tip the mince into a bowl, add the oats, spring onions, spices and the coriander stalks, then lightly knead the ingredients together until well mixed. Shape into 12 ping-pong- sized balls. Heat the oil in a non-stick frying pan, add the meatballs and cook, turning them frequently, until golden. Remove from the pan.

STEP 2

Tip the onion and garlic into the pan with the pepper and stir-fry until softened. Stir in the cumin and chilli paste, then pour in the stock. Return the meatballs to the pan and cook, covered, over a low heat for 10 mins. Stir in the tomatoes and beans, and cook, uncovered, for a few mins more. Toss the avocado chunks in the lime juice and serve the meatballs topped with the avocado and coriander leaves.

Smoky veggie nachos

Prep: 25 mins **Cook:** 15 mins plus cooling

Serves 6

Ingredients

- 7 soft corn tortillas
- 1 tbsp rapeseed oil
- 1 tsp sweet smoked paprika , plus extra to serve
- 2 red peppers , halved and deseeded
- 400g can black beans , drained and rinsed
- ½ bunch of parsley , very finely chopped
- 50g fat-free yogurt
- 1 jalapeño , finely sliced

For the salsa

- 4 spring onions , finely sliced
- 4 medium tomatoes , deseeded and finely chopped
- 1 small avocado , peeled, stoned and chopped
- ½ small bunch of coriander , finely chopped
- 1 small garlic clove , finely grated
- 1 lime , zested and juiced
- 1 tbsp rapeseed oil

Method

STEP 1

Heat the oven to 180C/160C fan/ gas 4. Cut each of the tortillas into 8-10 triangles and spread over two large baking sheets. Drizzle with the oil and sprinkle over the paprika. Bake for 7-8 mins until crisp and leave to cool.

STEP 2

Heat the grill to high. Grill the peppers, skin-side up, for 7-10 mins until charred and soft. Leave to cool. Peel off and discard the skins, slice into strips and toss with the beans and parsley.

STEP 3

To make the salsa, combine the ingredients. Pile the nachos on a large plate, top with the bean mix, salsa, yogurt and jalapeño and sprinkle over some paprika to serve.

Pea & leek open lasagne

Prep: 10 mins **Cook:** 15 mins

Serves 2

Ingredients

- 2 tbsp rapeseed oil
- 2 leeks , washed and sliced into half moons
- 2 garlic cloves , finely chopped
- 250g frozen peas
- 100g kale
- 1 tbsp wholegrain mustard
- 2 tbsp low-fat crème fraîche
- 1 lemon , zested
- 4 fresh lasagne sheets

Method

STEP 1

Put a frying pan over a medium heat. Pour in the oil and add the leeks, garlic and a pinch of salt. Cook, stirring occasionally, until collapsed and soft. Meanwhile, bring a pan of water to the boil.

STEP 2

Tip the peas and kale into the pan with the leeks and add a splash of water. Cook until the kale has wilted and peas are defrosted. Turn down the heat to low. Stir in the mustard, crème fraîche and ¾ of the lemon zest. Add enough water to make a sauce. Give everything a good mix and season to taste.

STEP 3

Drop the lasagne into the water and cook following pack instructions, then drain well. Put one lasagne sheet on each plate, top with half the leek and pea mix then layer up the second lasagne sheet and the remaining greens. Scatter over the remaining lemon zest and add a good grinding of black pepper.

Penne with broccoli, lemon & anchovies

Prep: 10 mins **Cook:** 17 mins

Serves 2

Ingredients

- 170g wholemeal penne
- 1 leek , washed and sliced
- 180g broccoli , cut into small florets
- 2 tsp oil from the anchovy can, plus 15g anchovies, chopped
- 1 red pepper , seeded, quartered and sliced
- ½ tsp finely chopped rosemary
- 1 red chilli , seeded and sliced
- 3 garlic cloves , sliced
- ½ lemon , zested and juiced
- 4 tbsp ricotta
- 2 tbsp sunflower seeds

Method

STEP 1

Boil the pasta with the sliced leek for 7 mins, then add the broccoli and boil for 5 mins until everything is just tender.

STEP 2

Meanwhile, heat the oil from the anchovies and fry the red pepper with the rosemary, chilli and garlic in a large non-stick pan for 5 mins until softened.

STEP 3

Drain the pasta, reserving a little water, then tip the pasta and veg into the pan and add the lemon juice and zest, anchovies and ricotta. Toss well over the heat, using the pasta water to moisten. Toss through the sunflower seeds and serve.

Miso burgers with mint & pomegranate slaw

Prep: 15 mins **Cook:** 25 mins

Serves 4

Ingredients

- 75g bulghar wheat
- 1 tbsp rapeseed oil
- 2 onions, chopped
- 4 garlic cloves, chopped
- 2 carrots, coarsely grated
- 1 large red chilli, deseeded and finely chopped
- 1 tsp cumin seeds
- 1 tbsp ground coriander
- 30g pack coriander, stalks and leaves chopped but kept separate
- 1 lime, zested, 1/2 juiced, 1/2 cut into 4 wedges
- 2 x cans chickpeas, drained
- 2 large eggs
- 2 tbsp white miso paste

For the slaw

- ½ small white cabbage, shredded
- 1 red onion, halved and thinly sliced
- 2 carrots, shredded (ideally with a julienne peeler)
- 1 pomegranate seeds only
- 2 tbsp chopped mint
- 1 tbsp cider vinegar
- 1 tbsp extra virgin rapeseed oil

Method

STEP 1

Heat oven to 220C/200C fan/gas 7. Cook the bulghar in a small pan of water for 5 mins. Meanwhile, heat the oil in a large non-stick frying pan and fry the onions and garlic, stirring, for 5 mins or until starting to turn golden. Add the carrots and chilli, and cook, stirring frequently, for 5 mins until the carrots soften. Add the cumin, ground coriander, coriander stalks and lime zest, and stir well.

STEP 2

Tip the chickpeas into a bowl and crush with a masher or fork, then add the eggs and miso to form a chunky paste.

STEP 3

Drain the bulghar well and stir into the spicy vegetables. Take off the heat, shape into eight burgers and place on a baking sheet lined with baking parchment. Bake in the oven for 15-20 mins or until firm and starting to turn golden.

STEP 4

For the slaw, combine all the ingredients in a big bowl with the lime juice and coriander leaves. Serve with the burgers and lime wedges for squeezing over.

Mozzarella, pepper & aubergine calzone

Prep: 15 mins **Cook:** 35 mins

Serves 4

Ingredients

- 400g strong wholewheat bread flour , plus extra for dusting
- ⅛ tsp salt (optional)

For the filling

- 2 tsp rapeseed oil
- 1 red and 1 yellow pepper , deseeded and cut into small chunks
- 1 large aubergine , halved lengthways and thinly sliced
- 2 large garlic cloves , finely chopped
- 1 tbsp tomato purée

- 7g sachet fast-action dried yeast
- 2 tsp rapeseed oil , plus extra for the baking sheet

- 1 tbsp balsamic vinegar
- small bunch basil , roughly torn
- 8 pitted Kalamata olives , halved
- 125g ball mozzarella (drained weight), quartered
- milk or beaten egg, for brushing

Method

STEP 1

Put the flour, salt (if using), yeast, oil and 300ml lukewarm water in a bowl and mix until soft. Knead into a ball (try not to add any extra flour) – it will be sticky but the flour will absorb some moisture. Return to the bowl, cover and leave somewhere warm.

STEP 2

Meanwhile, make the filling. Heat the oil in a large non-stick pan, then stir-fry the peppers for about 1 min until they start to soften. Add the aubergine and garlic and continue to cook over a medium heat for 8-10 mins, gently pressing the veg with a wooden spoon until it breaks down a little. If it doesn't, fry, covered, for a few extra mins.

STEP 3

Stir in the tomato purée, vinegar and 2 tbsp water. When the veg is soft, remove the pan from the heat and stir through the basil.

STEP 4

Heat the oven to 220C/200C fan/gas 7. Quarter the risen dough and roll each piece out to a 20cm circle on a lightly floured surface. Spoon a quarter of the filling over one side, scatter over a quarter of the olives, top with a quarter of the cheese, and brush the edges with the milk or beaten egg. Fold the dough over the filling and pinch the edges together at the side, a bit like making a Cornish pasty. Lift onto a lightly oiled baking sheet and brush with more milk or beaten egg. Repeat with the remaining dough and filling to make four calzones, then bake for 15-20 mins until golden. Leave to cool slightly and serve at room temperature.

Wild salmon & avocado triangles

Prep: 2 mins **Cook:** 8 mins - 10 mins

Serves 2

Ingredients

- 3 triangular bread thins
- 1 lemon , halved
- a few dill sprigs, plus extra to serve
- 1 small red onion , 1/2 sliced, the rest finely chopped
- 2 skinless, boneless wild salmon fillets
- 1 small avocado

Method

STEP 1

Follow our triangular bread-thins recipe to make your own. While they bake, bring a small pan of water to the boil and add a good squeeze of lemon, a few dill sprigs and the sliced onion. Add the fish and leave to poach for 8-10 mins or until it flakes easily. Lift from the pan and and flake into pieces.

STEP 2

Scoop the avocado into a bowl and roughly mash with a generous squeeze of lemon. Cut the bread triangles in half, put cut-side up and top with the avocado, scatter over half the chopped onion, then top with salmon, more onions and some snipped dill. Squeeze over some lemon to serve.

Baked falafel & cauliflower tabbouleh with pickled carrot, cucumber & chilli salad

Prep: 35 mins **Cook:** 20 mins

Serves 2

Ingredients

- 400g can chickpeas , drained (or 85g dried chickpeas soaked in 500ml cold water overnight, then drained)
- 1 tsp ground cumin
- 1 tsp ground coriander
- ¼ tsp cayenne pepper
- ½ small red onion , quartered
- 1 garlic clove
- 1 tbsp sesame seeds
- ½ tsp baking powder (gluten free if you like)
- small pack parsley , stalks and leaves separated, leaves chopped
- 1 tbsp olive oil
- ½ small cauliflower , cut into florets
- ½ small pack mint , leaves chopped
- ½ lemon , juiced
- 2 carrots , peeled into ribbons
- 1 cucumber , peeled into ribbons, seedy core removed
- 1 small red chilli , deseeded and sliced
- 1½ tbsp rice or white wine vinegar
- pinch sugar
- ½ small pack coriander , leaves picked
- 2 tbsp % fat natural yogurt

Method

STEP 1

Heat oven to 200C/180C fan/gas 6, line a baking sheet with baking parchment. Tip the chickpeas, ½ tsp ground cumin, ½ tsp ground coriander, cayenne pepper, red onion, garlic, sesame seeds, baking powder, parsley stalks and ½ tbsp water into a food processor. Blitz until everything is combined but not mushy – you want the falafel to have some texture, rather than being like hummus. Season to taste then roll into 18 even-sized balls. Flatten each ball into a disc shape and put onto the baking trays (the more surface area the crisper they will become). Brush them with ½ tbsp oil. Bake for 20 mins, turning halfway, until golden and crisp.

STEP 2

Meanwhile, clean the food processor. Briefly pulse the cauliflower until you have a couscous consistency. Mix the cauliflower with the remaining ground spices, olive oil and seasoning. Tip onto a baking tray and roast for 10-12 mins, stirring occasionally, until slightly toasted. Once cool, mix through the chopped parsley, mint and a squeeze of lemon juice. Season to taste.

STEP 3

Mix the carrot, cucumber, red chilli, vinegar, sugar and a pinch of salt in a bowl. Stir through the coriander and divide between the baked falafel and tabbouleh with a dollop of yogurt.

Lamb & squash biryani with cucumber raita

Prep: 10 mins **Cook:** 25 mins

Serves 4

Ingredients

- 4 lean lamb steaks (about 400g), trimmed of all fat, cut into chunks
- 2 garlic cloves, finely grated
- 8 tsp chopped fresh ginger
- 3 tsp ground coriander
- 4 tsp rapeseed oil
- 4 onions, sliced
- 2 red chillies, deseeded and chopped
- 170g brown basmati rice
- 320g diced butternut squash
- 2 tsp cumin seeds
- 2 tsp vegetable bouillon powder
- 20cm length cucumber, grated
- 100ml bio yogurt
- 4 tbsp chopped mint, plus a few extra leaves
- handful coriander, chopped

Method

STEP 1

Mix the lamb with the garlic, 2 tsp chopped ginger and 1 tsp ground coriander and set aside.

STEP 2

Heat 2 tsp oil in a non-stick pan. Add the onions, the remaining ginger and chilli and stir-fry briefly over a high heat so they start to soften. Add the rice and squash and stir over the heat for a few mins. Tip in all the remaining spices, then stir in 500ml boiling water and the bouillon. Cover the pan and simmer for 20 mins.

STEP 3

Meanwhile, mix the cucumber, yogurt and mint together in a bowl to make a raita. Chill half for later.

STEP 4

About 5 mins before the rice is ready, heat the remaining oil in a non-stick frying pan, add the lamb and stir for a few mins until browned but still nice tender. Toss into the spiced rice with the coriander and serve with the raita and a few mint or coriander leaves on top.

Roasted asparagus & pea salad

Prep: 10 mins **Cook:** 10 mins

Serves 2

Ingredients

- 3 tbsp natural yogurt
- 1 tsp wholegrain mustard
- ½ tsp honey
- ½ lemon , zested and juiced
- 100g watercress
- 1 large slice sourdough bread
- 200g asparagus , tough ends removed
- 1 ½ tbsp cold-pressed rapeseed oil
- 2 eggs
- 200g frozen peas

Method

STEP 1

Heat oven to 220C/200C fan/gas 7. Mix the yogurt, mustard and honey together. Add the lemon zest, then add the juice and some seasoning to taste. Squeeze any remaining lemon juice over the watercress.

STEP 2

Tear the bread into rough chunks and put them on a large roasting tray with the asparagus. Toss both in the rapeseed oil and seasoning, and roast for 10 mins until the asparagus is tender and croutons are golden.

STEP 3

Meanwhile, cook the eggs in a pan of boiling water for 6 mins, then add the frozen peas and cook for 1 min more. Drain and rinse both under cold water until cool. Peel the eggs, then cut into quarters.

STEP 4

To assemble, mix the asparagus and peas through the watercress, then toss through the creamy dressing. Nestle in the eggs and croutons, and serve.

Roasted red pepper & tomato soup with ricotta

Prep: 10 mins **Cook:** 30 mins

Serves 2

Ingredients

- 400g tomatoes , halved
- 1 red onion , quartered
- 2 Romano peppers , roughly chopped
- 2 tbsp good quality olive oil
- 2 garlic cloves , bashed in their skins
- few thyme sprigs
- 1 tbsp red wine vinegar
- 2 tbsp ricotta
- few basil leaves
- 1 tbsp mixed seeds , toasted
- bread , to serve

Method

STEP 1

Heat oven to 200C/180C fan/gas 6. Put the tomatoes, onion and peppers in a roasting tin, toss with the oil and season. Nestle in the garlic and thyme sprigs, then roast for 25-30 mins until all the veg has softened and slightly caramelised. Squeeze the garlic cloves out of their skins into the tin, strip the leaves off the thyme and discard the stalks and garlic skins. Mix the vinegar into the tin then blend everything in a bullet blender or using a stick blender, adding enough water to loosen to your preferred consistency (we used around 150ml).

STEP 2

Reheat the soup if necessary, taste for seasoning, then spoon into two bowls and top each with a spoonful of ricotta, a few basil leaves, the seeds and a drizzle of oil. Serve with bread for dunking.

Sesame chicken noodles

Prep: 10 mins No cook

Serves 2

Ingredients

- 1 tbsp tahini
- 1 lime , juiced
- 2 tsp soy sauce
- 2 roasted garlic cloves
- 1 tsp sesame oil
- ½ tsp chilli flakes , plus extra to serve
- 200g cooked rice noodles
- 200g leftover roast chicken
- 1 roasted aubergine
- 1 carrot , grated
- ½ cucumber , seeds removed and cut into half moons
- ½ small pack mint , roughly chopped

Method

STEP 1

Whisk together the tahini, lime juice, soy sauce, flesh from the roasted garlic, sesame oil and chilli flakes in a large bowl, adding enough water to make a creamy dressing.

STEP 2

Add the noodles, leftover roast chicken, aubergine and carrot and toss everything to combine, then gently fold through the cucumber and mint. Divide between two containers, then sprinkle over a few extra chilli flakes to serve.

Healthier risotto primavera

Prep: 40 mins **Cook:** 35 mins

Serves 4

Ingredients

- 350g bunch asparagus
- 2 tbsp olive oil
- 1 bunch (about 9) spring onions , ends trimmed, sliced
- 175g fresh or frozen pea
- 250g shelled fresh or frozen broad bean
- 2 tbsp shredded basil
- 2 tbsp snipped chive
- 1 tbsp finely chopped mint
- finely grated zest 1 lemon
- 1.7 litres/3 pints vegetable bouillon (we used Marigold)
- 4 shallots , finely chopped
- 3 plump garlic cloves , finely chopped
- 300g carnaroli or arborio rice
- 150ml dry white wine
- 25g parmesan (or vegetarian alternative), grated
- 25g rocket leaves

Method

STEP 1

Cut the woody ends off the asparagus, then slice the stems into 5cm diagonal lengths. Heat half the oil in a large, wide non-stick frying pan. Tip in the asparagus and stir-fry over a medium-high heat for about 4 mins or until nicely browned all over (Step 1). Stir in the spring onions and fry for 1-2 mins with the asparagus until browned. Remove, season with pepper and set aside. Cook the peas and beans separately in a little boiling water for 3 mins each, then drain each through a sieve. When the broad beans are cool enough to handle, pop them out of their skins. Set the peas and beans to one side. Mix the basil, chives, mint and lemon zest together in a small bowl and season with pepper (Step 2). Set aside.

STEP 2

Pour the stock into a saucepan and keep it on a very low heat. Pour the remaining oil into a large, wide sauté pan. Tip in the shallots and garlic, and fry for 3-4 mins until soft and only slightly brown. Stir in the rice and continue to stir for 1-2 mins over a medium-high heat. As it starts to sizzle, pour in the wine and stir again until the wine has been absorbed. Start to stir in the hot stock, 1½ ladlefuls at a time (Step 3), so it simmers and is absorbed after each addition. To tell when it is ready to have the next 1½ ladlefuls added, drag the spoon across the bottom of the pan and it should leave a clear line. Keep stirring the whole time, to keep the risotto creamy. Continue adding the stock as above – after 20 mins the rice should be soft with a bit of chew in the middle. If it isn't, add more stock – you should still have at least a ladleful of stock left at this point. Season with pepper, you shouldn't need to add any salt.

STEP 3

Take the pan off the heat. Pour over a ladleful of the remaining stock to keep the mixture fluid, then scatter over all the vegetables, a grinding of pepper, half of the herb mix (Step 4) and half the cheese. Cover with the pan lid and let the risotto sit for 3-4 mins to rest. Gently stir everything together, if necessary adding a drop more remaining stock for good consistency. Ladle into serving dishes and serve topped with a small pile of rocket and the rest of the herbs and cheese scattered over.

Spicy peanut pies

Prep: 15 mins **Cook:** 1 hr

Makes 2 pies, each serves 2

Ingredients

For the mash

- 500g potatoes , peeled and chopped
- 2 x 400g cans cannellini beans , drained
- 3 tbsp chopped fresh coriander
- 1 tsp chilli powder

For the filling

- 320g cauliflower , cut into small florets
- 2 tsp rapeseed oil
- 2 tbsp finely chopped ginger
- 1 red chilli , seeded unless you like it very spicy
- 2 tbsp cumin seeds
- 2 tbsp ground coriander
- 1 tsp chilli powder
- 400g leeks , thickly sliced
- 1 red pepper , deseeded and diced
- 1 green pepper , deseeded and diced
- 400g can chopped tomatoes
- 2 tbsp tomato purée
- 2 tsp vegetable bouillon
- 85g chunky peanut butter (with no sugar or palm oil)

Method

STEP 1

Heat oven to 200C, 180C fan, gas 6. Steam the potatoes for the mash for 20 mins until tender, adding the cauliflower to the steamer after 10 mins. Heat the oil for the filling in a non-stick pan, add the ginger and chilli and stir around the pan until starting to soften. Stir in the dried spices then add the leeks and peppers and cook, stirring frequently, until they are softening.

STEP 2

Tip in the tomatoes and tomato purée with the cauliflower and 150ml water, and the bouillon. Cover and simmer for 10 mins.

STEP 3

Stir the peanut butter with 100ml water to loosen the consistency, then stir into stew and cook 5 mins more. Spoon equally into 25cm by 18cm pie dishes.

STEP 4

For the mash, tip the beans into a bowl, add the coriander and chilli powder and mash well. Add the potatoes and roughly mash into the beans so it still has a little texture. Pile on top of the filling in the pie dishes and carefully spread over the filling to enclose it.

STEP 5

Bake one for 35 mins and chill the other for another day. It will keep for 3 days. Reheat the remaining pie as above, adding an extra 15 mins as you're cooking it from cold.

Meal prep: pasta

Prep: 20 mins **Cook:** 30 mins

Each box serves 1

Ingredients

For the pasta base

- 2 red onions , halved and thinly sliced
- 150g wholemeal penne
- 1 lemon , zested and juiced
- 1 tbsp rapeseed oil , plus a little extra for drizzling
- 2 large garlic cloves , finely grated
- 30g pack basil , chopped, stems and all

For the salmon pasta box

- ½ red pepper , sliced
- 1 salmon fillet
- 1 tsp capers
- big handful rocket
- For the chicken pasta box
- 1 large courgette , sliced

- 1 skinless chicken breast fillet, thickly sliced (150g)
- 2 tsp pesto
- 5 large cherry tomatoes , halved (80g)

For the aubergine pasta box

- 1 small aubergine , sliced then diced (about 275g)
- 5 large cherry tomatoes , quartered (80g)
- 5 kalamata olives , halved

Method

STEP 1

Heat oven to 200C/180C fan/gas 6. Arrange the red onions, red pepper, courgette and aubergine in lines on a large baking sheet. Drizzle with a little oil and roast for 15 mins.

STEP 2

Cook the pasta for 10-12 mins until al dente. While the pasta is cooking, loosely wrap the salmon fillet in foil and do the same with the chicken and pesto in another foil parcel, then put them on another baking tray.

STEP 3

When the veg have had their 15 mins, put the salmon and chicken in the oven and cook for a further 12 mins (or until the chicken is cooked through). Drain the pasta, put in a bowl and toss really well with the lemon zest and juice, rapeseed oil, garlic and two-thirds of the basil. When everything is cooked, add the red onions to the pasta. Toss together and divide between three lunch boxes.

STEP 4

Top the first box with the salmon fillet (remove the skin first), then add the red pepper from the tray. Scatter over the capers and add the rocket. To the second box, add the chicken and pesto with any juices, the roasted courgette and the halved cherry tomatoes. In the third box, toss the aubergine into the pasta with the quartered cherry tomatoes, olives and the remaining basil. Seal up each container and chill. Eat within three days, preferably in the order of the salmon, then the chicken and then the aubergine.

Fennel spaghetti

Prep: 15 mins **Cook:** 30 mins

Serves 2

Ingredients

- 1 tbsp olive oil , plus extra for serving
- 1 tsp fennel seeds
- 2 small garlic cloves , 1 crushed, 1 thinly sliced
- 1 lemon , zested and juiced
- 1 fennel bulb , finely sliced, fronds reserved
- 150g spaghetti
- ½ pack flat-leaf parsley , chopped
- shaved parmesan (or vegetarian alternative), to serve (optional)

Method

STEP 1

Heat the oil in a frying pan over a medium heat and cook the fennel seeds until they pop. Sizzle the garlic for 1 min, then add the lemon zest and half the fennel slices. Cook for 10-12 mins or until the fennel has softened.

STEP 2

Meanwhile, bring a pan of salted water to the boil and cook the pasta for 1 min less than pack instructions. Use tongs to transfer the pasta to the frying pan along with a good splash of pasta water. Increase the heat to high and toss well. Stir through the remaining fennel slices, the parsley and lemon juice, season generously, then tip straight into two bowls to serve. Top with the fennel fronds, extra olive oil and parmesan shavings, if you like.

Three bean spring minestrone

Prep: 10 mins **Cook:** 15 mins

Serves 3

Ingredients

- 2 tbsp olive oil , plus extra for drizzling
- 1 banana shallot , chopped
- 1 fennel bulb , thinly sliced
- 2 garlic cloves , chopped
- 400g can cannellini beans
- 400g can borlotti beans
- 700ml vegetable stock
- 100g green beans , chopped

- rind of a vegetarian hard cheese, plus 30g, grated
- 150g frozen peas
- 1 lemon, zested
- handful basil leaves, torn to serve

Method

STEP 1

Put the oil in a saucepan over a medium heat, add the shallot, fennel, garlic and a pinch of salt and cook until softened. Drain the beans, reserving the starchy water from half of one can. Tip these into the pan along with the stock, green beans and cheese rind. Cook for 15 mins until the green beans are completely softened.

STEP 2

Stir in the peas, cook for a couple of mins more, then stir in the lemon zest and grated cheese.

Chicken & veg bowl

Prep: 15 mins **Cook:** 15 mins

Serves 4

Ingredients

- 250g brown basmati rice
- 1 tbsp rapeseed oil
- 1 garlic clove, crushed
- 2 chicken breasts, sliced
- 2 tbsp hoisin sauce
- 100g frozen edamame beans or peas, defrosted
- 100g frozen sweetcorn
- 100g grated carrots
- 100g red peppers, cut into small cubes
- 1 avocado, stoned and sliced
- 1 lemon, cut into quarters, to serve (optional)

Method

STEP 1

Cook the rice following pack instructions, then drain and return to the pan to keep warm. Heat the oil in a frying pan or wok, add the garlic and fry for 2 mins or until golden. Tip in the chicken and fry until the pieces are cooked through, then stir in the hoisin sauce, season and continue cooking for a further 2 mins. Cook the edamame beans and sweetcorn in simmering water for 2 mins, then drain.

STEP 2

Divide the rice between four bowls and top with the chicken slices in a strip down the middle, with the carrot, red pepper, beans or peas, sweetcorn and avocado down either side. Serve with the lemon to squeeze over, if you like.

Black-eyed bean mole with salsa

Prep: 15 mins **Cook:** 5 mins - 8 mins

Serves 2

Ingredients

For the salsa

- 1 red onion , finely chopped
- 2 large tomatoes , chopped
- 2 tbsp fresh coriander
- ½ lime , zest and juice

For the mole

- 2 tsp rapeseed oil
- 1 red onion , halved and sliced
- 1 garlic clove , finely grated
- 1 tsp ground coriander
- 1 tsp mild chilli powder
- ½ tsp ground cinnamon
- 400g can black-eyed beans in water
- 2 tsp cocoa
- 1 tsp vegetable bouillon
- 1 tbsp tomato purée

Method

STEP 1

Tip all the salsa ingredients into a bowl and stir together.

STEP 2

For the mole, heat the oil in a non-stick pan, add the onion and garlic and fry stirring frequently until softened. Tip in the spices, stir then add the contents of the can of beans with the cocoa, bouillon and tomato purée. Cook, stirring frequently to make quite a thick sauce.

STEP 3

Spoon into shallow bowls, top with the salsa and serve.

Walnut & almond muesli with grated apple

Prep: 10 mins **Cook:** 2 mins

Serves 4

Ingredients

- 85g porridge oats
- 15g flaked almonds
- 15g walnut pieces
- 15g pumpkin seeds
- 1 tsp ground cinnamon
- 80g raisins
- 15g high fibre puffed wheat (we used Good Grain)
- 4 apples , no need to peel, grated
- milk , to serve

Method

STEP 1

Put the porridge oats in a saucepan and heat gently, stirring frequently until they're just starting to toast. Turn off the heat, then add all of the nuts, pumpkin seeds, and cinnamon, then stir everything together well.

STEP 2

Tip into a large bowl, stir to help it cool, then add the raisins and puffed wheat and toss together until well mixed. Tip half into a jar or airtight container and save for another day – it will keep at room temperature. Serve the rest in two bowls, grate over 2 apples and pour over some cold milk (use nut milk if you're vegan) at the table. Save the other apples for the remaining muesli.

Avocado hummus & crudités

Prep: 10 mins No cook

Serves 2

Ingredients

- 1 avocado , peeled and stoned
- 210g chickpeas , drained

- 1 garlic clove , crushed
- pinch chilli flakes , plus extra to serve
- 1 lime , juiced
- handful coriander leaves
- 2 carrots , cut into strips
- 2 mixed peppers , cut into strips
- 160g sugar snap peas

Method

STEP 1

Blitz together the avocado, chickpeas, garlic, chilli flakes and lime juice, and season to taste. Top the hummus with the coriander leaves and a few more chilli flakes, and serve with the carrot, pepper and sugar snap crudités. Make the night before for a great take-to-work lunch.

Spinach dhal with harissa yogurt

Prep: 5 mins **Cook:** 10 mins

Serves 2

Ingredients

- 1 tsp harissa
- 60g Greek yogurt
- 1 tbsp flaked almonds
- 500g leftover basic lentils
- 200g spinach

Method

STEP 1

Swirl the harissa through the Greek yogurt. Toast the flaked almonds in a dry frying pan until golden. Reheat the leftover lentils and stir through the spinach. Once wilted, spoon into bowls, and top with the yogurt and almonds.

Thai green pork lettuce cups

Prep: 10 mins **Cook:** 15 mins

Serves 4

Ingredients

- 1 tbsp sesame oil
- 500g pork mince
- 1 tbsp green curry paste
- 1 red onion , finely chopped

- juice 1 lime
- 1 tbsp fish sauce
- ½ small pack mint, leaves only, roughly chopped
- ½ small pack coriander, leaves only, roughly chopped
- 4 Little Gem lettuces, leaves separated
- rice, to serve (optional)

Method

STEP 1

Heat the oil in a frying pan and cook the pork for 8-10 mins or until cooked through. Stir in the green curry paste and 2 tbsp water, then cook for 1-2 mins.

STEP 2

Remove from the heat and stir in the red onion, lime juice, fish sauce and herbs. Spoon the pork into the lettuce leaves and serve with rice, if you like.

Tarka dhal

Prep: 10 mins **Cook:** 1 hr

Serves 2

Ingredients

- 200g red lentils
- 2 tbsp ghee, or vegetable oil if you're vegan
- 1 small onion, finely chopped
- 3 garlic cloves, finely chopped
- ¼ tsp turmeric
- ½ tsp garam masala
- coriander, to serve
- 1 small tomato, chopped

Method

STEP 1

Rinse the lentils several times until the water runs clear, then tip into a saucepan with 1 litre water and a pinch of salt. Bring to the boil, then reduce the heat and simmer for 25 mins, skimming the froth from the top. Cover with a lid and cook for a further 40 mins, stirring occasionally, until it's a thick, soupy consistency.

STEP 2

While the lentils are cooking, heat the ghee or oil in a non-stick frying pan over a medium heat, then fry the onion and garlic until the onion is softened, so around 8 mins. Add the turmeric and garam masala, then cook for a further minute. Set aside.

STEP 3

Tip the lentils into bowls and spoon half the onion mixture on top. Top with the coriander and tomato to serve.

Lentil ragu with courgetti

Prep: 15 mins **Cook:** 40 mins

Serves 4 - 6

Ingredients

- 2 tbsp rapeseed oil, plus 1 tsp
- 3 celery sticks, chopped
- 2 carrots, chopped
- 4 garlic cloves, chopped
- 2 onions, finely chopped
- 140g button mushrooms from a 280g pack, quartered
- 500g pack dried red lentils
- 500g pack passata
- 1l reduced-salt vegetable bouillon (we used Marigold)
- 1 tsp dried oregano
- 2 tbsp balsamic vinegar
- 1-2 large courgettes, cut into noodles with a spiraliser, julienne peeler or knife

Method

STEP 1

Heat the 2 tbsp oil in a large sauté pan. Add the celery, carrots, garlic and onions, and fry for 4-5 mins over a high heat to soften and start to colour. Add the mushrooms and fry for 2 mins more.

STEP 2

Stir in the lentils, passata, bouillon, oregano and balsamic vinegar. Cover the pan and leave to simmer for 30 mins until the lentils are tender and pulpy. Check occasionally and stir to make sure the mixture isn't sticking to the bottom of the pan; if it does, add a drop of water.

STEP 3

To serve, heat the remaining oil in a separate frying pan, add the courgette and stir-fry briefly to soften and warm through. Serve half the ragu with the courgetti and chill the rest to eat on another day. Can be frozen for up to 3 months.

Pesto-crusted cod with Puy lentils

Prep: 15 mins **Cook:** 8 mins - 10 mins

Serves 2

Ingredients

- large pack basil , leaves only
- 4 garlic cloves , 2 whole, 2 crushed
- 25g pine nuts
- 1 lemon
- 50ml olive oil
- 2 cod fillets
- 2 red chillies , finely chopped
- 2large tomatoes , roughly chopped
- 250g ready-to-eat puy lentils

Method

STEP 1

First, make the pesto. In a food processor, pulse the basil, whole garlic cloves, pine nuts, the juice of half the lemon and some seasoning, gradually adding most of the oil. Taste and adjust the seasoning.

STEP 2

Heat oven to 180C/160C fan/ gas 4 and line a roasting tin with foil. Season the cod on both sides and coat each fillet in the pesto. Cook for 8-10 mins until a crust has formed and the cod is cooked through.

STEP 3

Meanwhile, heat the remaining oil in a small saucepan. Add the crushed garlic and the chillies, and cook for a couple of mins to release the flavour. Add the tomatoes and cook for 1 min more. Tip in the lentils, squeeze over the other half of the lemon, then season. Cook until piping hot and serve with the pesto cod.

Squash & spinach fusilli with pecans

Prep: 10 mins **Cook:** 40 mins

Serves 2

Ingredients

- 160g butternut squash, diced
- 3 garlic cloves, sliced
- 1 tbsp chopped sage leaves
- 2 tsp rapeseed oil
- 1 large courgette, halved and sliced
- 6 pecan halves
- 115g wholemeal fusilli
- 125g bag baby spinach

Method

STEP 1

Heat oven to 200C/180C fan/gas 6. Toss the butternut squash, garlic and sage in the oil, then spread out in a roasting tin and cook in the oven for 20 mins, add the courgettes and cook for a further 15 mins. Give everything a stir, then add the pecans and cook for 5 mins more until the nuts are toasted and the vegetables are tender and starting to caramelise.

STEP 2

Meanwhile, boil the pasta according to pack instructions – about 12 mins. Drain, then tip into a serving bowl and toss with the spinach so that it wilts in the heat from the pasta. Add the roasted veg and pecans, breaking up the nuts a little, and toss again really well before serving.

Coronation chicken salad

Prep: 5 mins No cook

Serves 2

Ingredients

- 3 tbsp low-fat Greek yogurt
- 1 tsp curry powder
- 1 tsp mango chutney
- ½ lemon, zested and cut into 2 wedges
- 250g pre-cooked grain pouch
- 150g leftover roast chicken
- 2 roasted red onions
- 1 large courgette, peeled into ribbons
- 1 small pack coriander, roughly chopped
- 1 tbsp flaked almonds

Method

STEP 1

Mix together the yogurt, curry powder, mango chutney and lemon zest with some seasoning in a large bowl. Add the grains, breaking them up with your fingers as you go, then add the chicken, onions, courgette and most of the coriander. Give everything a good stir and divide between two containers. Sprinkle over the remaining coriander, flaked almonds and nestle a lemon wedge into each lunchbox.

Spring tabbouleh

Prep: 20 mins **Cook:** 25 mins

Serves 4

Ingredients

- 6 tbsp olive oil
- 1 tbsp garam masala
- 2 x 400g cans chickpeas , drained and rinsed
- 250g ready-to-eat mixed grain pouch
- 250g frozen peas
- 2 lemons , zested and juiced
- large pack parsley , leaves roughly chopped
- large pack mint , leaves roughly chopped
- 250g radishes , roughly chopped
- 1 cucumber , chopped
- pomegranate seeds , to serve

Method

STEP 1

Heat oven to 200C/180C fan/ gas 6. Mix 4 tbsp oil with the garam masala and some seasoning. Toss with the chickpeas in a large roasting tin, then cook for 15 mins until starting to crisp. Tip in the mixed grains, peas and lemon zest. Mix well, then return to the oven for about 10 mins until warmed through.

STEP 2

Transfer to a large bowl or platter, then toss through the herbs, radishes, cucumber, remaining oil and lemon juice. Season to taste and scatter over the pomegranate seeds. Any leftovers will be good for lunch the next day.

Salmon & purple sprouting broccoli grain bowl

Prep: 10 mins **Cook:** 10 mins

Serves 2

Ingredients

- 2½ tbsp cold pressed rapeseed oil
- ½ tsp honey
- ½ tsp wholegrain mustard
- 1 lemon, juiced
- 200g purple sprouting broccoli, each stem cut into three pieces
- 1-2 garlic cloves, sliced
- 250g pouch mixed grains
- handful parsley, roughly chopped
- handful dill, roughly chopped
- 160g radishes, cut into chunks
- 200g cooked salmon, broken into chunks

Method

STEP 1

Mix 2 tbsp oil with the honey, mustard, lemon juice and some seasoning. Bring a pan of water to the boil. Add the broccoli, cook for 3-4 mins until tender but with a slight bite, then drain.

STEP 2

Heat the remaining oil in a frying pan. Add the garlic, sizzle for a min, then tip in the mixed grain pouch, using the back of your spoon to separate the grains. Add the broccoli, mustard dressing, herbs and radishes. Give everything a mix to combine, season to taste, then gently stir through the salmon. Serve warm or cold.

Sweet potato jackets with pomegranate & celeriac slaw

Prep: 5 mins **Cook:** 35 mins - 40 mins

Serves 2

Ingredients

- 2 sweet potatoes (about 195g each)
- 90g pomegranate seeds

- 8 walnut halves, broken
- small handful coriander, chopped

For the slaw

- 1 small red onion, halved and thinly sliced
- 160g peeled celeriac, thinly sliced into matchsticks
- 2 celery sticks, chopped
- 1 tbsp lemon juice
- 120g pot bio yogurt
- 1 tbsp rapeseed oil
- 2 tsp balsamic vinegar
- 0.5 - 1 tsp English mustard powder (optional)
- 2 tbsp chopped parsley

Method

STEP 1

Heat oven to 200C/180C fan/gas 6. Roast the sweet potatoes for 35-40 mins until a knife slides in easily.

STEP 2

Meanwhile, pour boiling water over the onion and leave for 5 mins, then rinse under the cold tap and pat dry with kitchen paper. Tip into a bowl and add the celeriac and celery with all but 4 tbsp yogurt along with the remaining slaw ingredients and toss together.

STEP 3

Cut into the potatoes and gently squeeze to open them. Top with the remaining yogurt, pomegranate and walnuts. Scatter over the coriander. Serve with the slaw.

Mexican chicken stew with quinoa & beans

Prep: 25 mins **Cook:** 30 mins

Serves 4 - 5

Ingredients

- 1 tbsp olive oil
- 1 onion, sliced
- 2 red peppers, deseeded and chopped into largish chunks
- 3 tbsp chipotle paste
- 2 x 400g cans chopped tomatoes
- 4 skinless chicken breasts
- 140g quinoa
- 2 chicken stock cubes
- 1 x 400g can pinto beans, drained

- small bunch coriander, most chopped, a few leaves left whole
- juice 1 lime
- 1 tbsp sugar
- natural yogurt, to serve

Method

STEP 1

Heat the oil in a deep frying pan and fry the onions and peppers for a few mins until softened. Stir in the chipotle paste for a minute, followed by the tomatoes. Add up to a tomato can-full of water to cover the chicken and bring to a gentle simmer. Add the chicken breasts and gently simmer, turning the chicken occasionally, for 20 mins until the chicken is cooked through.

STEP 2

Bring a large saucepan of water to the boil with the stock cubes. Add the quinoa and cook for 15 mins until tender, adding the beans for the final min. Drain well and stir in the coriander and lime juice, then check for seasoning before covering to keep warm.

STEP 3

Lift the chicken out onto a board and shred each breast using two forks. Stir back into the tomato sauce with the sugar and season. Serve with the quinoa, scattering the stew with some coriander leaves just before dishing up and eating with a dollop of yogurt on the side.

Lemony chicken stew with giant couscous

Prep: 25 mins **Cook:** 1 hr plus longer cooking if needed

Serves 4

Ingredients

- 1 tbsp olive oil
- 2 onions, chopped
- 500g skinless boneless chicken thighs, each cut into 2-3 chunks
- 3 tbsp tagine paste or 2 tbsp ras el hanout
- 2 x 400g cans tomato with chopped mixed olives
- small handful fresh oregano, leaves picked and chopped
- 2 preserved lemons, flesh removed, skin rinsed and finely chopped
- 2 tbsp clear honey
- 1 chicken stock cube
- 200g giant couscous

- handful parsley, chopped

Method

STEP 1

Heat the oil in a large flameproof casserole dish with a lid. Add the onions and cook for 10 mins until starting to caramelise. Push the onions to one side of the dish and add the chicken. Cook over a high heat for 5 mins or so until the chicken is browning.

STEP 2

Add the tagine paste, tomatoes, oregano, preserved lemons and honey, and crumble in the stock cube. Fill one of the tomato cans halfway with water and pour this into the dish. Season with a little salt and plenty of black pepper. Give everything a good stir, then cover with a lid and simmer for 40 mins, on a gentle bubble, or for up to 4 hrs over a very low heat if you're eating at different times.

STEP 3

Add the couscous 10 mins before you're ready to serve, cover and simmer for 10 mins or until cooked. If you're eating at different times, scoop your portion into a pan, add 50g couscous and cook in the same way. Stir in some parsley just before serving.

Porridge with quick berry compote, figs & pistachios

Prep: 5 mins **Cook:** 5 mins

Serves 2

Ingredients

- 150g porridge oats
- 100ml milk
- 120g frozen berries
- ½ orange , zested and juiced
- 1 fig , sliced
- 1 tbsp pistachios , toasted and chopped

Method

STEP 1

Put the oats, milk and 450ml water in a pan with a pinch of salt. Cook for about 5 mins until thick and creamy. Meanwhile, microwave the berries, orange juice and zest for 2-3 mins.

STEP 2

Divide the porridge between bowls and top each with the berry compote, fig and pistachios.

Microwave shakshuka

Prep: 5 mins **Cook:** 5 mins

Serves 1

Ingredients

- 1 tbsp olive oil
- 200ml passata or canned tomatoes, whizzed to a paste
- 1 garlic clove, finely sliced
- 1 heaped tbsp red pepper salsa (we used Gran Luchito) or ¼-½ red pepper, chopped
- 1 medium egg
- 1 tbsp chopped coriander and pitta bread, to serve

Method

STEP 1

Brush a microwave bowl or dish with a little of the oil. Stir the passata, garlic and salsa together and season well. Tip into the bowl and make a dip in the centre. Break in the egg, then prick the yolk with the tip of a sharp knife.

STEP 2

Cover the bowl with its lid or clingfilm. Microwave on high for 1 min, and then in 20 sec bursts until the white is set. Scatter over the coriander and serve with the warmed pitta.

Cabbage koshimbir

Prep: 10 mins **Cook:** 2 mins

Serves 6

Ingredients

- 1 tbsp sunflower oil
- 1 tsp black mustard seed
- 1 tsp cumin seeds
- ½ white cabbage , finely shredded or coarsely grated
- 1 red onion , finely sliced
- 1 green chilli , chopped (optional)
- ½ lemon , juiced

Method

STEP 1

Heat the oil in a frying pan and warm the mustard and cumin seeds until they sizzle and crackle, then remove from the heat. Combine everything together in a mixing bowl with a large pinch of salt and serve. (Can be made a day ahead and kept in the fridge.)

Baked carrot & nigella seed bhajis with raita

Prep:30 mins **Cook:**25 mins

Serves 12, as a snack or canapé

Ingredients

- 100g gram flour (chickpea flour)
- 1 tsp ground turmeric
- 2 tsp nigella seeds
- ½ tsp ground cumin
- ½ tsp ground coriander
- ½ tsp ground ginger
- ½ tsp chilli powder
- 2 large eggs
- 4 large carrots (about 400g), peeled, ends trimmed and spiralized into thin noodles
- 2 tsp vegetable oil

For the raita

- ½ cucumber , grated
- 150g pot of natural yogurt
- ½ small pack of mint , leaves finely chopped

Method

STEP 1

Heat oven to 200C/180C fan/gas 6.Line one large or two medium baking trays with baking parchment.

STEP 2

Mix all the ingredients for the carrot bhajis, apart from the carrot and oil, together in a large bowl to form a thick batter. If the mixture looks a little dry add a splash of water. Stir in the sprialized carrots, cutting any large spirals in half, and season.

STEP 3

Dollop 12 spoonfuls of the mixture onto the baking tray, leaving enough space to flatten the bhajis with the back of a spoon. Drizzle over the oil and bake for 25 mins or until golden brown, flipping the bhajis halfway.

STEP 4

While the bhajis are cooking, squeeze any excess moisture from the cucumber using a tea towel then combine all the ingredients for the raita together in a small bowl, seasoning to taste. Serve alongside the baked bhajis.

Fish pie with pea & dill mash

Prep: 10 mins **Cook:** 55 mins

Serves 2

Ingredients

- 375g potatoes , cut into chunks
- 175g leeks , thickly sliced
- 160g frozen peas
- 2 tbsp half-fat crème fraîche
- ½ lemon , zested and juiced
- 2 tbsp chopped fresh dill
- ½ tsp vegetable bouillon powder
- 100g cherry tomatoes , halved
- 250g skinless cod loin , cut into large chunks
- 50g Atlantic prawns (thawed if frozen)
- veg , to serve (optional)

Method

STEP 1

Heat oven to 200C/180C fan/gas 6. Cook the potatoes in a pan of boiling water for 10 mins, with the leeks in a covered steamer over the pan. Remove the steamer, add the peas to the potatoes and cook for 10 mins more. Drain the peas and potatoes, then mash with ½ tbsp crème fraîche, the lemon zest and juice, dill and bouillon.

STEP 2

Arrange the leeks in a shallow ovenproof pie dish (about 18 x 24cm). Add the tomatoes, cod and prawns, then dot over the rest of the crème fraîche. Spoon over the mash, then spread it lightly to the edges with a fork.

STEP 3

Bake for 30-35 mins until bubbling round the sides of the dish. Serve with veg, if you like. If you make this ahead and are cooking from cold, bake for about 10 mins longer.

Vegetable tagine with chickpeas & raisins

Prep: 10 mins **Serves 4**

Ingredients

- 2 tbsp olive oil
- 2 onions , chopped
- ½ tsp each ground cinnamon , coriander and cumin
- 2 large courgettes , cut into chunks
- 2 chopped tomatoes
- 400g can chickpea , rinsed and drained
- 4 tbsp raisin
- 425ml vegetable stock
- 300g frozen pea
- chopped coriander , to serve

Method

STEP 1

Heat the oil in a pan, then fry the onions for 5 mins until soft. Stir in the spices. Add the courgettes, tomatoes, chickpeas, raisins and stock, then bring to the boil. Cover and simmer for 10 mins. Stir in the peas and cook for 5 mins more. Sprinkle with coriander, to serve.

Asian pulled chicken salad

Prep: 20 mins No cook

Serves 5

Ingredients

- 1 small roasted chicken , about 1kg
- ½ red cabbage , cored and finely sliced
- 3 carrots , coarsley grated or finely shredded

- 5 spring onions, finely sliced on the diagonal
- 2 red chillies, halved and thinly sliced
- small bunch coriander, roughly chopped, including stalks
- 2 heaped tbsp roasted salted peanuts, roughly crushed

For the dressing

- 3 ½ tbsp hoisin sauce
- 1 ½ tbsp toasted sesame oil

Method

STEP 1

Combine the dressing ingredients in a small bowl and set aside.

STEP 2

Remove all the meat from the chicken, shred into large chunks and pop in a large bowl. Add the cabbage, carrots, spring onions, chillies and half the coriander. Toss together with the dressing and pile onto a serving plate, then scatter over the remaining coriander and peanuts.

Chicken piccata with garlicky greens & new potatoes

Prep: 5 mins **Cook:** 15 mins

Serves 2

Ingredients

- 200g new potatoes, halved or quartered
- 300g green beans, trimmed
- 200g spring greens, shredded
- 2 skinless chicken breasts
- 3 tsp olive oil
- 100ml chicken stock or water
- 1 tbsp drained capers
- 1 lemon, zested and juiced
- 2 small garlic cloves, sliced
- 1 tbsp grated parmesan

Method

STEP 1

Cook the new potatoes in a large pan of boiling salted water for 8-10 mins until tender. Add the green beans and spring greens for the last 3 mins. Drain, then separate the greens from the potatoes.

STEP 2

While the potatoes are cooking, cut the chicken breasts through the centre lengthways, leaving one side attached so it opens out like a book. Brush each one with 1 tsp of the olive oil, then season.

STEP 3

Heat a large frying pan over a medium-high heat and cook the chicken for 4 mins on each side until golden. Pour over the stock, capers, lemon juice and zest, then simmer gently for a few minutes to reduce. Add the cooked potatoes and simmer for another minute.

STEP 4

Heat the remaining 1 tsp oil in another frying pan and fry the garlic for 1 min until lightly golden and fragrant. Tip in the drained greens, and toss in the garlicky oil. Season, then scatter over the parmesan and serve with the chicken and potatoes.

Chicken & aubergine shawarma pittas

Prep: 20 mins **Cook:** 30 mins

Serves 4

Ingredients

- 6 boneless and skinless chicken thighs
- 3 tbsp za'atar
- 1 tsp chilli flakes
- 2 tbsp olive oil
- 2 aubergines , cut into 1cm rounds
- large bunch parsley
- 100g natural yogurt
- 1 tbsp mayonnaise
- 1 small garlic clove , finely grated
- ½ red onion , thinly sliced
- 1 small lemon , juiced
- 4 large brown pitta breads
- hummus , sliced chilli and pickled gherkins, to serve

Method

STEP 1

Heat the grill to medium. Open out the chicken thighs and gently bash them with a rolling pin to flatten them slightly. Mix together the za'atar, chilli flakes and oil, then toss with the chicken and aubergine in a large bowl. Season generously.

STEP 2

Line a large baking sheet with foil and lay the chicken on top. Grill for 10-15 mins or until cooked through and beginning to char around the edges. Meanwhile, heat a griddle pan or non-stick frying pan over a high heat until really hot. Add the aubergine slices in batches and cook on each side for 4-6 mins or until charred and softened.

STEP 3

Finely chop half the parsley and tear the remaining leaves. Mix the yogurt, mayonnaise and garlic, stir through the chopped parsley and season to taste with salt. Combine the torn parsley leaves in a separate bowl with the sliced onion and lemon juice, and season to taste.

STEP 4

Lightly toast the pittas and split in half. Serve the chicken at the table, sliced into strips, along with the aubergine, pittas, hummus, chilli, pickles, parsley salad and garlic yogurt for everyone to assemble their own shawarmas.

Little beef & mushroom pies

Prep: 30 mins **Cook:** 50 mins

Serves 4

Ingredients

- 30g dried porcini mushroom , finely chopped
- 1 tbsp vegetable bouillon powder
- 1 tbsp balsamic vinegar
- 2 medium baking potatoes , cut into chunks (475g)
- 1 small celeriac , peeled and cut into large chunks (500g)
- ½ tsp ground white pepper
- 2 tsp rapeseed oil
- 2 large onions , halved and sliced
- 400g 5% lean beef mince
- 125g baby chestnut mushrooms , halved if large
- 2 tsp chopped sage
- 25g stilton , crumbled (optional)
- 320g spinach or chard
- 320g frozen peas

Method

STEP 1

Tip the dried mushrooms, bouillon and vinegar into a bowl and pour over 400ml boiling water. Boil the potatoes and celeriac together for 18-20 mins until very tender, then drain and leave to steam-dry. Mash with the white pepper.

STEP 2

Meanwhile, heat the oil in a large, deep, non-stick frying pan and fry the onions for 10 mins, stirring occasionally, until golden. Add the mince and fresh mushrooms and fry for 5-10 mins until the mince is browned. Tip in the dried mushroom mixture and the sage, then half-cover the pan and simmer for 20 mins, stirring occasionally, until thickened.

STEP 3

Spoon the mixture into four 175ml pie dishes and top with the mash and stilton, if using.

STEP 4

If eating straightaway, heat the grill to high. Put the pies on a baking tray (in case they bubble over) and grill for 5 mins. To make ahead, leave to cool completely, cover and freeze for up to three months. Reheat in the oven until piping hot. Wilt the spinach in a pan or the microwave and cook the peas following pack instructions. Serve the pies with the veg on the side.

Herby Persian frittata

Prep: 10 mins **Cook:** 10 mins

Serves 2

Ingredients

- 3 eggs
- ½ tsp baking powder
- ¼ tsp turmeric
- 1 small pack of coriander and parsley, roughly chopped
- ½ small pack dill , roughly chopped
- 4 spring onions , thinly sliced
- 1 tbsp currants or barberries, if you can find them
- 1 tbsp toasted walnuts (optional), roughly chopped
- 1 tbsp cold pressed rapeseed oil

- 30g feta, crumbled

Method

STEP 1

Heat grill to high. Whisk the eggs together in a large bowl, add the baking powder and turmeric, then season with salt and pepper. Stir in most of the herbs, then add the spring onions, currants and walnuts.

STEP 2

Drizzle the oil into a small ovenproof, non-stick frying pan over a medium heat. Pour in the herby egg mixture and cook for 8-10 mins until the egg is nearly set, then put the frittata under the grill for a final minute until cooked through. Sprinkle over the remaining herbs and the crumbled feta to serve.

Spiced black bean & chicken soup with kale

Prep: 10 mins **Cook:** 15 mins

Serves 4

Ingredients

- 2 tbsp mild olive oil
- 2 fat garlic cloves, crushed
- small bunch coriander stalks finely chopped, leaves picked
- zest 1 lime, then cut into wedges
- 2 tsp ground cumin
- 1 tsp chilli flakes
- 400g can chopped tomatoes
- 400g can black beans, rinsed and drained
- 600ml chicken stock
- 175g kale, thick stalks removed, leaves shredded
- 250g leftover roast or ready-cooked chicken
- 50g feta, crumbled, to serve
- flour & corn tortillas, toasted, to serve (see tip)

Method

STEP 1

Heat the oil in a large saucepan, add the garlic, coriander stalks and lime zest, then fry for 2 mins until fragrant. Stir in the cumin and chilli flakes, fry for 1 min more, then tip in the tomatoes, beans and stock. Bring to the boil, then crush the beans against the bottom of the pan a few times using a potato masher. This will thicken the soup a little.

STEP 2

Stir the kale into the soup, simmer for 5 mins or until tender, then tear in the chicken and let it heat through. Season to taste with salt, pepper and juice from half the lime, then serve in shallow bowls, scattered with the feta and a few coriander leaves. Serve the remaining lime in wedges for the table, with the toasted tortillas on the side. The longer you leave the chicken in the pan, the thicker the soup will become, so add a splash more stock if you can't serve the soup straight away.

Chicken waldorf

Prep: 15 mins **Cook:** 12 mins

Serves 4

Ingredients

- 170g wholemeal penne
- 2 x 120g pots bio yogurt
- 4 tsp sherry vinegar
- 2 tsp English mustard powder
- 4 spring onions , finely chopped
- 6 celery sticks (320g), finely chopped
- 4 cooked chicken breasts (600g), cut into bite-sized chunks
- 8 walnut halves (22g), broken into pieces
- 150g black seedless grapes , halved
- 8 crisp lettuce leaves from an iceberg lettuce

Method

STEP 1

Boil the penne for 12 mins until al dente. Meanwhile, make a dressing by mixing the yogurt with the vinegar, mustard and spring onions.

STEP 2

Add the celery, cooked penne and chicken to the dressing and stir until everything is well coated.

STEP 3

If you're following our Healthy Diet Plan and eating straight away, add half the walnuts and grapes to half the salad and serve with half of the crisp lettuce leaves, either as a base or as lettuce wraps. Keep the remainder in the fridge, well covered, for up to three days, then add the nuts, grapes and lettuce when ready to serve.

Avocado & strawberry ices

Prep: 5 mins Plus freezing

Serves 4

Ingredients

- 200g ripe strawberries, hulled and chopped
- 1 avocado, stoned, peeled and roughly chopped
- 2 tsp balsamic vinegar
- ½ tsp vanilla extract
- 1-2 tsp maple syrup (optional)

Method

STEP 1

Put the strawberries (save four pieces for the top), avocado, vinegar and vanilla in a bowl and blitz using a hand blender (or in a food processor) until as smooth as you can get it. Have a taste and only add the maple syrup if the strawberries are not sweet enough.

STEP 2

Pour into containers, add a strawberry to each, cover with cling film and freeze. Allow the pots to soften for 5-10 mins before eating.

Toddler recipe: Mild split pea & spinach dhal

Prep: 10 mins **Cook:** 1 hr and 15 mins

Makes 5 toddler portions

Ingredients

- 175g yellow split peas
- ½ tbsp coconut oil
- 1 small onion, finely chopped
- 1 fat garlic clove, crushed
- ½ tsp yellow mustard seeds
- ¼ tsp turmeric

- 1 ½ tsp mild curry powder
- 50g unsalted cashew nuts , chopped
- 1 very low salt vegetable stock cube (we used Kallo)
- 100g frozen chopped spinach
- plain yogurt , pitta bread or rice, to serve

Method

STEP 1

Soak the yellow split peas in a bowl of water for 20 mins. Rinse thoroughly in a few changes of water.

STEP 2

Heat the oil in a large heavy-based saucepan. Cook the onion for 5-10 mins, stirring from time to time until softened and starting to caramelise. Add the garlic and spices and cook for a further 1-2 mins allowing the aromas to release.

STEP 3

Pulse the cashews in a food processor into fine pieces – make sure you do this well so that there is no risk of choking. Add the split peas and cashews to the pan, then pour in enough water to cover it by a few cms. Crumble in the veg stock cube. Bring to the boil, then simmer for 1hr or until the split peas are tender, stirring from time to time. If they start to look a little dry, add in more water as needed during the cooking. Stir through the frozen chopped spinach and once the dhal is hot throughout, serve with a dollop of yogurt on top, pitta or brown rice.

Moroccan harira

Prep:15 mins **Cook:**40 mins

Serves 4

Ingredients

- 1-2 tbsp rapeseed oil
- 2 large onions , finely chopped
- 4 garlic cloves , chopped
- 2 tsp turmeric
- 2 tsp cumin
- ½ tsp cinnamon
- 2 red chillies , deseeded and sliced
- 500g carton passata
- 1.7l reduced-salt vegetable bouillon
- 175dried green lentils

- 2 carrots, chopped into small pieces
- 1 sweet potato, peeled and diced
- 5 celery sticks, chopped into small pieces
- ⅔ small pack coriander, few sprigs reserved, the rest chopped
- 1 lemon, cut into 4 wedges, to serve

Method

STEP 1

Heat the oil in a large non-stick sauté pan over a medium heat and fry the onions and garlic until starting to soften. Tip in the spices and chilli, stir briefly, then pour in the passata and stock. Add the lentils, carrots, sweet potato and celery, and bring to the boil.

STEP 2

Cover the pan and leave to simmer for 30 mins, then cook uncovered for a further 5-10 mins until the vegetables and lentils are tender. Stir in the chopped coriander and serve in bowls with lemon wedges for squeezing over, and the reserved coriander sprinkled over.

Spinach & tuna pancakes

Prep: 15 mins **Cook:** 10 mins

Serves 2

Ingredients

- 2 tsp rapeseed oil
- 2 garlic cloves, chopped
- 250g baby spinach
- 1 tbsp tomato purée
- 120g can tuna steak in spring water, drained
- 200g cottage cheese
- 2 large eggs
- 4 tbsp plain wholemeal flour

For the salad

- 200g can sweetcorn (no added salt or sugar), rinsed and drained
- 1 small red onion, finely chopped
- 85g cherry tomatoes, quartered
- 10 basil leaves, chopped
- 4 pitted Kalamata olives, sliced
- 2 tsp balsamic vinegar

Method

STEP 1

Mix all the ingredients for the salad and set aside. Heat 1 tsp oil in a large non-stick pan and fry the garlic briefly. Stir in the spinach to wilt, then mix in the tomato purée, tuna and cottage cheese. Set aside.

STEP 2

Beat the eggs with the flour and 2 tbsp water. Heat the remaining oil in a medium non-stick pan, add half the batter and swirl round the pan to coat the base. Cook briefly until set, then flip over with a palate knife to cook the other side for 1 min. Repeat with the remaining batter. Put the pancakes on serving plates, spoon the filling down one side, roll up and serve with the salad.

Celeriac, hazelnut & truffle soup

Prep: 20 mins **Cook:** 45 mins

Serves 6

Ingredients

- 1 tbsp olive oil
- small bunch thyme
- 2 bay leaves
- 1 onion, chopped
- 1 fat garlic clove, chopped
- 1 celeriac (about 1kg), peeled and chopped
- 1 potato (about 200g), chopped
- 1l veg stock (check the label to ensure it's vegan – we used Marigold)
- 100ml soya cream
- 50g blanched hazelnuts, toasted and roughly chopped
- 1 tbsp truffle oil, plus an extra drizzle to serve

Method

STEP 1

In a large saucepan, heat the oil over a low heat. Tie the thyme sprigs and bay leaves together with a piece of string and add them to the pan with the onion and a pinch of salt. Cook for about 10 mins until softened but not coloured.

STEP 2

Stir in the garlic and cook for 1 min more, then tip in the celeriac and potato. Give everything a good stir and season with a big pinch of salt and white pepper. Pour in the stock, bring to the boil, then simmer for around 30 mins until the vegetables are completely soft.

STEP 3

Discard the herbs, then stir through the cream, remove from the heat and blitz until completely smooth. Stir through 1/2 tbsp truffle oil at a time and taste for seasoning – the strength of the oil will vary, so it's better to start with less oil and add a little at a time.

STEP 4

To serve, reheat the soup until piping hot, then ladle into bowls and top with the hazelnuts, some black pepper and an extra drizzle of truffle oil.

Noodle salad with sesame dressing

Prep: 7 mins **Cook:** 5 mins

Serves 2

Ingredients

For the dressing

- 1 tbsp sesame oil
- 2 tsp tamari
- 1 lemon , juiced
- 1 red chilli , deseeded and finely chopped

For the salad

- 1 small onion , finely chopped
- 2 wholemeal noodle nests (about 100g)
- 160g sugar snap peas
- 4 small clementines , peeled and chopped
- 160g shredded carrots
- large handful of coriander , chopped
- 50g roasted unsalted cashews

Method

STEP 1

Mix all the dressing ingredients together in a large bowl, then stir in the onion. Meanwhile, cook the noodles in a pan of boiling water for 5 mins, adding the sugar snap peas halfway through the cooking time – the noodles and peas should be just tender. Drain, cool under cold running water and drain again. Snip or cut the noodles into smaller lengths to make them more manageable to eat.

STEP 2

Tip the noodles and peas into the bowl with the dressing, along with the clementines, carrots, coriander and cashews. Toss to combine, then serve in bowls or pack into rigid airtight containers to take to work.

Sesame prawn & smacked cucumber rice noodles

Prep: 10 mins **Cook:** 15 mins

Serves 2

Ingredients

- ½ cucumber
- 1 fat clove garlic, crushed
- 1 red chilli, finely chopped (deseeded, if you prefer)
- 1 tbsp sesame oil
- 3 tbsp rice wine vinegar
- 1 tsp low-sodium soy sauce
- pinch of sugar
- 100g rice noodles
- 160g frozen peas
- 160g frozen podded edamame beans
- 180g raw king prawns
- 160g mangetout
- 2 pak choi, white parts sliced and leaves left whole
- 1 tsp mustard seeds
- 1 tsp sesame seeds

Method

STEP 1

Lightly smack the cucumber with a rolling pin until it begins to break, then cut into pieces. Put in a sieve, sprinkle with a pinch of salt and leave to sit for 10 mins to draw out some of the moisture. To make the marinade, put the garlic in a large bowl along with the chilli, ½ tbsp sesame oil, the vinegar, soy and sugar. Set aside.

STEP 2

Meanwhile, boil the kettle. Put the rice noodles in a bowl along with the frozen peas and edamame beans. Pour over the boiling water. Set aside until the noodles have softened. Drain thoroughly, then tip back into the bowl along with the marinade. Add the cucumber and toss everything together.

STEP 3

Pour the remaining sesame oil into a frying pan over a high heat, then add the prawns, mangetout, pak choi, mustard and sesame seeds with a splash of water. Cook for 2-3 mins until the prawns have changed colour. Tip into the bowl with the cucumber and toss to combine.

Banana & tahini porridge

Prep: 5 mins **Cook:** 5 mins

Serves 2

Ingredients

- 1 tbsp tahini
- 150ml milk of your choice, plus 1 tbsp
- 100g porridge oats
- 2 small bananas, sliced
- seeds from 2 cardamom pods, crushed
- 1 tbsp toasted sesame seeds

Method

STEP 1

Mix the tahini with 1 tbsp milk and 1 tbsp water. Put the oats, 1 sliced banana, cardamom, 100ml milk and 300ml water in a pan with a pinch of salt. Cook over a medium heat for 5 mins, stirring, until creamy and hot.

STEP 2

Divide between two bowls. Pour over the remaining milk, then top with the remaining sliced banana. Drizzle over the tahini mixture and sprinkle over the toasted sesame seeds.

Bombay lamb wraps

Prep: 5 mins **Cook:** 50 mins

Serves 4

Ingredients

- 1 tbsp vegetable oil
- 1 large red onion , chopped
- 3 fat garlic cloves , crushed
- 200g frozen lamb mince
- 3 tbsp curry paste (we used tikka)
- 400g can chopped tomatoes
- 2 large potatoes , cut into 2cm/0.75in cubes
- 250g frozen peas
- 8 flour wraps or chapatis , warmed
- 140g natural yogurt

Method

STEP 1

Heat the oil in a large pan, add the onion and cook for a few mins to soften. Add the garlic, stir for 1 min, then add the frozen mince. Cook until defrosted and nicely browned, then stir in the curry paste, tomatoes, potatoes and half a can of water. Season well, then cover with a lid and simmer for 20 mins or until the potatoes are nearly cooked.

STEP 2

Remove the lid and simmer for a further 10-15 mins until the liquid has reduced and the sauce clings to the potatoes and mince. Add the peas, stir through until defrosted, then serve with the warm wraps and yogurt.

Creamy leek & bean soup

Prep: 10 mins **Cook:** 20 mins

Serves 4

Ingredients

- 1 tbsp rapeseed oil
- 600g leeks , well washed and thinly sliced
- 1l hot vegetable bouillon
- 2 x 400g cans cannellini beans , drained
- 2 large garlic cloves , finely grated
- 100g baby spinach
- 150ml full-fat milk

Method

STEP 1

Heat the oil in a large pan, add the leeks and cook on a low-medium heat for 5 mins. Pour in the bouillon, tip in the beans, cover and simmer for 10 mins.

STEP 2

Stir in the garlic and spinach, cover the pan and cook for 5 mins more until the spinach has wilted but still retains its fresh green colour.

STEP 3

Add the milk and plenty of pepper, and blitz with a stick blender until smooth. Ladle into bowls and chill the remainder.

Chicken and mushrooms

Prep: 15 mins **Cook:** 25 mins

Serves 4

Ingredients

- 2 tbsp olive oil
- 500g boneless, skinless chicken thigh
- flour, for dusting
- 50g cubetti di pancetta
- 300g small button mushroom
- 2 large shallots, chopped
- 250ml chicken stock
- 1 tbsp white wine vinegar
- 50g frozen pea
- small handful parsley, finely chopped

Method

STEP 1

Heat 1 tbsp oil in a frying pan. Season and dust the chicken with flour, brown on all sides. Remove. Fry the pancetta and mushrooms until softened, then remove.

STEP 2

Add the final tbsp oil and cook shallots for 5 mins. Add the stock and vinegar, bubble for 1-2 mins. Return the chicken, pancetta and mushrooms and cook for 15 mins. Add the peas and parsley and cook for 2 mins more, then serve.

Spicy 'vedgeree'

Prep: 10 mins **Cook:** 1 hr and 10 mins

Serves 4

Ingredients

- 350g long grain brown rice
- 150g green beans, trimmed and halved
- 4 medium eggs
- 2 tbsp rapeseed oil
- 2 onions, sliced
- 2 garlic cloves, crushed
- 2 heaped tbsp medium curry powder
- 1 tsp ground turmeric
- 2 bay leaves
- 200g spinach
- 100g cherry tomatoes, halved
- ½ small bunch coriander, chopped
- 1 green chilli, sliced
- 1 lemon, cut into wedges

Method

STEP 1

Rinse the rice under cold running water, rubbing with your fingers to remove any excess starch. Cook following pack instructions, then drain well.

STEP 2

Bring another pan of water to a simmer. Cook the green beans for 2 mins, then transfer to a bowl with a slotted spoon and set aside. Boil the eggs in the pan for 7 mins, then drain and transfer to a bowl of cold water to cool.

STEP 3

Meanwhile, heat the oil in a large frying pan over a medium heat. Fry the onions for 10-15 mins until golden. Add the garlic, curry powder, turmeric and bay leaves and cook for 1 min more. Stir in the spinach, tomatoes and a splash of water and cook for another 5 mins until the spinach has wilted.

STEP 4

Fold the cooked rice and green beans through the spinach mixture and cook for a few minutes until the rice is warmed through. Drain and gently peel the eggs, then slice in half.

STEP 5

Top the rice mixture with the eggs, coriander and chilli. Serve the vedgeree with the lemon wedges on the side for squeezing over.

Creamy mustard mushrooms on toast with a glass of juice

Prep: 5 mins **Cook:** 5 mins

Serves 1

Ingredients

- 1 slice wholemeal bread
- 1 ½ tbsp light cream cheese
- 1 tsp rapeseed oil
- 3 handfuls sliced, small flat mushrooms
- 2 tbsp skimmed milk
- ¼ tsp wholegrain mustard
- 1 tbsp snipped chives
- 150ml orange juice freshly squeezed or from a carton

Method

STEP 1

Toast the bread, then spread with a little of the cheese (don't use butter).

STEP 2

Meanwhile, heat the oil in a non-stick pan and cook the mushrooms, stirring frequently, until softened. Spoon in the milk, remaining cheese and the mustard. Stir well until coated. Tip onto the toast, top with chives and serve with the juice.

Spicy meatball tagine with bulgur & chickpeas

Prep: 10 mins **Cook:** 45 mins plus chilling

Serves 4

Ingredients

- 2 onions, 1 quartered, 1 halved and sliced
- 2 tbsp tomato purée
- 2 garlic cloves
- 1 egg
- 1 tbsp chilli powder
- 500g pack extra-lean beef mince
- 2 tsp rapeseed oil
- 4 large carrots, cut into batons
- 1 tsp ground cumin
- 2 tsp ground coriander
- 400g can chopped tomatoes

- 1 lemon, zest removed with a potato peeler, then chopped
- 12 Kalamata olives, chopped

For the bulgur

- 200g bulgur wheat
- 400g can chickpeas
- 1 tbsp vegetable bouillon powder
- ⅓ pack fresh coriander, chopped
- 2 tsp vegetable bouillon powder
- 2 tsp ground coriander

Method

STEP 1

Put the quartered onion in the food processor and process to finely chop it. Add the minced beef, 1 tbsp tomato purée, the garlic, egg and chilli powder and blitz to make a smoothish paste. Divide the mixture into 26 even-sized pieces and roll into balls.

STEP 2

Heat the oil in a large frying pan and cook the meatballs for about 5-10 mins to lightly brown them. Tip from the pan onto a plate.

STEP 3

Now add the sliced onion and carrots to the pan and stir fry briefly in the pan juices to soften them a little. Add the spices and pour in the tomatoes with 1 ½ cans of water then stir in the chopped lemon zest, remaining tomato purée, olives and bouillon powder. Return the meatballs to the pan then cover and cook for 15 mins until the carrots are just tender. Stir in the coriander.

STEP 4

While the tagine is cooking, tip the bulgur into a pan with the chickpeas and water from the can. Add 2 cans of water, the bouillon and coriander. Cover and cook for 10 mins until the bulgur is tender and the liquid had been absorbed. If you're doing the Healthy Diet Plan (serving two people), serve half with half of the tagine and chill the remainder for another night if you like.

Curried pork bulgur salad

Prep: 5 mins **Cook:** 8 mins

Serves 2

Ingredients

- 50g bulgur wheat
- 1 tsp Madras curry powder
- ¼ tsp cumin seeds (optional)
- 1 tsp vegetable bouillon
- 2 medjool dates, sliced
- 3 spring onions, sliced
- 4 tsp chopped mint
- handful coriander, chopped
- ¼ cucumber, diced
- 2 tomatoes, cut into wedges
- 120g leftover cooked pork, chopped
- ½ lemon, cut into wedges

Method

STEP 1

Tip the bulgur into a small pan with the curry powder, cumin seeds (if using), bouillon, dates and spring onions. Pour over 300ml boiling water and cook, covered, for 5-8 mins or until the liquid has been absorbed and the bulgur is tender. Leave to cool completely.

STEP 2

Stir in the mint, coriander, cucumber, tomatoes and pork. Spoon into containers and top with lemon wedges to squeeze over and mix through just before eating. Will keep for two-three days in the fridge.

Brown rice tabbouleh with eggs & parsley

Prep: 10 mins **Cook:** 20 mins

Serves 2

Ingredients

- 75g brown basmati rice
- fresh thyme, a sprig
- 160g celery, chopped
- 2 large eggs
- 1 tsp vegetable bouillon
- 1 small lemon, zest and juice
- 1 small red onion, finely chopped
- 3 tbsp parsley, chopped
- 1/2 pomegranate, seeds only

Method

STEP 1

Simmer the rice with the thyme and celery for 20 mins until tender. Meanwhile, boil the eggs for 7 mins, then cool in cold water and carefully peel off the shell.

STEP 2

Drain the rice and tip into a bowl. Add the bouillon, lemon zest and juice, and red onion, then stir well and scatter over the parsley and pomegranate. Spoon onto plates or into lunchboxes, then halve or quarter the eggs and arrange on top.

Lean turkey burger with sweet potato wedges

Prep: 15 mins **Cook:** 25 mins

Serves 2

Ingredients

- 1 large sweet potato (about 190g), cut into wedges
- 260g turkey breast mince (under 5% fat)
- 1 small red onion, diced
- 1 garlic clove, grated
- 1 large egg, beaten
- 1 apple (about 70g), peeled and grated
- 2 tsp dried oregano
- 1 tsp paprika
- 15g coconut oil
- 135g green vegetables (spinach, kale, broccoli, mangetout or green beans)

Method

STEP 1

Heat oven to 180C/160C fan/gas 4. Zap the sweet potato wedges in the microwave for about 6 mins on full power until just turning soft. Leave to rest for 30 secs.

STEP 2

While the sweet potato is spinning in the microwave, mix the mince in a bowl with the onion, garlic, egg and apple. Get your hands stuck in and work the ingredients together with a good pinch of salt and pepper, the oregano and paprika. Shape the mixture into two burgers about 3cm thick. Place on a baking tray in the oven for 15-20 mins until cooked through.

STEP 3

Heat the coconut oil in a large frying pan over a high heat. Add the sweet potato wedges and shallow-fry for about 3 mins each side until they are nicely browned all over and cooked through to the centre. (Alternatively, toss in the oil and roast in the oven for 15-20 mins.) Drain on kitchen paper, then season with a good pinch of salt.

STEP 4

Serve the burgers with the sweet potato wedges and a portion of green veg either steamed, blanched or boiled.

Broccoli pasta salad with eggs & sunflower seeds

Prep: 10 mins **Cook:** 10 mins

Serves 2

Ingredients

- 2 large eggs
- 75g wholewheat penne
- 160g broccoli florets
- 160g fine beans, trimmed and halved
- 1 tbsp white miso paste
- 1 tsp grated ginger
- 1 tbsp rapeseed oil
- 2 tbsp sunflower seeds

Method

STEP 1

Hard-boil the eggs for 8 mins, then shell and halve. Meanwhile, boil the pasta for 5 mins, add the broccoli and beans, and cook 5 mins more or until everything is tender.

STEP 2

Drain, reserving the water, then tip the pasta and veg into a bowl and stir in the miso, ginger, oil and 4 tbsp pasta water. Serve topped with the eggs and seeds.

Vegan bolognese

Prep: 20 mins **Cook:** 1 hr

Serves 3

Ingredients

- 15g dried porcini mushrooms
- 1 ½ tbsp olive oil
- ½ onion, finely chopped
- 1 carrot, finely chopped
- 1 celery stick, finely chopped
- 2 garlic cloves, sliced
- 2 thyme sprigs
- ½ tsp tomato purée

- 50ml vegan red wine (optional)
- 125g dried green lentils
- 400g can whole plum tomatoes
- 125g chestnut mushrooms, chopped
- 125g portobello mushrooms, sliced
- ½ tsp soy sauce
- ½ tsp Marmite
- 270g spaghetti
- handful fresh basil leaves

Method

STEP 1

Pour 400ml boiling water over the dried porcini and leave for 10 mins until hydrated. Meanwhile pour 1 tbsp oil into a large saucepan. Add the onion, carrot, celery and a pinch of salt. Cook gently, stirring for 10 mins until soft. Remove the porcini from the liquid, keeping the mushroomy stock and roughly chop. Set both aside.

STEP 2

Add the garlic and thyme to the pan. Cook for 1 min then stir in the tomato purée and cook for a min more. Pour in the red wine, if using, cook until nearly reduced, then add the lentils, reserved mushroom stock and tomatoes. Bring to the boil, then reduce the heat and leave to simmer with a lid on.

STEP 3

Meanwhile, heat a large frying pan. Add the remaining oil, then tip in the chestnut, portobello and rehydrated mushrooms. Fry until all the water has evaporated and the mushrooms are deep golden brown. Pour in the soy sauce. Give everything a good mix, then scrape the mushrooms into the lentil mixture.

STEP 4

Stir in the Marmite and continue to cook the ragu, stirring occasionally, over a low-medium heat for 30-45 mins until the lentils are cooked and the sauce is thick and reduced, adding extra water if necessary. Remove the thyme sprigs and season to taste.

STEP 5

Cook the spaghetti in a large pan of salted water for 1 min less than packet instructions. Drain the pasta, reserving a ladleful of pasta water, then toss the spaghetti in the sauce, using a little of the starchy liquid to loosen up the ragu slightly so that the pasta clings to the sauce. Serve topped with fresh basil and some black pepper.

Sweet potato, coconut & lemongrass soup with coriander sambal

Prep: 15 mins **Cook:** 30 mins

Serves 4

Ingredients

- 2 tbsp groundnut oil
- 4 spring onions , sliced
- 2 large garlic cloves , sliced
- 2 lemongrass stalks , outer leaves removed and stalk finely chopped
- finger-sized piece ginger , sliced
- 900g sweet potatoes , peeled and chopped into small pieces
- 215ml coconut milk
- 285ml vegetable stock (we used Bouillon)
- 1 green chilli , deseeded
- 1 tsp caster sugar
- 2 limes , juiced
- 1 small pack coriander

Method

STEP 1

Heat the oil in a large pan, then add the spring onions, garlic, lemongrass and three-quarters of the ginger and cook for 2 mins until aromatic, then tip in the sweet potato. Give everything a good mix so the sweet potato is well coated, then add the coconut milk, stock and 500ml water. Bring to the boil, then simmer for around 25 mins until the sweet potato is cooked through.

STEP 2

Meanwhile, tip the remaining ginger, the chilli, sugar, three-quarters of the lime juice and most of the coriander (reserving a few leaves for a garnish) into a food processor and blitz until smooth. Transfer the sambal to a small jug and set aside.

STEP 3

Blitz the soup with a hand blender until smooth, then season to taste with the remaining lime juice and some salt and pepper. Divide the soup between bowls and top with the coriander sambal. Garnish with the reserved coriander leaves.

Beetroot latkes

Prep: 25 mins **Cook:** 20 mins

Serves 2

Ingredients

- 1 tbsp rapeseed oil
- 4 tbsp fat-free Greek yogurt
- ½ small bunch mint leaves, finely chopped

For the latkes

- 400g raw beetroot, peeled, trimmed and coarsely grated
- 1 large egg, beaten
- 1 tbsp plain flour
- 150g mixed rocket salad leaves
- 130g cherry tomatoes, halved
- 1 large garlic clove, grated
- 1 tsp caraway seeds
- ½ tsp ground cumin
- 1 lemon, zested

Method

STEP 1

Heat the oven to 180C/160C fan/gas 4. Make the latkes by combining all of the ingredients.

STEP 2

Heat the oil in a large non-stick pan. Spoon in the mixture to make six round latkes. Fry for 4-5 mins on each side, then transfer to a baking sheet and bake for 10 mins.

STEP 3

Combine the yogurt and mint in a small bowl. Toss the salad leaves and tomatoes together, then serve the latkes with the mint yogurt and salad.

Baked piri-piri tilapia with crushed potatoes

Prep: 10 mins **Cook:** 25 mins

Serves 4

Ingredients

- 600g small new potatoes
- 2 red peppers, cut into chunky pieces
- 1 tbsp red wine vinegar

For the piri-piri sauce

- 6 hot pickled peppers (I used Peppadew)
- 1 tsp chilli flakes
- 2 garlic cloves
- drizzle of extra virgin olive oil
- 4 large pieces tilapia or cod
- green salad, to serve

- juice and zest 1 lemon
- 1 tbsp red wine vinegar
- 2 tbsp extra virgin olive oil
- 1 tbsp smoked paprika

Method

STEP 1

Heat oven to 220C/200C fan/gas 7. Boil the potatoes until knife-tender, then drain. Spread out on a large baking tray and gently crush with the back of a spatula. Add the peppers, drizzle with the vinegar and oil, season well and roast for 25 mins.

STEP 2

Put the piri-piri ingredients in a food processor with some salt. Purée until fine, then pour into a bowl. Put the fish on a baking tray and spoon over some of the piri-piri sauce. Season and bake for the final 10 mins of the potatoes' cooking time. Serve everything with the extra sauce and a green salad on the side.

Lighter aubergine Parmigiana

Prep: 35 mins **Cook:** 55 mins

Serves 4

Ingredients

- 2 tbsp rapeseed oil , plus 1 tsp
- 2 tbsp lemon juice
- 3 aubergines (750g/1lb 10oz total weight), stalk ends trimmed, cut into 1cm/1/2in lengthways slices
- 1 small onion , chopped
- 3 garlic cloves , finely chopped
- 400g can plum tomatoes
- 225g can plum tomatoes
- 1 tbsp tomato purée
- 2 tbsp chopped fresh oregano
- 100g ricotta
- 50g mozzarella , torn into small pieces
- handful basil leaves , roughly torn

- 2 medium tomatoes, sliced
- 25g vegetarian-style parmesan, grated

Method

STEP 1

Heat oven to 200C/180C fan/gas 6. Measure the 2 tbsp of oil into a small bowl. Brush just a little of it onto 2 large, non- stick baking sheets (if you only have 1 tray, bake the aubergines in batches). Mix the lemon juice into the measured oil. Lay the aubergine slices snugly in a single layer on the baking sheets, brush the tops with half the oil and lemon, season with pepper and bake for 20 mins. Turn the slices over, give the remaining oil and lemon mixture a good stir as it will have separated, and brush it over again. Season with pepper and bake for 10-15 mins more or until softened.

STEP 2

Meanwhile, heat the remaining 1 tsp oil in a medium saucepan. Add the onion and garlic and fry for 3-4 mins, stirring often, until the onion is softened and starting to brown. Tip in the cans of tomatoes, stir to break them up, then mix in the purée, pepper and a pinch of salt. Simmer uncovered for about 10-12 mins until thickened and saucy, then stir in the oregano.

STEP 3

Spread a little of the tomato sauce in the bottom of a shallow ovenproof dish (about 25 x 20 x 5cm). Start by laying a third of the aubergine slices widthways across the dish, spread over a third of the remaining sauce and put half the ricotta on top in small spoonfuls, then half the mozzarella. Scatter over half the torn basil and season well with pepper. Repeat the layering of aubergine slices, tomato sauce, ricotta, mozzarella and basil, and finish with the final aubergine slices, the sliced tomatoes and the last of the sauce. Season with pepper and scatter over the Parmesan. Bake for about 20 mins, or until the cheese is golden and the juices are bubbling.

Peruvian toasted sweetcorn, avocado & quinoa salad

Prep: 10 mins **Cook:** 20 mins

Serves 2

Ingredients

- 75g uncooked quinoa
- 140g frozen sweetcorn
- 1 tbsp extra-virgin olive oil
- 75g cherry tomatoes , quartered
- 1 small pack coriander , leaves roughly chopped
- 2 spring onions , trimmed and finely sliced
- finely grated zest and juice 1 lime
- 1/2 long red chilli , finely chopped (deseeded if you don't like it too hot)
- 1 ripe but firm avocado
- 25g mixed nuts , such as brazils, almonds, hazelnuts, pecans and walnuts

Method

STEP 1

Half fill a medium pan with water and bring to the boil. Rinse the quinoa in a fine sieve then add to the water, stir well and simmer for about 12 mins or until just tender.

STEP 2

While the quinoa is cooking, put the sweetcorn in a dry frying pan and place over a medium-high heat. Cook for 5-6 mins, turning every now and then until lightly toasted. Set aside.

STEP 3

Rinse the cooked quinoa in a sieve under cold water, then press hard with a ladle or serving spoon to remove as much of the excess water as possible.

STEP 4

Tip the quinoa into a bowl and toss with the olive oil, sweetcorn, tomatoes, coriander, spring onions, lime zest and chilli. Season well with black pepper.

STEP 5

Halve and stone the avocado. Scoop out the flesh with a large metal spoon and cut into slices. Toss with the lime juice. Add the avocado and nuts to the salad and toss gently together before serving.

Egg & rocket pizzas

Prep: 10 mins **Cook:** 15 mins - 20 mins

Serves 2

Ingredients

- 2 seeded wraps
- a little olive oil , for brushing
- 1 roasted red pepper , from a jar
- 2 tomatoes
- 2 tbsp tomato purée
- 1 tbsp chopped dill
- 2 tbsp chopped parsley
- 2 eggs
- 65g pack rocket
- ½ red onion , very thinly sliced

Method

STEP 1

Heat oven to 200C/180C fan/gas 6. Lay the tortillas on two baking sheets, brush sparingly with the oil then bake for 3 mins. Meanwhile chop the pepper and tomatoes and mix with the tomato purée, seasoning and herbs. Turn the tortillas over and spread with the tomato mixture, leaving the centre free from any large pieces of pepper or tomato.

STEP 2

Break an egg into the centre then return to the oven for 10 mins or until the egg is just set and the tortilla is crispy round the edges. Serve scattered with the rocket and onion.

Apple & penne slaw with walnuts

Prep: 15 mins **Cook:** 12 mins

Serves 4

Ingredients

- 200g wholemeal penne
- 2 x 150g pots bio yogurt
- 4 tsp sherry vinegar
- 2 tsp English mustard powder
- 4 spring onions , finely chopped
- 6 celery sticks (320g), finely chopped
- 400g and 210g cans chickpeas , drained
- 30g raisins
- 2 apples
- 12 walnut halves (35g), broken up
- 8 crisp lettuce leaves from an iceberg lettuce

Method

STEP 1

Boil the penne for 12 mins until al dente. Meanwhile, make a dressing by mixing the yogurt with the vinegar, mustard and spring onions.

STEP 2

Add the celery, penne, chickpeas and raisins to the dressing and stir until everything is well coated. If you're following our Healthy Diet Plan, chop 1 apple and add to half the salad with half the nuts and serve with half of the crisp lettuce leaves, either as a base or as wraps. Chill the remainder for up to three days, then add the apple, nuts and lettuce on the day you're eating it. If you do it ahead, the nuts will soften and the apples will turn brown.

Butternut & bacon fusilli

Prep: 10 mins **Cook:** 50 mins

Serves 4

Ingredients

- ½ x 160g pack pancetta di cubetti
- 1 ½ tbsp olive oil
- 750g butternut squash , deseeded and cut into 2cm cubes
- 2 rosemary sprigs, leaves finely chopped
- ¼ tsp chilli flakes
- 3 garlic cloves , finely chopped
- 350g fusilli bucati (or fusilli)
- 100g young leaf spinach , roughly chopped
- grated parmesan , to serve

Method

STEP 1

Tip the pancetta into a large frying pan set over a medium heat and cook for 5-8 mins until really crisp. Remove using a slotted spoon, leaving the fat in the pan. Add the oil to the pan, along with the squash, rosemary, chilli and garlic. Cover and cook for 25 mins, stirring now and then, until the squash is tender. Season well, and gently crush some of the butternut squash with the back of a spoon.

STEP 2

Bring a large pan of salted water to the boil 15 mins before the squash is ready, and cook the pasta following pack instructions. Drain, reserving the cooking water. Add 1-2 ladles of pasta water to the squash and let it bubble for a few mins. Tip in the drained pasta and toss together. Stir through the spinach, then divide between plates. Sprinkle over the pancetta, some grated Parmesan and a good grinding of black pepper.

Prawn fried rice

Prep: 5 mins **Cook:** 25 mins

Serves 4

Ingredients

- 250g long-grain brown rice
- 150g frozen peas
- 100g mangetout
- 1½ tbsp rapeseed oil
- 1 onion , finely chopped
- 2 garlic cloves , crushed
- thumb-sized piece of ginger , finely grated
- 150g raw king prawns
- 3 medium eggs , beaten
- 2 tsp sesame seeds
- 1 tbsp low-salt soy sauce
- ½ tbsp rice or white wine vinegar
- 4 spring onions , trimmed and sliced

Method

STEP 1

Cook the rice following pack instructions. Boil a separate pan of water and blanch the peas and mangetout for 1 min, then drain and set aside with the rice.

STEP 2

Meanwhile, heat the oil in a large non-stick frying pan or wok over a medium heat and fry the onion for 10 mins or until golden brown. Add the garlic and ginger and fry for a further minute. Tip in the blanched vegetables and fry for 5 mins, then the prawns and fry for a further 2 mins. Stir the rice into the pan then push everything to one side. Pour the beaten eggs into the empty side of the pan and stir to scramble them. Fold everything together with the sesame seeds, soy and vinegar, then finish with the spring onions scattered over.

Avocado & bean triangles

Prep: 5 mins No cook

Serves 2

Ingredients

- 3 triangluar bread thins
- 210g can red kidney beans , drained
- 1 tbsp finely chopped dill , plus extra for garnish
- 1/2 lemon , for squeezing
- 1 tomato , chopped
- 1 small avocado
- 1 small red onion , finely chopped

Method

STEP 1

Follow our triangular bread thins recipe to make your own. While they bake, roughly mash the beans with the dill and a good squeeze of lemon then stir in the tomato.

STEP 2

Cut the bread triangles in half and top with the beans. Scoop the avocado into a bowl and roughly mash with a squeeze more lemon. Spoon the avocado onto the beans, scatter over the chopped onion, then garnish with the remaining dill.

White velvet soup with smoky almonds

Prep: 10 mins **Cook:** 25 mins

Serves 2

Ingredients

- 2 tsp rapeseed oil
- 2 large garlic cloves , sliced
- 2 leeks , trimmed so they're mostly white in colour, washed well, then sliced (about 240g)
- 200g cauliflower , chopped
- 2 tsp vegetable bouillon powder
- 400g cannellini beans , rinsed
- fresh nutmeg , for grating
- 100ml whole milk
- 25g whole almonds , chopped
- ½ tsp smoked paprika
- 2 x 25g slices rye bread , to serve

Method

STEP 1

Heat the oil in a large pan. Add the garlic, leeks and cauliflower and cook for about 5 mins, stirring frequently, until starting to soften (but not colouring).

STEP 2

Stir in the vegetable bouillon and beans, pour in 600ml boiling water and add a few generous gratings of the nutmeg. Cover and leave to simmer for 15 mins until the leeks and cauliflower are tender. Add the milk and blitz with a hand blender until smooth and creamy.

STEP 3

Put the almonds in a dry pan and cook very gently for 1 min, or until toasted, then remove from the heat. Scatter the paprika over the almonds and mix well. Ladle the soup into bowls, top with the spicy nuts and serve with the rye bread.

Summer pistou

Prep: 10 mins **Cook:** 25 mins

Serves 4

Ingredients

- 1 tbsp rapeseed oil
- 2 leeks, finely sliced
- 1 large courgette, finely diced
- 1l boiling vegetable stock (made from scratch or with reduced-salt bouillon)
- 400g can cannellini or haricot beans, drained
- 200g green beans, chopped
- 3 tomatoes, chopped
- 3 garlic cloves, finely chopped
- small pack basil
- 40g freshly grated parmesan

Method

STEP 1

Heat the oil in a large pan and fry the leeks and courgette for 5 mins to soften. Pour in the stock, add three-quarters of the haricot beans with the green beans, half the tomatoes, and simmer for 5-8 mins until the vegetables are tender.

STEP 2

Meanwhile, blitz the remaining beans and tomatoes, the garlic and basil in a food processor (or in a bowl with a stick blender) until smooth, then stir in the Parmesan. Stir the sauce into the soup, cook for 1 min, then ladle half into bowls or pour into a flask for a packed lunch. Chill the remainder. Will keep for a couple of days.

Chicken with rice & peas

Prep: 15 mins **Cook:** 30 mins

Serves 4

Ingredients

- 1 tbsp rapeseed oil
- 2 red onions , halved and sliced
- 4 chicken legs (about 1 kg in total), skin removed
- 1 tbsp fresh thyme leaves
- 1 tbsp Madras curry powder
- 1 tsp ground allspice
- 4 large tomatoes , chopped
- 1 red chilli , deseeded and sliced
- 2 garlic cloves , chopped
- 2 tsp vegetable bouillon

For the rice & peas

- 125g brown basmati
- 1 red onion , chopped
- 2 garlic cloves , chopped
- 1 tbsp fresh thyme leaves , plus extra to serve
- 1 tsp vegetable bouillon
- 400g can black-eyed beans

Method

STEP 1

Heat the oil in a very large non-stick frying pan and cook the onions for 5 mins or until soft. Meanwhile, coat the chicken thoroughly with the thyme, curry powder and allspice. Add to the pan and briefly brown the chicken, then tip in the tomatoes, chilli, garlic and bouillon. Pour over 450ml water, cover and simmer for 30 mins or until the chicken is tender.

STEP 2

Meanwhile, tip the rice into a medium-sized pan with the onion, garlic, thyme and bouillon. Pour in 600ml water, cover and cook for 25 mins or until the liquid has been absorbed and the rice is tender. Check toward the end of the cooking time to ensure it isn't starting to catch on the pan. Stir in the beans and heat through. If you're following our Healthy Diet Plan, serve half the rice with half the chicken (saving the leftovers for a second meal later in the week). Otherwise you can serve four portions, scattered with a few extra thyme leaves, if you like.

Chargrilled chicken & kale Caesar salad

Prep: 20 mins **Cook:** 20 mins

Serves 4

Ingredients

- 1 anchovy
- 1 garlic clove
- 1 tsp Dijon mustard
- 100ml buttermilk
- 1 lemon , zested and juiced
- 200g bag kale , large tough stalks removed
- 200g defrosted frozen peas
- 6 skinless and boneless chicken thighs
- 2 thick slices crusty bread
- 3 tbsp cold pressed rapeseed oil
- 400g long-stem broccoli , cut in half lengthways
- 30g parmesan

Method

STEP 1

Mash the anchovy and garlic together using a pestle and mortar, then tip the mixture into a bowl and whisk in the mustard, buttermilk, lemon zest and juice, and season with black pepper. Put the kale and peas in a large bowl, pour over ¾ of the dressing, then massage into the kale so each leaf is coated.

STEP 2

Put the chicken thighs between two pieces of baking parchment, then bash out with a rolling pin to 1cm thickness.

STEP 3

Heat a griddle pan until searing hot. Brush the bread slices with a little oil, then griddle until lightly charred on all sides. Set aside.

STEP 4

Next, season the broccoli and brush the cut side of each piece with a little oil. Griddle, cut-side down, in batches for 3-4 mins until tender. Lastly, brush the remaining oil over the chicken thighs and season, then griddle the chicken for 3-4 mins on each side until cooked through.

STEP 5

Distribute the kale between four plates. Slice the chicken diagonally and break the bread into pieces. Top each of the plates with ¼ of the chicken, broccoli and croutons. Grate over the parmesan in large shavings and drizzle with the remaining dressing to serve.

Loaded baked potatoes with slaw

Prep: 20 mins **Cook:** 1 hr and 45 mins

Serves 4

Ingredients

- 4 baking potatoes (about 700g)
- 1 tbsp olive oil
- 30g butter
- 150g plain 0% fat yogurt, plus extra to serve
- 6 small spring onions, washed, outer layer removed and finely sliced
- 200g can no added sugar sweetcorn, drained
- 150g reduced-fat strong cheddar, grated
- small bunch chives, finely chopped

For the healthy coleslaw

- 125g plain 0% fat yogurt
- ½ tsp wholegrain mustard
- ½ small white cabbage, about 400g
- 2 medium carrots, about 150g
- 1 small red onion

Method

STEP 1

Heat oven to 180C/160C fan/gas 4. Wash and pierce the skins of the potatoes a few times with a sharp knife. Rub the skin with a little olive oil and bake for 1 hr 30 mins until soft inside and crisp on the outside.

STEP 2

Meanwhile, make the coleslaw. Mix the yogurt and mustard together in a bowl. Then, use a grating attachment on a food processor, or a box grater, to grate the cabbage and carrots. Either grate the onion or chop as finely as you can. Tip all of the vegetables into the bowl and stir through the yogurt and mustard.

STEP 3

Once the potatoes are crisp on the outside and soft inside, remove from the oven and cut in half. Scoop out the flesh and mash with the butter and yogurt, stir in the spring onion and sweetcorn and most of the cheese, reserving a little of the cheese for topping. Season if needed.

STEP 4

Turn the oven up to 200C/180C fan/gas 6. Load the filling back into the crisp potato skins, top with the remaining cheese and put them back in the oven on a baking sheet for about 10-15 mins, or until the cheese is melted and the edges are browning. To serve, sprinkle with chives and serve alongside the coleslaw with a dollop of natural yogurt.

Potato pancakes with chard & eggs

Prep: 10 mins **Cook:** 15 mins

Serves 2

Ingredients

- 300g mashed potato
- 4 spring onions , very finely chopped
- 25g plain wholemeal flour
- ½ tsp baking powder
- 3 eggs
- 2 tsp rapeseed oil
- 240g chard , stalks and leaves roughly chopped, or baby spinach, chopped

Method

STEP 1

Mix the mash, spring onions, flour, baking powder and 1 of the eggs in a bowl. Heat the oil in a non-stick frying pan, then spoon in the potato mix to make two mounds. Flatten them to form two 15cm discs and fry for 5-8 mins until the undersides are set and golden, then carefully ip over and cook on the other side.

STEP 2

Meanwhile, wash the chard and put in a pan with some of the water still clinging to it, then cover and cook over a medium heat for 5 mins until wilted and tender. Poach the remaining eggs.

STEP 3

Top the pancakes with the greens and egg. Serve while the yolks are still runny.

Garden salmon salad

Prep: 15 mins No cook

Serves 4

Ingredients

- 2 courgettes
- 100g fresh shelled peas
- 8 radishes , halved
- 3 tbsp rapeseed oil
- 1 large lemon , zested and juiced
- 2 tbsp fat-free natural yogurt
- 75g pea shoots
- 4 poached salmon fillets, skin removed and flaked into large chunks
- 2 tbsp mixed seeds
- 1/2 small bunch dill , fronds picked

Method

STEP 1

Cut the courgettes into long thin strips using a peeler, and discard the soft, seeded core. Toss the courgette ribbons, peas and radishes together in a large bowl. Whisk the oil, lemon zest and juice, and yogurt together, then toss with the veg.

STEP 2

Put the pea shoots, dressed veg and large flakes of salmon on a large platter. Finish with a good grinding of black pepper, and scatter over the mixed seeds and dill to serve.

Lighter vegetable lasagne

Prep: 40 mins - 45 mins **Cook:** 1 hr and 15 mins

Serves 4

Ingredients

For the roast vegetables

- 1 small aubergine , about 250g, cut into approx 3cm chunks
- 1 medium courgette , about 200g, cut into 2-3cm chunks
- 1 red pepper , deseeded and chopped into 2.5cm pieces
- 1 medium onion , halved lengthways, sliced into thin wedges
- pinch of chilli flakes
- 1 tbsp rapeseed oil

For the tomato sauce

- 400g can plum tomatoes
- 1 medium carrot , chopped into small dice
- 3 garlic cloves , finely chopped
- 2 tbsp tomato purée (or sundried tomato purée – see tip)
- 400g can green lentils (with no added salt), drained
- 2 tbsp chopped basil , plus extra leaves to garnish

For the other layers

- 300g fresh spinach
- 1 medium egg
- 250g tub ricotta
- 1 rounded tbsp chopped oregano , plus extra leaves to garnish
- good pinch of ground nutmeg
- 9 dried lasagne sheets, each 17.5cm x 8cm
- 125g ball mozzarella , roughly chopped
- 25g parmesan or vegetarian alternative, grated
- 100g cherry tomatoes on the vine

To serve

- green salad

Method

STEP 1

Heat oven to 220C/200C fan/gas 7. Put the aubergine, courgette, pepper and onion in a large, shallow roasting tin. Scatter with the chilli flakes and season with pepper and a pinch of salt. Pour the oil over, toss together to coat (you can use your hands for this), then spread the vegetables out in a single layer. Roast for 15 mins, then give them a stir and spread them out again. Roast for another 10-15 mins until softened and turning golden.

STEP 2

While the vegetables are roasting, make the tomato sauce. Tip the tomatoes into a medium pan, then pour 100ml water into the empty can, swirl it round and pour into the saucepan. Add the carrot and garlic, and simmer gently for 20-25 mins, partly covered with the lid and stirring occasionally, until the carrot is just tender. Stir in the tomato purée and the lentils, season with pepper and simmer for 2 mins more. Remove from the heat, stir in the basil and set aside.

STEP 3

Tip the spinach into a large heatproof bowl, pour over boiling water, press the leaves into the water and leave for 30 secs. Drain in a large colander and rinse under cold water briefly to cool it down quickly. Squeeze the spinach to remove the excess water, then roughly chop. Beat the egg in a bowl and stir in the ricotta, oregano, nutmeg and some pepper.

STEP 4

Lay the lasagne sheets, spread well out, in a large shallow roasting tin and pour boiling water over to cover. Move them around with a wooden spoon to make sure they aren't sticking, then leave for 5 mins. ('No pre-cook' lasagne sheets benefit from a brief soaking, which improves the texture and makes them more pliable for layering in the dish.) Drain well and immediately separate them out to prevent them sticking.

STEP 5

When the vegetables have finished roasting, lower the heat to 200C/180C fan/ gas 6. Spread a very thin layer of the tomato sauce (about 2 big spoonfuls) over the bottom of an ovenproof dish, about 25 x 18 x 7cm deep and 2 litres capacity. Lay 3 lasagne sheets across the width of the dish and spread over half of the remaining sauce and half of the roasted vegetables. Cover with 3 more lasagne sheets, then spread the spinach over the top and season with pepper. Put the ricotta mixture on top in spoonfuls and spread out over the spinach. Cover with the last 3 lasagne sheets. Spread over the rest of the tomato sauce and then the remaining roasted vegetables. Scatter over the mozzarella and Parmesan to cover the vegetables and sauce as much as possible, then top with the cherry tomatoes. Season with pepper and lay a piece of foil loosely over the top. Can be made up to a day ahead and chilled – allow an extra few mins when baking the next day. Or freeze for up to 1 month and thaw overnight in the fridge.

STEP 6

Bake for 35 mins, then remove the foil and bake for a further 5-10 mins until everything is bubbling around the edges. Scatter with oregano and basil leaves, and serve with a green salad.

Zingy teriyaki beef skewers

Prep: 20 mins **Cook:** 25 mins plus marinating

Serves 2

Ingredients

- 1 tbsp tamari or soy sauce
- 3 tbsp freshly squeezed orange juice
- 15g chunk ginger , peeled and very finely grated
- 2 garlic cloves , crushed

For the salad

- 100g long-grain brown rice
- ⅓ cucumber , cut into small cubes
- 2 medium carrots , peeled and sliced into ribbons with a peeler
- 4 spring onions , trimmed and diagonally sliced
- 100g radishes , trimmed and sliced

- 1 tsp honey (preferably raw)
- ¼ tsp chilli flakes
- 300g beef sirloin steak , trimmed of hard fat and cut into long, thin strips

- 20g coriander , leaves roughly chopped, plus extra to garnish
- 10g mint leaves , plus extra to garnish
- 1 tbsp cold-pressed rapeseed oil
- zest and juice 1 lime
- 25g unsalted cashew nuts , toasted and roughly chopped

Method

STEP 1

Put the tamari, orange juice, ginger, garlic, honey and chilli flakes in a small saucepan with 100ml cold water and bring to the boil. Cook for 3-5 mins, boiling hard until well reduced, glossy and slightly syrupy. Remove from the heat, pour into a shallow dish and leave to cool.

STEP 2

Thread the beef onto 4 soaked wooden or metal skewers. Place in the marinade, turn and brush until well coated. Cover with cling film and marinate for 30 mins.

STEP 3

While the beef is marinating, prepare the salad. Half-fill a medium pan with water and bring to the boil. Cook the rice for about 20 mins or following pack instructions until tender. Rinse in a sieve under running water until cold, then drain well. Tip into a large bowl.

STEP 4

Add the cucumber, carrots, spring onions, radishes, coriander, mint, oil, lime zest and juice, and toss well together well. Season with a little black pepper. Divide between two plates and top with a sprinkling of nuts and extra herbs to garnish.

STEP 5

Heat the grill to high. (You could also cook the skewers on a non-stick griddle pan.) Put the skewers on a rack above a foil-lined baking tray, reserving any excess marinade. Grill the skewers close to the heat for 3-5 mins each side or until done to your liking. Brush with more marinade when they are turned. They should look sticky and glossy when cooked. Serve hot or cold with the rice salad.

Toasted soda bread with blue cheese & pear

Prep: 10 mins **Cook:** 2 mins

Serves 2

Ingredients

- 2 slices seeded wholemeal soda bread (see goes well with)
- 50g Danish blue cheese
- 2 tsp rapeseed oil
- 1 tsp apple cider vinegar
- pinch of English mustard powder
- 1 small garlic clove , finely grated
- 85g bag mixed leaf salad (choose one with curly endive and radicchio)
- 1 large or 2 small pears , halved, cored and sliced (no need to peel)
- 20g walnuts , roughly chopped

Method

STEP 1

Toast the bread while you make the dressing: mash 15g blue cheese with the oil, vinegar, mustard powder, garlic and 1 tbsp water.

STEP 2

Pile the salad leaves onto two plates. Spread the remaining cheese over the toast (it doesn't matter if it goes cold), top with the pear and scatter with the walnut pieces. Drizzle the dressing over the salad leaves and serve.

Harissa trout, beetroot & grapefruit salad with whipped feta

Prep: 20 mins **Cook:** 45 mins

Serves 2

Ingredients

- 300g raw beetroot , scrubbed, skin left on
- 30g feta
- 2 tbsp 0% fat natural yogurt
- 1 lemon , zested and juiced
- 2 tbsp quinoa (optional)
- 1 pink grapefruit
- 1 tbsp extra virgin olive oil
- 1 tbsp harissa
- 2 trout fillets
- 2 red chicory , separated into leaves
- ½ small pack dill , leaves picked

Method

STEP 1

Bring a saucepan of water to the boil. Season the water, drop in the beetroot and cover the pan with a lid. Cook for 30-45 mins, depending on their size, until a cutlery knife can be easily inserted into them.

STEP 2

Meanwhile, heat oven to 200C/180C fan/gas 6. Put the feta in a bowl and mash with a fork, then beat in the yogurt and season with the lemon juice and zest to taste. In a dry frying pan, toast the quinoa, if using, until it pops. Set both aside.

STEP 3

Segment the grapefruit over a bowl to catch the juices, squeezing out as much as possible. Put the segments to one side, then whisk the olive oil with the juice. Season to taste with lemon juice, salt and pepper. You want it to be really tangy, as all the acidity will be absorbed by the beets.

STEP 4

Rub the harissa over the trout, season, then roast in the oven for 8-10 mins until just cooked.

STEP 5

Drain the beetroot. Once cool enough to handle, peel off the skin – it should come away easily. Cut into segments, then put onto a salad plate along with the chicory leaves. Pour the dressing over the warm beets and toss together. Nestle in the grapefruit segments, trout, harissa and dill, then add dollops of the feta and scatter over the toasted quinoa, if using.

Spicy harissa chicken with lentils

Prep: 10 mins **Cook:** 45 mins

Serves 4

Ingredients

- 1 tbsp olive oil
- 1 red onion , chopped
- 1 garlic clove , crushed
- 50g harissa
- 500g chicken thigh , skin removed, boned and diced
- 1 medium carrot , grated
- 200g dried puy lentils
- 2 x 400g cans chopped tomatoes
- 1.2l stock , made from 1 chicken or vegetable stock cube
- flat-leaf parsley , to serve (optional)

Method

STEP 1

Heat the oil in a large frying pan. Fry the onion on a low heat for 5-6 mins until softened and translucent. Add the garlic and cook for 1 min more.

STEP 2

Stir in the harissa, add the chicken and cook until well browned all over. Stir in the carrot, lentils and tomatoes, then add the stock so the chicken is fully immersed.

STEP 3

Reduce the heat and cook, uncovered, for 30-35 mins until the chicken is thoroughly cooked, and the lentils are tender and have absorbed the liquid. Season well, scatter with parsley (if using) and serve.

Carrot cake overnight oats

Prep: 10 mins plus overnight soaking, no cook

Serves 1

Ingredients

- 40g grated carrot
- a big pinch of mixed spice
- ¼ tsp cinnamon
- 50g rolled porridge oats
- 1 tsp honey
- 1 tsp sultanas
- 1 tbsp Greek yogurt

Method

STEP 1

Mix the grated carrot, mixed spice and cinnamon with the oats, 150ml water and a pinch of salt, then cover and chill in the fridge overnight.

STEP 2

The next day, stir in the honey and sultanas then top with Greek yogurt.

Balsamic beef with beetroot & rocket

Prep: 15 mins **Cook:** 25 mins

Serves 2

Ingredients

- 240g beef sirloin , fat trimmed
- 1 tbsp balsamic vinegar
- 2 tsp thyme leaves
- 2 garlic cloves , 1 finely grated, 1 sliced
- 2 tsp rapeseed oil
- 2 red onions , halved and sliced
- 175g fine beans , trimmed
- 2 cooked beetroot , halved and cut into wedges
- 6 pitted Kalamata olives , quartered
- 2 handfuls rocket

Method

STEP 1

Beat the steak with a rolling pin until it is about the thickness of two £1 coins, then cut into two equal pieces. In a bowl, mix the balsamic, thyme, grated garlic, half the oil and a grinding of black pepper. Place the steaks in the marinade and set aside.

STEP 2

Heat the remaining 1 tsp oil in a large non-stick frying pan, and fry the onions and garlic for 8-10 mins, stirring frequently, until soft and starting to brown. Meanwhile, steam the beans for 4-6 mins or until just tender.

STEP 3

Push the onion mixture to one side in the pan. Lift the steaks from the bowl, shake off any excess marinade, and sear in the pan for 2½-3 mins, turning once, until cooked but still a little pink inside. Pile the beans onto plates and place the steaks on top. Add the beetroot wedges, olives and remaining marinade to the pan and cook briefly to heat through, then spoon on top and around the steaks. Add the rocket and serve.

Wasabi chicken rice salad

Prep: 15 mins No cook

Serves 1

Ingredients

- 70g frozen edamame
- ½ tsp wasabi paste
- 2 tbsp fat-free natural yogurt
- 1 lime , juiced
- 1 tbsp sesame oil
- 70g cooked rice
- 3 radishes , quartered
- 1 tsp sesame seeds
- 1 cooked boneless, skinless chicken breast, sliced
- ¼ sheet dried seaweed , sliced into strips

Method

STEP 1

Put the edamame in a heatproof bowl and cover with boiling water. Leave for 10 mins, then drain. Mix the wasabi paste with the yogurt, lime juice and sesame oil.

STEP 2

Toss the rice with the edamame and radishes. Top with the sesame seeds, chicken and seaweed, then drizzle over the dressing to serve.

Chicken taco salad

Prep: 10 mins no cook

Serves 1

Ingredients

- ¼ tsp olive oil
- 2 tbsp low-fat soured cream
- 1 tsp white wine vinegar
- 1 Baby Gem lettuce, shredded
- 50g sweetcorn, drained
- 5 cherry tomatoes, halved
- 75g cooked BBQ chicken
- juice 1 lime
- ½ small avocado, peeled and chopped
- 1 corn taco shell, broken into pieces

Method

STEP 1

Make the dressing by combining the oil, soured cream and vinegar. Keep in the fridge.

STEP 2

Put the lettuce, sweetcorn, tomatoes and chicken in a lunchbox. Stir the lime juice into the avocado and put on top. Pack the dressing on the side.

STEP 3

Scatter the taco over the salad to serve.

Parsnip gnocchi

Prep: 40 mins **Cook:** 55 mins

Serves 4

Ingredients

- 400g parsnip, peeled and cut into chunks
- 600g potatoes, peeled and cut into chunks

- 60ml olive oil , plus a drizzle to serve
- 3 unpeeled garlic cloves
- 1 tsp ground nutmeg (around 1 clove)
- 100g '00' flour
- 2 tbsp nutritional yeast
- ½ small pack thyme , leaves picked, to serve
- 30g walnuts , toasted and chopped, to serve

Method

STEP 1

Heat oven to 220C/200C fan/gas 7. Toss the parsnips and potatoes in 2 tbsp of the olive oil and tip into a roasting tin along with the garlic cloves. Roast for 40 mins or until the veg is completely soft. Remove from the oven and leave to cool a little. Squeeze the garlic from their skins, then discard the skins. Tip everything into a food processor, along with the nutmeg, flour and nutritional yeast, season well, then pulse until well combined and holding together as a dough.

STEP 2

Bring a large pan of salted water to the boil. Tip the dough onto a floured surface, cut into four chunks and roll each into a sausage about 35cm long and 2.5cm wide. Use the back of a table knife to cut each sausage into small pillow-shaped gnocchi, each around 2cm long. Cook the gnocchi in batches for 1 min or until they float to the surface. Remove from the water with a slotted spoon and drain on kitchen paper.

STEP 3

In a frying pan, heat the rest of the oil over a medium heat until shimmering. Add half the gnocchi and fry until lightly golden on each side, around 3-4 mins. Transfer them to a tray using a slotted spoon while you cook the second batch. When all the gnocchi are golden, return them all to the pan to warm through before dividing between four plates. Sprinkle over some black pepper, then top with the thyme leaves, toasted walnuts and a drizzle of olive oil, if you like.

Pork & apple stew with parsley & thyme dumplings

Prep: 25 mins **Cook:** 1 hr and 35 mins

Serves 4

Ingredients

For the stew

- 1 tbsp rapeseed oil
- 2 onions, halved and sliced
- 3 celery sticks, thickly sliced
- 2 bay leaves
- 1 tbsp picked thyme leaves
- 500g lean pork fillet, cut into large chunks
- 2 tsp English mustard powder
- 4 large garlic cloves, grated
- 2 tbsp spelt flour
- 4 tbsp cider vinegar
- 800ml bouillon or chicken stock
- 1 Granny Smith apple, peeled, cored and cut into chunks
- 2 leeks, thickly sliced
- 4 carrots, cut into chunks

For the dumplings

- 140g spelt flour
- 1 tsp baking powder
- 1 tsp English mustard powder
- 2 tbsp finely chopped flat-leaf parsley
- 1 tbsp picked thyme leaves, plus a few sprigs to garnish
- 2 tbsp bio yogurt
- 2 tbsp rapeseed oil

Method

STEP 1

Heat 1 tbsp of the oil in a flameproof and ovenproof dish. Add the onions, celery, bay and thyme, and fry for about 8 mins until softened. Add the pork and cook for a few mins until it changes colour, but it doesn't need to brown as you don't want to overcook it.

STEP 2

Stir in the mustard powder, garlic, flour and vinegar, then pour in the bouillon, stirring to prevent any lumps forming.

STEP 3

Add the apple, leeks and carrots, bring the liquid to the boil, then reduce to a simmer. Cover the pan and simmer for 1 hr, stirring occasionally, until the pork and vegetables are tender.

STEP 4

When the stew is nearly cooked, heat oven to 190C/170C fan/gas 5. To make the dumplings, tip the flour, baking powder, mustard powder, parsley and thyme into a bowl and stir to combine. Put the yogurt in a jug, make up to 100ml with water, then stir in the oil. Lightly stir the liquid into the flour to make a soft, slightly sticky dough. Divide the dough equally into eight and shape into balls. Drop them on top of the stew, drizzling each one with the remaining oil. Bake for 20 mins until the dumplings are golden. Scatter with the extra thyme, if you like, before serving.

Roasted squash, pancetta & chestnut risotto

Prep: 5 mins **Cook:** 45 mins

Serves 3 - 4

Ingredients

- 1 large butternut squash (about 1.5kg), peeled, ends trimmed, cut in half widthways and spiralized into thin noodles
- 1 ½ tbsp olive oil
- 1 tsp chilli flakes
- 100g cooked chestnuts , quartered
- ½ small pack sage , leaves picked
- 8 slices pancetta
- 2 banana shallots , finely chopped
- 2 garlic cloves , finely chopped
- 200g pearl barley
- 850ml low-sodium vegetable stock (we used bouillon)
- parmesan , to serve

Method

STEP 1

Heat oven to 200C/180C fan/gas 6. Toss the squash with 1/2 tbsp of oil, chilli flakes and some seasoning on a large roasting tray. Roast for 15 mins, then add the chestnuts and nestle the sage and pancetta around the squash so that they touch the baking sheet. Return to the oven for 8–10 mins until the pancetta and sage are crisp. Remove from the oven and set aside. When cool, tear the pancetta and sage leaves into pieces.

STEP 2

Heat the remaining oil in a sauté pan over a low heat. Add the shallots and cook for 8 mins until softened but not coloured. Add the garlic and cook for 1 min. Tip in the pearl barley, toast for a minute, then pour in the stock.

STEP 3

Working in small amounts, add the stock to the pan and cook, stirring over a medium heat until all the liquid is absorbed by the barley – about 20 mins. When there is only a little liquid left, stir in the roasted ingredients to warm through. Season to taste. Serve with Parmesan.

Bean & pepper chilli

Prep: 15 mins **Cook:** 30 mins

Serves 4

Ingredients

- 1 tbsp olive oil
- 1 onion , chopped
- 350g pepper , deseeded and sliced
- 1 tbsp ground cumin
- 1-3 tsp chilli powder , depending on how hot you want your chilli to be
- 1 tbsp sweet smoked paprika
- 400g can kidney bean in chilli sauce
- 400g can mixed bean , drained
- 400g can chopped tomato
- rice , to serve (optional)

Method

STEP 1

Heat the oil in a large pan. Add the onion and peppers, and cook for 8 mins until softened. Tip in the spices and cook for 1 min.

STEP 2

Tip in the beans and tomatoes, bring to the boil and simmer for 15 mins or until the chilli is thickened. Season and serve with rice, if you like.

Cod & smashed celeriac

Prep: 10 mins **Cook:** 45 mins

Serves 2

Ingredients

- 1 small celeriac , peeled and chopped
- 3 tbsp olive oil
- 1 tsp fennel seeds
- 4 spring onions , each cut into 3 on the diagonal
- 1 courgette , grated
- 1 garlic clove , crushed

- 2 x 125g skinless cod fillets
- 1 lemon, ½ juiced and ½ cut into wedges, to serve
- 1 tbsp chopped parsley leaves, to serve
- rocket leaves, to serve

Method

STEP 1

Heat oven to 200C/180C fan/gas 6. Put the celeriac into a roasting tin, drizzle with 2 tbsp oil, then sprinkle over the fennel seeds. Season and bake in the oven for 45 mins, stirring halfway through, until lightly charred.

STEP 2

While the celeriac cooks, put the spring onions in a dry pan and cook over a high heat for 3-4 mins, turning occasionally, until starting to char. Spread two large sheets of foil out on your work surface. Divide the spring onions between the foil sheets, then top with the grated courgette, garlic and fish. Season and drizzle over the lemon juice and the remaining 1 tbsp olive oil. Scrunch up the edges of the foil to seal and create two parcels. Put the parcels on a baking sheet and bake in the oven for 10-12 mins.

STEP 3

When the celeriac is cooked, mash the pieces with a potato masher or a fork and season well. Pile the smashed celeriac onto plates, then carefully open the fish parcels – the contents will be hot – and gently slide onto the plates next to the celeriac. Garnish with parsley and serve with rocket leaves and lemon wedges.

Thai broccoli rice

Prep: 25 mins **Cook:** 10 mins

serves 4 (or 6 as a side)

Ingredients

- 100g salted peanuts
- 1 head of broccoli, cut into florets and the stem cut in half
- 2 tbsp olive oil
- 1 red onion, finely diced
- 1 garlic clove, crushed
- 1 tbsp grated ginger

- 1 medium red chilli, deseeded and finely diced
- ½ small red cabbage, shredded
- 1 red pepper, deseeded and sliced into strips
- small pack coriander, roughly chopped

For the dressing

- zest and juice 1 lime
- 2 tbsp tamari
- ½ tbsp golden caster sugar
- 2 tbsp olive oil

Method

STEP 1

Heat a frying pan over a medium heat and add the peanuts. Toast evenly, regularly shaking the pan, then remove and set aside. Put the broccoli in a food processor and pulse until it looks like green couscous grains. Empty into a large bowl and set aside.

STEP 2

Heat the oil in a large frying pan and fry the onion, garlic, ginger and chilli until soft and aromatic. Add the broccoli rice to the pan and mix through, making sure everything is well coated. Sauté for 3-4 mins until al dente. Transfer to a large bowl and add the red cabbage, red pepper, half the coriander and half the toasted peanuts. Mix to combine.

STEP 3

To make the dressing, whisk the lime zest and juice, tamari, sugar and oil together until combined. Toss the dressing through the broccoli rice and transfer to a serving bowl or individual bowls. To serve, garnish with the remaining coriander and peanuts.

Sausage & butternut squash shells

Prep: 15 mins **Cook:** 35 mins

Serves 4

Ingredients

- 1 medium butternut squash, peeled and cut into medium chunks
- 1 ½ tbsp olive oil
- 2 garlic cloves, crushed
- 1 fennel bulb, thinly sliced (keep the green fronds to serve)

- 4 spring onions, thinly sliced
- 2 tsp chilli flakes
- 1 tsp fennel seeds
- 300g large pasta shells
- 3 pork sausages

Method

STEP 1

Put the squash in a microwaveable bowl with a splash of water. Cover with cling film and cook on high for 10 mins until soft. Tip into a blender.

STEP 2

Meanwhile, put a frying pan over a medium heat and pour in 1 tbsp olive oil. Add the garlic, sliced fennel, spring onions, half the chilli flakes, half the fennel seeds and a splash of water. Cook, stirring occasionally, for 5 mins until softened. Scrape into the blender with squash. Blitz to a smooth sauce, adding enough water to get to a creamy consistency. Season to taste.

STEP 3

Bring a pan of water to the boil and cook the pasta for 1 min less than the pack instructions. Put the frying pan back on the heat (don't bother washing it first – it's all flavour). Pour in the remaining oil, squeeze the sausagemeat from the skins into the pan and add the remaining chilli and remaining fennel seeds. Fry until browned and crisp, breaking down the sausagemeat with a spoon.

STEP 4

Drain the pasta and return to its pan on the heat. Pour in the butternut sauce and give everything a good mix to warm the sauce through. Divide between bowls and top with the crispy sausage mix and fennel fronds.

Caramelised onion & goat's cheese pizza

Prep: 20 mins **Cook:** 30 mins

Serves 2

Ingredients

For the base

- 125g wholemeal flour , plus a little for kneading if necessary
- ½ tsp instant yeast

For the topping

- 2 onions , halved and thinly sliced
- 2 tsp rapeseed oil
- 2 tsp balsamic vinegar
- 160g baby spinach leaves (not the very tiny ones), chopped

- pinch of salt
- 1 tsp rapeseed oil , plus extra for greasing

- 2 large garlic cloves , finely grated
- 50g soft goat's cheese
- 4 pitted Kalamata olives , quartered
- few soft thyme leaves
- 1 tsp sunflower seeds

Method

STEP 1

Heat oven to 220C/200C fan/gas 7. Tip the flour into a mixer with a dough hook, or a bowl. Add the yeast, salt, oil and just under 100ml warm water then mix to a soft dough. Knead in the food mixer for about 5 mins, but if making this by hand, tip onto a work surface and knead for about 10 mins. The dough is sticky, but try not to add too much extra flour. Leave in the bowl and cover with a tea towel while you make the topping. There is no need to let the dough prove for a specific time – just let it sit while you get on with the next step.

STEP 2

Tip the onions into a non-stick wok and add the oil, 4 tbsp water and balsamic vinegar. Cover with a saucepan lid that sits inside the pan to help the onions soften, then cook for 15 mins, stirring about 3 times and replacing the lid quickly so as not to lose too much moisture. After the time is up, the onions should be golden and all the liquid gone. Tip onto a plate. Add the spinach and garlic to the pan and stir-fry until the spinach has wilted.

STEP 3

Take the dough from the bowl and cut in half with an oiled knife, then press each piece into a 25-15 cm oval on a large greased baking sheet with oiled hands. Don't knead the dough first otherwise it will be too elastic and it will keep shrinking back.

STEP 4

Spread with the spinach followed by the onions, then dot with the cheese and scatter with the olives, thyme and sunflower seeds. Bake for 15 mins until golden and the base is cooked through.

Herby quinoa, feta & pomegranate salad

Prep: 10 mins **Cook:** 15 mins

Serves 4 or 6-8 as a side

Ingredients

- 300g quinoa
- 1 red onion, finely chopped
- 85g raisins or sultana
- 100g feta cheese, crumbled
- 200g pomegranate seeds from tub or fruit
- 85g toasted pine nuts or toasted flaked almonds
- small pack each coriander, flat leaf parsley and mint, roughly chopped
- juice 3 lemon
- 1 tsp sugar

Method

STEP 1

Cook the quinoa following pack instructions – it should be tender but with a little bite. Drain well and spread over a platter or wide, shallow bowl to cool quickly and steam dry.

STEP 2

When the quinoa is just about cool stir through all of the remaining ingredients with plenty of seasoning.

Beef goulash soup

Prep: 15 mins **Cook:** 1 hr

Serves 2 - 3

Ingredients

- 1 tbsp rapeseed oil
- 1 large onion, halved and sliced
- 3 garlic cloves, sliced
- 200g extra lean stewing beef, finely diced
- 1 tsp caraway seeds
- 2 tsp smoked paprika
- 400g can chopped tomatoes
- 600ml beef stock
- 1 medium sweet potato, peeled and diced
- 1 green pepper, deseeded and diced

Supercharged topping

- 150g pot natural bio yogurt
- good handful parsley, chopped

Method

STEP 1

Heat the oil in a large pan, add the onion and garlic, and fry for 5 mins until starting to colour. Stir in the beef, increase the heat and fry, stirring, to brown it.

STEP 2

Add the caraway and paprika, stir well, then tip in the tomatoes and stock. Cover and leave to cook gently for 30 mins.

STEP 3

Stir in the sweet potato and green pepper, cover and cook for 20 mins more or until tender. Allow to cool a little, then serve topped with the yogurt and parsley (if the soup is too hot, it will kill the beneficial bacteria in the yogurt).

Falafel burgers

Prep: 10 mins **Cook:** 6 mins

Serves 4

Ingredients

- 400g can chickpeas, rinsed and drained
- 1 small red onion, roughly chopped
- 1 garlic clove, chopped
- handful of flat-leaf parsley or curly parsley
- 1 tsp ground cumin
- 1 tsp ground coriander
- ½ tsp harissa paste or chilli powder
- 2 tbsp plain flour
- 2 tbsp sunflower oil
- toasted pitta bread, to serve
- 200g tub tomato salsa, to serve
- green salad, to serve

Method

STEP 1

Drain the chickpeas and pat dry with kitchen paper. Tip into a food processor along with the onion, garlic, parsley, cumin, coriander, harissa paste, flour and a little salt. Blend until fairly smooth, then shape into four patties with your hands.

STEP 2

Heat the sunflower oil in a non-stick frying pan, and fry the burgers for 3 mins on each side until lightly golden. Serve with the toasted pitta bread, tomato salsa and green salad.

Buckwheat with charred baby aubergines

Prep: 15 mins **Cook:** 20 mins

Serves 4

Ingredients

- 350g baby aubergines, halved
- 8 whole spring onions, tops trimmed
- 250g buckwheat
- 2 tbsp cold pressed rapeseed oil
- 1 x 400g can green lentils, drained
- 30g dried cherries, roughly chopped
- 8 walnut halves, finely chopped
- 1 lemon, juiced
- ½ tsp chilli flakes
- small bunch dill, finely chopped
- 30g soft goat's cheese, crumbled

Method

STEP 1

Heat the grill to its highest setting. Spread the aubergines out on a baking sheet, cut-side up, and grill for 10-15 mins until they begin to soften and blister.

STEP 2

Meanwhile, heat a griddle pan over a high heat. Add the spring onions and cook on each side for 5-6 mins until softened and charred. Remove with tongs and set aside.

STEP 3

Bring a medium-sized pan of water to the boil. Tip the buckwheat into a frying pan and dry fry over a medium heat for 3 mins until lightly toasted. Add the buckwheat to the boiling water and cook for 4-5 mins. Drain and toss with the oil. Leave to cool down for 5 mins.

STEP 4

Toss the warm buckwheat, lentils, cherries, walnuts, lemon juice, chilli and most of the dill in a bowl. Spread out on a serving plate and top with the aubergines, charred spring onions, remaining dill and goat's cheese.

Chickpea Bombay mix

Prep: 2 mins **Cook:** 10 mins

Serves 1

Ingredients

- 60g curried chickpeas (see recipe below)
- 1 tbsp unsalted peanuts
- 1 tsp raisins

Method

STEP 1

Mix the curried chickpeas (see recipe here) with the unsalted peanuts. Place in the oven at 200C/180C fan/gas 6 for 10 mins, then mix with the raisins.

Green shakshuka

Prep: 10 mins **Cook:** 25 mins

Serves 4

Ingredients

- 3 tbsp olive oil
- 2 leeks , washed and sliced
- 200g bag baby spinach
- 250g frozen peas
- 2 fat garlic cloves , finely chopped
- 1 tbsp cumin seeds
- small pack parsley , roughly chopped
- small pack coriander , roughly chopped
- small pack mint , leaves picked and roughly chopped, reserving a few leaves to garnish
- 8 medium eggs
- 150g pot natural yogurt
- 1 tbsp harissa
- flatbread , to serve

Method

STEP 1

Heat the oil in a wide, shallow frying pan over a medium heat. Add the leeks with a pinch of salt and cook for 4 mins until softened. Add handfuls of spinach to the pan, stirring until wilted.

STEP 2

Stir in the peas, garlic, cumin, herbs and some seasoning. Cook for a few mins until it smells fragrant, then create four gaps and crack two eggs into each. Cover and cook for 10 mins or until the whites are set but the yolks are runny – they will carry on cooking slightly as you take them to the table.

STEP 3

Season the eggs with flaky sea salt, dollop spoonfuls of the yogurt interspersed with the harissa, and scatter over a few mint leaves. Serve with a pile of flatbread for scooping.

Curried parsnip soup shots

Prep: 10 mins **Cook:** 25 mins

Makes 12 shots

Ingredients

- 1 tbsp cold pressed rapeseed oil
- 1 onion , chopped
- ½ tbsp garam masala or curry powder
- 1 garlic clove , grated

For the crispy kale topping

- 50g kale , torn into small pieces
- ½ tbsp cold pressed rapeseed oil

For the crispy prosciutto topping

- 1 slice prosciutto

- small piece ginger , grated
- 4 parsnips , peeled and sliced
- 600ml low-sodium veg stock

- ¼-½ tsp chilli powder

Method

STEP 1

Heat oven to 180C/160C/gas 4. For the kale topping, massage the kale with the oil, chilli powder and a pinch of salt and pepper, then spread out on a baking tray. Roast for 8 mins until crisp, checking halfway through.

STEP 2

Heat the oil in a saucepan over a medium heat. Add the onion and fry until soft and lightly coloured, then add the garam masala (or curry powder), garlic and ginger. Cook for 1 min, then tip in the parsnips and stock. Bring to the boil, then simmer for 15 mins until the parsnip is completely soft. Blitz, adding enough water to get to your desired thickness, and season to taste.

STEP 3

To make the crispy prosciutto topping, put the prosciutto slice in a dry non-stick frying pan over a medium-high heat. Use a fish slice to keep it flat and fry for a couple of mins until crisp. Set aside to cool, then break into six pieces.

STEP 4

Divide the soup between 12 shot glasses. Top half with the roasted kale and the other half with the prosciutto.

Chilli tempeh stir-fry

Prep: 10 mins **Cook:** 15 mins

Serves 2

Ingredients

- 300g long-stem broccoli
- ½ tbsp toasted sesame oil
- 150g tempeh, sliced and cut into 2cm cubes
- 2 garlic cloves, thinly sliced
- 1 thumb-sized piece ginger, peeled and finely grated
- ½ small red chilli, deseeded and finely chopped
- ½ tbsp gochujang paste
- 1 tsp sesame seeds
- steamed brown rice, to serve (optional)

Method

STEP 1

Boil the broccoli for 1 min 30 secs. Drain.

STEP 2

Heat the oil in a non-stick pan. Stir-fry the tempeh for 2-3 mins, then put on a plate. Fry the garlic, ginger and chilli for 2 mins. Tip in the broccoli and toss.

STEP 3

Mix the gochujang with 2 tbsp water and the tempeh. Add to the pan with the seeds. Cook for 2 mins. Serve with rice, if you like.

Broccoli pasta salad with salmon & sunflower seeds

Prep: 10 mins **Cook:** 10 mins

Serves 2

Ingredients

- 75g wholewheat penne
- 125g broccoli florets
- 125g fine beans, trimmed and halved
- 1 tbsp white miso paste
- 1 tsp grated ginger
- 2 tbsp sunflower seeds
- 1 tbsp extra virgin rapeseed oil
- 2 x skinless cooked wild salmon fillets

Method

STEP 1

Boil the pasta for 5 mins, then add the broccoli and beans, and cook 5 mins more or until everything is tender.

STEP 2

Drain, reserving the water, then tip the pasta and veg into a bowl and add the miso, ginger, seeds, oil and 3 tbsp pasta water. Flake the salmon into the pasta in large pieces and toss well. Spoon into containers and keep in the fridge until ready to eat.

Creamy sprout, hazelnut & leek pasta

Prep: 15 mins **Cook:** 25 mins

Serves 4

Ingredients

- ½ tbsp rapeseed oil
- 3 leeks, halved and sliced
- 200g Brussels sprouts, ½ chopped and ½ quartered
- 2 garlic cloves, rushed
- 50ml low-salt vegetable stock
- 3 tbsp low-fat crème fraîche
- 350g short pasta (riciolli or fusilli work well)
- 1 tbsp grated parmesan or veggie alternative
- 1 lemon, zested
- ½ small bunch of parsley, finely chopped
- 1 tbsp chopped hazelnuts, toasted

Method

STEP 1

Heat the oil in a large frying pan over a low heat. Add the leeks and sprouts and cook for 10-15 mins or until softened. Add the garlic and cook for 1 min. Stir through the hot stock and crème fraîche.

STEP 2

Cook the pasta following pack instructions. Drain and toss with the leeks and sprouts, parmesan, lemon, parsley and hazelnuts, adding a ladleful of the pasta cooking water if needed to loosen. Season to taste and spoon into four bowls.

Roast potatoes with paprika

Prep: 15 mins **Cook:** 1 hr and 25 mins

Serves 6

Ingredients

- 1 ½kg floury potatoes (such as Maris Piper, King Edward or Desirée), peeled and cut into halves or quarters, depending on size
- 100ml olive oil
- 2 tsp smoked paprika

Method

STEP 1

Heat oven to 200C/180C fan/gas 6. Add the potatoes to a pan of cold salted water, bring to a boil, then simmer for 5 mins until partly tender. Drain and steam dry for a few mins in a colander.

STEP 2

Return the potatoes to the saucepan, and add the oil, paprika and plenty of salt and pepper. Cover with a lid, then shake the pan around to roughen the edges of the potatoes and thoroughly coat them in the paprika and oil. Tip the potatoes into a large roasting tin, making sure they are evenly spaced apart. Scrape in all the fluffy potato mess – these make the best crispy bits!

STEP 3

Roast the potatoes for 1 hr 15 mins, turning halfway, until extremely fluffy and crisp.

Poached eggs with broccoli, tomatoes & wholemeal flatbread

Prep: 5 mins **Cook:** 6 mins

Serves 2

Ingredients

- 100g thin-stemmed broccoli, trimmed and halved
- 200g cherry tomatoes on the vine
- 4 medium free-range eggs (fridge cold)
- 2 wholemeal flatbreads (see Goes well with for recipe)
- 2 tsp mixed seeds (such as sunflower, pumpkin, sesame and linseed)
- 1 tsp cold-pressed rapeseed oil
- good pinch of chilli flakes

Method

STEP 1

Boil the kettle. Heat oven to 120C/100C fan/gas 1/2 and put an ovenproof plate inside to warm up. Fill a wide-based saucepan one-third full of water from the kettle and bring to the boil. Add the broccoli and cook for 2 mins. Add the tomatoes, return to the boil and cook for 30 secs. Lift out with tongs or a slotted spoon and place on the warm plate in the oven while you poach the eggs.

STEP 2

Return the water to a gentle simmer. Break the eggs into the pan, one at a time, and cook for 2 1/2 - 3 mins or until the whites are set and the yolks are runny.

STEP 3

Divide the flatbreads between the two plates and top with the broccoli and tomatoes. Use a slotted spoon to drain the eggs, then place on top. Sprinkle with the seeds and drizzle with the oil. Season with a little black pepper and the chilli flakes, and serve immediately.

Curried squash, lentil & coconut soup

Prep: 10 mins **Cook:** 25 mins

Serves 6

Ingredients

- 1 tbsp olive oil
- 1 butternut squash, peeled, deseeded and diced
- 200g carrot, diced
- 1 tbsp curry powder containing turmeric
- 100g red lentil
- 700ml low-sodium vegetable stock
- 1 can reduced-fat coconut milk
- coriander and naan bread, to serve

Method

STEP 1

Heat the oil in a large saucepan, add the squash and carrots, sizzle for 1 min, then stir in the curry powder and cook for 1 min more. Tip in the lentils, the vegetable stock and coconut milk and give everything a good stir. Bring to the boil, then turn the heat down and simmer for 15-18 mins until everything is tender.

STEP 2

Using a hand blender or in a food processor, blitz until as smooth as you like. Season and serve scattered with roughly chopped coriander and some naan bread alongside.

Bang bang chicken cups

Prep:10 mins No cook

Serves 2

Ingredients

- 3 tbsp crunchy peanut butter
- 1 tbsp Thai sweet chilli dipping sauce
- juice ½ lime
- 2 cooked skinless chicken breasts
- 2 Little Gem lettuces , leaves separated
- 4 spring onions , trimmed and cut into very fine matchsticks
- 0.3 cucumber , cut into very fine matchsticks

1 medium carrot , peeled and cut into very fine matchsticks

Method

STEP 1

Put the peanut butter in a small bowl and stir in 3 tbsp of just-boiled water until smooth. Add the chilli sauce and lime juice, and mix well.

STEP 2

Cut the chicken breasts into thin slices and place on a board with the bowl of peanut sauce. Put the lettuce leaves, spring onions, cucumber and carrot in separate piles alongside.

STEP 3

Put slices of chicken into the lettuce leaves, then top with the vegetables and peanut sauce.

Meatballs with fennel & balsamic beans & courgette noodles

Prep: 35 mins **Cook:** 40 mins

Serves 4

Ingredients

- 400g lean beef steak mince
- 2 tsp dried oregano
- 1 large egg
- 8 garlic cloves , 1 finely grated, the other sliced
- 1-2 tbsp rapeseed oil
- 1 fennel bulb , finely chopped, fronds reserved
- 2 carrots , finely chopped
- 500g carton passata
- 4 tbsp balsamic vinegar
- 600ml reduced-salt vegetable bouillon

For the courgette noodles

- 1 tsp rapeseed oil
- 1-2 large courgettes , cut into noodles with a julienne peeler or spiralizer
- 350g frozen soya beans , thawed

Method

STEP 1

Put the mince, oregano, egg and grated garlic in a bowl and grind in some black pepper. Mix together thoroughly and roll into 16 balls.

STEP 2

Heat the oil in a large sauté pan over a medium-high heat, add the meatballs and fry, moving them around the pan so that they brown all over – be careful as they're quite delicate and you don't want them to break up. Once brown, remove them from the pan. Reduce the heat slightly and add the fennel, carrots and sliced garlic to the pan and fry, stirring until they soften, about 5 mins.

STEP 3

Tip in the passata, balsamic vinegar and bouillon, stir well, then return the meatballs to the pan, cover and cook gently for 20-25 mins.

STEP 4

Meanwhile, heat the 1 tsp of oil in a non-stick pan and stir-fry the courgette with the beans to heat through and soften. Serve with the meatballs and scatter with any fennel fronds.

Berry yogurt pots

Prep: 5 mins No cook

Serves 2

Ingredients

- 150g bio yogurt
- 160g blueberries, raspberries or cherries (or a combination)
- 1 tbsp pumpkin seeds, sunflower seeds or flaked almonds
- a little chopped mint (optional)

Method

STEP 1

Spoon the yogurt into two tumblers. Mix the fruit, seeds or nuts of your choice with the mint, if using, and pile into the tumblers.

Summer porridge

Prep: 20 mins no cook

Serves 2

Ingredients

- 300ml almond milk
- 200g blueberries
- ½ tbsp maple syrup
- 2 tbsp chia seeds
- 100g jumbo oats
- 1 kiwi fruit, cut into slices
- 50g pomegranate seeds
- 2 tsp mixed seeds

Method

STEP 1

In a blender, blitz the milk, blueberries and maple syrup until the milk turns purple. Put the chia and oats in a mixing bowl, pour in the blueberry milk and stir very well. Leave to soak for 5 mins, stirring occasionally, until the liquid has absorbed, and the oats and chia thicken and swell.

STEP 2

Stir again, then divide between two bowls. Arrange the fruit on top, then sprinkle over the mixed seeds. Will keep in the fridge for 1 day. Add the toppings just before serving.

Harissa salmon with zesty couscous

Prep: 10 mins **Cook:** 15 mins

Serves 2

Ingredients

- 2 skinless salmon fillets
- zest and juice 1 orange
- 1 tbsp olive oil
- 1-2 tsp rose harissa (depending on how spicy you like it)
- 100g couscous
- ¼ cucumber, finely diced
- 1 small red onion, finely diced
- small pack parsley, chopped, or 1/2 handful mint
- 1 tbsp flaked almond, toasted (optional)

Method

STEP 1

Heat oven to 200C/180C fan/gas 6 and arrange the salmon in a shallow ovenproof dish. Mix the orange juice with the oil and harissa, then pour over the salmon and bake for 10-12 mins until the fish flakes easily, but is still moist.

STEP 2

Meanwhile, put the couscous in a pan with the orange zest, 200ml water and a sprinkling of salt. Heat until the water bubbles round the edges of the pan, then cover and turn off the heat. After 5 mins, tip the couscous into a bowl, add the cucumber, onion, parsley and almonds (if using) and toss together ready to serve with the salmon and spicy juices.

Bone broth

Prep: 20 mins **Cook:** 45 mins

Serves 4

Ingredients

- 1 meaty chicken carcass, plus any jellified roasting juices from it, skin and fat discarded
- 1 large onion , halved and sliced
- zest and juice 1 lemon
- 2 bay leaves
- 1-2 red chillies , halved, deseeded and sliced
- 1 tsp ground coriander
- ½ tsp ground cumin
- small pack coriander , stems and leaves chopped and separated
- 1 large garlic clove , finely grated

Optional topping

- 250g pouch wholegrain basmati rice

Method

STEP 1

Break the chicken carcass into a large pan and add the onion, 1.5 litres of water, the lemon juice and bay leaves. Cover and simmer for 40 mins. Remove from the heat and allow to cool slightly, to make things a bit easier to handle.

STEP 2

Place a colander over a bowl and scoop out all the bones into the colander. Pick through them, stripping off the chicken and returning it with any onion as you work your way down the pile of bones.

STEP 3

Return any broth from the bowl to the pan – and any jellified roasting juices – along with the chilli, ground coriander, cumin, coriander stems, lemon zest and garlic. Cook for a few mins until just bubbling – don't overboil as you will spoil the delicate flavours. Taste, and season only if you need to. Meanwhile, heat the rice following pack instructions, then toss with the coriander leaves. Ladle the broth into bowls and top with the rice.

Blueberry & nut oat bake

Prep: 5 mins **Cook:** 35 mins

Serves 6

Ingredients

- 500ml almond milk
- 200g jumbo porridge oats
- 2 tbsp almond butter
- 1 tsp baking powder
- 1 egg, beaten
- 1 small ripe banana, mashed
- ½ tsp almond extract or 1 tsp vanilla extract (optional)
- 450g blueberries, plus extra to serve
- 30g whole, skin-on almonds, roughly chopped
- milk or fat-free yogurt and honey, to serve (optional)

Method

STEP 1

Heat the oven to 200C/180C fan/gas 6. Mix all of the ingredients together in a large bowl.

STEP 2

Tip the mixture into a 2-litre ovenproof dish, then bake for 30-35 mins until piping hot in the middle. Serve warm with a little milk or yogurt, honey and extra blueberries, if you like.

Chicken korma

Prep: 10 mins **Cook:** 25 mins

Serves 4

Ingredients

- 1 onion, chopped
- 2 garlic cloves, roughly chopped
- thumb-sized piece ginger, roughly chopped
- 4 tbsp korma paste
- 4 skinless, boneless chicken breasts, cut into bite-sized pieces
- 50g ground almonds, plus extra to serve (optional)
- 4 tbsp sultanas
- 400ml chicken stock
- ¼ tsp golden caster sugar
- 150g pot 0% fat Greek yogurt
- small bunch coriander, chopped

Method

STEP 1

Put 1 chopped onion, 2 roughly chopped garlic cloves and a roughly chopped thumb-sized piece of ginger in a food processor and whizz to a paste.

STEP 2

Tip the paste into a large high-sided frying pan with 3 tbsp water and cook for 5 mins. Add 4 tbsp korma paste and cook for a further 2 mins until aromatic.

STEP 3

Stir 4 skinless, boneless chicken breasts, cut into bite-sized pieces, into the sauce. Add 50g ground almonds, 4 tbsp sultanas, 400ml chicken stock and ¼ tsp golden caster sugar.

STEP 4

Give everything a good mix, then cover and simmer for 10 mins or until the chicken is cooked through.

STEP 5

Remove the pan from the heat, stir in a 150g pot Greek yogurt and some seasoning, then scatter over a small bunch of chopped coriander and more ground almonds, if using. Serve with brown or white basmati rice.

Prawn jalfrezi

Prep: 10 mins **Cook:** 22 mins

Serves 2

Ingredients

- 2 tsp rapeseed oil
- 2 medium onions , chopped
- thumb-sized piece ginger , finely chopped
- 2 garlic cloves , chopped
- 1 tsp ground coriander
- ½ tsp ground turmeric
- ½ tsp ground cumin
- ¼ tsp chilli flakes (or less if you don't like it too spicy)
- 400g can chopped tomato
- squeeze of clear honey
- 1 large green pepper , halved, deseeded and chopped
- small bunch coriander , stalks and leaves separated, chopped
- 140g large cooked peeled tiger prawns
- 250g pouch cooked brown rice
- minty yogurt or chutney, to serve (optional)

Method

STEP 1

Heat the oil in a non-stick pan and fry the onions, ginger and garlic for 8-10 mins, stirring frequently, until softened and starting to colour. Add the spices and chilli flakes, stir briefly, then pour in the tomatoes with half a can of water and the honey. Blitz everything in the pan with a hand blender until almost smooth (or use a food processor). Stir in the pepper and coriander stalks, cover the pan and leave to simmer for 10 mins. (The mixture will be very thick and splutter a little, so stir frequently.)

STEP 2

Stir in the prawns and scatter over the coriander leaves. Heat the rice following pack instructions. Serve both with a minty yogurt or chutney, if you like.

Broccoli and kale green soup

Prep: 15 mins **Cook:** 20 mins

Serves 2

Ingredients

- 500ml stock , made by mixing 1 tbsp bouillon powder and boiling water in a jug
- 1 tbsp sunflower oil
- 2 garlic cloves , sliced
- thumb-sized piece ginger , sliced
- ½ tsp ground coriander
- 3cm/1in piece fresh turmeric root, peeled and grated, or 1/2 tsp ground turmeric
- pinch of pink Himalayan salt
- 200g courgettes , roughly sliced
- 85g broccoli
- 100g kale , chopped
- 1 lime , zested and juiced
- small pack parsley , roughly chopped, reserving a few whole leaves to serve

Method

STEP 1

Put the oil in a deep pan, add the garlic, ginger, coriander, turmeric and salt, fry on a medium heat for 2 mins, then add 3 tbsp water to give a bit more moisture to the spices.

STEP 2

Add the courgettes, making sure you mix well to coat the slices in all the spices, and continue cooking for 3 mins. Add 400ml stock and leave to simmer for 3 mins.

STEP 3

Add the broccoli, kale and lime juice with the rest of the stock. Leave to cook again for another 3-4 mins until all the vegetables are soft.

STEP 4

Take off the heat and add the chopped parsley. Pour everything into a blender and blend on high speed until smooth. It will be a beautiful green with bits of dark speckled through (which is the kale). Garnish with lime zest and parsley.

Smashed cannellini bean tartine

Prep: 15 mins No cook

Serves 2

Ingredients

- 400g can cannellini beans, drained and rinsed
- 2 tbsp rapeseed oil
- 1 large lemon, zested and juiced
- 1 small garlic clove, finely grated
- 1 small red chilli, deseeded and finely chopped
- 1/2 small bunch parsley, finely chopped
- 8 cherry tomatoes, halved
- 2 slices sourdough
- 15g feta, crumbled
- 50g rocket

Method

STEP 1

Put the beans, 1 tbsp of the oil, the lemon zest and juice and the garlic in a food processor and blitz to create a chunky texture. Transfer to a bowl and stir through the chilli, parsley and cherry tomatoes.

STEP 2

Lightly toast the bread and pile on the cannellini bean smash, scatter over the feta and drizzle with the remaining oil. Serve with the rocket on the side.

Stir-fry with broccoli & brown rice

Prep: 10 mins **Cook:** 20 mins

Serves 2

Ingredients

- 200g trimmed broccoli florets (about 6) halved
- 0.5 x 300g pack Quorn chicken-style pieces (or similar vegetarian product), diced
- 15g ginger, cut into shreds
- 2 garlic cloves, cut into shreds
- 1 red onion, sliced
- 1 roasted red pepper, from a jar, cut into cubes
- 2 tsp olive oil
- 1 tsp mild chilli powder
- 1 tbsp reduced-salt soy sauce
- 1 tbsp honey
- 250g pack cooked brown rice

Method

STEP 1

In a medium pan, pour boiling water over the broccoli then boil for 4 mins.

STEP 2

Heat the olive oil in a non-stick wok and stir-fry the ginger, garlic and onion for 2 mins, add the mild chilli powder and stir briefly. Add the vegetarian, chicken-style pieces and stir-fry for 2 mins more. Drain the broccoli and reserve the water. Tip the broccoli into the wok with the soy, honey, red pepper and 4 tbsp broccoli water then cook until heated through. Meanwhile, heat the rice following the pack instructions and serve with the stir-fry.

Chicken meatballs

Prep: 30 mins **Cook:** 30 mins

Serves 4

Ingredients

- 500g skinless boneless chicken thighs, cut into pieces
- 100g fresh breadcrumbs
- 1 large egg, beaten
- 1 onion, grated
- 25g parmesan, finely grated plus more to serve
- 4 garlic cloves, crushed
- ½ small bunch oregano, finely chopped
- 2 tbsp olive oil, plus extra to grease tray and serve
- 2 x 400g cans chopped tomatoes
- 1 tsp sugar
- 300g spaghetti

Method

STEP 1

Heat the oven to 200C/180C fan/gas 6. Put the chicken in a food processor and pulse until finely chopped. Scrape into a bowl and add the breadcrumbs, egg, onion, parmesan, half the crushed garlic, and half the oregano. Season really well, and mix with clean hands until everything is evenly distributed. Shape into 20 meatballs, and put onto an oiled baking tray. Brush the meatballs with 1½ tbsp oil. Bake for 20 minutes until cooked through and golden brown.

STEP 2

Meanwhile, heat the remaining ½ tbsp oil in a deep frying pan. Fry the remaining garlic for 30 secs, then add the chopped tomatoes and reserved oregano. Season with salt, pepper, and a pinch of sugar. Simmer for 10-15 mins stirring frequently, until the tomatoes break down and you get a thick sauce.

STEP 3

Bring a large pot of salted water to a boil. Add the spaghetti and cook for 10 mins until al dente.

STEP 4

Add the cooked meatballs to the tomato sauce and gently stir through. Heat for a few minutes while you drain the spaghetti and spoon into warmed pasta bowls. Serve the meatballs and sauce on top. Drizzle over a little olive oil and a grating of more parmesan, if you wish.

Roasted chickpea wraps

Prep: 20 mins **Cook:** 25 mins

Serves 4

Ingredients

- 2 x 400g cans chickpeas
- 2 tsp olive oil
- 2 tsp ground cumin
- 2 tsp smoked paprika
- 2 avocados, stoned, peeled and chopped
- juice 1 lime
- small pack coriander, chopped
- 8 soft corn tortillas
- 1 small iceberg lettuce, shredded
- 150g pot natural yogurt
- 480g jar roasted red peppers, chopped

Method

STEP 1

Heat oven to 220C/200C fan/gas 7. Drain the chickpeas and put in a large bowl. Add the olive oil, cumin and paprika. Stir the chickpeas well to coat, then spread them onto a large baking tray and roast for 20-25 mins or until starting to crisp – give the tray a shake halfway through cooking to ensure they roast evenly. Remove from the oven and season to taste.

STEP 2

Toss the chopped avocados with the lime juice and chopped coriander, then set aside until serving. Warm the tortillas following pack instructions, then pile in the avocado, lettuce, yogurt, peppers and toasted chickpeas at the table.

Creamy squash linguine

Prep: 5 mins **Cook:** 1 hr

Serves 4

Ingredients

- 350g chopped butternut squash
- 3 peeled garlic cloves
- 3 tbsp olive oil
- 350g linguine
- small bunch sage

Method

STEP 1

Heat oven to 200C/180C fan/gas 6. Put the squash and garlic on a baking tray and drizzle with the olive oil. Roast for 35-40 mins until soft. Season.

STEP 2

Cook the pasta according to pack instructions. Drain, reserving the water. Use a stick blender to whizz the squash with 400ml cooking water. Heat some oil in a frying pan, fry the sage until crisp, then drain on kitchen paper. Tip the pasta and sauce into the pan and warm through. Scatter with sage.

Easy creamy coleslaw

Prep: 20 mins No cook

Serves 4

Ingredients

- ½ white cabbage, shredded
- 2 carrots, grated
- 4 spring onions, chopped
- 2 tbsp sultanas

- 3 tbsp low-fat mayonnaise
- 1 tbsp wholegrain mustard

Method

STEP 1

Put the cabbage, carrots, spring onions and sultanas in a large bowl and stir to combine.

STEP 2

Mix the mayonnaise with the mustard in another small bowl and drizzle over the veg. Fold everything together to coat in the creamy sauce, then season to taste.

Healthier beef wellington

Prep: 1 hr **Cook:** 55 mins Plus cooling and resting

Serves 6

Ingredients

- 1kg thick, lean fillet of beef
- 3 tbsp rapeseed oil
- good handful dried porcini mushrooms
- 2 shallots , finely chopped
- 2 garlic cloves , finely chopped
- 140g chestnut mushroom , very finely chopped
- 2 tbsp finely chopped flat-leaf parsley
- 1 tbsp finely chopped tarragon
- 100g mix of watercress, baby spinach and rocket (or use just watercress or spinach)
- 6 filo pastry sheets, each about 38 x 30cm
- 1 tsp plain flour
- 5 tbsp red wine
- 350ml chicken stock
- 2 tsp Dijon mustard

Method

STEP 1

Heat oven to 220C/200C fan/gas 7. Unless the butcher has already done so, tie the meat around with string at even intervals to hold it together. Heat 2 tsp of the oil in a large non-stick frying pan. Lay the beef in the pan and fry over a high heat for 5 mins to seal, turning often. Transfer it to a roasting tin, season with pepper and a pinch of salt, then roast for 17-18 mins (this roasts to medium-rare).

STEP 2

Meanwhile, put the porcini in a small heatproof bowl, cover with boiling water and leave for 20-30 mins to soak. Pour 1 tbsp of the remaining oil into the same frying pan (don't wash it) that the meat was cooked in. Tip in the shallots, garlic and chestnut mushrooms and fry for 4-5 mins, stirring often, over a high-ish heat, so all the liquid is first released from the mushrooms then evaporated, and all are softened. Remove from the heat, stir in the parsley and tarragon, season with pepper and a pinch of salt, and leave to cool.

STEP 3

Put the mix of leaves in a large heatproof bowl, pour over boiling water, leave for 30 secs, then tip into a colander, rinse under the cold tap and drain. Squeeze out all the moisture with your hands and pat dry with kitchen paper. Chop and set aside. Drain the porcini, reserving 5 tbsp of the soaking liquid. Chop the porcini finely and stir into the mushroom mix. Line a baking sheet with baking parchment.

STEP 4

When the beef is done, remove from the oven and let it sit in the tin for 10 mins for any juices to be released. Lower the oven to 200C/180C fan/gas 6. Lift the beef from the tin (keep all the juices in the tin for the gravy) and lay it on kitchen paper. Leave until dry and cool enough to wrap in the filo.

STEP 5

Lay 1 of the filo sheets on the work surface with the short end facing you. Brush all over with a little of the remaining oil (you will have 1 tbsp and 1 tsp left). Layer up and oil 4 more filo sheets in the same way. Remove the string from the cooled beef. Spread the chopped leaves down the middle of the pastry, so it is the same length and width as the fillet. Top with the mushroom mix and lightly press down. Lay the beef over this, with the top of the beef facing down. Bring the long sides of the filo over the beef to enclose it, then turn it over so the join is underneath. Tuck both ends of the pastry under (trim first if necessary to reduce any excess) and place on the lined baking sheet so all the joins are on the bottom. Brush with more oil.

STEP 6

Lay the last sheet of filo on the work surface in front of you, with one of the longest sides towards you, then cut across its width into 5 strips. Lay these one by one, slightly overlapping, over the wrapped beef, scrunching up an edge of each strip slightly as you go to give a bit of height. Carefully brush with the last of the oil, then bake for 30 mins until golden. If the pastry starts to brown too quickly, loosely lay a piece of foil over the top. Remove the meat and let sit for 5-10 mins before slicing.

STEP 7

Meanwhile, make the gravy. Heat the saved roasting juices in the roasting tin, stirring to deglaze. Stir in the flour. Gradually pour in the wine, stirring all the time to blend in the flour. Stir in the stock and reserved porcini liquid and bubble for about 8-10 mins to reduce a little. It should have body, but be thinner like a 'jus'. Stir in the mustard and season with pepper. Transfer the beef to a platter, then slice thickly with a sharp knife and serve with a spoonful or two of the gravy.

Sweet potato pancakes with orange & grapefruit

Prep: 10 mins **Cook:** 15 mins

Serves 4

Ingredients

- 325g sweet potatoes , peeled and coarsely grated
- ½ tsp vanilla extract
- 2 oranges , 1 zested, both cut into segments
- 150g ricotta or bio yogurt
- 2 large eggs
- ½ tsp baking powder
- 2 tsp rapeseed oil
- 2 grapefruits , cut into segments
- small handful mint leaves

Method

STEP 1

Put the sweet potato in a bowl, cover with cling film and cook in the microwave on high for 5 mins (or steam them). Mash the potato with a fork. When cooled a little, beat in the vanilla, orange zest, ricotta, eggs and baking powder to make a batter.

STEP 2

Heat the oil in a non-stick frying pan and fry spoonfuls of the batter for a few mins. Carefully flip the pancakes to cook the other side. When done, set aside on a plate and cook the remaining batter, aiming for eight pancakes in total.

STEP 3

If you are following our Healthy Diet Plan, you should serve four on the first day and set aside four for another day – keep in the fridge and reheat in a microwave or in a pan. Alternatively, cook half the batter now, reserving the rest for another day – but you will need to add ¼ tsp baking powder to the mixture before using it.

STEP 4

Mix the grapefruit and orange segments with mint and serve with the pancakes.

Vitality chicken salad with avocado dressing

Prep: 5 mins **Cook:** 3 mins

Serves 1

Ingredients

- handful frozen soya beans
- 1 skinless cooked chicken breast, shredded
- ¼ cucumber, peeled, deseeded and chopped
- ½ avocado, flesh scooped out
- few drops Tabasco sauce
- juice ½ lemon, plus a lemon wedge
- 2 tsp extra-virgin olive oil
- 5-6 Little Gem lettuce leaves
- 1 tsp mixed seed

Method

STEP 1

Blanch the soya beans for 3 mins. Rinse in cold water and drain thoroughly. Put the chicken, beans and cucumber in a bowl.

STEP 2

Blitz the avocado, Tabasco, lemon juice and oil in a food processor or with a hand blender. Season, pour into the bowl and mix well to coat.

STEP 3

Spoon the mixture into the lettuce leaves (or serve it alongside them) and sprinkle with the seeds. Chill until lunch, then serve with a lemon wedge.

Dried fruit energy nuggets

Prep: 10 mins No cook

Makes 6

Ingredients

- 50g soft dried apricot
- 100g soft dried date
- 50g dried cherry
- 2 tsp coconut oil
- 1 tbsp toasted sesame seed

Method

STEP 1

Whizz apricots with dates and cherries in a food processor until very finely chopped. Tip into a bowl and use your hands to work in coconut oil. Shape the mix into walnut-sized balls, then roll in sesame seeds. Store in an airtight container until you need a quick energy fix.

Spicy seed mix

Prep: 5 mins **Cook:** 20 mins

Makes 250g

Ingredients

- 250g mixed seed (sunflower, pumpkin, linseed)
- 1 tsp rapeseed oil
- 1 tsp ras-el-hanout
- ¼ tsp low-sodium salt
- 1 tsp reduced salt soy sauce
- 1 tsp agave syrup
- pinch cayenne

Method

STEP 1

Preheat the oven to 160C/ 140 fan/ Gas mark 3.

STEP 2

Mix all the ingredients together in a bowl and spread onto a baking sheet. Cook for 15 - 20 mins until dry and golden. Stir once during cooking. Allow to cool and store in a sealed container for up to 3 weeks.

Prawn & pink grapefruit noodle salad

Prep: 25 mins No cook

Serves 6

Ingredients

- 200g thin rice noodle (vermicelli)
- 12 cherry tomatoes , halved
- 1 tbsp fish sauce
- juice 1 lime
- 2 tsp palm sugar or soft brown sugar
- 1 large red chilli , ½ diced, ½ sliced
- 2 pink grapefruits , segmented
- ½ cucumber , peeled, deseeded and thinly sliced
- 2 carrots , cut into matchsticks
- 3 spring onions , thinly sliced
- 400g cooked large prawn
- large handful mint , leaves picked
- large handful coriander , leaves picked

Method

STEP 1

Put the noodles in a bowl, breaking them up a little, and cover with boiling water from the kettle. Leave to soak for 10 mins until tender. Drain, rinse under cold running water, then leave the noodles to drain thoroughly.

STEP 2

In the same bowl, lightly squash the cherry tomatoes – we used the end of a rolling pin. Stir in the fish sauce, lime juice, sugar and diced chilli. Taste for the right balance of sweet, sour and spicy – adjust if necessary (see tip, below).

STEP 3

Toss through the noodles, then add all the remaining ingredients, except the sliced chilli. Season and give everything a good stir, then divide the noodle salad between 6 serving dishes and sprinkle over the chilli before serving.

Stuffed Moroccan pitta

Prep: 5 mins No cook

Serves 2

Ingredients

- 2 wheat-free pitta bread pockets
- 4 falafels , halved (from Falafels with hummus recipe, in 'goes well with', below right)
- 4 tbsp hummus (from Falafels with hummus recipe, see 'goes well with')
- ½ red pepper , deseeded and sliced
- handful rocket leaves

Method

STEP 1

Spread the hummus on the inside of each pitta, then layer with the falafels, pepper and rocket.

Spicy bean tostadas with pickled onions & radish salad

Prep: 15 mins **Cook:** 12 mins

Serves 4

Ingredients

- 2 red onions , 1 thinly sliced, 1 finely chopped
- 2 limes , juice of 1 and 1 cut into wedges
- 1 ½ tbsp sunflower oil
- 2 garlic cloves , finely chopped
- 2 tsp ground cumin
- 1 tbsp tomato purée
- 1 tbsp chipotle paste
- 400g can kidney bean , drained and rinsed
- 4 corn tortillas
- 140g radish , thinly sliced
- large handful coriander , roughly chopped

Method

STEP 1

Heat oven to 220C/200C fan/gas 7. Put the sliced onion, lime juice and seasoning in a bowl, and set aside.

STEP 2

Heat 1 tbsp of the oil in a pan and fry the chopped onion and garlic until tender. Stir in the cumin and fry for 1 min more. Add the tomato purée, chipotle paste and beans, stir, then tip in half a can of water. Simmer for 5 mins, season, then roughly mash to a purée. (You can cook for a few mins more if it is a bit runny, or add a few splashes of water to thin.)

STEP 3

Meanwhile, brush the tortillas with the remaining oil and place on a baking sheet. Bake for 8 mins until crisp. Spread the tortillas with the bean mixture. Mix the radishes and coriander with the pickled onions, then spoon on top. Serve with lime wedges.

Artichoke, red onion & rosemary risotto

Prep: 15 mins **Cook:** 35 mins

Serves 4

Ingredients

- 1 tbsp olive oil
- 2 red onions, sliced into thin wedges
- 2 red peppers, cut into chunks
- 2 tbsp rosemary needles
- 140g arborio risotto rice
- 150ml white wine
- 850ml low-salt vegetable stock
- 400g tin artichoke heart in water, drained and halved
- 2 tbsp grated parmesan or vegetarian alternative
- 2 tbsp toasted pine nuts

Method

STEP 1

Heat the oil in a large frying pan or wok. Cook the onions gently for 6-7 mins until softened and browning. Add the peppers and rosemary and cook for a further 5 mins. Add rice and stir well.

STEP 2

Pour in the wine and of the stock. Bring to the boil then reduce the heat and simmer gently, stirring occasionally until almost all the liquid is absorbed.

STEP 3

Stir in another of the stock and simmer again, until it's all absorbed. Add the final with the artichokes and simmer again until rice is tender.

STEP 4

Season and stir in the Parmesan and ½ the pine nuts. Scatter over the remainder and serve.

Lighter massaman chicken curry

Prep: 35 mins **Cook:** 35 mins

Serves 4

Ingredients

For the curry paste

- 1 tbsp coriander seed
- 2 tsp cumin seed
- seeds from 5 cardamom pods
- 3 cloves
- ½ tsp crushed dried chilli
- 2 tsp rapeseed oil
- 100g shallot , finely chopped
- 3 garlic cloves , finely chopped
- 2.5cm piece ginger , finely grated
- 1 plump lemongrass stalk, tough ends and outside layer removed, finely chopped
- 4 tbsp light coconut milk (from the can, below)
- ¼ tsp ground black pepper

For the curry

- 25g unsalted, unroasted peanut
- 2 tsp rapeseed oil
- 140g small shallot (6-7), halved
- 1 cinnamon stick , broken in half
- 400ml can light coconut milk
- 500g skinless, boneless chicken breast , cut into bite-sized pieces
- 200g sweet potato , cut into 2.5cm chunks
- 175g green bean , stem ends trimmed
- 1 tbsp fish sauce
- 2 tsp tamarind paste
- 75ml chicken stock
- coriander or Thai basil leaves (or both), to garnish
- a small handful of peanuts , to garnish

Method

STEP 1

To make the curry paste, heat a small heavy-based frying pan and drop in all the seeds and the cloves. Dry-fry over a medium heat, shaking the pan often, for 1-2 mins to release their flavours – until they start popping in the pan. Mix in the chillies, then grind finely using a pestle and mortar or a spice grinder. Set aside.

STEP 2

Heat the oil in the same pan. Tip in the shallots and garlic, and fry over a medium heat for 5-6 mins, stirring occasionally, until a deep, rich golden brown. Stir in the ground spices and stir-fry for 1 min. Spoon into a mini processor with the ginger, lemongrass and coconut milk. Blitz until it is as smooth as you can get it, then stir in the black pepper. Can be kept in the fridge for several days.

STEP 3

To make the curry, dry-fry the peanuts in a small frying pan for about 2 mins to give them extra colour and flavour. Set aside. Heat the oil in a large sauté pan, tip in the shallots and fry over a medium heat, turning occasionally, for 8-10 mins until they are well browned all over and softened. Remove and set aside. Put the cinnamon stick and curry paste in the sauté pan and cook for 1 min. Pour in 100ml of the coconut milk. Let it bubble for 2 mins, stirring occasionally, until it's like a thick paste. Tip in the chicken and stir-fry in the paste over a high-ish heat for 6-8 mins or until cooked.

STEP 4

Meanwhile, steam the sweet potato chunks for 8-10 mins and the beans for about 5 mins. Remove the pan of chicken from the heat and stir in the remaining coconut milk, the fish sauce, tamarind paste and stock. Lay the sweet potatoes and shallots in the curry and warm through gently over a very low heat – overheating or overcooking may cause the coconut milk to curdle and thicken. If you need to thin the sauce slightly, stir in 1-2 spoons of water. Remove the cinnamon.

STEP 5

Lay a bunch of the beans to one side of each serving bowl or plate. Spoon the curry over one end of the beans and serve scattered with the coriander, Thai basil and peanuts.

Sesame, edamame & chicken noodle salad

Prep: 15 mins **Cook:** 5 mins

Serves 3 (or 2 adults and 2 children)

Ingredients

- 2 chicken legs, cooked
- 1½ tbsp sesame seeds
- 4 wholewheat noodle nests
- 160g frozen edamame beans
- 160g long-stemmed broccoli, cut into small florets
- 1 tbsp tahini
- 2 tbsp sesame oil
- 2 tsp honey
- 1½ tbsp low-sodium soy sauce
- 1 tbsp rice wine vinegar

Method

STEP 1

Boil the kettle. Remove the chicken skin, then shred the meat and discard the bones. Set aside. In a large pan, toast the sesame seeds for 1 min until golden, then tip into a large bowl (big enough to hold the noodles).

STEP 2

Fill the pan with water from the kettle and bring back to the boil. Add the noodles and cook following pack instructions. Tip in the beans and broccoli for the last 2 mins.

STEP 3

Meanwhile, mix the tahini, sesame oil, honey, soy sauce and vinegar into the sesame seeds. Drain the noodles, reserving a cup of the cooking water, and run under cold water to cool. Drain again and toss through the sauce along with the chicken. Add a splash of the cooking water to make the sauce thin enough to coat the noodles (it will thicken as it cools). Transfer to containers and chill until ready to eat, if not eating straight away.

Peach crumble

Prep: 10 mins **Cook:** 35 mins

Serves 6

Ingredients

- 3 x 410g cans peach slices in juice
- zest 1 lemon, plus juice ½
- 1 tbsp agave syrup
- 140g plain flour

- 50g porridge oat
- 25g cold butter, grated

Method

STEP 1

Heat oven to 200C/180C fan/gas 6. Drain the peaches, but reserve the juice. Tip the peaches into a deep baking dish, roughly 20 x 30cm. Scatter over the lemon zest and juice and 1 tbsp of the agave, then toss everything together.

STEP 2

In a bowl, combine the flour, oats, butter, remaining agave and 4 tbsp of the reserved peach juice. Mix together, first with a spoon, then with your fingers, until you have a rough crumbly mixture. Scatter over the peaches, then bake for 35 mins until golden and crunchy on top.

Smoked salmon & avocado sushi

Prep: 20 mins **Cook:** 10 mins

Makes 32

Ingredients

- 300g sushi rice
- 2 tbsp rice or white wine vinegar
- 1 tsp caster sugar
- 1 large avocado
- juice ½ lemon
- 4 sheets nori seaweed
- 4 large slices smoked salmon
- 1 bunch chives
- sweet soy sauce (kecap manis), to serve

Method

STEP 1

Put the rice in a small pan with 600ml water. Bring to the boil and cook for 10 mins until the water is absorbed and the rice is tender. Stir through the vinegar and sugar, cover and cool.

STEP 2

Skin, stone and slice the avocado. Put in a bowl and squeeze over the lemon juice, turning the avocado to ensure the pieces are covered.

STEP 3

Divide the rice between the nori sheets and spread it out evenly, leaving a 1cm border at the top and bottom. Lay the salmon over the rice, followed by the chives and finally position the avocado across the centre.

STEP 4

Fold the bottom edge of the seaweed over the filling, then roll it up firmly. Dampen the top border with a little water to help it seal the roll. Repeat to make 4 rolls. At this stage, the rolls can be wrapped individually in cling film and chilled until ready to serve.

STEP 5

Using a serrated knife, cut each roll into 8 rounds. Serve with sweet soy sauce for dipping.

Hot & sour broth with prawns

Prep: 10 mins **Cook:** 5 mins

Serves 4

Ingredients

- 3 tbsp rice vinegar or white wine vinegar
- 500ml chicken stock
- 1 tbsp soy sauce
- 1-2 tbsp golden caster sugar
- thumb-size piece ginger, peeled and thinly sliced
- 2 small hot red chillies, thinly sliced
- 3 spring onions, thinly sliced
- 300g small raw peeled prawns, from a sustainable source

Method

STEP 1

Put the vinegar, stock, soy sauce, sugar (start with 1 tbsp and add the second at the end if you want the soup sweeter), ginger, chillies and spring onions in a saucepan and bring to a simmer. Cook for 1 min, then add the prawns to heat through. Serve in small bowls or cups.

Herby celery & bulgur salad

Prep: 30 mins No cook

Serves 6

Ingredients

- 200g bulgur wheat
- 1 bunch celery
- 1 dessert apple
- juice 1 lemon
- 4 tbsp olive oil
- handful toasted hazelnuts , roughly chopped
- 1 red chilli , deseeded and chopped
- large handful pomegranate seeds
- small bunch parsley , chopped
- small bunch mint , chopped
- small bunch tarragon , chopped

Method

STEP 1

Put the bulgur wheat in a large bowl and just cover with boiling water. Cover the bowl with cling film and leave for 30 mins to absorb all the water.

STEP 2

Meanwhile, separate the sticks of celery and set the leaves aside. Very finely slice the celery and roughly chop the leaves. Cut the apple into fine matchsticks and toss in a little lemon juice. In a bowl, mix the remaining lemon juice with the oil and some seasoning to make a dressing.

STEP 3

Gently fluff up the bulgur with a fork. Mix the sliced celery and apple through the bulgur, followed by the nuts, chilli, pomegranate seeds and herbs. Drizzle over the dressing and toss everything together gently. Scatter with the celery leaves and serve.

Crispy fried chicken

Prep: 15 mins **Cook:** 20 mins plus 1 hr or overnight marinating

Serves 4

Ingredients

- 150ml buttermilk
- 2 plump garlic cloves, crushed
- 4 x skinless, boneless chicken breasts (total weight 550g), preferably organic
- 50g Japanese panko breadcrumbs
- 2 tbsp self-raising flour
- ½ rounded tsp paprika
- ¼ rounded tsp English mustard powder
- ¼ rounded tsp dried thyme
- ¼ tsp hot chilli powder
- ½ tsp ground black pepper
- 3 tbsp rapeseed oil

Method

STEP 1

Pour the buttermilk into a wide shallow dish and stir in the garlic. Slice the chicken into chunky slices, about 9.5cm long x 3-4cm wide. Lay the chicken in the dish and turn it over in the buttermilk so it is well coated. Leave in the fridge for 1-2 hrs, or preferably overnight.

STEP 2

Meanwhile, heat a large, non-stick frying pan and tip in the panko crumbs and flour. Toast them in the pan for 2-3 mins, stirring regularly so they brown evenly and don't burn. Tip the crumb mix into a bowl and stir in the paprika, mustard, thyme, chilli powder, pepper and a pinch of fine sea salt. Set aside.

STEP 3

When ready to cook, heat oven to 230C/210C fan/gas 8. Line a baking tin with foil and sit a wire rack (preferably non-stick) on top. Transfer half the crumb mix to a medium-large plastic bag. Lift half the chicken from the buttermilk, leaving the marinade clinging to it. Transfer it to the bag of seasoned crumbs. Seal the end of the bag and give it a good shake so the chicken gets well covered (you could do all the crumbs and chicken together if you prefer, but it's easier to coat evenly in 2 batches).

STEP 4

Remove the chicken from the bag. Heat 1 tbsp of the oil in a large, non-stick frying pan, then add the chicken pieces and fry for 1½ mins without moving them. Turn the chicken over, pour in another ½ tbsp of the oil to cover the base of the pan and fry for 1 min more, so both sides are becoming golden. Using tongs, transfer to the wire rack. Repeat with the remaining seasoned crumbs, oil and chicken.

STEP 5

Bake all the chicken on the rack for 15 mins until cooked and crisp, then serve with the Crunchy coleslaw (see 'Goes well with', below right).

Chickpea mash

Prep: 5 mins **Cook:** 1 hr and 10 mins plus overnight soaking

Serves 6

Ingredients

- 500g pack of dried chickpeas
- 1 tsp fennel seeds
- 1 banana shallot , quartered lengthways
- 1 red chilli , deseeded and halved lengthways
- 2 rosemary sprigs
- 2 bay leaves
- 250ml white wine
- 1.3l vegetable stock (we used Marigold bouillon)
- extra virgin olive oil , to serve

Method

STEP 1

In a large bowl, cover the chickpeas with cold water and soak overnight. The next day, drain and rinse well.

STEP 2

Tip the chickpeas into a large pan with all the other ingredients except the olive oil. Bring to the boil, then leave to simmer for 1 hr-1 hr 10 mins until the chickpeas are tender but not mushy.

STEP 3

Remove the bay leaves and rosemary sprigs. Working in batches, blitz the chickpeas in a food processor along with their cooking liquid and the shallot until smooth.

STEP 4

Reheat the mash if necessary and serve sharing-style with a generous drizzle of olive oil and some cracked black pepper on top.

Lentil, walnut & apple salad with blue cheese

Prep: 30 mins **Cook:** 25 mins

Serves 4

Ingredients

- 250g Puy lentil
- 1l chicken stock or water
- 1 celery heart, finely chopped
- 1 Granny Smith , peeled, cored and finely sliced
- 2 shallots , finely sliced

- 25g walnut , toasted and chopped
- 2 tbsp flat-leaf parsley , finely chopped
- a few handfuls mixed leaf salad
- 1 tbsp strong blue cheese , crumbled (we used Roquefort)

For the vinaigrette

- 2 tbsp extra-virgin olive oil or walnut oil
- 2 tbsp red wine vinegar
- 1 tsp Dijon mustard
- 1 garlic clove , crushed

Method

STEP 1

Put the lentils and stock or water in a large saucepan and bring to the boil. Reduce the heat and simmer for 20-25 mins, or until al dente. Drain and pour into a bowl. Add the celery, apple, shallots, walnuts, parsley and salad leaves, then mix together well.

STEP 2

To make the vinaigrette, put all the ingredients in a small glass jar with a lid. Season and shake well. Keep the lid on until ready to serve. Pour the dressing over the salad, toss well, then scatter over the blue cheese.

Mango chicken with spiced pilau

Prep: 10 mins **Cook:** 30 mins

Serves 4

Ingredients

- 4 skinless, boneless chicken breasts
- 4 tbsp chunky mango chutney
- 1 tbsp medium curry powder
- 4 tsp cumin seeds
- 4 tsp sunflower oil
- 2 small onions, thinly sliced
- 4 bay leaves
- 1 cinnamon stick
- 200g basmati rice
- 4 tbsp chopped coriander
- lime wedges, to serve (optional)

Method

STEP 1

Heat oven to 200C/180C fan/gas 6 and line a baking tray with foil. Cut a horizontal pocket in each chicken breast, taking care not to cut all the way through to the other side. Stuff with the mango chutney, then seal the pocket closed around the chutney with a cocktail stick.

STEP 2

Mix the curry powder and 2 tsp cumin seeds with 3 tsp oil, then brush all over the chicken. Place on the baking tray and roast for 25-30 mins until cooked through.

STEP 3

Meanwhile, heat remaining oil and fry the onions for 6-8 mins until golden. Add remaining cumin, bay and cinnamon then cook, stirring, for 1 min. Stir in the rice. Pour over 450ml boiling water, add a pinch of salt, bring to the boil, stir and cover. Reduce heat; simmer for 15 mins.

STEP 4

Remove bay and cinnamon, stir in coriander and serve with the chicken.

Stir-fry green curry beef with asparagus & sugar snaps

Prep: 10 mins **Cook:** 10 mins

Serves 2

Ingredients

- 250g very lean sirloin steak , sliced
- 1 tsp Thai fish sauce
- zest and juice 1/2 lime
- ½ tsp green peppercorns in brine, rinsed and chopped
- 3 garlic cloves , chopped
- 1 tbsp rapeseed oil
- 1 large banana shallot , chopped
- 10 asparagus spears , sliced at an angle
- 4 handfuls sugar snap peas
- 4 broccoli florets (about 275g/10oz), cut into smaller pieces
- 175ml reduced-fat coconut milk
- 2-3 tsp green Thai curry paste (if you like it spicy, use a yellow paste)
- good handful basil leaves (about 25)

Method

STEP 1

Stir the beef with the fish sauce, lime zest, peppercorns and garlic, then set aside. Heat half the oil in a large non-stick wok and pile in the shallot, asparagus, sugar snaps and broccoli. Stir-fry over a high heat for 5 mins. (There are a lot of vegetables, so you can speed up the process by adding a dash of water to the wok every now and then to steam them at the same time.)

STEP 2

Stir the coconut milk, curry paste and lime juice together, pour into the pan and stir well. Simmer for 2 mins, adding a few tbsp water until the vegetables are tender but still have a lot of bite. Tip into bowls and keep warm.

STEP 3

Add the remaining oil to the pan, tip in the beef and stir-fry for 1-2 mins until just cooked. Stir through the basil leaves and serve on top of the vegetables.

Chicken, butter bean & pepper stew

Prep: 10 mins **Cook:** 55 mins

Serves 4

Ingredients

- 1 tbsp olive oil
- 1 large onion , chopped
- 2 celery sticks, chopped
- 1 yellow pepper , deseeded and diced
- 1 red pepper , deseeded and diced
- 1 garlic clove , crushed
- 2 tbsp paprika
- 400g can chopped tomato
- 150ml chicken stock
- 2 x 400g cans butter beans , drained and rinsed
- 8 skinless chicken thighs

Method

STEP 1

Heat oven to 180C/160C fan/gas 4. Heat the oil in a large flameproof casserole dish. Add the onion, celery and peppers, and fry for 5 mins. Add the garlic and paprika, and cook for a further 3 mins.

STEP 2

Stir in the tomatoes, stock and butter beans, and season well. Bring to the boil, then nestle the chicken thighs into the sauce. Cover with a tight-fitting lid and put in the oven for 45 mins.

Cheesy turkey nuggets with smoking chips

Prep: 15 mins **Cook:** 30 mins

Serves 4

Ingredients

- 1 egg
- 3 tbsp finely grated parmesan
- 3 garlic cloves , 1 crushed, 2 finely chopped
- 500g pack turkey breast pieces, large chunks halved to make 16 pieces in all
- 750g large potato , cut into thick chips
- 2 tbsp sunflower oil
- 65g fresh breadcrumb (all crusts if possible)
- ½-1 tsp smoked paprika
- salad , to serve

Method

STEP 1

Heat oven to 220C/200C fan/gas 7. Beat the egg in a bowl with the Parmesan, crushed garlic and some seasoning, then stir in the turkey pieces.

STEP 2

Toss potatoes in the oil, then spread out on a baking tray and bake for 15 mins.

STEP 3

Meanwhile, toss the turkey into the breadcrumbs and spread out on another baking tray. Take the chips from the oven and tip in a bowl with the chopped garlic, paprika and sea salt. Mix well, then spread back out on the tray and return to the oven with the turkey. Bake for 10-12 mins, then serve with a salad.

Beetroot hummus

Prep: 15 mins **Cook:** 45 mins Plus cooling

Serves 8-10

Ingredients

- 500g raw beetroot , leaves trimmed to 1 inch, but root left whole
- 2 x 400g cans chickpeas , drained
- juice 2 lemons
- 1 tbsp ground cumin
- yogurt, toasted cumin seeds, mint and crusty bread, to serve

Method

STEP 1

Cook the beetroot in a large pan of boiling water with the lid on for 30-40 mins until tender. When they're done, a skewer or knife should go all the way in easily. Drain, then set aside to cool.

STEP 2

Pop on a pair of rubber gloves. Pull off and discard the roots, leaves/stalk and peel of the cooled beetroot. Roughly chop the flesh. Whizz the beetroot, chickpeas, lemon juice, cumin,

2 tsp salt and some pepper. Serve swirled with a little yogurt, some toasted cumin seeds, a little torn mint and some crusty bread.

Spiced cod with quinoa salad & mint chutney

Prep: 5 mins **Cook:** 25 mins

Serves 2

Ingredients

- 40g quinoa (or 85g pre-cooked quinoa)
- 3 tbsp chopped mint
- 3 tbsp chopped coriander
- 150g pot 0% natural yogurt
- 1 garlic clove
- ¼ tsp turmeric
- pinch of cumin seeds
- 2 x 150g chunky fillets skinless white fish, such as sustainable cod
- ¼ cucumber, finely diced
- 1 small red onion, finely chopped
- 4 tomatoes, chopped
- good squeeze of lemon juice

Method

STEP 1

Tip the quinoa (if not pre-cooked) into a pan, cover with water and boil, covered, for 25 mins, checking the water level to make sure it doesn't boil dry. Drain well.

STEP 2

Meanwhile, put 2 tbsp each of the mint and coriander in a bowl. Add the yogurt and garlic, and blitz with a hand blender until smooth. Stir 2 tbsp of the herby yogurt with the turmeric and cumin, then add the fish and turn in the mixture to completely coat.

STEP 3

Turn the grill to High. Arrange the fish in a shallow heatproof dish and grill for 8-10 mins, depending on thickness, until it flakes. Toss the quinoa with the cucumber, onion, tomatoes, lemon juice and remaining herbs. Spoon onto a plate, add the fish and spoon round the mint chutney, or add it at the table.

Spicy tuna quinoa salad

Prep:10 mins **Cook:**10 mins

Serves 4

Ingredients

- 1 onion , sliced
- 350g pepper , sliced
- 1 tbsp olive oil
- 1 red chilli , finely chopped
- 225g pouch ready-to-eat quinoa
- 350g cherry tomato , halved
- handful black olives , chopped
- 225g jar albacore tuna in olive oil, flaked

Method

STEP 1

Fry the onion and peppers in the oil until soft. Add the chilli and cool slightly.

STEP 2

Mix the quinoa, onion mixture, cherry tomatoes, olives and tuna together. Divide between 4 plates, pour over a little of the oil from the tuna jar, season and serve.

Mediterranean chicken with roasted vegetables

Prep:50 mins - 55 mins **Serves 2**

Ingredients

- 250g baby new potatoes, thinly sliced
- 1 large courgette, diagonally sliced
- 1 red onion, cut into wedges
- 1 yellow pepper, seeded and cut into chunks
- 6 firm plum tomatoes, halved
- 12 black olives, pitted
- 2 skinless boneless chicken breast fillets, about 150g/5oz each
- 3 tbsp olive oil
- 1 rounded tbsp green pesto

Method

STEP 1

Preheat the oven to 200C/ Gas 6/fan oven 180C. Spread the potatoes, courgette, onion, pepper and tomatoes in a shallow roasting tin and scatter over the olives. Season with salt and coarsely ground black pepper.

STEP 2

Slash the flesh of each chicken breast 3-4 times using a sharp knife, then lay the chicken on top of the vegetables.

STEP 3

Mix the olive oil and pesto together until well blended and spoon evenly over the chicken. Cover the tin with foil and cook for 30 minutes.

STEP 4

Remove the foil from the tin. Return to the oven and cook for a further 10 minutes until the vegetables are juicy and look tempting to eat and the chicken is cooked through (the juices should run clear when pierced with a skewer).

Spring salmon with minty veg

Prep: 10 mins **Cook:** 10 mins

Serves 4

Ingredients

- 750g small new potato , thickly sliced
- 750g frozen pea and beans (we used Waitrose pea and bean mix, £2.29/1kg)
- 3 tbsp olive oil
- zest and juice of 1 lemon
- small pack mint , leaves only
- 4 salmon fillets about 140g/5oz each

Method

STEP 1

Boil the potatoes in a large pan for 4 mins. Tip in the peas and beans, bring back up to a boil, then carry on cooking for another 3 mins until the potatoes and beans are tender. Whizz the olive oil, lemon zest and juice and mint in a blender to make a dressing(or finely chop the mint and whisk into the oil and lemon).

STEP 2

Put the salmon in a microwave-proof dish, season, then pour the dressing over. Cover with cling film, pierce, then microwave on High for 4-5 mins until cooked through. Drain the veg, then mix with the hot dressing and cooking juices from the fish. Serve the fish on top of the vegetables.

Tomato & tamarind fish curry

Prep: 10 mins **Cook:** 25 mins

Serves 4

Ingredients

- 6 garlic cloves
- 1 red chilli , roughly chopped (deseeded if you don't like it too hot)
- thumb-sized piece ginger , peeled and roughly chopped
- 1 tsp turmeric
- 1 tbsp ground coriander
- 1 tbsp rapeseed oil
- 2 tsp cumin seed
- 1 tsp fennel seed
- 2 x 400g cans chopped tomatoes
- 200g green bean , trimmed and halved
- 1 tbsp tamarind paste
- 4 firm white fish fillets (we used hake)
- handful coriander leaves, roughly chopped
- cooked basmati rice , to serve

Method

STEP 1

Blitz together the garlic, chilli, ginger, turmeric and ground coriander with 3 tbsp water. Heat the oil in a large pan and toast the cumin and fennel seeds, letting them sizzle until aromatic. Add the ginger paste and fry for 3 mins.

STEP 2

Empty the tomatoes into the spice pan, plus a can of water. Add the beans, bring to the boil, then turn down the heat and simmer for 5 mins. Stir in the tamarind paste. Add the fish fillets, generously season with ground black pepper, cover and simmer for 10 mins. Take off the lid, carefully turn the fillets, then bubble the sauce until the fish is cooked through and the sauce is thick. Sprinkle over the coriander leaves and serve with rice.

Indian rice salad with chicken

Prep: 20 mins **Cook:** 20 mins

Serves 6 - 8

Ingredients

- 500g bag long grain rice
- 1 tsp turmeric
- small bunch coriander , leaves roughly chopped, stalks reserved
- 100g bag toasted cashew , ½ very roughly chopped
- 1 cucumber , deseeded and cut into chunks
- 1 large red onion , finely chopped
- about 110g pack pomegranate seeds
- 400g can black bean , drained and rinsed
- 2 x roughly 130g packs cooked chicken tikka pieces, chopped
- natural yogurt and mini poppadum crisps, to serve (optional)

For the dressing

- 4 tbsp mango chutney
- 1 tbsp sunflower oil
- 1 tbsp brown sugar
- 1 tbsp medium curry powder , plus 1 tsp for the rice
- juice 1½-2 lemon , depending on size

Method

STEP 1

Cook the rice following pack instructions but add the turmeric and 1 tsp curry powder to the cooking water. Drain well and spread on a tray lined with kitchen paper to cool.

STEP 2

Meanwhile, finely chop the coriander stalks and whisk with all the other dressing ingredients, plus seasoning.

STEP 3

Tip the rice into a big mixing bowl. Using a fork, break up any large lumps, then mix in the cashews, cucumber, onion, coriander leaves, pomegranate seeds, beans and chicken. Pour over the dressing and lightly stir in, then cover and keep in the fridge. Eat over the next 2 days (as long as it's within the chicken use-by date). Keep a big spoon in the bowl so kids can easily help themselves. Top with a dollop of yogurt and add a handful of poppadum crisps, if you like.

Japanese-style brown rice

Prep: 5 mins **Cook:** 25 mins

Serves 4

Ingredients

- 250g brown rice
- 175g frozen soya bean
- 1 tbsp low-salt soy sauce
- 1 tbsp extra virgin olive oil
- 2 tsp finely grated ginger
- 1 garlic clove , crushed
- 4 spring onions , thinly sliced on the diagonal

Method

STEP 1

Cook the brown rice following pack instructions, adding the soya beans for the final 2 mins of cooking. Meanwhile, mix together the soy sauce, olive oil, ginger and garlic.

STEP 2

Drain the cooked rice and beans, transfer to a serving bowl and stir in the soy sauce mixture. Scatter with the spring onions and serve.

Curried chickpeas

Prep: 15 mins **Cook:** 15 mins

Serves 4

Ingredients

- 2 tbsp vegetable oil
- 1 tsp cumin seeds
- 1-2 red chillies , deseeded and chopped
- 1 clove
- 1 small cinnamon stick
- 1 bay leaf
- 1 onion , finely chopped
- ½ tsp ground turmeric
- 2 garlic cloves , finely chopped
- 400g can chickpeas , rinsed and drained
- 1 tsp paprika
- 1 tsp ground coriander
- 2 small tomatoes , chopped
- 1 tbsp chopped coriander

Method

STEP 1

Heat the oil in a heavy-bottomed pan. Fry the cumin, chillies, clove, cinnamon and bay leaf together until the cumin starts to crackle. Tip in the onion, turmeric and a pinch of salt. Cook for 2 mins until starting to soften, then add the garlic.

STEP 2

Continue cooking 4-5 mins until the onion is soft, then add chickpeas, paprika, black pepper and ground coriander. Give everything a good stir so the chickpeas are well coated in the spices.

STEP 3

Add the tomatoes and 2 tbsp water. Cook on a medium heat until tomatoes are soft and the sauce is thick and pulpy. Take off the heat and sprinkle on the coriander.

Stir-fried beef with hoisin sauce

Prep: 20 mins - 25 mins Plus 20 minutes marinating

Serves 2

Ingredients

- 1 tbsp soy sauce
- 1 tbsp dry sherry
- 2 tsp sesame oil
- 1 fat garlic clove , crushed
- 1 tsp finely chopped fresh root ginger (or fresh ginger paste in a jar)
- 200g lean sirloin steak , thinly sliced across the grain
- 1 tbsp sesame seeds
- 1 tbsp sunflower oil
- 1 large carrot , cut into matchsticks
- 100g mangetout , halved lengthways
- 140g mushrooms , sliced
- 3 tbsp hoisin sauce
- Chinese noodles , to serve

Method

STEP 1

Mix together the soy sauce, sherry, sesame oil, garlic and ginger in a shallow dish. Add the steak and leave to marinate for about 20 minutes (or longer, if you have time).

STEP 2

Heat a large heavy-based frying pan or wok, add the sesame seeds and toast over a high heat, stirring, for a few minutes until golden. Tip on to a plate.

STEP 3

When ready to cook, heat the sunflower oil in a large frying pan or wok until hot. Add the steak with the marinade and stir fry for 3-4 minutes over a high heat until lightly browned. Remove, using a slotted spoon, on to a plate, leaving the juices in the pan.

STEP 4

Toss the carrots in the pan and stir fry for a few minutes, then add the mangetout and cook for a further 2 minutes.

STEP 5

Return the steak to the pan, add the mushrooms and toss everything together. Add the hoisin sauce and stir fry for a final minute. Sprinkle with the toasted sesame seeds and serve immediately.

For-the-freezer ratatouille

Prep: 15 mins **Cook:** 1 hr and 55 mins for the basic ratatouille

Serves 10

Ingredients

- 250g red onion , cut into 3cm chunks
- 250g white onion , cut into 3cm chunks
- 600g red and yellow pepper - after deseeding and removing stalks, cut into chunks
- 1kg courgette , cut into 3cm chunks
- 1kg aubergine
- 20g garlic clove , crushed
- 800g cherry tomato
- 3 x 400g cans chopped tomatoes
- 1 tbsp sugar
- 2 tbsp red wine vinegar

To serve as Greek veg bake with feta (serves 1)

- 1 tsp dried thyme or oregano, plus a pinch extra
- 1 tbsp wholemeal breadcrumb
- 25g light feta cheese

To serve as veggie chilli jackets (serves 1)

- 1 small baking potato weighing 100g
- 1 tsp cumin seed
- 1 tsp mild chilli powder
- 2 tbsp chopped coriander

To serve as cheesy stuffed peppers (serves 2)

- 2 small peppers of any colour
- 25g lighter mature cheddar
- 200g cooked broccoli

- 30g Little Gem lettuce leaves
- 25g sliced spring onion
- 50g sliced cucumber
- squeeze of lemon juice

- 25g fat-free Greek yogurt
- 10g rocket leaves
- squeeze of lemon juice

- 20g baby spinach leaves
- 1 tsp balsamic vinegar

Method

STEP 1

Heat oven to 200C/180C fan/gas 6. Scatter the onions in a roasting tin, season and roast for 25 mins, stirring occasionally, until charred and softened. Repeat with the peppers for 20 mins, then the courgette for just 15 mins.

STEP 2

Heat a non-stick frying pan. Slice the aubergines into 2-3cm thick rounds and arrange in the pan (only cut what you can fit in your pan at a time – cooking freshly cut slices in batches should prevent them going brown). Cook over a high heat until charred on both sides, then remove to a microwave-proof plate. Repeat in batches until all are nicely crisped and browned. Cover the plate with cling film, poke in a couple of holes, then microwave the aubergines on High for about 5 mins until soft. You may need to do this in batches. Quarter the slices, or cut into chunks. (Because you're frying without oil, they'll burn before they're cooked through, so finishing in a microwave is ideal. If you don't have one, just add to the sauce for the final 10-15 mins simmering, but they may break up a bit.)

STEP 3

While roasting the veg, put the garlic in the non-stick frying pan or a large pan with a small glass of water. Simmer until the water is nearly gone, then tip in the cherry and chopped tomatoes, sugar, vinegar and plenty of seasoning. Simmer for 20 mins until thickened and saucy. Taste for seasoning, then turn off and combine with the veg. Cool, divide into 10 portions and freeze.

STEP 4

To serve as Greek veg bake with feta (serves 1, prep 10 mins, cook 15 mins): Stir herbs through 1 serving defrosted ratatouille and tip into a small dish. Sprinkle with breadcrumbs, then add feta with a pinch more herbs. Bake at 200C/180C fan/gas 6 for 15 mins if defrosted, or 25-30 mins from frozen. Toss Baby Gem leaves with spring onion, cucumber and lemon juice. Serve with the bake.

Per serving: 236 kcals, protein 13g, carbs 34g, fat 5g, sat fat 3g, fibre 10g, sugar 20g, salt 1.0g

STEP 5

To serve as veggie chilli jackets (serves 1, prep 5 mins, cook about 1hr): Bake potato in the oven. Add a few tbsp water to a pan with cumin seeds and chilli powder. Simmer, and just before the water evaporates, stir in 1 serving of defrosted ratatouille. Heat through, then stir in coriander. Halve the potato, top with veggie chilli and Greek yogurt. Serve with rocket leaves dressed with lemon juice.

Per serving: 270kcals, protein 14g, carbs 50g, fat 3g, sat fat 0g, fibrew 12g, sugar 20g, salt 0.4g

STEP 6

To serve as cheesy stuffed peppers (serves 2, prep 15 mins, cook 20 mins): Halve peppers down the stalks and scrape out any seeds. Divide 1 serving of defrosted ratatouille between the pepper halves. Grate over cheddar, then bake for 15-20 mins at 200C/180C fan/gas 6. Serve with broccoli and spinach tossed with balsamic vinegar.

Per serving: 173 kcals, protein 12g, carbs 21g, fat 4g, sat fat 2g, fibre 10g, sugar 20g, salt 0.4g

Ceviche

Prep: 20 mins Plus 1hr 30 mins in lime juice no cook

Serves 6 as a starter

Ingredients

- 500g firm white fish fillets, such as haddock, halibut or pollack, skinned and thinly sliced
- juice 8 limes (250ml/9fl oz), plus extra wedges to serve
- 1 red onion , sliced into rings
- handful pitted green olives , finely chopped
- 2-3 green chillies , finely chopped
- 2-3 tomatoes , seeded and chopped into 2cm pieces
- bunch coriander , roughly chopped
- 2 tbsp extra-virgin olive oil
- good pinch caster sugar
- tortilla chips , to serve

Method

STEP 1

In a large glass bowl, combine the fish, lime juice and onion. The juice should completely cover the fish; if not, add a little more. Cover with cling film and place in the fridge for 1 hr 30 mins.

STEP 2

Remove the fish and onion from the lime juice (discard the juice) and place in a bowl. Add the olives, chilies, tomatoes, coriander and olive oil, stir gently, then season with a good pinch of salt and sugar. This can be made a couple of hours in advance and stored in the fridge. Serve with tortilla chips to scoop up the ceviche and enjoy with a glass of cold beer.

Summer vegetable minestrone

Prep: 10 mins **Cook:** 30 mins

Serves 4

Ingredients

- 3 tbsp olive oil
- 2 leeks , finely sliced
- 2 celery sticks, finely chopped
- 2 courgettes , quartered lengthways then sliced
- 4 garlic cloves , finely chopped
- 1l vegetable stock
- 250g asparagus , woody ends removed, chopped
- 100g pea , fresh or frozen
- 200g broad bean , double-podded if you have time
- small bunch basil , most chopped
- crusty bread , to serve

Method

STEP 1

Heat the oil in a large saucepan, add the leeks and celery, and cook for 8 mins until soft. Add the courgettes and garlic. Cook gently for 5 mins more.

STEP 2

Pour in the stock and simmer, covered, for 10 mins. Add the asparagus, peas and broad beans, and cook for a further 4 mins, until just cooked through. Stir in the chopped basil and season well. Scatter with basil leaves and serve with crusty bread.

Spring greens with lemon dressing

Prep: 10 mins **Cook:** 5 mins

Serves 8

Ingredients

- 250g broccoli , thicker stalks halved
- 400g spring green , thick stalks removed and shredded

For the dressing

- 2 garlic cloves , crushed
- zest and juice 1 lemon
- 2 tbsp olive oil

Method

STEP 1

To make the dressing, mix the garlic, lemon juice and zest, olive oil and some seasoning together. Bring a large pan of water to the boil, then add the broccoli and greens, and cook for about 5 mins until tender. Drain well, then toss through the dressing and serve.

Harissa aubergine kebabs with minty carrot salad

Prep: 10 mins **Cook:** 15 mins

Serves 2

Ingredients

- 2 tbsp harissa paste
- 2 tbsp red wine vinegar
- 1 aubergine , cut into 4cm cubes
- 2 carrots , finely shredded
- 1 small red onion , sliced
- small handful mint , chopped, plus extra leaves to serve
- 2 Middle Eastern flatbreads
- 2 heaped tbsp hummus
- Greek yoghurt , to serve

Method

STEP 1

Mix the harissa and vinegar in a bowl. Remove half and reserve. Toss the aubergine in the remaining harissa sauce and season. Thread onto metal or soaked wooden skewers. Heat a griddle or grill until hot, then cook the kebabs until golden on all sides and cooked through.

STEP 2

Meanwhile, mix together the carrots, onion and mint with some seasoning.

STEP 3

Top the flatbreads with the hummus, carrot salad and kebabs. Scatter over the extra mint and serve with yogurt and a drizzle of reserved harissa sauce.

Peanut hummus with fruit & veg sticks

Prep: 10 mins No cook

Serves 2

Ingredients

- 380g carton chickpeas
- zest and juice 0.5 lemon (use the other 1/2 to squeeze over the apple to stop it browning, if you like)
- 1 tbsp tahini
- 0.5-1 tsp smoked paprika
- 2 tbsp roasted unsalted peanuts
- 1 tsp rapeseed oil
- 2 crisp red apples , cored and cut into slices
- 2 carrots , cut into sticks
- 4 celery sticks, cut into batons lengthways

Method

STEP 1

Drain the chickpeas, reserving the liquid. Tip three-quarters of the chickpeas into a food processor and add the lemon zest and juice, tahini, paprika, peanuts and oil with 3 tbsp chickpea liquid. Blitz in a food processor until smooth, then stir in the reserved chickpeas. Serve with the fruit and veg sticks.

Bean & pesto mash

Prep: 5 mins **Cook:** 5 mins

Serves 4

Ingredients

- 1 tbsp olive oil , plus a drizzle to serve (optional)
- 2 x 400g cans cannellini beans , rinsed and drained
- 2 tbsp pesto

Method

STEP 1

Heat the oil in a large saucepan. Add the beans and cook for 3-4 mins until hot through. Lightly mash with a potato masher for a chunky texture. Stir through the pesto and season. To serve, drizzle with a little olive oil, if you like.

Super-green mackerel salad

Prep: 10 mins **Cook:** 10 mins

Serves 1

Ingredients

- 85g green bean
- 85g thin-stemmed broccoli
- large handful baby spinach leaves
- 2 hot-smoked mackerel fillets (about 75g), skinned and flaked
- 2 tsp sunflower seed , toasted

For the dressing

- 75ml low-fat natural yogurt
- 1 tsp lemon juice
- 1 tsp wholegrain mustard
- 2 tsp dill, chopped, plus extra to serve

Method

STEP 1

Boil a pan of water. Add the green beans and cook for 2 mins, then add the broccoli and cook for 4 mins more. Drain, run under cold water until cool, then drain well.

STEP 2

To make the dressing, combine all the ingredients in a small jam jar with a twist of black pepper, put the lid on and give it a good shake.

STEP 3

To serve, mix together the cooked veg with the spinach and mackerel and pack into a lunchbox. Just before eating, pour over the dressing, scatter over the sunflower seeds and add a grind of black pepper and extra dill.

Yellow lentil & coconut curry with cauliflower

Prep: 15 mins **Cook:** 50 mins

Serves 4

Ingredients

- 1 tbsp vegetable oil
- 1 onion, thinly sliced
- 2 garlic cloves, crushed
- thumb-sized piece ginger, finely chopped
- 3 tbsp curry paste (we used Bart Veeraswamy Gujurat Masala curry paste)
- 200g yellow lentil, rinsed
- 1 ½l vegetable stock
- 3 tbsp unsweetened desiccated coconut, plus extra to sprinkle if you like
- 1 cauliflower, broken into little florets
- cooked basmati rice and coriander leaves, plus mango chutney and naan bread (optional), to serve

Method

STEP 1

Heat the oil in a large saucepan, then add the onion, garlic and ginger. Cook for 5 mins, add the curry paste, then stir-fry for 1 min before adding the lentils, stock and coconut. Bring the mixture to the boil and simmer for 40 mins or until the lentils are soft.

STEP 2

During the final 10 mins of cooking, stir in the cauliflower to cook. Spoon rice into 4 bowls, top with the curry and sprinkle with coriander leaves, and coconut if you like. Serve with mango chutney and naan bread (optional).

Charred broccoli, lemon & walnut pasta

Prep: 5 mins **Cook:** 15 mins

Serves 2

Ingredients

- 1 head broccoli , cut into small florets and stalk cut into small pieces
- 3 tsp olive oil
- 150g penne or fusilli
- 2 garlic cloves , crushed
- 1 tbsp roughly chopped walnuts
- pinch of chilli flakes
- ½ lemon , zested and juiced

Method

STEP 1

Heat the grill to high. Put the broccoli on a baking tray and drizzle over 1 tsp of the oil. Season, and toss together. Grill for 8-10 mins, tossing around halfway through, until crispy and charred.

STEP 2

Cook the pasta in salted water following pack instructions. Drain, reserving a cup of the cooking water.

STEP 3

In a frying pan, heat the remaining 2 tsp oil over a medium heat, and fry the garlic, walnuts and chilli for 3-4 mins until golden.

STEP 4

Tip in the pasta, broccoli, lemon zest and juice, reserving a little of the zest. Add a splash of the reserved cooking water and toss everything together to coat the pasta. Serve in warmed bowls with the remaining lemon zest scattered over.

Creamy yogurt porridge with pear, walnut & cinnamon topping

Prep: 6 mins **Cook:** 3 mins

Serves 1

Ingredients

For the porridge

- 3 tbsp (25g) porridge oat
- 150g 0% fat probiotic plain yogurt

For the topping

- 1 ripe pear , sliced (keep the skin on)
- 4 broken walnut halves
- couple pinches of cinnamon

Method

STEP 1

For the porridge: Tip 200ml water into a small non-stick pan and stir in porridge oats. Cook over a low heat until bubbling and thickened. (To make in a microwave, use a deep container to prevent spillage as the mixture will rise up as it cooks, and cook for 3 mins on High.) Stir in yogurt – or swirl in half and top with the rest.

STEP 2

For the topping: Add pear and walnut halves to the finished porridge, then sprinkle on cinnamon.

Beetroot & squash salad with horseradish cream

Prep: 30 mins **Cook:** 45 mins

Serves 12

Ingredients

- 1kg raw beetroot
- 6 red onions
- 1 ¼kg large butternut squash, peeled and deseeded

For the horseradish cream

- 175ml soured cream
- 3 tbsp creamed horseradish
- 2 tbsp red wine vinegar
- 1 tbsp soft brown sugar
- 50ml olive oil
- juice 1 lemon
- 85g watercress, large stalks removed

Method

STEP 1

Heat oven to 200C/180C fan/gas 6. Peel the beetroot and cut each into 8 wedges. Cut the onions and butternut squash into roughly the same size. Spread out in a large roasting tin. Mix the vinegar and sugar until dissolved, then whisk in the oil. Pour over the vegetables, toss and roast for 40-45 mins until charred and soft, stirring halfway through cooking.

STEP 2

To make the horseradish cream, mix together the soured cream, horseradish, lemon juice and some seasoning.

STEP 3

To serve, put the roasted veg in a large bowl or on a platter, followed by the watercress, then drizzle over the horseradish cream. Serve warm or cold.

Bean, feta & herb dip

Prep: 10 mins No cook

Serves 4

Ingredients

- 400g can cannellini bean
- 200g feta cheese
- 1 tbsp lemon juice
- 1 garlic clove, crushed

- 3 tbsp chopped dill, mint or chives (or 1 tbsp each)

Method

STEP 1

Drain and rinse beans. Tip into a food processor with feta, lemon juice and garlic, and whizz until smooth. Add dill, mint or chives, and season with pepper.

Easy chicken korma

Prep: 15 mins **Cook:** 20 mins

Serves 4

Ingredients

- small knob fresh ginger , peeled and finely sliced
- 1 garlic clove
- 1 onion , sliced
- 1 tbsp vegetable oil
- 4 skinless chicken breasts, cut into bite-size pieces
- 1 tsp garam masala
- 100ml chicken stock
- 3 tbsp low-fat fromage frais
- 2 tbsp ground almonds
- handful toasted, sliced almonds , to serve
- coriander leaves, plain rice , naan bread or chapatis, to serve

Method

STEP 1

Cook the ginger, garlic and onion in a large pan with the oil until softened. Tip in the chicken and cook until lightly browned, about 5 mins, then add in garam masala and cook for 1 min further.

STEP 2

Pour over the stock and simmer for 10 mins until the chicken is cooked through. Mix together the fromage frais and ground almonds. Take the pan off the heat and stir in the fromage frais mixture. Sprinkle over sliced almonds, garnish with coriander and serve with boiled rice, chapatis or plain naan bread.

Prawn, rice & mango jar salad

Prep: 15 mins No cook

Serves 1

Ingredients

- 125g cooked rice (we used brown basmati)
- handful baby spinach
- 50g cooked prawn
- ¼ ripe mango , cut into small pieces
- ½ red chilli , deseeded and finely chopped
- small handful coriander , roughly chopped

For the dressing

- ½ tbsp low-salt soy sauce
- 1 tsp sesame oil
- 1 tsp rice vinegar
- ½ tsp brown sugar

Method

STEP 1

Make the dressing by whisking together all the ingredients. Tip the dressing into the bottom of a big jar, top with the rice and put in the fridge if making the night before.

STEP 2

Layer the spinach, prawns, mango, chilli and coriander on top of the rice. Leave a little space at the top so that when lunchtime arrives, you can shake up the salad to eat.

Orzo with spinach & cherry tomatoes

Prep: 5 mins **Cook:** 25 mins

Serves 4

Ingredients

- 400g orzo pasta
- 2 tbsp olive oil
- 1 celery heart, chopped
- 1 red onion , chopped
- 3 garlic cloves , chopped
- 2 x 400g cans cherry tomato
- 250g baby spinach
- 10 black olives , halved
- small handful dill , chopped
- small handful mint , chopped

Method

STEP 1

Cook the orzo following pack instructions. Drain, rinse under cold water, drain again and toss with half the olive oil.

STEP 2

Meanwhile, heat the remaining oil in a large sauté pan. Add the celery, onion and some seasoning, and cook for 8 mins until soft. Add the garlic, cook for 1 min, then tip in the cherry tomatoes and simmer for 10 mins. Add the spinach, cover with a lid to wilt the leaves, then add the orzo, olives, dill and mint. Season and serve.

Kale & apple soup with walnuts

Prep: 20 mins **Cook:** 15 mins

Serves 2

Ingredients

- 8 walnut halves , broken into pieces
- 1 onion , finely chopped
- 2 carrots , coarsely grated
- 2 red apples , unpeeled and finely chopped
- 1 tbsp cider vinegar
- 500ml reduced-salt vegetable stock
- 200g kale , roughly chopped
- 20g pack of dried apple crisps (optional)

Method

STEP 1

In a dry, non-stick frying pan, cook the walnut pieces for 2-3 mins until toasted, turning frequently so they don't burn. Take off the heat and allow to cool.

STEP 2

Put the onion, carrots, apples, vinegar and stock in a large saucepan and bring to the boil. Reduce the heat and simmer for 10 mins, stirring occasionally.

STEP 3

Once the onion is translucent and the apples start to soften, add the kale and simmer for an additional 2 mins. Carefully transfer to a blender or liquidiser and blend until very smooth. Pour into bowls and serve topped with the toasted walnuts, and a sprinkling of apple crisps, if you like.

Mustardy greens

Prep: 10 mins **Cook:** 5 mins

Serves 4

Ingredients

- 300g spring green
- 300g frozen pea
- 25g butter
- 1 tbsp wholegrain mustard
- 2 tbsp Dijon mustard

Method

STEP 1

Heat 250ml water in a large pan. Add the greens and peas, cover with a lid and boil for 4 mins. Drain into a colander, put the pan back on the heat, and add the butter and mustards. When the butter has melted, add the veg back to the pan, season well and toss everything together. Serve straight away.

Full English frittata with smoky beans

Prep: 5 mins **Cook:** 30 mins

Serves 4

Ingredients

- 2 low-fat sausages, sliced
- 4 rashers extra lean bacon, all fat removed, chopped
- 150g pack button mushroom, halved, or larger ones quartered
- 8 egg whites, or use 350ml liquid egg whites from a carton
- 3 tbsp milk
- 140g cherry tomato, halved
- 2 x 400g cans reduced salt and sugar baked beans
- 1 ½ tsp smoked paprika
- small bunch chives, snipped

Method

STEP 1

Heat oven to 180C/160C fan/gas 4. Line a roasting tin about the size of A4 paper with enough baking parchment to cover the base and sides. Fry the sausages and bacon in a non-stick pan until golden, stirring them often to stop them sticking. Scoop into the tin.

STEP 2

Place the pan back on the heat and fry the mushrooms for about 5 mins until golden, then add these to the tray, too. Whisk the egg whites with the milk and lots of seasoning. Pour into the tin, then dot the tomatoes on top.

STEP 3

Bake in the oven for 20-25 mins, until set. Meanwhile, tip the beans into a pan with the paprika and heat through. Scatter the frittata with the chives and serve with the beans on the side.

Maple-roasted marrow on cavolo nero salad

Prep: 15 mins **Cook:** 30 mins

Serves 4

Ingredients

- 1 medium marrow
- 1 tbsp olive oil
- 1 garlic clove , crushed
- 1 tbsp maple syrup
- 3 tbsp hazelnuts , halved
- 2 slices toasted sourdough bread , blitzed into crumbs
- 200g cavolo nero , stalks removed, shredded
- 10 radishes , quartered
- 16 shavings of vegetarian-style Parmesan

For the dressing

- 2 tbsp red wine vinegar
- 1 tbsp lemon juice
- 3 tbsp extra virgin olive oil
- 1 shallot , finely diced
- 1 tsp Dijon mustard
- pinch golden caster sugar

Method

STEP 1

Heat oven to 220C/200C fan/gas 7. Slice the marrow open lengthways and scoop out the seeds. Cut the marrow into slices and place on a baking tray. Toss with the olive oil, garlic, maple syrup and some seasoning. Roast for 20 mins, then sprinkle the hazelnuts and breadcrumbs over. Roast for another 8 mins, then remove.

STEP 2

While the marrow is roasting, prepare the rest of the salad. Shred the cavolo nero leaves into bite-sized pieces. Put on a large platter or shallow bowl and top with the radishes.

STEP 3

Combine the dressing ingredients in a small bowl, adding some salt. Mix well.

STEP 4

Just before the marrow has finished cooking, drizzle the dressing over the cavolo nero. Use your hands to massage it into the cavolo nero for a few mins so that it softens it, then top with the marrow, breadcrumbs and hazelnuts. Sprinkle the Parmesan shavings over and serve.

Griddled lettuce & peas

Prep: 5 mins **Cook:** 10 mins

Serves 2

Ingredients

- 3 tsp white wine vinegar
- 1 tbsp olive oil
- 1 garlic clove , crushed
- 1 tbsp chopped parsley
- 1 tbsp chopped mint
- 2 Baby Gem lettuces , halved
- 140g frozen peas

Method

STEP 1

To make a dressing, mix the vinegar, 2 tsp of the oil, the garlic and herbs in a small bowl. Heat a griddle pan. Brush the lettuces in the remaining oil and cook on the griddle for 3 mins each side until charred. Bring a small pan of water to the boil, add the peas and cook for 3 mins. Drain the peas and mix with the lettuce and dressing. Serve straight away.

Thai chicken cakes with sweet chilli sauce

Total time 25 mins Ready in 20-25 minutes

Serves 2 - 3

Ingredients

- 2 large boneless, skinless chicken breasts (about 175g), cubed
- 1 garlic clove , roughly chopped
- small piece fresh root ginger , peeled and roughly chopped
- 1 small onion , roughly chopped
- 4 tbsp fresh coriander , plus a few sprigs to garnish
- 1 green chilli , seeded and roughly chopped
- 2 tbsp olive oil
- sweet chilli sauce , lime wedges, shredded spring onion and red chilli, to serve

Method

STEP 1

Toss the chicken, garlic, ginger, onion, coriander and chilli into a food processor and season well. Blitz until the chicken is finely ground and everything is well mixed. Use your hands to shape six small cakes.

STEP 2

Heat the oil in a frying pan, then fry the cakes over a medium heat for about 6-8 mins, turning once. Serve hot, with sweet chilli sauce, lime wedges, coriander, shredded spring onion and red chilli.

Herbed lamb cutlets with roasted vegetables

Prep: 15 mins **Cook:** 45 mins

Serves 4

Ingredients

- 2 peppers , any colour, deseeded and cut into chunky pieces
- 1 large sweet potato , peeled and cut into chunky pieces
- 2 courgettes , sliced into chunks
- 1 red onion , cut into wedges
- 1 tbsp olive oil
- 8 lean lamb cutlets
- 1 tbsp thyme leaf , chopped
- 2 tbsp mint leaves, chopped

Method

STEP 1

Heat oven to 220C/200C fan/gas 7. Put the peppers, sweet potato, courgettes and onion on a large baking tray and drizzle over the oil. Season with lots of ground black pepper. Roast for 25 mins.

STEP 2

Meanwhile, trim the lamb of as much fat as possible. Mix the herbs with a few twists of ground black pepper and pat all over the lamb.

STEP 3

Take the vegetables out of the oven, turn over and push to one side of the tray. Place the cutlets on the hot tray and return to the oven for 10 mins.

STEP 4

Turn the cutlets and cook for a further 10 mins or until the vegetables and lamb are tender and lightly charred. Mix everything on the tray and serve.

Apple crisps

Prep: 5 mins **Cook:** 40 mins

Makes roughly 16

Ingredients

- 1 apple

Method

STEP 1

Heat oven to 140C/120C fan/gas 1. Thinly slice the apple through the core – use a mandolin, if you have one, to get thin slices. Arrange the slices on a baking tray lined with parchment and bake for 40 mins. Cool until crisp.

Hoisin pork with garlic & ginger greens

Prep: 10 mins **Cook:** 10 mins Plus marinating

Serves 4

Ingredients

- 500g pork loin steak , cut into 2cm-thick slices
- 4 tbsp hoisin sauce
- 1 tbsp light soy sauce , plus a dash
- 350g thin-stemmed broccoli
- 1 tbsp sunflower oil
- 2 garlic cloves , thinly sliced
- 5cm-piece ginger , shredded
- 1 bunch spring onion , halved lengthways
- 350g bok choi , halved lengthways
- rice or noodles, to serve (optional)

Method

STEP 1

Put the pork, hoisin and soy sauce in a bowl and allow to stand for 10 mins. Heat the grill to high, shake off any excess sauce, then lay the pork on a tray. Grill for 5 mins, turning halfway, until cooked through. Remove and leave to rest in a warm place for 5 mins.

STEP 2

Meanwhile, put the broccoli in a microwave-safe bowl with 4 tbsp water, cover with cling film, then microwave on High for 3 mins. Heat the oil in a wok, add the garlic and ginger, and stir-fry for 1 min. Add the spring onions and bok choi, then stir-fry for a further 2 mins. Tip in the broccoli with a dash of soy sauce and stir-fry for 1-2 mins more until the veg is warmed through. Serve the pork with the greens, a drizzle of any resting pork juices and rice or noodles, if you like.

Roasted balsamic cauliflower

Prep: 5 mins **Cook:** 25 mins - 30 mins

Serves 2

Ingredients

- 1 large cauliflower, cut into bite-sized florets
- 2 tbsp olive oil
- 1 garlic clove, finely chopped
- 2 tbsp balsamic glaze
- 1 red chilli (deseeded if you don't like it too hot), finely sliced

Method

STEP 1

Heat oven to 200C/180C fan/gas 6. Put the cauliflower on a large baking sheet. Combine the oil and garlic, and drizzle over the cauliflower and roast in the oven for 10 mins.

STEP 2

Drizzle the balsamic glaze over the cauliflower and roast for a further 15-20 mins until it is cooked through. Serve immediately with the chilli scattered over.

Squash & coconut curry

Prep: 10 mins **Cook:** 20 mins Ready in 30 minutes

Serves 2

Ingredients

- 2 tbsp Madras curry paste
- 1 large butternut squash (600g/1lb 5oz peeled weight), chopped into medium size chunks
- 1 red pepper, halved, deseeded and roughly chopped into chunks
- 400g can reduced-fat coconut milk
- small bunch coriander, roughly chopped

Method

STEP 1

Heat a large frying pan or wok, tip in the curry paste and fry for 1 min. Add the squash and red pepper, then toss well in the paste.

STEP 2

Pour in the coconut milk with 200ml water and bring to a simmer. Cook for 15-20 mins or until the butternut squash is very tender and the sauce has thickened. Season to taste, then serve scattered with chopped coriander and naan bread or rice.

Beetroot & mint dip

Prep: 10 mins No cook

Serves 4

Ingredients

- 250g vacuum-packed beetroot
- ½ tsp ground cumin
- 2 tsp chopped mint , plus a few leaves for sprinkling
- squeeze lemon juice
- 3 tbsp half-fat crème fraîche
- a few pinches nigella seeds

Method

STEP 1

Put beetroot and cumin in the small bowl of a food processor, season and blend until smooth. Tip into a bowl, add the mint and lemon juice, then gently stir through crème fraîche to get a rippled effect. Sprinkle with mint leaves and nigella seeds.

Super berry smoothie

Prep: 10 mins No cook

Serves 4

Ingredients

- 450g bag frozen berry
- 450g pot fat-free strawberry yogurt
- 100ml milk
- 25g porridge oat
- 2 tsp honey (optional)

Method

STEP 1

Whizz the berries, yogurt and milk together with a stick blender until smooth. Stir through the porridge oats, then pour into 4 glasses and serve with a drizzle of honey, if you like.

Basque-style salmon stew

Prep: 10 mins **Cook:** 25 mins

Serves 4

Ingredients

- 1 tbsp olive oil
- 3 mixed peppers , deseeded and sliced
- 1 large onion , thinly sliced
- 400g baby potatoes , unpeeled and halved
- 2 tsp smoked paprika
- 2 garlic cloves , sliced
- 2 tsp dried thyme
- 400g can chopped tomatoes
- 4 salmon fillets
- 1 tbsp chopped parsley , to serve (optional)

Method

STEP 1

Heat the oil in a large pan and add the peppers, onion and potatoes. Cook, stirring regularly for 5-8 mins until golden. Then add the paprika, garlic, thyme and tomatoes. Bring to the boil, stir and cover, then turn down heat and simmer for 12 mins. Add a splash of water if the sauce becomes too thick.

STEP 2

Season the stew and lay the salmon on top, skin side down. Place the lid back on and simmer for another 8 mins until the salmon is cooked through. Scatter with parsley, if you like, and serve.

Layered hummus & griddled vegetable salad

Prep: 15 mins **Cook:** 45 mins

Serves 4

Ingredients

- 3 red peppers, halved
- 3 tbsp olive oil
- 2 courgettes, thinly sliced lengthways
- 1 large aubergine, thinly sliced lengthways
- 8 tbsp hummus
- juice 1 lemon
- small garlic clove, crushed
- 1 tsp sumac
- 2 large handfuls rocket
- ciabatta, to serve

Method

STEP 1

Heat oven to 200C/180C fan/ gas 6. Rub the peppers with a little oil and roast for 30 mins, turning halfway through, until soft and slightly charred. Place in a bowl, cover with cling film and set aside.

STEP 2

Meanwhile, heat a large griddle pan (or two, if you have them, for speed) until hot. Drizzle the courgettes and aubergine with oil, then griddle for a few mins each side until char lines appear. Peel the peppers and discard the seeds. Tear the peppers into thick strips.

STEP 3

Spread the hummus over a serving plate. Mix together the lemon juice and garlic. Toss with the vegetables and half the sumac, then arrange over the hummus. Top with the rocket leaves and sprinkle over the remaining sumac. Serve with ciabatta.

Storecupboard pasta salad

Prep:5 mins **Serves 2**

Ingredients

- 2 tsp finely chopped red onion
- 1 tsp caper
- 1 tbsp pesto
- 2 tsp olive oil
- 185g can of tuna in spring water, drained
- 100g leftover pasta shapes
- 3 sundried tomatoes, chopped

Method

STEP 1

Mix the onion, capers, pesto and oil. Flake the tuna into a bowl with the pasta and tomatoes, then stir in the pesto mix.

Energy bites

Prep: 10 mins Plus chilling no cook

Makes 8

Ingredients

- 100g pecan
- 75g raisin
- 1 tbsp ground flaxseed (or a mix- we used milled flaxseed, almond, Brazil nut and walnut mix)
- 1 tbsp cocoa powder
- 1 tbsp agave syrup
- 50g desiccated coconut
- 2 tbsp peanut butter

Method

STEP 1

Put pecans in a food processor and blitz to crumbs. Add raisins, peanut butter, flaxseeds, cocoa powder and agave syrup, then pulse to combine.

STEP 2

Shape mixture into golf ball-sized balls and roll in desiccated coconut to coat. Put in the fridge to firm for 20 mins, then eat whenever you need a quick energy boost.

Fruity pork steaks

Prep: 10 mins **Cook:** 22 mins

Serves 4

Ingredients

- 4 boneless pork loin steaks , trimmed of any fat
- 2 tsp Chinese five-spice powder
- 1 tbsp sunflower oil
- 1 large red onion , cut into thin wedges through the root
- 4 red apples , cored and cut into eighths
- 2 tbsp redcurrant jelly
- 1 tbsp red wine vinegar or cider vinegar

- 200ml chicken stock

Method

STEP 1

Dust the pork steaks with the Chinese five-spice powder. Heat half the oil in a frying pan and fry the pork for about 3 mins on each side until browned and cooked through. Transfer to a plate.

STEP 2

Add the remaining oil to the frying pan, reduce the heat slightly, then fry the onion wedges for 2 mins. Add the apples and cook, stirring occasionally, for another 3 mins.

STEP 3

Add the redcurrant jelly to the pan, followed by the vinegar and then the stock. Bring to the boil and simmer rapidly, uncovered, for 8-10 mins until the sauce is slightly syrupy and the apples are tender. Gently reheat the pork in the sauce, turning to glaze each side.

Avocado pizza crisps

Prep: 15 mins **Cook:** 28 mins

Serves 2

Ingredients

For the topping

- 2 tsp rapeseed oil
- 1 red or orange pepper , deseeded, quartered and sliced
- 2 garlic cloves , finely chopped
- 160g cherry tomatoes
- 1 small avocado , halved, destoned and sliced
- 2 good handfuls of rocket
- 1 small red onion , thinly sliced
- 4 Kalamata olives , sliced
- 1 tsp balsamic vinegar

For the base

- 150g wholemeal flour
- 1 ½ tsp baking powder
- 2 tsp rapeseed oil

Method

STEP 1

Heat oven to 200C/180C fan/gas 6 and line two baking sheets with baking parchment. Heat the oil in a non-stick pan and fry the pepper for 5 mins, stirring every now and then until softened. Add the garlic, stir well and remove from the heat. Stir in the cherry tomatoes.

STEP 2

Meanwhile, make the base. Tip the flour into a bowl with the baking powder. Mix 80ml water with the oil, then add to the flour and stir in with the blade of a knife. Set aside for 5 mins.

STEP 3

Cut the dough in half and knead on the work surface until smooth – you shouldn't need to add any extra flour. Roll out to a very thin 20cm circle, then lift onto the baking sheet. Do the same with the other half of the dough. Bake the two bases for 8 mins, then turn them over and top with the pepper and tomato mixture. Return to the oven for 10 mins more.

STEP 4

Toss the avocado, rocket, onion and olives with the balsamic vinegar. Remove the bases from the oven and squash the tomatoes a little to fill any areas that aren't covered with the topping. Pile the avocado mixture on top and eat while still hot.

Chicken tikka with spiced rice

Prep: 10 mins **Cook:** 20 mins Plus marinating

Serves 4

Ingredients

- 4 skinless chicken breasts
- 150g pot low-fat natural yogurt
- 50g tikka paste
- 100g/4oz cucumber, diced
- 1 tbsp roughly chopped mint leaves
- 1 red onion, cut into thin wedges

- 140g easy-cook long grain rice
- 1 tbsp medium curry powder
- 50g frozen pea
- 1 small red pepper, diced

Method

STEP 1

Slash each chicken breast deeply with a knife 3-4 times on one side. Put in a bowl and add 50g of the yogurt and the tikka paste. Mix well, cover and marinate in the fridge for 30 mins. Make the raita by stirring the cucumber and most of the mint into the rest of the yogurt. Season with black pepper, cover and chill.

STEP 2

Heat oven to 240C/220C fan/gas 9. Scatter the onion wedges over a foil-lined baking tray. Remove the chicken from the marinade, shake off any excess and place on top of the onion wedges. Cook for 20 mins.

STEP 3

Meanwhile, tip the rice, curry powder, peas and pepper into a pan of boiling water and simmer for 10 mins or until the rice is just tender. Drain well and divide the rice between 4 plates. Add the chicken, roasted onion and remaining mint. Serve with the cucumber raita.

Chicken & vegetable curry

Prep: 15 mins **Cook:** 30 mins Plus marinating

Serves 2

Ingredients

- 100g coconut yogurt
- 2 heaped tbsp tandoori spice mix
- 2 skinless chicken breasts, cut into chunks
- 1 large onion, chopped
- 1 red pepper, cut into chunks
- 250ml passata
- 250g pouch cooked basmati rice
- 100g frozen pea
- small bunch coriander, roughly chopped

Method

STEP 1

Mix together 75g of the yogurt with 1 tbsp of the spice mix and some seasoning. Add the chicken and leave to marinate for at least 15 mins or up to overnight in the fridge. Heat the remaining spices, the onion and a good splash of water, and soften for 5 mins, stirring often.

STEP 2

Tip in the pepper chunks and passata, and simmer while you cook the chicken. Heat the grill to High, remove the chicken from the marinade and shake off any excess. Grill under a high heat until starting to char at the edges.

STEP 3

Tip the rice and peas into a pan with a splash of water and heat through. Stir most of the coriander into the sauce. Serve the rice alongside the chicken and sauce, scattered with the remaining coriander and the remaining yogurt on the side.

Pork with sweet & sour onion sauce

Prep: 10 mins **Cook:** 20 mins

Serves 4

Ingredients

- 250g mixed basmati rice and wild rice
- 600g pork fillet , cut into 4cm-thick slices
- 2 tbsp coarse black pepper (freshly ground)
- 2 tbsp olive oil
- 1 large red onion , halved and sliced
- 150ml cider vinegar
- 75ml maple syrup
- small bunch parsley , chopped

Method

STEP 1

Boil the rice in plenty of water, following pack instructions, until cooked. Drain, return to the pot and cover to keep warm.

STEP 2

Meanwhile, sprinkle the meat on all sides with the black pepper and some salt. Heat 1 tbsp of the oil in a large frying pan. Sear the meat on both sides until nicely browned. Remove from the pan.

STEP 3

Add the remaining oil and the onion to the pan. Cook for 5 mins, then pour in the vinegar and let reduce for 1 min. Stir in the maple syrup, then return the pork to the pan and heat for 5 mins until cooked through. Serve the pork and sauce spooned over the rice and scattered with the parsley.

Spicy pepper & tomato soup with cucumber yogurt

Prep: 15 mins **Cook:** 25 mins - 30 mins

Serves 4

Ingredients

- 2 tbsp olive oil , plus extra to serve
- 2 onions , finely sliced
- 1 carrot , finely chopped
- 3 red peppers , roughly chopped
- 3 garlic cloves , sliced
- 1 red chilli , sliced
- 400g can chopped tomato
- 850ml-1 litre/1½-1¾pts vegetable stock or bouillon
- 4 tbsp Greek-style yogurt
- ½ cucumber , halved, deseeded, coarsely grated and squeezed of excess water
- a few mint leaves, chopped

Method

STEP 1

Heat the oil in a large saucepan. Tip in the onions, carrot and peppers. Cook gently for 15 mins, to soften. Add the garlic and chilli, and cook for a few mins more. Pour over the chopped tomatoes and 800ml of the stock. Bring to the boil and simmer for 10-15 mins until the veg is completely tender.

STEP 2

Meanwhile, mix the yogurt, cucumber and mint in a bowl, and season.

STEP 3

Blitz the soup with a hand blender until smooth, using the extra stock to thin if it has become too thick. Heat through, season and spoon into bowls. Serve with a dollop of the yogurt mixture on top and a drizzle of olive oil.

Mustardy beetroot & lentil salad

Prep: 5 mins **Cook:** 20 mins plus cooling

Serves 5 - 6

Ingredients

- 200g puy lentils (or use 2 x 250g packs pre-cooked lentils)
- 1 tbsp wholegrain mustard (or gluten-free alternative)
- 1 ½ tbsp extra virgin olive oil
- 300g pack cooked beetroot (not in vinegar), sliced
- large handful tarragon , roughly chopped

Method

STEP 1

If not using pre-cooked lentils, cook the lentils following pack instructions, drain and leave to cool. Meanwhile, combine the mustard, oil and some seasoning to make a dressing.

STEP 2

Tip the lentils into a bowl, pour over the dressing and mix well. Stir through the beetroot, tarragon and some seasoning, then serve.

Warm lemony courgette salad

Prep: 10 mins **Cook:** 5 mins

Serves 2

Ingredients

- 2 courgettes
- 1 tbsp olive oil
- zest 1 lemon , plus a squeeze of lemon
- 1 garlic clove , crushed
- ¼ small pack basil , roughly torn

Method

STEP 1

Use a vegetable peeler to slice the courgettes into wide strips, discarding the central, seedy part. Heat the oil in a large frying pan, add the lemon zest and garlic, and fry over a medium heat for 1 min. Add the courgette strips and cook, stirring regularly, for a further 1-2 mins until the courgettes are slightly softened. Add a squeeze of lemon juice and toss the basil through.

Broccoli & sage pasta

Prep: 5 mins **Cook:** 12 mins

Serves 2

Ingredients

- 140g quick-cook spaghetti
- 140g long-stem broccoli , trimmed and cut into 5cm lengths
- 3 tbsp olive oil
- 2 shallots , sliced
- 1 garlic clove , finely chopped
- ¼ tsp crushed chillies
- 12 sage leaves, shredded
- grated parmesan (or vegetarian alternative), to serve (optional)

Method

STEP 1

Boil the spaghetti for 1 min. Add the broccoli and cook for 4 mins more.

STEP 2

Meanwhile, heat the oil in a frying pan and add the shallots and garlic. Gently cook for 5 mins until golden. Add the chillies and sage to the pan and gently cook for 2 mins. Drain the pasta, mix with the shallot mixture in the pan, then scatter with Parmesan, if you like.

Chicken & avocado salad with blueberry balsamic dressing

Prep: 15 mins **Cook:** 5 mins

Serves 2

Ingredients

- 1 garlic clove
- 85g blueberries
- 1 tbsp extra virgin rapeseed oil
- 2 tsp balsamic vinegar
- 125g fresh or frozen baby broad beans
- 1 large cooked beetroot , finely chopped
- 1 avocado , stoned, peeled and sliced
- 85g bag mixed baby leaf salad
- 175g cooked chicken
- **Method**

STEP 1

Finely chop the garlic. Mash half the blueberries with the oil, vinegar and some black pepper in a large salad bowl.

STEP 2

Boil the broad beans for 5 mins until just tender. Drain, leaving them unskinned.

STEP 3

Stir the garlic into the dressing, then pile in the warm beans and remaining blueberries with the beetroot, avocado, salad and chicken. Toss to mix, but don't go overboard or the juice from the beetroot will turn everything pink. Pile onto plates or into shallow bowls to serve.

Coleslaw with tahini yogurt dressing

Prep: 15 mins No cook

Serves 6

Ingredients

- 1 ½ tbsp tahini paste
- 5 tbsp Greek-style natural yogurt
- ½ garlic clove , crushed
- 1 small red cabbage , quartered and finely sliced
- 3 small carrots , cut into fine matchsticks
- 1 small onion , halved and finely sliced

Method

STEP 1

Put the tahini, yogurt, garlic, and some seasoning in a large bowl and mix until smooth. The dressing will thicken so add 2-3 tbsps cold water to loosen it. Add the vegetables to the dressing, and toss together until everything is well coated.

Spiced chickpea soup

Prep: 10 mins **Cook:** 25 mins

Serves 4

Ingredients

- 1 tbsp olive oil
- 1 onion, chopped
- 2 garlic cloves, crushed
- 1 red chilli, deseeded and roughly chopped
- 1 tbsp grated fresh ginger
- 1 tsp cumin
- 1 tsp ras-el-hanout
- ¼ tsp cinnamon
- 200g roasted red pepper, from a jar
- 2 x 400g cans chopped tomato
- 400ml vegetable stock
- 400g can chickpea, drained and rinsed
- 2 preserved lemons, rind chopped (discard the pulp and seeds)
- 1 tbsp clear honey
- 50g wholewheat couscous

Method

STEP 1

Heat the oil in a large lidded pan. Add the onion and garlic, put on the lid and cook for 5 mins, stirring halfway through. Stir the chilli, ginger, cumin, ras el hanout and cinnamon into the pan and cook for 1 min. Add the peppers, tomatoes and stock. Bring to the boil, turn down to a simmer, put on the lid and cook for 10 mins.

STEP 2

Blitz the soup with a stick blender, or in a food processor until smooth. Return to the pan and add more liquid to thin the soup, if you like. Stir in the chickpeas, preserved lemons, honey and some seasoning. If eating straight away, add the couscous and heat through for 5 mins. (If taking to work, add the couscous just before reheating).

Egg & Puy lentil salad with tamari & watercress

Prep: 10 mins **Cook:** 35 mins plus optional overnight soaking

Serves 2

Ingredients

- 75g dried puy lentils
- 175g cauliflower florets , broken into smaller pieces
- 1 tbsp rapeseed oil , plus a drizzle
- 1 large carrot , chopped into small pieces
- 2 celery sticks , chopped into small pieces
- 2 garlic cloves
- 3 omega-3 enriched eggs
- 1 tbsp wheat-free tamari
- 10 cherry tomatoes , halved
- 4 spring onions , finely sliced
- 2 generous handfuls watercress , large stems removed

Method

STEP 1

If you want to activate the lentils (see tip below), do this the night, or up to 8 hrs, before eating. Pour water over them and leave to soak at room temperature. Drain and rinse.

STEP 2

When ready to eat, heat oven to 220C/ 200C fan/gas 7. Toss the cauliflower with a drizzle of the oil, then roast for 20 mins on a parchment-lined baking tray until tender and tinged with gold round the edges.

STEP 3

Meanwhile, put the drained lentils in a pan with the carrot and celery. Pour in water to cover, put on a lid and boil for 20 mins until the lentils are tender. Check before they are ready in case they are boiling dry and, if necessary, top up with a little more water.

STEP 4

While they are cooking, finely grate the garlic and set aside in a large bowl. Boil the eggs for 6 mins, this will give you eggs with a soft yolk. When they are ready, plunge into cold water, then shell.

STEP 5

Mix the tamari and oil into the garlic to make a dressing. Check the lentils and drain, if necessary, then toss in the bowl with the dressing, tomatoes, spring onions and watercress. Pile onto plates and top with the eggs, adding any remaining dressing from the bowl over the top.

Melon & crunchy bran pots

Prep: 10 mins No cook

Serves 1

Ingredients

- ½ x 200g pack melon medley
- 150g pot fat-free yogurt
- 2 tbsp fruit & fibre cereal
- 1 tbsp mixed seed
- 1 tsp clear honey

Method

STEP 1

Top melon medley with yogurt, then sprinkle over cereal mixed with seeds. Drizzle over honey and eat immediately.

Apple & sultana muffins

Prep: 15 mins **Cook:** 25 mins

Makes 12

Ingredients

- 200g self-raising flour
- 1 tsp baking powder
- 1 tsp cinnamon
- 50g wholemeal flour
- 100g golden caster sugar
- 2 eggs
- 125ml semi-skimmed milk
- 4 tbsp sunflower oil
- 2 apples , grated
- 100g sultana

Method

STEP 1

Heat oven to 180C/160C fan/gas 4. In a large bowl mix the self-raising flour, baking powder, cinnamon, wholemeal flour and golden caster sugar.

STEP 2

In another bowl, mix the eggs, semi-skimmed milk and sunflower oil. Pour the wet ingredients into the dry and mix well, then stir in the grated apples and sultanas.

STEP 3

Divide the mix between 12 muffin cases and bake for 25 mins. Cool on a wire rack, then pack in a container for lunch.

Homemade burgers with sweet potato wedges

Prep: 15 mins **Cook:** 40 mins Plus chilling

Serves 6

Ingredients

For the burgers

- 1 tbsp olive oil , plus extra for drizzling
- 1 red onion , finely chopped
- 500g lean minced beef or turkey
- 1 egg
- 12 cream crackers, bashed to fine crumbs
- 2 tsp chilli paste
- 2 tsp garlic paste
- 1 tsp each, tomato ketchup and brown sauce
- 2 tbsp plain flour
- 6 hamburger rolls , toasted, to serve
- toppings of your choice (relish, chutney and salad), to serve

For the wedges

- 4 sweet potatoes , cut into wedges
- 2 tbsp olive oil
- 1 tsp paprika

Method

STEP 1

Heat the oil in a frying pan and fry the onion for about 5 mins or until soft. Leave to cool slightly. When cool, put the onion in a large bowl with the mince, egg, bashed crackers, chilli, garlic, ketchup and brown sauce, and mix well to combine. Divide the mince into 6, roll into balls and flatten each into a nice fat burger.

STEP 2

Put the flour on a plate, dab each burger to the flour on both sides, then transfer to a baking tray. Wrap with cling film and pop in the fridge for a couple of hours.

STEP 3

Heat oven to 200C/180C fan/gas 6. To make the wedges, put the sweet potato on a baking tray and drizzle with olive oil. Sprinkle with paprika, season, then give them a good shake or shuffle around with your hands to make sure they're well coated. Roast for 30-40 mins depending on how crisp you like them. Make sure you give them a good shake a couple of times to ensure they cook evenly.

STEP 4

When the wedges have been cooking for 10 mins, drizzle the burgers with a little olive oil and put them in the oven to cook with the wedges for the remaining 20-30 mins, flipping them halfway. 5 Serve the burgers in the rolls with your choice of toppings, and a good helping of wedges on the side.

Salmon with new potato & corn salad & basil dressing

Prep: 15 mins **Cook:** 15 mins

Serves 4

Ingredients

- 400g baby new potatoes
- 2 sweetcorn cobs
- 4 skinless salmon fillets
- 2 very large tomatoes , like beefsteak

For the dressing

- 2 tbsp red wine vinegar
- 2 tbsp extra-virgin olive oil
- 1 shallot, finely chopped
- 1 tbsp capers, finely chopped
- handful basil leaves

Method

STEP 1

Cook potatoes in boiling water until tender, adding corn for final 5 mins, then drain and allow to cool a little.

STEP 2

For the dressing, mix the vinegar, oil, shallot, capers, basil and some seasoning.

STEP 3

Heat grill to high. Rub a little dressing on the salmon and cook, skinned-side down, for 7-8 mins. Slice tomatoes and place on a serving plate. Slice the potatoes, cut the corn from the cobs and arrange over the tomatoes. Top with the salmon, then drizzle over the remaining dressing.

Steak, roasted pepper & pearl barley salad

Prep: 10 mins **Cook:** 30 mins

Serves 2

Ingredients

- 85g pearl barley, rinsed
- 1 red pepper, deseeded and cut into strips
- 1 yellow pepper, deseeded and cut into strips
- 1 red onion, cut into 8 wedges, leaving root intact
- 1 tbsp olive oil, plus a little extra
- 1 large lean steak, around 300g, trimmed of any excess fat
- ½ x 100g bag watercress, roughly chopped
- juice ½ lemon, plus wedges to serve (optional)

Method

STEP 1

Put the pearl barley in a large pan of water. Bring to the boil and cook vigorously for 25-30 mins or until tender. Drain thoroughly and transfer to a bowl.

STEP 2

Meanwhile, heat oven to 200C/ 180C fan/gas 6. Put the peppers on a baking tray with the onion wedges, toss in 1 tbsp olive oil and roast for about 20 mins until tender.

STEP 3

While the peppers are roasting, rub the steak with a little bit of oil and season. Cook in a non-stick frying pan for 3-4 mins each side, or to your liking. Set aside to rest for a few mins. Mix the cooked peppers and onions into the barley. Stir though the watercress, lemon juice and some seasoning. Thinly slice the steaks, place on top of the salad and serve with lemon wedges, if you like.

Herbed pork fillet with roast vegetables

Total time 1 hr and 45 mins Takes around 1½ - 1¾ hours

Serves 4

Ingredients

- 4 medium parsnips, peeled and quartered lengthways
- 1 butternut squash (about 650g/1lb 7oz), peeled, seeded and cut into chunks
- 2 red onions, each cut into 8 wedges
- 1 tbsp olive oil
- grated zest of 1 lemon
- 2 tsp pork seasoning or dried mixed Italian herbs
- 500g lean pork tenderloin, in one or two pieces
- 1 medium Bramley apple
- 400ml hot chicken stock

Method

STEP 1

Preheat the oven to 200C/ gas 6/fan 180C. Put all the vegetables into a roasting tin. Drizzle with the olive oil, season with salt and pepper, then toss everything together.

STEP 2

On a plate, mix together the lemon zest and pork seasoning or herbs. Roll the pork tenderloin in the mixture, then put it on top of the vegetables. Roast for 40 minutes.

STEP 3

Peel and core the apple and cut it into chunks. Scatter the pieces into the roasting tin, then pour in the hot stock and cook for a further 15-20 minutes. Slice the pork, arrange on a platter with the veg, then spoon the pan juices on top.

Spiced parsnip & cauliflower soup

Prep: 15 mins **Cook:** 50 mins

Serves 6 - 8

Ingredients

- 1 tbsp olive oil
- 1 medium cauliflower, cut into florets
- 3 parsnips, chopped
- 2 onions, chopped
- 1 tbsp fennel seed
- 1 tsp coriander seed
- ½ tsp turmeric
- 3 garlic cloves, sliced
- 1-2 green chillies, deseeded and chopped
- 5cm piece ginger, sliced
- zest and juice 1 lemon
- 1l vegetable stock
- handful coriander, chopped

Method

STEP 1

Heat the oil in a large saucepan and add the vegetables. Cover partially and sweat slowly for 10-15 mins until soft but not brown. In a separate pan, dry-roast the spices with a pinch of salt for a few mins until fragrant. Grind with a pestle and mortar to a fine powder.

STEP 2

Add the garlic, chilli, ginger and spices to the vegetables, and cook for about 5 mins, stirring regularly. Add the lemon zest and juice. Pour in the stock, topping up if necessary to just cover the veg. Simmer for 25-30 mins until all the vegetables are tender.

STEP 3

Purée with a blender until smooth. Dilute the consistency with more water if needed, until you get a thick but easily pourable soup. Season generously, stir in the coriander and add more lemon juice to balance the taste. Eat straight away or chill in the fridge to reheat. This also freezes beautifully. Serve with crusty bread, if you like.

Chilli chicken & peanut pies

Prep: 15 mins **Cook:** 1 hr

Makes 2 pies, each serves 2

Ingredients

For the mash

- 500g potatoes , peeled and chopped
- 2 x 400g cans cannellini beans , drained
- 3 tbsp chopped fresh coriander
- 1 tsp chilli powder

For the chicken filling

- 2 tsp rapeseed oil
- 2 tbsp finely chopped ginger
- 1 red chilli , deseeded for less spice
- 2 tbsp cumin seeds
- 2 tbsp ground coriander
- 1 tsp chilli powder
- 400g leeks , thickly sliced
- 1 red pepper , deseeded and diced
- 1 green pepper , deseeded and diced
- 2 large skinless chicken breasts , about 400g, diced
- 400g can chopped tomatoes
- 2 tbsp tomato purée
- 2 tsp vegetable bouillon
- 3 tbsp peanut butter (with no sugar or palm oil)
- 320g broccoli , to serve

Method

STEP 1

Heat oven to 200C/180C fan/gas 6. Cook the potatoes in a steamer for 15 mins until tender. Meanwhile, start the chicken filling. Heat the oil in a non-stick pan, add the ginger and chilli, and stir over a medium heat until starting to soften. Stir in the dried spices, leeks and peppers. Cook, stirring frequently, until softened.

STEP 2

Add the chicken and stir-fry until it begins to colour, then tip in the tomatoes, squeeze in some tomato purée and add the bouillon and 150ml water. Cover and simmer for 10 mins.

STEP 3

Mix the peanut butter with 100ml water, then stir into the stew and cook for 5 mins more. Spoon the mixture equally into two 24 x 18cm shallow pie dishes.

STEP 4

For the mash, tip the beans into a bowl, add the coriander and chilli powder and mash well. Add the steamed potatoes and roughly mash into the beans so it still has a little texture. Pile on top of the filling in the pie dishes and carefully spread over the filling to enclose it. Bake one of the pies for 35 mins.

STEP 5

Meanwhile, cook half of the broccoli and serve with the pie. Chill the other pie with the remaining broccoli for another day. Will keep chilled for up to three days. Reheat the remaining pie as above, adding an extra 15 mins to the cooking time.

Veggie okonomiyaki

Prep: 15 mins **Cook:** 10 mins

Serves 2

Ingredients

- 3 large eggs
- 50g plain flour
- 50ml milk
- 4 spring onions, trimmed and sliced
- 1 pak choi, sliced
- 200g Savoy cabbage, shredded
- 1 red chilli, deseeded and finely chopped, plus extra to serve
- ½ tbsp low-salt soy sauce
- ½ tbsp rapeseed oil
- 1 heaped tbsp low-fat mayonnaise
- ½ lime, juiced
- sushi ginger, to serve (optional)
- wasabi, to serve (optional)

Method

STEP 1

Whisk together the eggs, flour and milk until smooth. Add half the spring onions, the pak choi, cabbage, chilli and soy sauce. Heat the oil in a small frying pan and pour in the batter. Cook, covered, over a medium heat for 7-8 mins. Flip the okonomiyaki into a second frying pan, then return it to the heat and cook for a further 7-8 mins until a skewer inserted into it comes out clean.

STEP 2

Mix the mayonnaise and lime juice together in a small bowl. Transfer the okonomiyaki to a plate, then drizzle over the lime mayo and top with the extra chilli and spring onion and the sushi ginger, if using. Serve with the wasabi on the side, if you like.

Curried chicken & baked dhal

Prep: 20 mins **Cook:** 35 mins

Serves 2

Ingredients

- 2 garlic cloves
- thumb-sized piece ginger
- 100g red split lentils
- 2 red onions, cut into small wedges
- 1 small cauliflower, cut into florets
- ½ tsp turmeric
- 2 tsp cumin seeds
- 4 boneless and skinless chicken thighs
- 1 tsp cold pressed rapeseed oil
- 2 tsp medium curry powder
- 100g baby leaf spinach
- 2 tomatoes, chopped
- ½ lemon, cut into wedges
- 2 tbsp natural yogurt

Method

STEP 1

Heat oven to 200C/180C fan/gas 6. Grate the garlic and ginger into a large roasting dish. Add the lentils, onions, cauliflower, turmeric and cumin seeds. Pour over 500ml boiling water and give everything a good mix. Rub the chicken thighs with the oil, curry powder and a pinch of salt and pepper. Nestle these into the lentils, then cook in the oven for 40 mins until the lentils and chicken are cooked through.

STEP 2

Add the spinach and tomatoes to the dish, remove the chicken and return to the oven briefly for a couple of mins until the spinach has wilted. Season to taste. Serve with the lemon wedges and yogurt.

Broccoli & pea soup with minty ricotta

Prep: 20 mins **Cook:** 20 mins - 25 mins

Serves 2

Ingredients

- 1 tbsp olive oil , plus extra for drizzling
- 1 onion , finely chopped
- 2 celery sticks, chopped
- 1 garlic clove , crushed
- 200g broccoli , broken into florets
- 150g fresh or frozen peas
- 500ml hot low-salt vegetable stock
- 1 lemon , zested and juiced
- 100g ricotta
- 1 tbsp finely chopped mint , plus a few whole leaves to serve
- 1 tbsp toasted pine nuts
- 2 slices bread , to serve (optional)

Method

STEP 1

Heat the oil in a flameproof casserole pot and fry the onion and celery for 10 mins. Add the garlic and fry for 1 min more.

STEP 2

Add the broccoli, peas and stock, bring to a simmer and cook, covered, for 10-15 mins, or until the broccoli is tender. Tip the mix into a blender and blitz until smooth, or use a hand blender. Season. Stir in half the lemon zest and juice, then taste, and add the rest, if you like.

STEP 3

Mix the ricotta with the mint and a pinch of salt. Ladle the soup into bowls, then top with the minty ricotta and the pine nuts. Drizzle over the extra olive oil and scatter with mint leaves, then serve with sliced bread, if you like.

Caponata with cheesy polenta

Prep: 15 mins **Cook:** 30 mins

Serves 2

Ingredients

- 1-2 tbsp olive oil
- 1 red onion , cut into thin wedges
- 1 courgette , cut into rounds
- 1 aubergine , cut into chunks
- 2 garlic cloves , crushed
- 2 tsp dried oregano
- ¼ tsp chilli flakes
- 400g can chopped tomatoes
- 30g pitted green olives , halved
- ½ tbsp capers , drained and rinsed
- ½ small bunch of basil , finely chopped, plus extra to serve
- 100g instant polenta
- a little milk , to loosen (optional)
- 40g parmesan or vegetarian Italian-style hard cheese, grated

Method

STEP 1

Heat the oil in a medium pan set over a medium heat, and fry the onion, courgette and aubergine for 5-10 mins, or until beginning to soften. Stir in the garlic, oregano and chilli flakes, followed by the tomatoes, olives and capers. Season to taste, then simmer, covered, for 20 mins, or until all the veg is soft and cooked through. Stir in the basil and taste for seasoning.

STEP 2

Meanwhile, cook the polenta following pack instructions – you may need to loosen with some water or milk if it's too thick. Mix with the parmesan, then spoon and spread over two plates. Top with the caponata and extra basil. Season.

Cauliflower & squash fritters with mint & feta dip

Prep: 30 mins **Cook:** 40 mins

Serves 4

Ingredients

- 100g gram (chickpea) flour
- 1 tsp turmeric

- 1 tsp ground cumin
- small bunch coriander, finely chopped (optional)
- oil, for shallow frying
- 150g natural yogurt

For the roast cauliflower & squash base

- 1 cauliflower, split into florets, the stalk cut into cubes
- 1 garlic clove, crushed
- 75g vegetarian feta, mashed
- 2 tbsp finely chopped mint
- pitta breads and salad, to serve

- ½ large butternut squash, cut into cubes
- 1 tbsp oil

Method

STEP 1

Heat oven to 180C/160C fan/gas 4. Toss the cauliflower and squash in oil and spread it out on a large oven tray. Roast for 25 mins, or until tender. If you're making the base ahead of time, you can leave it to cool at this stage then freeze in an airtight container for up to a month. (Defrost fully before using in the next step.)

STEP 2

Put the flour in a bowl and gradually stir in 125-150ml water to make a batter as thick as double cream. Stir in the turmeric and cumin and some seasoning. Break up the cauliflower and squash a little and mix it gently into the batter. Add the coriander, if using.

STEP 3

Heat a little oil in a frying pan and when it is hot, drop 2 heaped tbsps of the mixture into the pan, spaced apart. Fry until the fritters are dark golden, about 2-3 mins each side. Remove, keep warm and repeat with the remaining batter.

STEP 4

Mix the yogurt with the garlic, feta and mint. Serve the fritters with the mint & feta dip, some salad and pitta breads.

Lighter chicken cacciatore

Prep: 15 mins **Cook:** 50 mins

Serves 4

Ingredients

- 1 tbsp olive oil
- 3 slices prosciutto, fat removed, chopped
- 1 medium onion, chopped
- 2 garlic cloves, finely chopped
- 2 sage sprigs
- 2 rosemary sprigs
- 4 skinless chicken breasts (550g total weight), preferably organic
- 150ml dry white wine
- 400g can plum tomatoes in natural juice
- 1 tbsp tomato purée
- 225g chestnut mushrooms, quartered or halved if large
- small handful chopped flat-leaf parsley, to serve

Method

STEP 1

Heat the oil in a large non-stick frying pan. Tip in the prosciutto and fry for about 2 mins until crisp. Remove with a slotted spoon, letting any fat drain back into the pan, and set aside. Put the onion, garlic and herbs in the pan and fry for 3-4 mins.

STEP 2

Spread the onion out in the pan, then lay the chicken breasts on top. Season with pepper and fry for 5 mins over a medium heat, turning the chicken once, until starting to brown on both sides and the onion is caramelising on the bottom of the pan. Remove the chicken and set aside on a plate. Raise the heat, give it a quick stir and, when sizzling, pour in the wine and let it bubble for 2 mins to reduce slightly.

STEP 3

Lower the heat to medium, return the prosciutto to the pan, then stir in the tomatoes (breaking them up with your spoon), tomato purée and mushrooms. Spoon 4 tbsp of water into the empty tomato can, swirl it around, then pour it into the pan. Cover and simmer for 15-20 mins or until the sauce has thickened and reduced slightly, then return the chicken to the pan and cook, uncovered, for about 15 mins or until the chicken is cooked through. Season and scatter over the parsley to serve.

Vegan moussaka

Prep: 40 mins **Cook:** 1 hr and 45 mins

Serves 6

Ingredients

- 30g bag dried porcini mushrooms
- 8 tbsp olive oil
- 1 onion , finely chopped
- 2 carrots , finely chopped
- 2 celery sticks , finely chopped
- 4 garlic cloves , sliced
- few springs of thyme
- 1 tsp tomato purée
- 100ml vegan red wine (optional)
- 250g dried green lentils
- 2 x 400g cans whole plum tomatoes
- 250g pack chestnut mushrooms , chopped
- 250g pack portobello mushrooms , sliced
- 1 tsp soy sauce
- 1 tsp Marmite
- 1kg floury potato (such as Maris Piper), peeled and chopped
- 1 ½ tsp dried oregano
- 3 aubergines , sliced lengthways
- 150ml soya milk

Method

STEP 1

Pour 800ml boiling water over the dried porcini and leave for 10 mins until hydrated. Meanwhile, pour 1½ tbsp oil into a large saucepan. Add the onion, carrot, celery and a pinch of salt. Cook gently, stirring for 10 mins until soft. Remove the porcini from the liquid, keeping the mushroomy stock and roughly chop. Set both aside.

STEP 2

Add the garlic and thyme to the pan. Cook for 1 min, then stir in the tomato purée and cook for a minute more. Pour in the red wine, if using, cook until nearly reduced, then add the lentils, reserved mushroom stock and tomatoes. Bring to the boil, then reduce the heat and leave to simmer with the lid on.

STEP 3

Meanwhile, heat a large frying pan. Add 1½ tbsp oil and tip all of the mushrooms into the pan, including the rehydrated ones. Fry until all the water has evaporated and the mushrooms are deep golden brown. Pour in the soy sauce. Give everything a good mix, then scrape the mushrooms into the lentil saucepan.

STEP 4

Stir in the Marmite, then continue to cook the ragu, stirring occasionally, over a low-medium heat for 30-45 mins until the lentils are cooked and the sauce is thick and reduced, adding extra water if necessary. Remove the thyme sprigs and season to taste.

STEP 5

Heat oven to 180C/160C fan/gas 4. Put the potatoes into a pan of cold salted water. Bring to the boil, then cook until mashable.

STEP 6

Meanwhile, mix the remaining 5 tbsp oil with the oregano, then brush the aubergine slices with most of it and sprinkle with sea salt. Griddle for 3 mins on each side until soft.

STEP 7

Drain and mash the potatoes with the soya milk. Season to taste.

STEP 8

Spoon the ragu into a large lasagne dish (or two smaller ovenproof dishes), layer in ½ the aubergine, followed by the mash. Brush the remaining oregano oil across the mash, then finish by topping with the remaining aubergine slices. Bake in the oven for 25-35 mins until golden and bubbling.

Lebanese-style meatballs with mujadara

Prep: 15 mins **Cook:** 55 mins plus chilling

Serves 4

Ingredients

- 250g lamb mince (10% fat or lower)
- 2 large onions (320g), 1 very finely chopped, 1 halved and thinly sliced
- 1 garlic clove , finely grated
- 3 tsp ground cumin
- 1 lemon , half zested and juiced, half cut into four wedges to serve
- 2 tsp rapeseed oil
- 200g brown basmati rice
- 1 tbsp bouillon powder
- 390g can green lentils , drained
- 2 tbsp tahini

For the salad

- 4 tomatoes , cut into wedges
- ¼ cucumber (about 150g), sliced
- 12 Kalamata olives , quartered
- 1 tbsp chopped mint , plus a few small leaves to serve

Method

STEP 1

Tip the lamb into a bowl with ¼ of the chopped onion, the garlic, ½ tsp cumin, the lemon zest and some black pepper. Mix well with your hands, then shape into 16 small meatballs. Chill for at least 30 mins.

STEP 2

Heat 1 tsp oil in a non-stick frying pan over a medium-high heat. Reserve most of the remaining chopped onion for the salad, then fry the rest for 5 mins until golden. Stir in the remaining cumin, then tip in the rice, bouillon powder, 500ml water and some black pepper. Reduce the heat to a simmer, then cover and cook over a medium heat for 30 mins. Tip in the lentils, cover again and cook for 5-10 mins more until the rice is tender and all the water has been absorbed.

STEP 3

Meanwhile, heat the remaining oil in a non-stick pan over a medium-high heat. Add the meatballs and sliced onion, cover and cook for 5 mins. Stir, then cook for 5 mins more until the meatballs are cooked through and the onions are golden. Stir the tahini and lemon juice together with 3-4 tbsp water to make a sauce.

STEP 4

Mix all of the salad ingredients with the reserved chopped onion. If you're following our Healthy Diet Plan, divide half of the mujadara between two plates and top with half of the meatballs and onions. Spoon over half of the tahini sauce and serve with half of the salad, two lemon wedges and a few mint leaves. Cover and chill the remaining portions to eat another day. Will keep for two to three days in the fridge.

Super smoky bacon & tomato spaghetti

Prep:5 mins **Cook:**20 mins

Serves 4

Ingredients

- 400g spaghetti
- 1 tbsp olive oil
- 120g smoked streaky bacon, sliced into matchsticks
- 1 onion, finely chopped
- 1 garlic clove, finely chopped
- 2 tsp sweet smoked paprika
- 2 x 400g cans chopped tomatoes
- grated parmesan, to serve (optional)

Method

STEP 1

Bring a large pan of water to the boil and cook the spaghetti following pack instructions. Meanwhile, heat the oil in a large non-stick frying pan and cook the bacon for 3-4 mins until just starting to crisp. Stir in the onion and cook for another 3-4 mins, then add the garlic and smoked paprika, and cook for 1 min more.

STEP 2

Pour in the chopped tomatoes, bring to the boil and bubble for about 5 mins until thickened, stirring every so often to stop it catching on the bottom. Drain the pasta and toss with the sauce. Serve with Parmesan, if you like.

Slow cooker chilli

Prep: 10 mins **Cook:** 6 hrs - 7 hrs and 15 mins

Serves 4 adults + 2 - 4 children

Ingredients

- 1 tbsp rapeseed oil
- 1 large onion, finely chopped
- 2 garlic cloves, crushed
- 2 tsp ground cumin
- 1 ½ tsp sweet smoked paprika
- 1 tsp mild chilli powder (optional)
- 2 carrots, diced
- 2 sticks celery, diced
- 1 courgette, diced
- 1 red pepper, diced
- 400g lean beef mince
- 3 x 400g cans chopped tomatoes
- 1 beef stock cube
- 1 tbsp tomato purée
- 1 x 400g can green lentils, drained and rinsed
- 1 x 400g can flageolet beans, drained and rinsed

- a selection of the following to serve: rice or tacos, soured cream, grated cheese and sliced avocado

Method

STEP 1

Heat the oil in a heavy-based pan. Cook the onion for 10 mins until softened and starting to caramelise. Add the garlic and spices and cook for a further 1-2 mins.

STEP 2

Transfer to a slow cooker, along with the diced vegetables, mince, chopped tomatoes, stock cube and tomato purée. Stir well. Cook on low for 6-7 hours. About half an hour before serving, take off the lid and use a stick blender to blend in the vegetables (if your children aren't keen to eat veg) or leave chunky. Stir through the lentils and flageolet beans. Replace the lid and heat through for a further half hour. Stir and serve with rice or tacos, soured cream, grated cheese and sliced avocado.

Root veg lentil bowl with herb pistou

Prep: 30 mins **Cook:** 50 mins

Serves 4

Ingredients

- 600g leftover root veg (carrots and parsnips work well)
- 1 tbsp rose harissa
- 3 tbsp rapeseed oil
- 150g baby spinach
- ½ small bunch of coriander
- ½ small bunch of mint
- 1 small garlic clove
- 30g mixed nuts, toasted and cooled
- 1 lemon, zested and juiced
- cooked puy lentils (or 2 x 250g pouches)

Method

STEP 1

Heat the oven to 200C/180C fan/gas 6. Slice the carrots into chunks, or halve lengthways if they are small, and quarter the parsnips lengthways. Toss with the harissa and ½ tbsp oil and season. Tip onto a baking tray and roast for 40-45 mins or until tender. Toss the spinach and 1 tbsp of water through for the last 5 mins to wilt.

STEP 2

Blitz the remaining oil, the coriander, mint, garlic and nuts in a food processor until smooth – add 1 tbsp water if needed. Season and stir in the lemon zest and juice.

STEP 3

Warm the lentils through in the microwave or in a pan with a few tablespoons of water, then toss with the roots and spinach. Spoon into bowls and top with the herb pistou.

Vegan three-bean chilli with potato jackets

Prep: 15 mins **Cook:** 50 mins

Serves 2

Ingredients

- 2 baking potatoes (about 180g each)
- 1 tbsp cold-pressed rapeseed oil
- 1 yellow or orange pepper, deseeded and chopped
- 2 garlic cloves, finely grated
- 1 tsp cumin seeds
- ½ tsp chilli flakes
- 1 tsp smoked paprika
- 1 tsp ground coriander
- 1 tsp dried oregano
- 400g can chopped tomatoes
- 2 tsp vegetable bouillon powder
- 400g can three bean salad (cannellini, flageolet and adzuki), drained
- handful of coriander, chopped, plus extra leaves to serve
- 1 small avocado, stoned, halved and chopped or mashed
- 1 lime, cut into wedges

Method

STEP 1

Heat the oven to 200C/180C fan/gas 6 and bake the potatoes for 50 mins-1 hr, or until tender.

STEP 2

Meanwhile, heat the oil in a non-stick frying pan and fry the pepper and garlic for a few minutes. Stir in the cumin seeds, chilli flakes and spices, then tip in the tomatoes, bouillon powder and beans. Bring to a simmer, cover and cook for 15 mins, or until reduced to a thick sauce. Stir in the chopped coriander.

STEP 3

Cut a cross into the tops of the baked potatoes and gently press on the sides to open them out. Spoon over the chilli, then top with the avocado and squeeze over some of the lime wedges. Scatter over some coriander leaves and serve with the remaining lime wedges.

Oat & chia porridge

Prep: 10 mins **Cook:** 4 mins plus overnight soaking

Serves 4

Ingredients

- 150g gluten-free porridge oats
- 50g milled seeds with flax and chia
- 400ml almond or oat milk
- 200g dairy-free coconut yogurt
- 40g toasted flaked almonds
- 2 pink grapefruit, segmented and chopped (4 portions)

Method

STEP 1

Soak the oats and seeds in 800ml water overnight.

STEP 2

Tip into a pan with 200ml milk and heat, stirring, until bubbling and thick. If you're following our Healthy Diet Plan, save half for the next day. Will keep in the fridge for two days. Divide the rest between two bowls, along with 50ml milk each and topping with a quarter portion each of the yogurt, almonds and grapefruit.

STEP 3

The next day, prepare the second grapefruit and reheat the leftover porridge in a pan with a splash more milk before serving with the toppings as described in step 2.

Moroccan freekeh traybake

Prep: 5 mins **Cook:** 30 mins

Serves 2

Ingredients

- 2 tbsp olive oil
- 400g can chickpeas , rinsed and drained
- 1 tsp ground coriander
- 1 tsp ground cumin
- ½ tsp chilli flakes
- 270g cherry tomatoes
- ½ x 400g can apricot halves , drained and roughly chopped
- 70g green olives
- 250g pouch cooked freekeh
- 70g fat-free Greek yogurt
- small bunch dill , finely chopped

Method

STEP 1

Heat oven to 200C/180C fan/ gas 6. Toss the oil with the chickpeas, spices and chilli flakes in a medium roasting tin. Roast for 15 mins or until the chickpeas are beginning to crisp and turn golden brown. Add the tomatoes, apricots, olives and freekeh to the pan and toss everything together. Return to the oven for a final 10-15 mins until the tomatoes start to burst and everything is piping hot. Season to taste.

STEP 2

Combine the yogurt and most of the dill and season with salt. Serve the freekeh with any extra dill fronds scattered over and a dollop of the herby yogurt.

No-cook chickpea salad

Prep: 10 mins no cook

Serves 6

Ingredients

- 400g can chickpeas, drained and rinsed
- small pack coriander, roughly chopped
- small pack parsley, roughly chopped
- 1 red onion, thinly sliced
- 2 large tomatoes, chopped
- 2 tbsp olive oil

- 2 tbsp harissa
- 1 lemon, juiced

Method

STEP 1

Mix all the ingredients together, mashing a little so the chickpeas are a bit rough round the edges – this helps absorb the dressing. (Can be made a day ahead and kept in the fridge.) Try it with slow-cooked Greek lamb and tzatziki sauce.

Pepper & lemon spaghetti with basil & pine nuts

Prep: 7 mins **Cook:** 25 mins

Serves 2

Ingredients

- 1 tbsp rapeseed oil
- 1 red pepper, deseeded and diced
- 150g wholemeal spaghetti
- 2 courgettes (250g), grated
- 2 garlic cloves, finely grated
- 1 lemon, zested and juiced
- 15g basil, finely chopped
- 25g pine nuts, toasted
- 2 tbsp finely grated parmesan or vegetarian alternative (optional)

Method

STEP 1

Heat the oil in a large non-stick frying pan. Add the pepper and cook for 5 mins. Meanwhile, cook the pasta for 10-12 mins until tender.

STEP 2

Add the courgette and garlic to the pepper and cook, stirring very frequently, for 10-15 mins until the courgette is really soft.

STEP 3

Stir in the lemon zest and juice, basil and spaghetti (reserve some pasta water) and toss together, adding a little of the pasta water until nicely coated. Add the pine nuts, then spoon into bowls and serve topped with the parmesan, if using.

Cod puttanesca with spinach & spaghetti

Prep: 10 mins **Cook:** 17 mins

Serves 2

Ingredients

- 100g wholemeal spaghetti
- 1 large onion, sliced
- 1 tbsp rapeseed oil
- 1 red chilli, deseeded and sliced
- 2 garlic cloves, chopped
- 200g cherry tomatoes, halved
- 1 tsp cider vinegar
- 2 tsp capers
- 5 Kalamata olives, halved
- ½ tsp smoked paprika
- 2 skinless cod fillet or loins
- 160g spinach leaves
- small handful chopped parsley, to serve

Method

STEP 1

Boil the spaghetti for 10 mins until al dente, adding the spinach for the last 2 mins. Meanwhile, fry the onion in the oil in a large non-stick frying pan with a lid until tender and turning golden. Stir in the chilli and garlic, then add the tomatoes.

STEP 2

Add the vinegar, capers, olives and paprika with a ladleful of the pasta water. Put the cod fillets on top, then cover the pan and cook for 5-7 mins until the fish just flakes. Drain the pasta and wilted spinach and pile on to plates, then top with the fish and sauce. Sprinkle over some parsley to serve.

Baked falafel

Prep: 20 mins **Cook:** 20 mins

Serves 6

Ingredients

- 3 x 400g cans chickpeas, drained (or 250g dried chickpeas, soaked in 1 litre cold water overnight, then drained)
- 2 tsp ground cumin
- 1 tsp ground coriander
- 1 tsp cayenne pepper
- 1 red onion, quartered
- 3 garlic cloves
- 2 tbsp sesame seeds
- 1½ tsp baking powder
- 2 small packs parsley, stalks only

Method

STEP 1

Heat oven to 200C/180C fan/gas 6 and line two baking sheets with baking parchment. Tip the chickpeas, ground cumin, ground coriander, the cayenne pepper, onion, garlic, sesame seeds, baking powder, parsley stalks and 1 tbsp water into a food processor. Blitz until combined but not smooth (you want the falafel to have some texture, rather than being the consistency of hummus).

STEP 2

Season to taste, then roll into 18 evenly sized balls. Flatten each ball into a disc shape and arrange on the baking sheets, then brush the tops with 1 tbsp of the oil. Bake for 20 mins until golden and crisp, turning halfway through cooking.

Miso noodles with fried eggs

Prep: 10 mins **Cook:** 12 mins

Serves 2

Ingredients

- 2 nests wholemeal noodles (100g)
- 1 tbsp rapeseed oil , plus a drop extra for frying
- 30g ginger , cut into matchsticks
- 1 green pepper , deseeded and cut into strips
- 2 leeks (165g), thinly sliced
- 3 large garlic cloves , finely grated
- 1 tsp smoked paprika
- 1 tbsp brown miso
- 160g beansprouts
- 100g frozen peas , defrosted

- 160g baby spinach
- 2 large eggs
- 1 red chilli, deseeded and chopped (optional)

Method

STEP 1

Put the noodles in a bowl and cover with boiling water. Set aside to soften.

STEP 2

Meanwhile, heat the oil in a wok and stir-fry the ginger, pepper and leek for a few mins until softened. Add the garlic and paprika and cook for 1 min more. Drain the noodles, reserve 2 tbsp of the water and mix with the miso.

STEP 3

Add the drained noodles, miso liquid, beansprouts, peas and spinach to the wok and toss over a high heat until the spinach wilts. While you are doing this, fry the eggs in a little oil to your liking. Pile the noodles onto plates, top with the eggs and chilli, if using, and serve.

Chocolate chia pudding

Prep: 5 mins No cook, plus 4 hours chilling

Serves 4

Ingredients

- 60g chia seeds
- 400ml unsweetened almond milk or hazelnut milk
- 3 tbsp cacao powder
- 2 tbsp maple syrup
- ½ tsp vanilla extract
- cacao nibs, mixed
- frozen berries, to serve

Method

STEP 1

Put all the ingredients in a large bowl with a generous pinch of sea salt and whisk to combine. Cover with cling film then leave to thicken in the fridge for at least 4 hours, or overnight.

STEP 2

Spoon the pudding into four glasses, then top with the frozen berries and cacao nibs.

Rosemary, garlic & chilli popcorn

Prep: 5 mins **Cook:** 15 mins plus infusing

Serves 4

Ingredients

- 2 tbsp rapeseed oil
- 2 garlic cloves , lightly bashed
- 1 tsp chipotle or other chilli flakes
- ½ small bunch of rosemary , finely chopped
- 150g popcorn kernels

Method

STEP 1

Heat the oil in a saucepan over a medium heat, then fry the garlic, chilli and rosemary for 2-3 mins. Remove from the heat, set aside and leave the oil to infuse for 30 mins.

STEP 2

Cook the popcorn according to pack instructions. Scoop the garlic out of the infused oil and discard. Toss the popcorn with the oil, then season and serve straightaway.

Lime prawn cocktail pitta salad

Prep: 10 mins **Cook:** 15 mins

Serves 2

Ingredients

- ½ wholemeal pitta
- ½ tbsp rapeseed oil
- 1 tsp Tabasco
- 1 tsp low-sugar, low-salt ketchup
- 1 tbsp low-fat mayonnaise
- 1 tbsp fat-free natural yogurt
- ½ lime , zested and juiced, plus wedges to serve

- 60g cooked king prawns
- 1 Little Gem lettuce , leaves separated
- ¼ small cucumber , peeled into ribbons
- 4 cherry tomatoes , halved

Method

STEP 1

Heat the oven to 200C/180C fan/gas 6. Slice the pitta into triangles, put on a baking sheet and drizzle over the oil. Bake for 10-15 mins until golden and crisp.

STEP 2

Mix together the Tabasco, ketchup, mayo, yogurt and lime zest and juice. Toss the prawns in the dressing.

STEP 3

Layer the lettuce, cucumber, tomatoes and dressed prawns in a lunchbox or jar. Season, top with the pitta chips and serve with lime wedges.

Pasta e fagioli

Prep: 20 mins **Cook:** 7 hrs - 9 hrs plus overnight soaking

Serves 6 - 8

Ingredients

- 200g dried borlotti or cannellini beans , soaked for 6-8 hours
- 2 onions , cut into 1cm chunks
- 2 medium carrots , cut into 1cm chunks
- 3 celery stalks, cut into 1cm chunks
- 2 tbsp extra virgin olive oil , plus extra to serve (optional)
- 4 garlic cloves , crushed
- 1 litre fresh vegetable stock
- 400g can plum tomatoes
- 2 tbsp brown rice miso
- 6 rosemary sprigs
- 4 bay leaves
- 150g ditaloni rigati or other small pasta shapes
- 200g cavolo nero , stalks finely chopped and leaves torn
- 30g vegan parmesan , grated, to serve (optional)

Method

STEP 1

Drain the beans and bring to the boil in a pan of salted water. Cook for 10 mins, drain, rinse and put in a slow cooker with the onions, carrots and celery.

STEP 2

Stir in the olive oil, garlic, stock, tomatoes, half a can of water and the miso. Tie the herbs together with kitchen string and add these as well. Season. Cover and cook on low for 6-8 hrs, until the beans are cooked through and all of the veg is really tender.

STEP 3

Remove and discard the herbs and stir in the pasta. Cover and cook on high for another 30 mins. Add the cavolo nero stalks and leaves and cook for a final 30-40 mins, or until the pasta is cooked through and the greens are tender. Serve scattered with the cheese and drizzled with a little more olive oil, if you like.

Steak & Vietnamese noodle salad

Prep: 15 mins **Cook:** 10 mins

Serves 2

Ingredients

- 83g brown rice noodles (Clearspring contain no salt)
- 1 tsp rapeseed oil
- 250g fillet steak
- 2 carrots, peeled into ribbons

For the dressing

- 1 red chilli, seeds removed and thinly sliced
- 1 lime, juiced
- 2 tsp soft brown sugar

- ½ Chinese cabbage, shredded
- 4 spring onions, sliced
- 1 small pack coriander, roughly chopped

- 1 tsp rice wine vinegar
- 1 garlic clove, finely chopped
- ½ tbsp fish sauce

Method

STEP 1

Mix all the ingredients for the dressing together in a bowl with 1 tbsp water until the sugar has dissolved.

STEP 2

Cook the noodles following pack instructions, then plunge into a bowl of cold water to cool completely. Drain the noodles, then add the carrot, cabbage, spring onion and dressing, and toss to combine.

STEP 3

Heat the oil in a frying pan over a high heat. Season the steak, then cook to your liking; 2-3 mins on each side for medium rare. Leave to rest for 5 mins, then slice. Divide the salad and steak slices between bowls and scatter over some coriander to serve.

Turkey escalopes & giant couscous

Prep: 15 mins **Cook:** 45 mins

Serves 4

Ingredients

- 3 tbsp rapeseed oil
- 1 onion , finely chopped
- 1 aubergine , cut into 3cm cubes
- 2 large garlic cloves , crushed
- ¼ tsp chilli flakes
- 400g can chopped tomatoes
- 70g black olives , pitted and sliced
- 1 lemon , zested
- 4 turkey escalopes
- 250g giant couscous
- ½ small bunch basil , chopped, plus some extra torn leaves to serve
- 20g parmesan , shaved, to serve

Method

STEP 1

Heat 2 tbsp of the oil in a saucepan over a medium heat. Fry the onion and aubergine for 15-20 mins, or until softened. Add the garlic and chilli flakes and cook for 1 min more. Tip in the tomatoes and olives and cook for another 10 mins.

STEP 2

Meanwhile, heat the grill high. Mix the remaining oil and the lemon zest together, then rub on both sides of the turkey escalopes. Put the escalopes on a baking sheet and grill for 5-6 mins on each side serving until cooked through.

STEP 3

Cook the couscous following pack instructions, then drain and stir through the tomato sauce along with the basil. Slice the escalopes and serve with the couscous, parmesan and extra basil leaves.

Roasted cauli-broc bowl with tahini hummus

Prep: 10 mins **Cook:** 30 mins

Serves 2

Ingredients

- 400g pack cauliflower & broccoli florets
- 2 tbsp olive oil
- 250g ready-to-eat quinoa
- 2 cooked beetroots, sliced
- large handful baby spinach
- 10 walnuts, toasted and chopped
- 2 tbsp tahini
- 3 tbsp hummus
- 1 lemon, 1/2 juiced, 1/2 cut into wedges

Method

STEP 1

The night before, heat oven to 200C/180C fan/gas 6. Put the cauliflower and broccoli in a large roasting tin with the oil and a sprinkle of flaky sea salt. Roast for 25-30 mins until browned and cooked. Leave to cool completely.

STEP 2

Build each bowl by putting half the quinoa in each. Lay the slices of beetroot on top, followed by the spinach, cauliflower, broccoli and walnuts. Combine the tahini, hummus, lemon juice and 1 tbsp water in a small pot. Before eating, coat in the dressing. Serve with the lemon wedges.

Creamy chicken, squash & pecan pasta

Prep: 15 mins **Cook:** 30 mins

Serves 4

Ingredients

- 1l chicken stock
- ½ butternut squash, peeled and chopped into small chunks
- 2 chicken breasts
- 400g pasta (we used casarecce)
- 50g cream cheese
- 75g pecans, chopped
- small pack flat-leaf parsley, chopped
- 25g parmesan grated, plus extra to serve

Method

STEP 1

Pour the stock into a pan and bring to a simmer. Add the squash and chicken, cover and bubble gently for 15 mins, or until the chicken and squash are cooked. If the chicken cooks first, remove from the pan, set aside and keep boiling the squash until tender. Scoop the squash out with a slotted spoon, leaving just the stock in the pan.

STEP 2

Bring the stock back to the boil and add the pasta; the liquid should just cover the pasta. Cook, stirring regularly, until the pasta is just tender and most of the stock has been absorbed (top up with water if necessary). Shred the chicken.

STEP 3

Return the squash to the pan and add the cream cheese, pecans, parsley and parmesan. Simmer for another min or two, then add the chicken. Season and serve with extra parmesan, if you like.

Squash & pesto pasta

Prep: 15 mins **Cook:** 25 mins

Serves 4

Ingredients

- 1 small butternut squash (750g), peeled, deseeded and cut into 2cm cubes
- 3 tbsp rapeseed oil
- large bunch of parsley
- large bunch of basil
- 20g cashew nuts, toasted and chopped
- 1 garlic clove, crushed
- 1 lemon, zested and juiced
- 1 tsp chilli flakes (optional)
- 350g pasta (casarecce or fusilli work well)
- 30g parmesan or vegetarian alternative, shaved

Method

STEP 1

Heat the oven to 200C/180C fan/gas 6. Toss the butternut cubes on a baking tray with ½ tbsp of the oil and some seasoning. Roast for 20-25 mins or until tender.

STEP 2

Put the parsley, basil, cashew nuts, garlic, lemon zest and juice and chilli (if using) in a food processor, along with the remaining oil and a splash of water, then whizz until very smooth. Season to taste.

STEP 3

Meanwhile, cook the pasta following pack instructions. Drain, reserving a little of the cooking water, then toss with the pesto and butternut squash and enough water to loosen the sauce. Finish with a little shaved parmesan, if you like.

Simple fish stew

Prep: 10 mins **Cook:** 20 mins - 25 mins

Serves 2

Ingredients

- 1 tbsp olive oil
- 1 tsp fennel seeds
- 2 carrots, diced
- 2 celery sticks, diced
- 2 garlic cloves, finely chopped
- 2 leeks, thinly sliced
- 400g can chopped tomatoes
- 500ml hot fish stock, heated to a simmer
- 2 skinless pollock fillets (about 200g), thawed if frozen, and cut into chunks
- 85g raw shelled king prawns

Method

STEP 1

Heat the oil in a large pan, add the fennel seeds, carrots, celery and garlic, and cook for 5 mins until starting to soften. Tip in the leeks, tomatoes and stock, season and bring to the boil, then cover and simmer for 15-20 mins until the vegetables are tender and the sauce has thickened and reduced slightly.

STEP 2

Add the fish, scatter over the prawns and cook for 2 mins more until lightly cooked. Ladle into bowls and serve with a spoon.

Super-quick sesame ramen

Prep: 5 mins **Cook:** 10 mins

Serves 1

Ingredients

- 80g pack instant noodles (look for an Asian brand with a flavour like sesame)
- 2 spring onions , finely chopped
- ½ head pak choi
- 1 egg
- 1 tsp sesame seeds
- chilli sauce , to serve

Method

STEP 1

Cook the noodles with the sachet of flavouring provided (or use stock instead of the sachet, if you have it). Add the spring onions and pak choi for the final min.

STEP 2

Meanwhile, simmer the egg for 6 mins from boiling, run it under cold water to stop it cooking, then peel it. Toast the sesame seeds in a frying pan.

STEP 3

Tip the noodles and greens into a deep bowl, halve the boiled egg and place on top. Sprinkle with sesame seeds, then drizzle with the sauce or sesame oil provided with the noodles, and chilli sauce, if using.

Jerk-style chicken pilaf

Prep: 10 mins **Cook:** 20 mins

Serves 4

Ingredients

- 1 tbsp rapeseed oil
- 1 onion , finely sliced
- 4 boneless, skinless chicken thighs, cut into thick strips
- 1-2 tbsp jerk seasoning
- 1 green chilli , deseeded and sliced (optional)
- 2 large garlic cloves , crushed
- 2 x 250g pouches microwave basmati rice , cooked
- 400g can kidney beans , drained and rinsed
- 1 lime , zested and juiced, plus wedges to serve
- 3 spring onions , finely sliced
- ½ small bunch of coriander , finely chopped

Method

STEP 1

Heat the oil in a large flameproof casserole dish over a medium-high heat. Add the onion and a pinch of salt and fry for 5-6 mins. Add the chicken and fry for 7-8 mins more. Stir in the jerk seasoning, chilli, if using, and garlic, and cook for 1 min.

STEP 2

Stir in the rice, beans and lime zest and juice. Cook until heated through. Scatter over the spring onions, coriander and serve with the extra lime wedges.

Spinach & barley risotto

Prep: 10 mins **Cook:** 15 mins

Serves 2

Ingredients

- 2 tsp rapeseed oil
- 1 large leek (315g), thinly sliced
- 2 garlic cloves, chopped
- 2 x 400g can barley, undrained
- 1 tbsp vegetable bouillon powder
- 1 tsp finely chopped sage
- 1 tbsp thyme leaves
- 160g cherry tomatoes, halved
- 160g spinach
- 50g finely grated vegetarian Italian-style hard cheese

Method

STEP 1

Heat the oil in a non-stick pan and fry the leek and garlic for 5-10 mins, stirring frequently, until softened, adding a splash of water if it sticks.

STEP 2

Tip in the cans of barley and their liquid, then stir in the bouillon powder, sage and thyme. Simmer, stirring frequently, for 4-5 mins. Add the tomatoes and spinach and cook for 2-3 mins more until the spinach is wilted, adding a splash more water if needed. Stir in most of the cheese, then serve with the remaining cheese scattered over.

Chia & oat breakfast scones with yogurt and berries

Prep: 8 mins **Cook:** 20 mins

Serves 4

Ingredients

- 2 tsp cold pressed rapeseed oil, plus a little for the ramekins
- 50ml milk
- 1 tbsp lemon juice
- 2 tsp vanilla extract
- 160g plain wholemeal spelt flour
- 2 tbsp chia seeds
- 25g oats
- 2 tsp baking powder
- 2 x 120g pots bio Greek yogurt
- 400g strawberries, hulled and sliced

Method

STEP 1

Heat oven to 200C/180C fan/gas 6 and line the base of 4 x 185ml ramekins with a disc of baking parchment and oil the sides with the rapeseed oil. Measure the milk in a jug and make up to 300ml with water. Stir in the lemon juice, vanilla and the 2 tsp oil. Mix the flour, seeds and oats then blitz in a food processor to make the mix as fine as you can. Stir in the baking powder.

STEP 2

Pour in the liquid, then stir in with the blade of a knife until you have a very wet batter like dough. Spoon evenly into the ramekins then bake on a baking sheet for 20 mins until risen – they don't have to be golden but should feel firm. Cool for a few mins then run a knife round the inside of the ramekins to loosen the scones then carefully ease out.

STEP 3

The scones can be eaten immediately or cooled and stored for later. If you're following our Healthy Diet Plan, this recipe can be used for two people over two meals, use two scones straight away split in half and served topped with half the yogurt and two portions of the berries. Cool and pack the remainder to eat on another day on the plan.

Hearty mushroom soup

Prep: 30 mins **Cook:** 30 mins

Serves 4 - 6

Ingredients

- 25g pack porcini mushrooms
- 2 tbsp olive oil
- 1 medium onion , finely diced
- 2 large carrots , diced
- 2 garlic cloves , finely chopped
- 1 tbsp chopped rosemary , or 1 tsp dried
- 500g fresh mushroom , such as chestnut, finely chopped
- 1.2l vegetable stock (from a cube is fine)
- 5 tbsp marsala or dry sherry
- 2 tbsp tomato purée
- 100g pearl barley
- grated fresh parmesan , to serve (optional)

Method

STEP 1

Put the porcini in a bowl with 250ml boiling water and leave to soak for 25 mins. Heat the oil in a pan and add the onion, carrot, garlic, rosemary and seasoning. Fry for 5 mins on a medium heat until softened. Drain the porcini, saving the liquid, and finely chop. Tip into the pan with the fresh mushrooms. Fry for another 5 mins, then add the stock, marsala or sherry, tomato purée, barley and strained porcini liquid.

STEP 2

Cook for 30 mins or until barley is soft, adding more liquid if it becomes too thick. Serve in bowls with parmesan sprinkled over, if desired.

Printed in Great Britain
by Amazon